Performance Criticism
of the Pauline Letters

Biblical Performance Criticism Series
Orality, Memory, Translation, Rhetoric, Discourse, Drama

David Rhoads, Holly E. Hearon, and Kelly R. Iverson, Series Editors

The ancient societies of the Bible were overwhelmingly oral. People originally experienced the traditions now in the Bible as oral performances. Focusing on the ancient performance of biblical traditions enables us to shift academic work on the Bible from the mentality of a modern print culture to that of an oral/scribal culture. Conceived broadly, biblical performance criticism embraces many methods as means to reframe the biblical materials in the context of traditional oral cultures, construct scenarios of ancient performances, learn from contemporary performances of these materials, and reinterpret biblical writings accordingly. The result is a foundational paradigm shift that reconfigures traditional disciplines and employs fresh biblical methodologies such as theater studies, speech-act theory, and performance studies. The emerging research of many scholars in this field of study, the development of working groups in scholarly societies, and the appearance of conferences on orality and literacy make it timely to inaugurate this series. For further information on biblical performance criticism, go to www.biblicalperformancecriticism.org.

Books in the Series

Holly Hearon and Philip Ruge-Jones, editors
The Bible in Ancient and Modern Media

James Maxey
From Orality to Orality

Antoinette Clark Wire
The Case for Mark Composed in Performance

Robert D. Miller II, SFO
Oral Tradition in Ancient Israel

Pieter J. J. Botha
Orality and Literacy in Early Christianity

James A. Maxey and
Ernst R. Wendland, editors
Translating Scripture for Sound and Performance

J. A. (Bobby) Loubser
Oral and Manuscript Culture in the Bible

Joanna Dewey
The Oral Ethos of the Early Church

Richard A. Horsley
Text and Tradition in Performance and Writing

Kelly R. Iverson, editor
From Text to Performance

Annette Weissenrieder &
Robert B. Coote, editors
The Interface of Orality and Writing

Thomas E. Boomershine
The Messiah of Peace

Performance Criticism of the Pauline Letters

BERNHARD OESTREICH

FOREWORD BY
GLENN S. HOLLAND

TRANSLATED BY
LINDSAY ELIAS
AND
BRENT BLUM

CASCADE *Books* · Eugene, Oregon

PERFORMANCE CRITICISM OF THE PAULINE LETTERS

Biblical Performance Criticism Series 14

Copyright © 2016 Bernhard Oestreich. All rights reserved. Except for brief quotations in critical publications or reviews, no part of this book may be reproduced in any manner without prior written permission from the publisher. Write: Permissions, Wipf and Stock Publishers, 199 W. 8th Ave., Suite 3, Eugene, OR 97401.

Originally published in German as *Performanzkritik der Paulusbriefe*. Wissenschaftliche Untersuchungen zum Neuen Testament 296. Tübingen: Mohr Siebeck, 2012.

The translation was supported by the Theologische Hochschule Friedensau.

Cascade Books
An Imprint of Wipf and Stock Publishers
199 W. 8th Ave., Suite 3
Eugene, OR 97401

www.wipfandstock.com

PAPERBACK ISBN: 978-1-4982-9831-5
HARDCOVER ISBN: 978-1-4982-4885-3
EBOOK ISBN: 978-1-4982-9832-2

Cataloguing-in-Publication data:

Names: Oestreich, Bernhard, 1949–. | Elias, Lindsay. | Blum, Brent. | Holland, Glenn Stanfield, 1952–.

Title: Performance criticism of the Pauline letters / Bernhard Oestreich ; translated by Lindsay Elias and Brent Blum ; foreword by Glenn S. Holland.

Description: Eugene, OR: Cascade Books, 2016. | Series: Biblical Performance Criticism Series 14. | Includes bibliographical references and index.

Identifiers: ISBN 978-1-4982-9831-5 (paperback) | ISBN 978-1-4982-4885-3 (hardcover) | ISBN 978-1-4982-9832-2 (ebook).

Subjects: LCSH: Oral reading. | Performance in literature. | Letters. | Bible. N.T.—Performance criticism. | Bible. N.T.—Criticism, interpretation, etc. | Bible. Epistles of Paul.

Classification: BS2650.52 O37 2016 (print) | BS2650.52 (ebook).

Manufactured in the U.S.A.   10/28/16

Biblical references are taken from the New American Standard Bible.® Copyright© 1960, 1962, 1963, 1968, 1971, 1972, 1973, 1975, 1977, 1995 by The Lockman Foundation (www.Lockman.org). Used by permission.

Contents

Foreword by Glenn S. Holland | vii
Preface to the German Edition | xi
Preface to the English Translation | xv
Abbreviations | xvii

   Introduction | 1

1. Theory of Performance Criticism | 7
   History of the Method | 7
   The Essence of Performance | 50
   Methodology of Performance Criticism | 67

2. Influencing Audience Interaction by Use of Letters | 98
   Addressing a Divided Audience | 98
   Singling out Individual Listeners | 112
   Focusing on the Reader as Communication's Medium | 136

3. Strategies in Letter Writing to Achieve Reconciliation | 152
   Controversy in Rome over Diet (Romans 14:1—15:13) | 152
   Instituting Friendship (Plato, Sixth Letter) | 190
   Establishing Peace after Unrest (Claudius to the Alexandrians) | 193
   Tensions in Corinth Due to Spiritual Gifts (1 Corinthians 12:3) | 195
   The Relationship of the Leaders to Those Being Led | 210

4. Strategies in Letter Writing to Achieve Separation | 228
   Winning Back the Listeners (Galatians) | 228
   Expelling the Opponents (First Letter of Clement) | 259

   Summary and Perspectives | 275

Bibliography | 285
Author Index | 319
Subject Index | 329
Ancient Document Index | 335

Foreword

The English translation of Bernhard Oestreich's *Performanzkritik der Paulusbriefe* allows a new and expanded audience to benefit from his cogent and insightful introduction to performance criticism of the New Testament and other ancient texts, most notably the letters of the apostle Paul. As Prof. Oestreich demonstrates, the theory behind performance criticism arises both from other related critical methodologies on the one hand, and from long-standing scholarly awareness of the historical circumstances surrounding the composition, transmission, and reception of the biblical documents on the other.

In short, the texts of the New Testament were written to be read aloud to groups—to be performed—and were understood by the audience, not only in terms of their content (usually the primary concern of biblical analysis), but also in terms of the circumstances of the performance. Those circumstances included not only the words spoken but also the way they were spoken by a specific reader, mediated by the reader's use of voice and body, and the impression the reader's spoken words made on the audience as a group and as individuals. But the circumstances of performance also included the subjective perceptions of the audience members. These include the audience's impressions of the reader's performance and its individual members' awareness of the performance space, the reactions of other audience members to what they see and hear, the reaction of the reader to the audience in turn, and the ceaseless flow of various sensory stimuli that create the unique circumstances of every individual performance before any audience, in any place, at any time. It is easy to imagine how this array of factors surrounding the initial reading aloud of a letter of Paul to the assembled members of one of his congregations could and would influence how what Paul had written was ultimately heard and understood by the letter's intended recipients.

Performance criticism does not seek to either fully delineate or re-create the initial performance of a biblical text such as one of Paul's letters. Instead, it represents the imperative to be aware of and to accommodate in the modern interpretation of Paul's letters the exigencies of the situation that was the historical reality shaping the reception and understanding of each of those letters by its initial addressees. Since what is available to the modern interpreter is the texts that, when read aloud, formed the basis of each individual audience's experience of the letter, performance criticism focuses on how the text reflects its author's (or authors') attempts to use the fact that the letters would be read aloud to further the purpose for which the text was written. In the case of Paul's letters, the question is how Paul attempted through the content of his letters to create and shape an oral performance that would most effectively persuade the members of his congregations to acknowledge Paul's authority, to accept his interpretation of the situation that had prompted his letter, and to put into action Paul's proposed resolution of that situation.

In this book, Prof. Oestreich has given particular attention to the possible reactions of an audience as one of Paul's letters is read aloud. The audience members are to be understood, not only collectively as a congregation, but also as members of specific subgroups in the social network the congregation created, and as distinct individuals. This leads to serious consideration of the reactions among members of the congregation, both as groups and as individuals, while they listen to the performance of the letter and respond in their different ways. The reader of the letter reacts in turn to the response among the members of his audience while he is reading, and adjusts his performance accordingly. The reader, in the act of reading aloud, makes the written text of the letter for a brief time a living thing for the congregation. The reader in so doing implicitly assumes the role of "Paul" in front of his audience, sometimes personifying the apostle and invoking his "presence," and sometimes, by virtue of the realities of the reader's own person, standing in clear contrast to the image Paul presents of himself through the written text. In this way Paul can be both "present" and "absent" while the letter is read aloud, and use both his presence and his absence to his own advantage.

Foreword

Prof. Oestreich brings a full awareness of the exigencies of the performance of Paul's letters before his congregations to his analysis of specific passages, most of them contentious, and thereby reaches some new and compelling conclusions. In each case he discusses the likely circumstances of a letter's performance before its initial audience, and how Paul uses the fact of performance as part of the persuasive strategy embodied in the text and, later, in its performance by a reader, to bring about unity or to enforce the separation of those who have been a source of discord among the members of a congregation. Analysis of early Christian letters from outside the New Testament and some from outside the Christian movement altogether provides parallels to situations in Paul's letters and demonstrates the more general applicability of performance criticism to the analysis of other ancient texts.

Prof. Oestreich, like other scholars employing performance criticism as a means of generating nuanced and historically grounded interpretations of the New Testament and other biblical texts, is well aware that the work to be done is only beginning. But with the theoretical foundation this book provides, and the insightful examples of performance criticism as a means of interpreting specific passages, Prof. Oestreich has greatly benefitted those interested in comprehending the multiple contingencies at play in the reception of these texts by their initial audiences, or in advancing the work of encompassing those contingencies in the interests of developing a comprehensive and compelling interpretation of Paul's letters.

Glenn S. Holland

Bishop James Mills Thoburn
Professor of Religious Studies

Allegheny College

Meadville, Pennsylvania

Preface to the German Edition

The present study has arisen from a question that has occupied me for a long time: How did the word that we read in the Bible today achieve its effect with the original recipients? It is not a new discovery that something more took place than an intellectual reception of the information contained in the texts when the texts were received by the addressees. Form criticism has already assumed that the sayings and anecdotes that we read in the New Testament Gospels had their *Sitz im Leben* in oral communication that was at home in particular sociological situations. That means that the passing on of the traditional stories about Jesus—often dramatic episodes of his life or trenchant remarks that he made in sometimes volatile situations—were common experiences that moved the listeners on an emotional plane and evoked the reactions which the speakers desired. How do we have to imagine this event? The New Testament letters were also designed for oral communication. These letters were sent to Christian believers and read out aloud to the assembled congregation (1 Thess 5:27). That must have been a very special experience for the listeners and must have left a lasting impression on them (2 Cor 10:10). Is it possible to know more exactly how the impact of the letter was achieved?

A substantial impetus to pursue this question came from my interest in homiletics. I still consider the art of preaching to be fascinating. I enjoy working with students, pastors, and lay preachers in homiletics classes. I enjoy experimenting with my own preaching. Listening to a sermon is a communal experience. That is still valid for modern European culture, even if the listeners' reaction to the sermon is much more reserved in comparison with ancient times. If the sermon is successful, the traditional word becomes an event for the listener. This automatically has led me to the question of how the original listeners of the biblical message experienced the "reading event."

A strong impulse to research this question more deeply came from publications that seriously consider the fact that the New Testament came into being in a culture largely dominated by oral communication. I would like to specially mention the collection of essays edited by Gerhard Sellin and François Vouga, *Logos und Buchstabe: Mündlichkeit und Schriftlichkeit im Judentum und Christentum der Antike* [*Logos and Letter: Orality and Scribality in Antique Judaism and Christianity*] (Tübingen: Francke, 1997), and the articles edited by Joanna Dewey in *Semeia* 65 (1995) with the title *Orality and Textuality in Early Christian Literature*. I am thankful to these authors and many others, having followed them inquisitively, as if on a trail left by their footprints, into a world where the texts that are recorded in the Bible are not just written texts but rather mutually experienced events. The objective of this study is to explore this world a little further.

Many have contributed with suggestions and constructive criticism to the development of this book. As can be seen on every page, I have profited from the thoughts and hypotheses of many authors and built my study on their groundwork. Enriching discussions with colleagues and students of the theological department of Friedensau University broadened my horizons. My gratitude extends to Prof. Glenn S. Holland and the participants of the section "Performance Criticism of Biblical and Other Ancient Texts" of the Society of Biblical Literature. For years I have been benefiting from its various suggestions and constructive criticism. I would also like to thank the faculty and students of the New Testament department of the Martin-Luther-University of Halle-Wittenberg under the leadership of Prof. Udo Schnelle. They have repeatedly offered me the opportunity of discussing my research. My thanks also go to Friedensau University. They offered me the possibility of a sabbatical term in order to concentrate on working on this project. I would like to thank Prof. Jörg Frey for accepting this book into the first series of Wissenschaftliche Untersuchungen zum Neuen Testament. I would like to thank the Mohr/Siebeck publishing house for the very good cooperation in preparing the book for printing. My gratitude extends to my son Raimar Oestreich and all those who helped proofread and format the manuscript. I owe special thanks to my wife, Hannelore, my faithful companion of many years, who, as so often, supported me in this project and repeatedly released me from other duties.

Bernhard Oestreich

Friedensau, August 2012

Preface to the English Translation

It is with great delight that I see my book enter a larger discussion forum by being handed over to English-speaking biblical scholars. I have profited from many of them as this book reveals. I hope that I can provide a few stimuli to new thoughts in return.

My heartfelt thanks are extended to Prof. David Rhoads, who never got tired of encouraging me to press ahead with the translation, and who accepted the work in the Biblical Performance Criticism Series. I am thankful for the work of the translators, whose skill I admire greatly, and for the selfless help of many others. My thanks go also to K. C. Hanson and the staff of Cascade Books for their professional and friendly guidance in the publishing process. I thank also Friedensau Adventist University for a generous financial grant helping with the translation.

Bernhard Oestreich

Friedensau, May 2016

Abbreviations

AB	Anchor Bible
AGJU	Arbeiten zur Geschichte des antiken Judentums und des Urchristentums
ANRW	*Aufstieg und Niedergang der römischen Welt*
ANTC	Abingdon New Testament Commentaries
AUSS	*Andrews University Seminary Studies*
BBB	Bonner Biblische Beiträge
BETL	Bibliotheca Ephemeridum Theologicarum Lovaniensium
BFCT	Beiträge zur Förderung christlicher Theologie
Bib	*Biblica*
BNTC	Black's New Testament Commentaries
BPCS	Biblical Performance Criticism Series
BTB	*Biblical Theology Bulletin*
BWA(N)T	Beiträge zur Wissenschaft vom Alten (und Neuen) Testament
BZ	*Biblische Zeitschrift*
BZNW	Beihefte zur Zeitschrift für die neutestamentliche Wissenschaft
CBET	Contributions to Biblical Exegesis and Theology

CBQ	*Catholic Biblical Quarterly*
CJ	*The Classical Journal*
ConBNT	Coniectanea Biblica: New Testament Series
CTQ	*Concordia Theological Quarterly*
CurBS	*Currents in Research: Biblical Studies*
EKKNT	Evangelisch-Katholischer Kommentar zum Neuen Testament
EvT	*Evangelische Theologie*
FAT	Forschungen zum Alten Testament
FF	Foundations and Facets
FRLANT	Forschungen zur Religion und Literatur des Alten und Neuen Testaments
GBSNTS	Guides to Biblical Scholarship: New Testament Series
GRBS	*Greek, Roman, and Byzantine Studies*
GTA	Göttinger theologische Arbeiten
HNT	Handbuch zum Neuen Testament
HSCP	*Harvard Studies in Classical Philology*
HSM	Harvard Semitic Monographs
HThKNT	Herders Theologischer Kommentar zum Neuen Testament
HTS	*Hervormde teologiese studies*
HUT	Hermeneutische Untersuchungen zur Theologie
Int	*Interpretation*
JBL	*Journal of Biblical Literature*
JETS	*Journal of the Evangelical Theological Society*
JSHRZ	Jüdische Schriften aus hellenistisch-römischer Zeit
JSNT	*Journal for the Study of the New Testament*
JSNTSup	Journal for the Study of the New Testament Supplement Series
JSOTSup	Journal for the Study of the Old Testament Supplement Series
JTS	*Journal of Theological Studies*

Jud	*Judaica*
KEK	Kritisch-exegetischer Kommentar über das Neue Testament
LCL	Loeb Classical Library
LEC	Library of Early Christianity
Mnemosyne Sup	Mnemosyne: Bibliotheca Classica Batava Supplementum
Neot	*Neotestamentica*
NICNT	New International Commentary on the New Testament
NIGTC	The New International Greek Testament Commentary
NovT	*Novum Testamentum*
NovTSup	Novum Testamentum Supplements
NTAbh	Neutestamentliche Abhandlungen
NTD	Das Neue Testament Deutsch
NTL	New Testament Library
NTOA	Novum Testamentum et Orbis Antiquus
NTS	*New Testament Studies*
NTTS	New Testament Tools and Studies
Q J Speech	*The Quarterly Journal of Speech*
SBB	Stuttgarter Biblische Beiträge
SBL	Society of Biblical Literature
SBLDS	Society of Biblical Literature Dissertation Series
SBLRBS	Society of Biblical Literature Resources for Biblical Study
SBLSBS	Society of Biblical Literature Sources for Biblical Study
SBLSP	*Society of Biblical Literature Seminar Papers*
SNT	Studien zum Neuen Testament
SNTSMS	Society for New Testament Studies Monograph Series
SP	Sacra Pagina
ST	*Studia Theologica*
STRev	*Sewanee Theological Review*
STW	Suhrkamp Taschenbuch Wissenschaft

SUNT	Studien zur Umwelt des Neuen Testaments
TANZ	Texte und Arbeiten zum neutestamentlichen Zeitalter
ThHKNT	Theologischer Handkommentar zum Neuen Testament
TLZ	*Theologische Literaturzeitung*
TSAJ	Texts and Studies in Ancient Judaism
TU	Texte und Untersuchungen zur Geschichte der altchristlichen Literatur
USQR	*Union Seminary Quarterly Review*
UTB	Uni-Taschenbücher
WBC	Word Biblical Commentary
WMANT	Wissenschaftliche Monographien zum Alten und Neuen Testament
WUNT	Wissenschaftliche Untersuchungen zum Neuen Testament
ZNW	*Zeitschrift für die neutestamentliche Wissenschaft und die Kunde der älteren Kirche*
ZRGG	*Zeitschrift für Religions- und Geistesgeschichte*
ZTK	*Zeitschrift für Theologie und Kirche*

Introduction

This study is concerned with the performance of the Pauline letters in the early Christian churches: that is, the *oral* expression of *written* language. Is that not a contradiction? What did letters have in common with oral speech in the first century after Christ?

Written communication is very closely associated with spoken dialog in *De elocutione*, a treatise attributed to Demetrius of Phaleron (fourth century BCE) but of a later date.[1] There letters are characterized as follows (223–24):

> Artemon, the editor of Aristotle's *Letters*, says that a letter should be written in the same manner as a dialogue; the letter, he says, is like one of the two sides of a dialogue. There is perhaps some truth in what he says, but not the whole truth. The letter should be a little more formal than the dialogue, since the latter improvised conversation, while the former is written and sent as a kind of gift.[2]

It is significant that this oldest known comment on epistolary theory brings the letter into close connection with *oral communication*, although the letter is written and so also compared to a discourse written in the style of a dialog. This is demonstrated on the one hand by the affirmation of Artemon's opinion that a letter is comparable to a dialog. Just like a written dialog, the letter is also a text that portrays spoken language. On the other hand, this is also shown by the way Demetrius explains how a letter should *not* be written. He illustrates this with no less than four

---

1. Klauck, *Ancient Letters*, 184–85 assumes a date between 200 BCE and 100 CE; Malherbe, *Ancient Epistolary*, 5 and Poster, "Conversation Halved," 23 estimate the first century BCE.

2. Translation by Klauck, *Ancient Letters*, 185; cf. Thraede, *Grundzüge*, 17–19.

examples of *oral* communication, all of which portray public oration: A letter should correspond to a conversation with a friend, therefore being simple in style and not reminiscent of a pretentious public speech (225). It should also not be written in the style of a first-person dialog, which would be more fitting for an actor (226). The sentences should not be too long or complicated, as if written for a debate over legal paragraphs in court (229). Because they are unpretentious, proverbs may be used to encourage, but solemn wisdom and moralizing as might be heard from a *deus ex machina* in a theater[3] as a divine remedy for the entangled plot (232) are inappropriate. Thus for the author, who notably chose to address letter style in a digression in a treatise on the styles of spoken language, communication by letter was so closely associated with the spoken word that he used comparisons with spoken language to clarify his instructions on the art of letter writing.[4]

Heikki Koskenniemi and others assume that Demetrius uses rhetorical practice to show how language should *not* be used in letters because Demetrius sees such fundamental differences between letter and public oration "that one can not imagine that the writer of a letter is making a speech, however unadorned, for the recipient."[5] Others see a fundamental distinction between letter and public speech in the fact that a letter is written while a speech is delivered orally.[6] But does this correctly describe the distinction between letter and oral speech as made in *De elocutione*? Significantly, it is in his treatise on rhetoric, which in the ancient world was a discipline of spoken language,[7] that Demetrius dedicated an excursus to the letter. Thus he demonstrated that for himself, the letter remained closely tied to oral language. He therefore pleads for a style corresponding to an informal exchange between friends (225).[8]

---

3. On μηχανή, cf. Klauck, *Ancient Letters*, 188.

4. Cicero also compared the language of letters with forms of oral speech such as the debate in court and the public speech; see below pp. 22–23.

5. Koskenniemi, *Studien*, 43 (my translation); also Porter, "Theoretical Justification," 112; Stamps, "Rhetorical Criticism"; Byrskog, "Epistolography," 31–32. Also Bünker, *Briefformular*, 21 interprets Demetrius so that he "considered already the written form to be constitutive for the letter" (my translation).

6. Porter, "Theoretical Justification," 112: "Demetrius recognizes that there is something inherent in the written nature of the letter that is different from spoken discourse."

7. Malherbe, *Ancient Epistolary*, 3 concludes that epistolary theory only gradually came to be a part of rhetoric.

8. Cf. Cicero, *Att.* 8.14.1: "cum quasi tecum loquor." Cf. Seneca, *Ep.* 75.1–2: "I

The distinction he makes is therefore not between written and oral communication, but between an amicable conversation and public oration.

On the other hand, a letter is more than a spontaneous contribution to a conversation and should therefore be formulated with greater care (224). This stipulation means that one thing a letter requires is exactly what an informal conversation does not—something customary for *public speech* in Hellenistic and Roman times, namely, a careful, often written preparation used for oral presentation and could subsequently be published in a revised form.[9] So even with this rule, the letter remained comparable to oral speech. The fact that Demetrius uses examples from rhetorical practice to illustrate what is *not* appropriate for a letter does not mean that a letter has nothing to do with a speech, but rather that the occasion for a letter requires its own type of speech, distinguished from the classical categories of rhetoric: this speech lies somewhere between the style of a speaker in court or at a public event and colloquial language.

Ultimately, Demetrius argues that the written nature of the letter calls for greater care when composing a letter. Apparently, the conclusion is that the written nature of the letter makes it something material that therefore has a different status than purely spoken words. However, the written form was undoubtedly not considered to be more significant and better able to transport information—for example because the recipient could read the letter multiple times. In the estimate of the ancient culture, the significance and binding nature of the spoken word

---

prefer that my letters should be just what my conversation would be if you and I were sitting in one anothers's company or taking walks together,—spontaneous and easy ... Even if I were arguing a point, I should not stamp my foot, or toss my arms about, or raise my voice; but I should leave that sort of thing to the orator" (translation by Malherbe, *Ancient Epistolary*, 29). To stamp one's foot and toss arms about were typical behaviors for public orators, according to Quintilian, *Inst.* 10.3.21 and 10.7.26. Also Quintilian, *Inst.* 9.4.19–22 distinguishes the style of a speech from that of a letter or conversation, but in so doing always compares the letter with oral communication. Cf. Porter, "Theoretical Justification," 113–14 who also refers to Philostratus of Lemnos, *De epistolis* (third century CE).

9. On the significance of writing for a speaker, see Quintilian, *Inst.* 10.1.2: "Nam neque solida atque robusta fuerit unquam eloquentia, nisi multo stilo vires acceperit." ("For eloquence will never attain to its full development or robust health, unless it acquires strength by frequent practice in writing" [translation: H. E. Butler].) Similarly 1.1.28–29; 10.1.1–3; 10.3.1–18; 10.6.3; 10.7.28–29. On the view that the art of speaking is learned by reading, see Quintilian, *Inst.* 10.1.16–131, also Dormeyer, *Literaturgeschichte*, 32 with reference to Theon, *Prog.* 1.84–92. Cf. Fuhrmann, "Mündlichkeit"; Fantham, "Two Levels," 226, *passim*; Morstein-Marx, *Mass Oratory*, 25–30. On revising for publication, see Quintilian, *Inst.* 10.7.30–31.

was greater than of the written word.¹⁰ The high esteem for the letter was rather due to the fact that it was sent to the recipient as a gift (224). With a letter the recipient thus acquires something that can be held in the hand, something that endures. Since ancient times it has been part of the magic of the written word that it transforms language, which is otherwise immaterial and fleeting, into something material and enduring. Above all, it has been the cultures in which oral tradition plays a major role that have preserved a sense for the reification of language in the written word.¹¹ Therefore, that Demetrius demands special care for writing a letter does not indicate a separation between letter writing and oral language but highlights their closeness.¹²

In this study we take up an aspect of the link between written and oral communication that was taken for granted in the ancient world. We consider the letters of Paul and investigate the context in which they were read aloud to the recipients. The question is, How must we imagine what took place when a letter from Paul reached the recipients and its influence came to bear? This process is an event (or multiple events) involving several people: the speaker presenting the text, and the listeners. This is a typical performance situation. All those present are collectively involved in generating the meaning of the text that has reached them. How does this occur? What interaction takes place between the parties involved?¹³

---

10. Stirewalt, *Paul*, 6: "There was a general distrust of the written word: Isocrates, obviously referring to literary letters, gives three reasons why it is better to offer advice in person rather than by letter, one of which states that people believe things spoken more readily than things written because they take the spoken word as practical advice but the written as an artistic composition." Cf. Isocrates, *Ep.* 1.2–3. On the higher estimation of the spoken word, cf. Botha, "Living Voice"; on the critical view of the written word, cf. Alexander, "Living Voice"; Frede, "Mündlichkeit."

11. See e.g., Niditch, *Oral World*, 78–88.

12. Cf. the significance of the letter as a material object in Seneca, *Ep.* 40.1: "Numquam epistulam tuam accipio, ut non protinus una simus. Si imagines nobis amicorum absentium iucundae sunt, quae memoriam renovant et desiderium falso atque inani solacio levant, quanto iucundiores sunt litterae, quae vera amici absentis vestigia, veras notas adferunt? Nam quod in conspectu dulcissimum est, id amici manus epistulae inpressa praestat, agnoscere." ("I never receive a letter from you without being in your company forthwith. If the pictures of our absent friends are pleasing to us, though they only refresh the memory and lighten our longing by a solace that is unreal and unsubstantial, how much more pleasant is a letter, which brings us real traces, real evidences, of an absent friend! For that which is sweetest when we meet face to face is afforded by the impress of a friend's hand upon his letter—recognition" [translation in Malherbe, *Ancient Epistolary*, 29].)

13. On the role of the audience—both as conceived by the speaker and in

The author of the letter is indirectly involved because he has imagined the situation while preparing the text, and in this way his thoughts are also there together with those present (1 Cor 5:3). How did the letter writer's mental anticipation of the performance event influence the way the text of letter was shaped? From today's perspective we might ask, How does taking the performance of the letter into account help to better understand the text? These questions will be discussed in this study.

This will be done in three steps. First, previous studies will be introduced that have served as a foundation for the work presented here. A broad overview of the rich literature reveals several currents in New Testament research that flow together and are becoming increasingly established as *performance criticism*.[14] Here, the Pauline Epistles remain at the center of consideration, with incidental references to studies on performance of the Gospels or other biblical literature.

A second step will clarify how performance is understood in the context of this study. To understand what we mean by performance and how Paul's letters were likely performed, we will examine relevant findings from cultural anthropology and theatrical studies. From the current discussions, five central characteristics of performance have crystallized that help to define performance. Appropriate methods and procedures for performance criticism of the Pauline Epistles are then derived from these characteristics.

One insight resulting from the study of performance events is that they take place in a "performance arena" (Foley). Performance is an act within the framework of certain social conventions that make it possible for those who are present to define themselves either as presenter or audience, and only then is a performance constituted. Because it is part of the task of performance criticism to take this framework into consideration, a short description of the conventions for performing letters in Graeco-Roman times is included. This part is based on historical findings about the cultural traditions in the context of letter reception.

Finally, in the third step, the main part of this study presents examples of how this method can help us understand the Pauline letters today. Many more studies could be written, for example about the acoustic quality of the performance[15] or about the special role of those who

---

reality—and its influence on the speaker and thus on the result of the oral communication event, cf. Perelman and Olbrechts-Tyteca, *New Rhetoric*, 17–26.

14. Cf. Rhoads, "Performance Criticism."

15. Cf. Dean, "Grammar of Sound"; Dean, "Textured Criticism"; Harvey, *Listening*;

present the letter.[16] The examples here will concentrate on one aspect that is of great importance but has received little attention. We have selected texts in which the listeners are not addressed as a homogeneous group, but in which more or less problematic relationships between different groups among the listeners are assumed and addressed. The groups may distinguish themselves according to their social status in the community or congregation, or also according to different views they may have about theology or faith practice. Quite often, multiple aspects are involved. In the church at Corinth, for example, there were divisions between the followers of different personalities (1 Cor 1:10), as well as tensions between the wealthier and and poorer members (1 Cor 11) and between those who practiced different spiritual gifts (1 Cor 12).[17]

The examples presented will show how taking the performance situation into consideration helps us to recognize Paul's rhetorical and performance strategy and to understand what he has written. Comparisons with nonbiblical letters and other sources will make it clear that Paul's strategies were not unusual; they were common methods widely used to establish and shape not only the relationship between the one presenting the letter and the audience but also the relationships between the different parts of the audience.

Harvey, "Orality and Its Implications"; Esler, *Conflict and Identity*, 216–19; Sellin, "Ästhetische Aspekte."

16. Cf. Johnson, "Titus' Tearful Performance."

17. See Theissen, "Soziale Schichtung"; Theissen, "Starken"; Theissen, "Soziale Integration."

1

Theory of Performance Criticism

History of the Method

There are primarily three currents in the research on the letters of the New Testament that flow together and contribute to the investigation of the Pauline letters and their performance: epistolography, rhetoric and studies on oral tradition.

Epistolography

Since Adolf Deissmann, a major focus in the research on the New Testament letters has been on the question of how they can be classified in the context of the variety of ancient letter literature. Deissmann himself compared the Pauline letters with the papyrus letters found in Egypt and considered both to be "real letters," that is, occasional writings that, in contrast to "epistles," had been born of concrete situations, composed without literary considerations and without thinking about a readership beyond the immediate situation.[1] It has since become obvious that the distinction between real letters and epistles is too simplistic and adequately reflects neither the diversity of letter literature nor the complexity

---

1. Deissmann, *Licht vom Osten*, 198. Deissmann's distinction between letter and epistle can be found on pp. 194–95.

of the New Testament letters.² Nevertheless, Deissmann's approach has dominated research, mostly through the comparison of biblical and non-biblical letters and through references to ancient texts on epistolography to shed light on the nature and message of New Testament letters.³

Usually, the comparison has been restricted to the linguistic form of the letters,⁴ i.e., the conventional letter form and set phrases used,⁵ as well as the typical letter topics⁶ and the letter genre.⁷ Events associated with the letter—that is, the writing process, the delivery to the recipients, and the reception of the letter—have hardly received attention in these investigations.

Heikki Koskenniemi (1956) examined primarily Greek letters and the forms and conventions according to which they were composed and connected with the typical letter situation. According to him, the intent of a letter is to maintain a friendship by enabling an exchange of thoughts⁸ in the sense that a letter generates the spiritual presence (παρουσία) of a distant friend. Koskenniemi states,

---

2. Cf. Doty, "Classification"; Doty, *Letters*, 24–27; Stowers, *Letter Writing*, 18–20.

3. For example, Sykutris, "Epistolographie," 187–88; White, *Light* (a selection of papyrus letters compared with Christian letters); Malherbe, *Ancient Epistolary* (edition of important texts on ancient epistolography); Berger, "Apostelbrief," is more cautious. Cf. the overview of historical research in Conring, *Hieronymus*, 17–36.

4. Doty, *Letters*, 12–15, stresses the adherence to form and use of formulaic language: "amazingly stereotyped and bound to tradition" (12).

5. Koskenniemi, *Studien*; Thraede, *Grundzüge*; Bahr, "Paul and Letter Writing"; Bahr, "Subscription" (on the personal postscript in letters); Mullins, "Disclosure"; Mullins, "Greeting"; Mullins, "Formulas"; Mullins, "Benediction"; White, "Saint Paul"; White, "New Testament Epistolary Literature"; White, *Form and Function* (letter body); White, "Ancient Greek Letters" (with bibliography); Arzt, "Thanksgiving" (formula valetudinis, thanksgiving); Reed, "Are Paul's Thanksgivings"; Alexander, "Hellenistic Letter-Forms," on the Epistle to the Philippians; D. Hartman, "Epistolary Conventions" (petition and request); Müller, *Vom Schluss zum Ganzen* (closing of the letter body).

6. Koskenniemi, *Studien*, 34–47 identifies three themes: philophronesis, parousia, homilia. On parousia, cf. Funk, *Language, Hermeneutic*, 164–269 (travelogue); Funk, "Apostolic Parousia" (parousia); Mullins, "Visit Talk." On the use of typical formulas and thoughts of letters of friendship in 1 Thess, see Schoon-Janssen, *Umstrittene Apologien*; Schoon-Janssen, "On the Use of Elements."

7. For example letters of recommendation, family letters, official letters from rulers and administrators, letters of consolation; cf. White, "Ancient Greek Letters," 88–95. Vegge, *Paulus*, 225–29 sees a connection between New Testament letters and the philosophical letters of instruction.

8. Koskenniemi, *Studien*, 35–47.

> We can be fundamentally certain that the primary understanding was that the words of the author of a letter do not come from afar, but that he himself personally meets the recipient in his words, which means that the focus of attention was not on the point in time when the letter was written, but rather on the moment when the letter was received, when in a certain sense, the letter first became real.[9]

However, just exactly how that happens in the "moment of reception" is hardly given any consideration.

Taking a very similar approach, Klaus Thraede (1970) investigated Latin letter writing in order to throw light on the ancient educational tradition as reflected in the themes and phraseology of letters. Although Thraede speaks of an "independent 'letter situation' defined by education and society" and seeks to find out "in which concrete thoughts on the meaning, form and experience of the exchange of letters it has taken form in the course of time,"[10] he only deals with the experience of letter reception on the basis of Cicero's exchange of letters in the sense that the letter of friendship replaced real contact, creating a spiritual presence by the fact that writing or reading the letter creates the experience of a mental vision.[11] That fact that the receiving side of the "letter situation defined by education and society" was usually an event involving speaking and listening, including important components of social interaction, receives no consideration.

John L. White (1972, 1984, 1986) also examined the form and content of the New Testament letters in comparison to ancient epistolography.[12] More than anyone before him has, he emphasizes the social event of letter reception. He understands the letter as a means to maintain *oral* communication despite physical separation: "The letter arises because of the inability of two or more parties to communicate face to face. Thus, the letter becomes the written means of keeping oral conversation in

---

9. Ibid., 46 (my translation). Schnider and Stenger, *Studien*, 100 refer to 1 Cor 5:3: "The presence of the apostle as mediated by the letter has, as it were, legal consequences: 'Here the letter is intended to be a practically legally binding representation of the author'" (my translation; Thraede, *Grundzüge*, 147, is cited here).

10. Thraede, *Grundzüge*, 9.

11. Ibid., 39–47, with examples mainly from Cicero's correspondence.

12. White, *Form and Function*; White, "New Testament Epistolary Literature"; White, *Light*, 193–213.

motion."[13] White assumes that the bodies of the Pauline Epistles reflect the way Paul would explain the gospel in a sermon in the churches: "There is surely warrant for suggesting that the letter is the written equivalent of the oral presentation which Paul would have delivered to the congregation, if he had actually been present."[14] The situation of letter reception is therefore the assembly of the congregation, in which the apostle is present with all his authority by letter:

> The letter was the substitute for Paul's apostolic presence with his Christian communities. His use of Christian formulas shows, more exactly, that the setting for which the letter served as a surrogate was the Christian congregation at worship. Namely, it was in his capacity as God's representative that Paul addressed his congregations. Given the Jewish conception of the evocative power of the spoken word of God, one may understand Paul's reticence in using the letter as a surrogate medium for that message. On the other hand, the religious and cultic nuances of the letter, as well as Paul's use of rhetorical techniques that are reminiscent of oral argumentation, all make sense in this light.[15]

Hearers recognized the apostolic authority of the letter thanks to references to Paul's earlier admonitions and to his exemplary life conduct, through references to the letter itself or to the delegates sent by Paul, and also through the announcement of a personal visit to come.[16] The handwritten conclusion (1 Cor 16:21; Gal 6:11; Phlm 19, as well as Col 4:18; 2

---

13. White, "New Testament Epistolary Literature," 1731. On the development of the letter out of oral communication, cf. White, *Light*, 192–93; White, "Ancient Greek Letters," 87–88.

14. White, "New Testament Epistolary Literature," 1743; cf. Doty, *Letters*, 16–17: "In each case, then, the original situation implied by the language and by the form of the letter is the personal confrontation, the conversation, or the oral encounter."

15. White, *Light*, 19. Similarly in Doty, *Letters*, 44–45; Stirewalt, *Paul*, 13. See also White, "New Testament Epistolary Literature," 1743: "Therefore we can speak of the assembled congregation as the common recipient of Paul's letters and of Paul as an addressor who, in every case, writes in his official capacity as apostle." Similarly on p. 1739: "Apart from Philemon . . . all of Paul's letters are addressed to Christian congregations with an eye to their corporate setting in worship." On the Epistle to Philemon as a letter to a house church, cf. Schnider and Stenger, *Studien*, 22 and 50–51: "The Pauline Epistles are not in fact intended for individuals, but for a wider audience, which is also true of the Epistle to Philemon. Thus the Pauline Epistles are brought closer to the genus of *public speech* than is the Hellenistic private letter, which is better compared to the genus of a *conversation* among friends" (my translation, italics in the original).

16. White, "New Testament Epistolary Literature," 1746–47; cf. White, *Form and Function*, 29–31; Funk, "Apostolic Parousia."

Thess 3:17; probably also 1 Thess 5:26–27) also emphasizes the authority of the apostle.[17] Although White does address certain social aspects of letter reception, many other social aspects remain unconsidered in most studies. So White also lacks reflection on how Paul's apostolic authority is embodied in the situation of the letter reception—for example by the envoy or the reader presenting the letter, who lends the sender his voice. Most important, there is no discussion of the role that the recipients play.

Like White, Stanley K. Stowers (1986) also emphasizes the social context of communication by letter[18] and describes the function of letters in the honor culture of ancient times and in the philosophical practice of spiritual guidance.[19] Stowers analyzes a number of types of letters (oriented on Pseudo-Demetrius, *Formae epistolicae* and Pseudo-Libanius, *Characteres epistolici*) and places New Testament letters next to a plethora of nonbiblical letters.[20] However, his focus is on the letter as an *object* composed according to traditional forms in order to fulfill certain functions in the social context. Although Stowers writes in his introduction "that ancient letters will be difficult to understand on their own terms unless we also understand something about the contexts of Greco-Roman society in which the actions were performed and had their meanings,"[21] the letter as part of a performance, as a social *event*, does not receive attention.

This overview of some important studies shows that the research has given little consideration to the recipients' side of communication

---

17. White, "New Testament Epistolary Literature," 1741: "he would add his personal weight to the letter's message." On the personally written closing of letters and legal documents, see Bahr, "Paul and Letter Writing"; Bahr, "Subscription"; Doty, *Letters*, 41; Schnider and Stenger, *Studien*, 135–44 and 145–67; Kremendahl, *Botschaft der Form*, 42–49. On the fact that the personally written closing is mentioned in the text of Gal 6:11 and is therefore apparent for those who do not see, but rather hear the letter, see Kremendahl, *Botschaft der Form*, 118.

18. Bünker, *Briefformular*, 12 also emphasized the letter as a product of the sociocultural situation and sees his work as a contribution to the sociological study of Christianity.

19. Stowers, *Letter Writing*, 27–31 (honor culture), pp. 36–40 (philosophy and character formation).

20. Cf. also Fitzgerald, "Paul, Ancient Epistolary Theorists," who finds echoes of a number of ancient types of letter in 2 Cor 10–13. Klauck, *Ancient Letters* follows a similar approach. Aune, *Literary Environment*, 162 finds that a consideration of the official letters is missing in Stowers.

21. Stowers, *Letter Writing*, 16.

by letter, where "in a certain sense, the letter first became real."[22] Usually, the New Testament letters are viewed as objects that need to be studied to determine what their characteristics are, and to analyze how they were treated, because that can bring insights into the human communication that took place through these objects. The characteristics of a letter are primarily a result of the way letters are produced. As a result, the primary interest in research has been on the *creation of the text*, on the work of the author, who—perhaps together with a secretary[23]—conceives the content of the text, composes the formal structure, chooses linguistic forms, and gives the letter a certain character.[24] The dispatching and conveyance of the letter up to delivery to the recipients[25] also receive attention. But then just how the recipients gain knowledge of the contents of the letter remains widely ignored.[26]

This emphasis on the creation of the text results from our culture of written language, which is characterized by the concept that communication takes place through written texts that have been composed, that can be held in the hands, and whose meaning can be comprehended by interpreting the visual symbols.

Such a concept is problematic for two reasons: On the one hand, because the recipient of a letter is not passive but is rather actively involved in giving meaning to the written text. This fact has been emphasized above all by interpretation methods that focus on the reader.[27] On the other hand, it is a problem because in the culture in which the letters of the New Testament originated, communication did not focus on written

22. Koskenniemi, *Studien*, 46 (my translation).

23. Cf. Richards, *Secretary*.

24. The fact that the *creation* of the Pauline Epistles is also a social event has been emphasized by studies that give attention to the role of Paul's coauthors and scribes: Bahr, "Paul and Letter Writing"; Botha, "Verbal Art," 415–17; Murphy-O'Connor, *Paul the Letter-Writer*, 16–34; Stirewalt, *Paul*, 9–11; Richards, *Paul and First-Century Letter*, 26–27, 34–35, 59–93.

25. For example Riepl, *Nachrichtenwesen*; Llewelyn, "Sending Letters"; Llewelyn, "Directions"; Murphy-O'Connor, *Paul the Letter-Writer*, 37–41; Stirewalt, *Paul*, 11–12; Richards, *Paul and First-Century Letter*, 171–209.

26. For example, a discussion of letter reception is missing in Murphy-O'Connor, *Paul the Letter-Writer*. Richards, *Paul and First-Century Letter*, who describes the composition, dispatch and delivery of letters in the ancient world, makes only a few comments on the reception and presentation of letters (pp. 185 and 202; he calls it "performance").

27. Fundamentally described in Warning, *Rezeptionsästhetik*; Iser, *Akt des Lesens*.

texts but was conceived as an interpersonal event in which the written word played a significant but only indirect role.[28] One can hold a letter in one's hands and also preserve and reproduce it. But the actual communication event for which letters are intended cannot be conserved, for it is a social event. Private letters are a substitute for a personal conversation.[29] A letter from an apostle is brought to the recipients by a messenger and read aloud to them (1 Thess 5:27).[30] A letter serves an oral event.[31] This is always unique and unreproducible, even if the letter is read again later. The nature of the social event brought about by the reading of a letter aloud depends on the situation, on the environment, and above all on the one who reads aloud and on the listeners with their diverse reactions.

In a thin book by Martin Luther Stirewalt (2003) a decisive step is taken in this direction. The whole event in connection with the letters of Paul, including the composition and the situation of reception, is addressed as a social event.[32] This is enlightening for our understanding of the letters because social rules must be followed that stipulate how communication between persons or between groups of higher, equal, or

28. Hearon, "Implications of Orality," 4–6 speaks of the written text as "written remains" of the communication event.

29. Cicero, *Fam.* 2.4.1; *Att.* 9.10.1 ("quasi loquerer"). Cf. Klauck, *Ancient Letters*, 160, 191–92; in detail in Thraede, *Grundzüge*.

30. Cox, "Reading" assumes that letters were the first Christian texts that were read in Christian assemblies—next to the texts that were taken over from the synagogue. The Gospels came only later.

31. Aune, *Literary Environment*, 158: "The Greek word epistole ('epistle') originally referred to an *oral* communication sent by messenger." Funk, *Language, Hermeneutic*, 248: "The letter, consequently, is an appropriate substitute for oral word—it is as near oral speech as possible—yet it provides a certain distance on the proclamation as event." On pp. 264–69, Funk interprets the travel notes ("travelogue") of Paul as a promise that the written word would be followed by the—according to Funk—more highly esteemed oral word; e.g., p. 269: "It has already been suggested that the travelogue is related to the body in the same way that the promise (or threat) of oral word is related to the written word in Paul's disposition toward language." Cf. also Funk, "Apostolic Parousia"; Tsang, "Are We Misreading."

32. Stirewalt, *Paul*. In Stirewalt, *Studies*, 2, he calls it an "extended setting" when a letter, such as an official communiqué, involves a wider group of senders and listeners: "That is, a community exists at each end of the communication . . . The writer lives in a community the personnel of which he may include or exclude as he wills. The addressees represent the recipient community, the members of which the writer may also include or exclude as he wills." An important aspect of this social event, namely the role of the messengers who carried letters and delivered oral messages, has been discussed in Mitchell, "New Testament Envoys."

lower social rank must take place. The social status of the correspondents and the relationship between sender and recipient therefore affects *what* is being said and *how* it is said.[33]

Stirewalt also compares the Pauline epistles with ancient letters, but unlike Deissmann, he comes to the conclusion that Paul's epistles are not private letters but correspond more closely to *official* letters (*epistula principum*): "His [Paul's] letters were communal letters addressed to ecclesiae or house churches to whom he ministered in an authoritative capacity."[34] With that Stirewalt confirmed a presumption that had already been stated previously.[35] Official letters are letters that serve the administrative and political business of the state or other leading personalities and transport official notices or instructions or items of diplomatic interest.[36] They are expressions of authority. Paul has adapted and used this form for his own purposes.

Stirewalt supports his thesis by first examining the process of composition, delivery, and reception of the official letter (chapters 5-8) and then analyzing the Pauline Epistles for evidence of this process in the main part of his book (chapters 9-18). Such evidence includes additional designations besides Paul's name; mentions of coauthors; multiple addressees (among them churches, house churches, or groups of churches); separate sections within the main body of each letter (a background section and a section featuring the message or instruction); and a personally

---

33. Aune, *Literary Environment*, 158.

34. Stirewalt, *Paul*, 9. Long, *Ancient Rhetoric*, 100-101 agrees.

35. Doty, *Letters*, 26: "Paul, insofar as he was not writing as a private person but as an apostle, and not primarily to individual persons but to churches, did indeed write letters which had a public intent, bringing them closer to the official pronouncement than to the private letter." Cf. also Doty, "Classification," 198. Aune, *Literary Environment*, 160: "Their [early Christian letters'] very length suggests a comparison with the longer literary and official letters of antiquity . . ." Cf. Aune, *Literary Environment*, 164-65, where he discusses official letters. Similarly in Schnider and Stenger, *Studien*, 91-92, where the Pauline Epistles are compared with letters sent from Hellenistic kings to various cities. Cf. Güttgemanns, *Offene Fragen*, 111-15; Andresen, "Zum Formular," who assumes the official Jewish letter to the diaspora to be the model for the form of Acts 15:23-29 and other early Christian writings. In contrast, Dormeyer, *Literaturgeschichte*, 193 does not perceive any official letters in the body of New Testament letters, because the authors "do not consider themselves to be administrators higher up in the hierarchy" (my translation).

36. On official letters, cf. Stirewalt, *Studies*, 6-10; Stirewalt assumes that letter writing originates from official letters (p. 6). Cf. White, *Light*, 192; White, "Ancient Greek Letters," 85.

written postscript that repeats formal parts of the letter such as the salutation, briefly summarized contents, greetings, and closing greeting.

Stirewalt emphasizes that composing the letter was a communal act. "Paul wrote from within a community. He surrounded himself with helpers: co-senders named in the salutation, scribes, greeters from the local congregation, commissioners and visitors from other churches. This group of people provided a kind of voluntary ad hoc secretariat."[37] The coauthors were also with Paul responsible for and witnesses to the entire letter event.[38] The reception of an official letter was also a social event[39] that followed a traditional protocol as described by Thukydides (7.10), by Luke (Acts 15:30–32), and by other sources. This included the oral report of the messengers, the official presentation of the letter, the public reading—usually performed by an important personality from the addressee community—and further questions put to messengers.[40] The oral report, the spoken reading in front of the assembled addressees, and the oral questioning of and comments by the messengers embed the letter in a culture of oral communication. Above all, the one who read the letter aloud brought the written word to life and made the presence of the sender tangible for the hearers.[41] Stirewalt summarizes the event as follows:

> Through the centuries, then, in different communities and settings, the official, administrative letter was treated consistently. It was prepared by competent, authorized persons and was carried by envoys who delivered it with ceremony appropriate to the particular assignment. It was addressed and delivered to a constituted body and read before that assembly or its representatives. Carriers also delivered oral messages and answered inquiries related to the letter's content.[42]

---

37. Stirewalt, *Paul*, 10.

38. Ibid., 54.

39. On the conventions for reception of an official envoy, cf. Mitchell, "New Testament Envoys."

40. Stirewalt, *Paul*, 7; similarly in Tsang, "Are We Misreading," 216, however, the questioning of the messenger is missing. Cf. the protocol for delivering messages and the connections between the written and oral message in the ancient Orient in Meier, *Messenger*, esp. 137–226.

41. Stirewalt, *Paul*, 16; cf. Stirewalt, *Studies*, 5. Cf. presence by way of letter in Koskenniemi, *Studien*, 38–47, 172–80; Thraede, *Grundzüge*, 39–47, 55–61, 146–57. On the role of the one reading aloud, cf. Botha, "Letter Writing," 25–27.

42. Stirewalt, *Paul*, 8. On the oral supplement to the letter content by the messenger,

Stirewalt has made an important contribution to understanding the New Testament letters as events. He has shown how the joint preparation and careful composition of the letter—with consideration for the situation of the recipients, the role of the letter carrier, and the task of the one presenting the letter aloud—all work together to constitute a letter event scripted by social conventions. Thus the letter's reception must be conceived as a performance where the presenter and audience collectively consummate a unique event—an event determined in part by the performance situation even as it follows specific common conventions in a culture dominated by oral communication.

Rhetoric

If the reception of a letter in the ancient world was part of an oral event, and if Paul's letters therefore also only achieved their full effect by being read out loud to a church congregation, then they must be viewed in connection with ancient rhetoric.

Rhetorical aspects have been a natural part of the interpretation of the New Testament since ancient times.[43] Particular attention was paid to linguistic forms and stylistic devices that lend persuasive power to the spoken word.[44] At the end of the nineteenth century, rhetoric came to be labeled as mere ornamentation and disappeared into the background. It

---

cf. White, *Light*, 216 with reference to P. Col. III.6: "The rest please learn from the man who brings you the letter. For he is no stranger to us." See also Mitchell, "New Testament Envoys," 650; Richards, *Paul and First-Century Letter*, 183–84, 201–2; particularly Head, "Named Letter-Carriers," 288–89 who comes to the conclusion "that the trusted letter carrier often has an important role in extending the communication initiated by the letter. The letter carrier thus brings fuller personal knowledge into the communication process, which is only partly embodied in the letter" (p. 296). The importance of the oral message as a supplement to the written message is also demonstrated by the changes to the official postal service made by Augustus, as reported by Suetonius in *Augustus* 49.3: Augustus first stationed young men at short intervals along the military streets to carry letters, and later he stationed carriages there so that the man who was entrusted with the letter could also reach the addressee and answer his questions; cf. Llewelyn, "Sending Letters," 341.

43. Cf. Kennedy, *Classical Rhetoric*; Classen, "Paulus"; Classen, "St Paul's Epistles." On the history of the rhetoric in the interpretation of the New Testament, cf. Mack, *Rhetoric*, 9–24; Stamps, "Rhetorical Criticism," 130–41; Kern, *Rhetoric and Galatians*, 39–89. Lampe, "Rhetorical Analysis," also offers an overview of the rhetorical exegesis of the New Testament.

44. Examples from the nineteenth century include Wilke, *Die neutestamentliche Rhetorik*; Heinrici, *Zweite Sendschreiben an die Korinther*; Weiss, "Beiträge."

was primarily the commentary on the Epistle to the Galatians by Hans Dieter Betz (1979) that drew on a long tradition of rhetorical interpretation and brought the importance of rhetoric back into the awareness of New Testament scholars.[45] There followed a wealth of studies on the rhetorical interpretation of the New Testament Epistles.[46]

Betz oriented his interpretation of the Letter to the Galatians on *ancient* rhetoric as presented in the ancient rhetorical handbooks[47] and assumed that Paul's letters contain argumentation. In particular, he examined which rhetorical category[48] the letter could be assigned to, what arguments are used (*inventio*), and how the arguments are organized (*dispositio*). The stylistic form of the speech (*elocutio*), which was at the focus of earlier rhetorical interpretations, receded into the background. Betz and those following him take a historical interest in the epistles and try to reconstruct the rhetoric used by the author in the social context of the times in order to convince his audience.[49]

The method of rhetorical analysis was systematized and developed further by George A. Kennedy (1984).[50] Kennedy's methodological steps included determining the limits of the section of text understood to be a rhetorical unit; ascertaining the rhetorical situation and the problem it is dealing with; establishing which rhetorical category is used; analyzing the content (*inventio*), structure (*dispositio*) and style (*elocutio*) of the speech; and finally evaluating the success of the speech in the rhetorical situation.[51] Many studies using Kennedy's methods followed.[52]

Kennedy assumes that the laws of rhetoric, although originally intended for oral events, could also be applied to the interpretation of the New Testament writings, since in the Greco-Roman culture both oral and

45. Betz, *Galatians*. Also Betz, "Literary Composition," and later Betz, *2 Corinthians* to 2 Cor 8 and 9. Already prior to Betz: Wilder, *Language*.

46. Cf. the bibliography in Watson and Hauser, *Rhetorical Criticism*.

47. In contrast, Mitchell, *Paul and the Rhetoric*, 6 postulates that apart from the handbooks, real speeches must be taken into consideration; similarly Watson and Hauser, *Rhetorical Criticism*, 112.

48. Judicial, deliberative, or epideictic, cf. Aristotle, *Rhet.* 1.3.3.

49. Watson and Hauser, *Rhetorical Criticism*, 110.

50. Kennedy, *New Testament Interpretation*. Cf. also the methodical considerations of Mitchell, *Paul and the Rhetoric*, 6–7.

51. Kennedy, *New Testament Interpretation*, 33–38; cf. Wuellner, "Where Is," 455–58; Watson, *Invention*, 1–28; cf. the criticism by Black, "Keeping Up," 256–57.

52. For example Watson, *Invention*; Mitchell, *Paul and the Rhetoric*; Smit, "Argument and Genre"; Bakke, *Concord and Peace*; Long, *Ancient Rhetoric*.

written communication was widely organized according to these rules.[53] For him, rhetoric is a universal prerequisite for human communication.[54] He attempts to reconstruct the power of the texts in the ancient world.[55]

As a consequence of such considerations, the results of *modern* rhetorical science have also been applied in the rhetorical interpretation of biblical texts.[56] The work of Chaim Perelman and Lucie Olbrechts-Tyteca (1958) was especially influential in this respect. They understand rhetoric as the basis of any communication, oral or written, and concentrate primarily on the social discourse, that is, the question of how verbal communication achieved its effect in its social environment.[57] This impulse

---

53. Kennedy, *New Testament Interpretation*, 10: "He [Paul] and the evangelists as well would, indeed, have been hard put to escape an awareness of rhetoric as practiced in the culture around them, for the rhetorical theory of the schools found its immediate application in almost every form of oral and written communication: in official documents and public letters, in private correspondence, in the lawcourts and assemblies, in speeches at festivals and commemorations, and in literary composition in both prose and verse." Cf. Longenecker, *Galatians*, cxiii, cxix; Mack, *Rhetoric*, 28–31; Porter, "Theoretical Justification," 104–10.

54. Kennedy, *New Testament Interpretation*, 10.

55. Ibid., 158–59.

56. Classen, "St Paul's Epistles," 268: "When one turns to the categories of rhetoric as tools for a more adequate and thorough appreciation of texts, their general structure and their details, one should not hesitate to use the most developed and sophisticated form, as it will offer more help than any other. For there is no good reason to maintain that a text could and should be examined only according to categories known (or possibly known) to the author concerned. For rhetoric provides a system for the interpretation of all texts (as well as of oral utterances and even of other forms of communication), irrespectively of time and circumstances." Similarly Wuellner, "Paul's Rhetoric"; Wuellner, "Greek Rhetoric"; Wuellner, "Where Is"; Wuellner, "Argumentative Structure"; Anderson, *Ancient Rhetorical Theory*, 30–33. Against such an extension, see Mitchell, *Paul and the Rhetoric*, 6–7.

57. Perelman and Olbrechts-Tyteca, *New Rhetoric*. Cf. Wuellner, *Hermeneutics*, 33–34, 38: The important thing is not just what the contents of the texts say (hermeneutics), but above all what effect they have, how they provoke a response (rhetorics). Cf. also Wuellner, "Paul's Rhetoric," 330. Cf. Stamps, "Rhetorical Criticism," 167: "Rhetorical criticism would thus generally be defined by its attempt to identify the textually embedded strategies that seek to persuade the reader, to assess the effectiveness of these strategies, and then to evaluate the ideological positions to which the reader(s) is being moved." Porter, "Theoretical Justification," 107–8; Stamps, "Rhetorical Criticism," 151–54; Kern, *Rhetoric and Galatians*, 165–66, 256–59 also argue for a perhaps limited rhetorical analysis which is not governed by the ancient school of rhetoric. Anderson, *Ancient Rhetorical Theory*, 280–91: Even though Paul probably had little contact to rhetorical training, rhetoric was nevertheless influential and can help to understand the texts.

triggered a large number of valuable studies.[58] The studies concerning the Letter to the Galatians sometimes came to different conclusions than Betz's study had.[59]

Vernon K. Robbins (1993, 1996) and others have widened rhetorical analysis to a social-rhetorical interpretation.[60] According to these authors, rhetorical and sociological methods, together with methods from literary theory, communication theory, and ideological criticism make a comprehensive interpretation possible. For Robbins, it is important to consider not only the texts but also the sociocultural situation in which they are embedded. Using woven fabric as an illustration, Robbins points out that different levels of interaction can be found and examines how the individual building blocks within a text are linked with each other as well as how the text as a whole is linked with other texts, with the dominating sociocultural structures and their respective ideologies, and with the religious environment.

Concerning the present study, there are above all two problems with which the rhetorical criticism of the New Testament Epistles has to wrestle. First, it is confronted with the question of how to justify interpreting *written texts* using rules and conventions designed for a *speech made*

---

58. Examples include Wuellner, "Paul's Rhetoric"; Wuellner, "Greek Rhetoric"; Wuellner, "Paul as Pastor"; Wuellner, "Rhetorical Criticism"; Siegert, *Argumentation bei Paulus*; Jewett, *Thessalonian Correspondence*; Vouga, "Zur rhetorischen Gattung"; Watson, "Rhetorical Analysis"; Hughes, *Early Christian Rhetoric*; Thurén, *Rhetorical Strategy*; Thurén, *Derhetorizing*; Wanamaker, *Thessalonians*; Olbricht, "Aristotelian Rhetorical Analysis"; Wire, *Corinthian Women*; Elliott, *Rhetoric of Romans*; Crafton, *Agency*; Pogoloff, *Logos and Sophia*; Litfin, *St. Paul's Theology*; Hester, "Speaker, Audience"; combined with linguistic methods: Johanson, *To All the Brethren*; also Stamps, "Theological Rhetoric." Cf. the literature commented on in Mack, *Rhetoric*, 19–24; the list of rhetorical studies on letters in Porter, "Theoretical Justification," 102–3, n. 7; the bibliography in Watson and Hauser, *Rhetorical Criticism*; Watson, "Rhetorical Criticism"; and the overview in Robbins, "Rhetorical Analysis."

59. According to Kennedy, *New Testament Interpretation*, 145–46; Hall, "Rhetorical Outline"; and Smit, "Letter of Paul to the Galatians," 1–26 the Epistle to the Galatians is not a judicial but rather a deliberative speech. Longenecker, *Galatians*, cix–cxiii finds a mixture of differing genera; Hansen, *Abraham* defines the Epistle to the Galatians as a "rebuke letter"; Classen, "Paulus," 8–15, 29–33 holds that there is no sense in attributing it to any rhetorical genus; Anderson, *Ancient Rhetorical Theory*, 189 understands the Letter to the Galatians to be more the teachings of a philosopher than a speech according to the teachings of rhetoric. Overview by Anderson, *Ancient Rhetorical Theory*, 129–42; Surburg, "Ancient Rhetorical Criticism"; Tolmie, *Persuading*, 1–19.

60. Robbins, "Rhetoric and Culture"; Robbins, *Exploring*.

orally in front of an audience. The second problem is the inconsistency of the method, which is demonstrated in the fact that of the five tasks of a speaker, rhetorical criticism only considers the first three (*inventio, dispositio, elocutio*), simply ignoring the memorization (*memoria*) and presentation of the speech (*pronuntiatio* or *actio*).

What is the justification for using the rules of ancient rhetoric for the interpretation of New Testament letters?[61] After all, ancient rhetoric dealt with public speech—that is, an *oral* event.[62] However, the writing of a letter follows its own rules and produces at first only a *written* text, and that is what is available to interpreters today.

This question is a widely discussed topic. Lauri Thurén summarizes the different positions as follows:[63] First, there is the opinion that epistolography and rhetoric are to be kept separate.[64] This is opposed by interpreters who take a second position and understand the letters to be speeches that have been written down only because of the distance separating the author from the addressees.[65] So a letter would then be something like a speech with the introduction and conclusion of a letter.[66] A third position would apply both letter theory and rhetoric to the

---

61. Hübner, "Galaterbrief," 242, 245, 249 has already posed this question in his recension of Betz's Galatians commentary. Cf. also Stamps, "Rhetorical Criticism," 141; Anderson, *Ancient Rhetorical Theory*, 120.

62. Even the fact that the orator prepared the speech in writing only served the oral presentation, since the presentation is the speaker's most important task: Quintilian, *Inst.* 10.3; 11.3.6; Cicero, *De or.* 1.33.150; 3.56.213. On the written preparation of speeches, cf. Winter, *Philo*, 205–6; Long, *Ancient Rhetoric*, 31–32; Habinek, "Situating Literacy," 123.

63. Thurén, *Rhetorical Strategy*, 57–64. Watson and Hauser group similarly, *Rhetorical Criticism*, 120–21; also Klauck, *Ancient Letters*, 206–11; Kremendahl, *Botschaft der Form*, 15–20.

64. For example Anderson, *Ancient Rhetorical Theory*, 117–21; Classen, "Paulus," especially 1–7; Classen, "St Paul's Epistles," 265–91, where he particularly argues against a too-mechanical application of the rhetorical rules to the New Testament letters without denying that a consideration of rhetoric is fruitful in exegesis. Cf. also Reed, "Using Ancient Rhetorical Categories"; Porter, "Theoretical Justification"; Porter, "Paul as Epistolographer," 226–34; Byrskog, "Epistolography"; Kern, *Rhetoric and Galatians*, 14–34; Becker, *Schreiben und Verstehen*, 22–24. Porter, "Paul as Epistolographer," 248 remarks pointedly: "To be a letter-writer was to be doing something different than being a speechmaker in the Greco-Roman world."

65. Aune, *Literary Environment*, 158, 197–99; Schnider and Stenger, *Studien*, 51–52; Dabourne, *Purpose*, 78, 107.

66. Kennedy, *New Testament Interpretation*, 86–87. On the general relationship between speeches and writings, see Kennedy, *Classical Rhetoric*, 127–36; Berger,

New Testament letters. Both of these disciplines are considered to help gain more understanding of the letters, since they throw light on different aspects of them.⁶⁷

Representatives of the first approach point to the fact that the introduction and conclusion of a letter are not the same as the introduction and conclusion of a speech, since the letter as a written work follows its own rules.⁶⁸ It is certainly correct that the letter as a conventional form must be appreciated in its own right. However, if one bears in mind that the conventional letter, and especially the introduction therein, was derived from the traditional messenger formula, then it becomes apparent that the letter is part of what was originally an oral event. The beginning of a letter, which was delivered by an envoy and in which the sender and the recipient are named, corresponds to the introduction of a messenger, who begins his oral message by speaking in the name of the one who commissioned him: Thus *x* speaks to *y*. This oral aspect of the letter event especially holds for official letters to groups or communities, where oral presentation was the usual practice.⁶⁹

The main objection to the rhetorical criticism of the New Testament letters is that letter writing was not part of the ancient rhetorical handbooks and therefore it is not appropriate to analyze letters according to the rules of ancient rhetoric.⁷⁰

"Apostelbrief"; Wuellner, "Greek Rhetoric"; Hübner, "Galaterbrief"; Hübner, "Rhetorik und Theologie"; Hughes, *Early Christian Rhetoric*, 26–30; Aune, "Romans," 278–81. Berger, "Hellenistische Gattungen," 1334, calls the Pauline letters "apostolic speeches" (my translation) in written form.

67. For example Bünker, *Briefformular*; Johanson, *To All the Brethren*; Thurén, *Rhetorical Strategy*; Schoon-Janssen, *Umstrittene Apologien*; Kremendahl, *Botschaft der Form*, explicitly 4, 14; cf. Stowers, *Letter Writing*, 27–28, 51–57. Lampe, "Rhetorical Analysis," 10–17 laments that epistolographical (i.e., with focus on written aspects) and rhetorical (i.e., with focus on oral aspects) analysis of the Pauline letters are often discussed next to each other but without any interconnections, or are even understood to be irreconcilable. He points out the many connections between epistolography and rhetoric and thus continues devoloping Kremendahl's integrative approach.

68. Stamps, "Rhetorical Criticism," 147.

69. Cf. Stirewalt, *Studies*, 4–5; Stirewalt, *Paul*, 7; Sykutris, "Epistolographie," 191 and see above on pp. 14–15 what is said about the protocol for delivering an official letter.

70. So, e.g., Porter, "Theoretical Justification," 110–16; Porter, "Paul as Epistolographer," 232; Stamps, "Rhetorical Criticism," 145; Klauck, *Ancient Letters*, 207–10. More cautiously White, "Saint Paul," 435–36; Reed, "Using Ancient Rhetorical Categories," 311–14.

Indeed, letter writing is not dealt with in Aristotle's *Rhetoric* and is only mentioned in passing in Quintilian's work (*Inst.* 9.4.19–20). However, it should be borne in mind that Aristotle does indeed lecture on how texts that are destined to be read aloud should be written. He requires a carefully prepared style and distinguishes it from the style of a judicial speech or a speech in a competition, where the speaker performs in a style more similar to an actor.[71] Thus Aristotle can fundamentally compare a written text that is to be presented to an audience with an oral speech, but clearly emphasizes the differences in style. As discussed above, such a comparison of a letter with orally presented speeches and a similar delimitation of the two is also found in Demetrius's excursus concerning the letter (*Eloc.* 224), where he explains the style in which a letter should be written. Indeed, it is questions of style, discussed according to the rhetorical task of *elocutio*, which we find again and again in ancient treatises on letters. The question of an appropriate style for letters consistent with the rhetorical function of *elocutio* also finds repeated treatment in both of the known ancient texts on letter writing with collections of example letters: Pseudo-Demetrius's *Formae epistolicae* first recommends a style fitting to the occasion, and then a collection of example letters is provided.[72] Pseudo-Libanius, *Characteres epistolici* 46–50, advocates a moderate Attic style.[73]

Very similar thoughts are found in a letter from Cicero to his friend Paetus (*Fam.* 9.21.1): "Quid enim simile habet epistula aut iudicio aut contioni?"[74] This sentence is often cited and understood as an indication that, for the Greeks and the Romans, letters and speeches where completely different things.[75] But what is Cicero's concern with this question?[76] The letter to Paetus is concerned with *public speaking*. Cicero, flattered by his friend for his oratory skills, points out in feigned humility

---

71. Aristotle, *Rhet.* 3.12; cf. Sonkowsky, "Aspect of Delivery," 260–61; Gagarin, "Orality," 165–66.

72. Second century BCE to third century CE.

73. Fourth to sixth century CE. Both ancient works about letters provide example letters that can be classified into the three rhetorical genera, e.g., letters of praise or congratulations (epideictical), letters of accusation or defense (judicial), letters of advice or warning (deliberative).

74. "What does a letter have in common with a speech in court or at a public meeting?" (my translation).

75. Anderson, *Ancient Rhetorical Theory*, 118–19; Klauck, *Ancient Letters*, 161, 207; Kremendahl, *Botschaft der Form*, 15, n. 5.

76. On this, cf. Müller, *Sprachbewusstsein*, 85–86.

that he does not always use such elaborate language and refers to his letters to his friend, which have simpler language. Yes, Cicero continues, even in his public speeches in court he adapts to the matter in question and uses simpler style for less important cases. He only uses more embellished language for cases of life and death, or ones concerning a citizen's social honor. At the end of the section, Cicero summarizes: "epistulas vero cottidianis verbis texere solemus."[77] That means that for Cicero, although letters to friends and public speeches use a different style of language—at least in serious legal cases—, letters and speeches are, nevertheless, *fundamentally* comparable. That is why it is possible for him to react to his friend's praise of his oratory in court[78] with the reference to the simplicity of language in his letters. So there is no clear line between speech and letter.[79]

So it appears only natural that an excursus on the letter appears in the work from Julius Victor (fourth century CE) on rhetorics (27). The first sentence reads: "Epistolis conveniunt multa eorum, quae de sermone praecepta sunt."[80] It then continues, saying concerning official letters that all the rules of rhetorics apply with the exception that a not-too-elaborate style is to be used and a more normal way of talking should prevail in a letter. Concerning the private letter it says that it should be short and clear and in a style suited to the recipient. Julius Victor quite naturally assumes that there is a connection between spoken performance and letter writing.[81]

---

77. "As for letters, we usually weave them out of everyday words" (my translation).

78. According to Müller, *Sprachbewusstsein*, 86 probably the *Philippicae*, which Cicero had published in writing in 44 BCE.

79. Probst, *Paulus und der Brief*, 99 with reference to Philostrat (third century CE). Cf. Vegge, *Paulus*, 345: Rhetorical speech is the language of the educated, the difference between verbal and written language is of secondary importance.

80. "Many directives which pertain to oral discourse also apply to letters" (translation in Malherbe, *Ancient Epistolary*, 63).

81. Cf. Poster, "Conversation Halved," 35–37. Anderson, *Ancient Rhetorical Theory*, 118–19 assumes with R. Giomini and M. S. Celentano ("Praefatio," in G. Iulii Victoris: *Ars Rhetorica*, xxii–xxiii) that this excursus on the letter is borrowed from Julius Titianus, who lived in the late second century CE. This would mean that the correlation between letter and rhetoric is older (cf. also Koskenniemi, *Studien*, 31) and that the excursus on the letter in Demetrius, *Eloc.* 223–35 does not stand fully isolated in its time. Further ancient comments concerning the style of letters in comparison to oral speech are found in Isocrates (436–338 BCE), *Ep.* 2,13: "I have unawares gradually drifted beyond the due proportions of a letter and run into a lengthy discourse [εἰς λόγου μῆκος]" (translation by Norlin, Perseus Collection); Philostratus of Lemnos,

Proponents of the rhetorical interpretation can point to the fact that the letter serves to make communication possible despite a spatial separation. In his review of Betz's commentary on Galatians, it is this fact that leads Hans Hübner to the conclusion that, contrary to the rhetorical and epistological theory, a clearly defined separation between letter and speech is relativized in practice. "If the parousia of the letter writer belongs to the main functions of the letter, then it breaches the basic diastasis between letter and speech."[82] In addition, it must be remembered that the New Testament letters are apostolic writings:

> Additionally, in the case of Gal there is the fact that it is an apostolic letter, that is, a letter from someone who, as an apostle, is entrusted with the ministry of the oral proclamation; in other words, the apostolic letter is a substitute for preaching . . . , so that the diastase is even more problematic . . . The combination of (literary) speech and letter in Gal is understandable because Paul was an apostle and as such, when he wrote, he "wrote speaking.[83]

For Klaus Berger, "the apostolic letter is an authoritative apostolic speech in written form whose origins are attributed to God."[84]

Examples of such letters, which, although delivered in writing were nevertheless perceived as oral speeches, can be found in the works of

---

De epistulis (third century CE), II.257.29–258.28 speaks out for an Attic style of letter (Malherbe, *Ancient Epistolary*, 42–43); Libanius (fourth century CE), *Ep.* 528.4, notes: ἀλλ', ὦ δαιμόνιε, δεῖξον ἡμῖν πρὸ τοῦ σώματος τὸν ῥήτορα· δηλοῦται μὲν γὰρ ἡ τέχνη καὶ διὰ τῶν γραμμάτων. "But before you show us yourself in person, my dear man, show us the rhetor in you, for this art is also exhibited in letters" (translation by Klauck, *Ancient Letters*, 208).

82. Hübner, "Galaterbrief," 245 (my translation); Stirewalt, *Studies*, 9, n. 27 points out that letters were originally supplements to the emissaries' oral messages, and therefore "the written message accompanying the oral speech and secondary to it was naturally written in the rhetorical style." Cf. also Dormeyer, *Literaturgeschichte*, 62, 190–93. Cf. Sampley, "Ruminations," ix: "Because Paul (and his scribe[s]) knew that at their destination, the letters were to be read aloud, that is, performed, it is a necessity for us to treat them as letters *and as* speeches, because they were both from their beginnings, and intentionally so" (italics in the original).

83. Hübner, "Galaterbrief," 245 (my translation); cf. White, "Saint Paul," 439. Hübner, "Rhetorik und Theologie," 169 calls Paul's Letter to the Romans "a rhetorical masterpiece of theological argumentation" (my translation).

84. Berger, "Apostelbrief," 219, likewise 231; cf. 214: "Messenger style and letter style can sometimes be similar because both serve as a means to convey words" (my translation).

the famous orator Demosthenes.⁸⁵ In 323 BCE, while he was in exile, he addressed a meeting of the citizens of Athens and wrote in his third letter (*Ep.* 3.35): ταῦτ' εἰ μὲν παρῆν, λέγων ἂν ὑμᾶς ἐδίδασκον· ἐπειδὴ δ' ἐν τοιούτοις εἰμὶ ἐν οἷς, εἴ τις ἐμοῦ κατέψευσται ἐφ' οἷς ἀπόλωλα, γένοιτο, γράψας ἐπέσταλκα.⁸⁶ Isocrates also did not deliver his speeches publicly but disseminated them in written form and expected them to be presented orally by others.⁸⁷

The question arises as to whether Paul consciously views communication by letter as contrasting with oral communication—for example by deciding to solve the pending problems in Corinth not by speaking to the church himself but rather by writing them a letter (2 Cor 1:12—2:11).⁸⁸

---

85. Klauck, *Ancient Letters*, 206: "The letters of the great Attic orator (!) Demosthenes may be regarded as a form of deliberative self-defense, replacing speeches that could not be delivered because of time constraints." On their authenticity, cf. Klauck, *Ancient Letters*, 114. For a rhetorical analysis of the letters of Demosthenes—following Goldstein, *Letters of Demosthenes*—, cf. Probst, *Paulus und der Brief*, 77–83. See Long, *Ancient Rhetoric*, 21–22 for a list of speeches in the form of letters as well as the examples there on pp. 27–28.

86. "If I were present in person I should be trying to explain these matters to you by word of mouth, but since I am in such a plight as I pray may be the lot of anyone who has uttered falsehoods against me to my ruin, I have sent my message in the form of a letter." Text edited by W. Rennie, translation by N. W. DeWitt and N. J. DeWitt. Hughes, *Early Christian Rhetoric*, 19, 45–50 analyzes ancient speeches in written form from Isocrates and Demosthenes in comparison with Pauline letters. Kremendahl, *Botschaft der Form*, 133–40 compares the Letter to the Galatians with the second letter that Demosthenes sent from exile, which he identifies as a letter of self-defence. Long, *Ancient Rhetoric*, 102–12 analyzes letters from Demosthenes, Isocrates, and Plato as rhetorical pleas of defense. Cf. also Anderson, *Ancient Rhetorical Theory*, 121–23.

87. Kennedy, *Classical Rhetoric*, 86, 129; cf. Winter, "Philodemus," 326–27. Further examples of speeches conveyed in written form are found in Anderson, *Ancient Rhetorical Theory*, 122. On speeches in the form of letters, cf. Long, *Ancient Rhetoric*, 26–28. Fuhrmann, "Mündlichkeit," 56, emphasizes that the speeches given out in written form must of necessity bare traces of their oral background in order to make the authority of the author clear. "The oration genre, once it was documented in writing, was therefore subject to a certain improvement of its form, but not to fundamental changes—apparently because it was only then considered authentic when the situation under which it was delivered was clearly recognizable. Someone who had given a speech before the people or the court belonged to those who had been essential for the decision at the time; the speaker would have robbed himself of his own authority if he had come up with the idea of turning his speech into an edifice of lofty ideas disconnected from time and space" (my translation).

88. Cf. Bosenius, *Abwesenheit*. Becker, *Schreiben und Verstehen*, 141–205 examines Paul's reflections as an epistolary metacommunication. Stirewalt, *Paul*, 117 also reflects on why Paul chose the letter form, but against the background that the effect

The ambivalence of this question can be seen by the fact that Frank W. Hughes refers precisely to the Second Letter to the Corinthians as evidence that Paul's letters are very close to oral speeches.[89] Hughes takes the fact that according to 2 Cor 10:10 Paul's opponents felt that his letters, and especially the letter mentioned in 2 Cor 2:4, made a stronger impression than his performance as a speaker—an assessment that stands in contrast to the fact that in antiquity oral communication was normally valued more than written communication—as evidence that Paul's letters were powerful rhetorical documents.

Generally, the prepared text was not read but memorized and performed in the manner of a spontaneous speech.[90] There were, however, speakers who read out speeches prepared in writing.[91] Both possibilities are documented by the Roman statues, reliefs, and coins that have been found. One relief shows Emperor Hadrian holding a rolled-out scroll in his left hand and gesturing with the right.[92] The emperor is apparently presenting the contents of the document to his listeners. However, speakers are more often portrayed holding a rolled-up scroll in the left hand.[93]

For clarification of the relationship between rhetoric and epistolography, too little consideration has been given to the role written material plays in rhetorical practice, that is, in the preparation for the speech and then in the presentation in front of the audience.[94] In the process of preparing and delivering a speech, the written document and the oral presentation (the real goal of all rhetorical effort) become connected. For the study of letters this means that the letter as a written document must be seen in connection with the event that Koskenniemi calls "the moment

---

of an official letter, which had been brought by authorized messengers and performed by suitable persons, does not depend on the written document alone, but essentially on this performance situation. Cf. also Sampley, "Ruminations," xvi, who considers the advantages of a letter in comparison with personal presence and speech in a conflict situation in a church.

89. Hughes, *Early Christian Rhetoric*, 19.
90. Fuhrmann, "Mündlichkeit," 55.
91. Aldrete, *Gestures*, 46 with reference to Sueton, *Aug.* 48.
92. Ibid., 48.
93. Ibid., 46–48, 93, 95–96.
94. On this, see Sonkowsky, "Aspect of Delivery." On the performance of literary text, cf. Sonkowsky, "Oral Performance"; Sonkowsky, "Oral Interpretation." Speeches were often published in written form after the event; Long, *Ancient Rhetoric*, 23–24 provides a list. On the role of written presentations of problems (*controversiae*) in the preparation of rhetorical exercises, cf. Imber, "Practised Speech."

when the letter was received, when in a certain sense, the letter first became real."[95] That is especially valid for letters which, like Paul's letters, are directed to a group of people and are read aloud by an authorized and qualified person. In this event, which can be called the performance of the letter, epistolography and rhetoric are connected.[96]

Thus an ancient letter cannot be considered a written document in the way we think about written documents today, in an age dominated by written communication, when readers can identify the message directly in the written symbols. This fact has largely been disregarded in rhetorical analysis. In a society primarily characterized by oral communication, letters unfolded their influence by oral presentation.[97] The presentation of the letter was the actual letter event, during which it was as if the letter writer were present with the recipients,[98] embodied and made audible by the one giving the presentation.[99]

With that we have already addressed the second problem of rhetorical analysis up to the present, namely, that of the five tasks of an orator, the last two (memorizing and delivering) are generally ignored.[100] The rhetorical analysis of the New Testament letters has focused on those three aspects of rhetoric concerned with the production of the text, which Aristotle had treated comprehensively in his *Rhetoric*: *inventio*, *dispositio*, and *elocutio*. Traditionally, rhetorical interpretation has been concerned with characteristics of style (*elocutio*) that can also be applied to the written texts.[101] Since Betz's revival of rhetorical interpretation, the

95. Koskenniemi, *Studien*, 46 (my translation).

96. Kremendahl, *Botschaft der Form*, 19 suggests this when he writes: "At the same time, the horizon must be widened within which the relationship between epistolography and rhetoric in the Pauline letters is to be determined. This relationship is subordinate to the relationship between orality and scribality" (my translation). On orality, see the section below on pp. 31–40.

97. Kennedy, *New Testament Interpretation*, 87.

98. On parusia through letters, cf. above all Thraede, *Grundzüge*, 146–61.

99. Stirewalt's studies (*Studies*) concerning the delivery of official letters are especially important in this connection.

100. The *Rhetorica ad Herennium* 1.3 (approx. 80 BCE) names five tasks of the orator: *inventio*, the finding the material for the speech, *dispositio*, organizing the material and the arguments, *elocutio*, formulating the thoughts in an appropriate style, *memoria*, memorizing the speech, *pronuntiatio*, the presentation to the audience. Similarly Cicero, *De or.* 1.31.142. Cf. Ueding, *Klassische Rhetorik*, 39–41; Olbricht, "Delivery and Memory."

101. Wuellner, "Where Is," 452–53 has already lamented that rhetorical critic is often identical to literary critic. Sellin, "Ästhetische Aspekte" has given attention to the

structure of the text and the arrangement of the arguments (*dispositio*) have received particular attention. Such rhetorical analysis becomes essentially an analysis of the arguments with the methods of ancient rhetorics. This direction is consequently pursued by those who, following the New Rhetoric from Perelman and Olbrechts-Tyteca, integrate the results of modern rhetorical research into their analysis[102] or connect rhetorical interpretation to an analysis of sociological and ideological backgrounds.[103]

This limiting rhetorical analysis to *inventio*, *dispositio*, and *elocutio* is all the more remarkable because according to the opinion of the ancient orators, the presentation in front of an audience is the most important task for the speaker.[104] It is therefore inconsistent that rhetorical interpretation has paid so little attention to the situation in which the communication becomes real before an audience.[105] Sometimes the relevance of this event is even flatly denied.[106]

---

aesthetic side of the language and the linguistic idioms.

102. For example, Siegert, *Argumentation bei Paulus*; Wuellner, "Argumentative Structure."

103. For example, Robbins, "Rhetoric and Culture"; Robbins, *Exploring*; Amador, *Academic Constraints*.

104. Demosthenes, upon being asked which task of the orator was the most important, answered: the presentation, the presentation, the presentation. That was reported and accepted with approval by Philodemus, *Rhet.* 4, col. 15, ll. 3–6; Cicero, *De or.* 3.56.213; Cicero, *Or. Brut.* 56; and Quintilian, *Inst.* 11.3.6. On the importance of the presentation especially in the time of the Second Sophistic, see Winter, "Philodemus," 326–32.

105. Botha, "Letter Writing," 26 laments this limitation of rhetorical studies: "While many scholars have turned to Greco-Roman rhetoric for help in interpreting Paul's letter (with worthwhile results), the oral, performative aspect of ancient communication, and specifically ancient rhetoric have been neglected." Similarly Holland, "Playing," 322. Cf. Kelber, "Modalities of Communication," 200: "All discussions of rhetoric should commence with its oral underpinnings and oral aspirations." Similarly Loubser, "Reconciling."

106. Porter, "Theoretical Justification," 108, n. 21: "Several of the categories of the handbooks are neglected, including memory (*memoria*) and delivery (*pronuntiatio*), probably because they do not have ready application to letters." Reed, "Using Ancient Rhetorical Categories," 296: "The last two of this group [of the five tasks of rhetorical practice] had little, if any, place in letter writing, being irrelevant of the task." In a footnote, Reed adds that the letter reader, while presenting orally, may have to deal with this side of holding a speech, but not Paul as the writer. Betz, *Galatians*, 24: "Since it is simply a lifeless piece of paper, it eliminates one of the most important weapons of the rhetorician, the oral delivery."

The problem pointed out above can also clearly be seen in the work of George A. Kennedy. He is conscious of the problem that the rules of rhetoric actually apply to an oral event and that the art of rhetoric leads to an event of oral communication, not to a text. He emphasizes that interpreters of the New Testament must take into consideration that the text would usually have been read aloud to a group, and that the Bible has more strongly preserved an oral quality for the listeners than do modern texts.[107] Kennedy formulates the aim of the rhetorical interpretation as to hear the New Testament letters in the same way Greek-speaking listeners would have heard them in their time: "What we need to do is to try to hear his [Paul's] words as a Greek-speaking audience would have heard them, and it involves some understanding of classical rhetoric."[108] This goal of reconstructing the oral event has hardly been achieved by rhetorical interpretation. Despite his insights into the importance of the oral aspects of the rhetorical event, Kennedy does not give attention to the presentation of the letter.[109]

Further evidence that the rhetorical interpretation focuses on the formation of the text becomes apparent in the discussion of the rhetorical situation. Following Lloyd F. Bitzer, Kennedy defines the rhetorical situation as a condition of acute or potential urgency, which can, at least in part, be solved by an oral statement.[110] The persons involved are also a part of this situation, whereby the listeners are especially important for Kennedy. "The critic needs to ask of what this audience consists, what the audience expects in the situation, and how the speaker or writer manipulates these expectations."[111] Then, however, the perspective only includes

---

107. Kennedy, *New Testament Interpretation*, 5. Funk, *Language, Hermeneutic*, 248 has already emphasized that a letter is close to an oral conversation and creates a spoken event.

108. Kennedy, *New Testament Interpretation*, 10. However, anachronistically, it appears that the presupposition on p. 5 is that the letters would be read by individuals for themselves, "reading the Bible as it would be read by an early Christian, by an inhabitant of the Greek-speaking world in which rhetoric was the core subject of formal education and in which even those without formal education necessarily developed cultural preconceptions about appropriate discourse."

109. Ibid., 14, deliberately excludes *memory* and *delivery* from his study.

110. Ibid., 35. Watson, "Contributions" discusses how rhetorical analysis can throw a light on what has been captured in the text regarding the rhetorical situation and the historical situation behind it. Cf. Bitzer, "Rhetorical Situation" and the critique from Amador, *Academic Constraints*, 29–31 following Vatz, "Myth."

111. Kennedy, *New Testament Interpretation*, 35.

how the *speaker* intends to react to the situation with his utterances—that is, on his strategy to win over the listeners and present his concern. The listeners remain passive. Their reactions during the presentation and their interaction with the presenter and with each other are not taken into consideration.

Wilhelm Wuellner, on the other hand, does speak of active recipients of the oral statements: "Rhetorical criticism changes the status of readers to that of judges and critics to that of validators."[112] However, since Wuellner is not thinking of listeners, but rather of readers, he does not give consideration to the lively and interactive reaction of the listeners. Indeed, this is a general problem in rhetorical analysis up to this point. Because the focus lies on the written texts available to us, it is assumed that the texts develop their effect through the written form. As a result, research is usually confined to those aspects of rhetoric that are also easy to recognize in written texts. Elements of communication that are not encoded in written text—gestures and facial expressions, many emotional elements, and also the reaction of the audience—generally remain unconsidered.

There are exceptions, however. Thomas H. Olbricht argues that exegetes should include the situation of the presentation in their interpretation of texts: "What if at some stage in trying to understand the text the critic read aloud while at the same time visualising appropriate vocal and physical responses to the text?"[113] Regarding New Textament texts, J. Eugene Botha presents some preliminary considerations for an intensive study of gestures and other elements of nonverbal communication that not only accompany a speech but at the same time show and consolidate social values and positions.[114] Margaret E. Lee (previously under the name Margaret E. Dean) explores the effect that the sound of speech has.[115] She criticizes Robbins's social-rhetorical interpretation for the fact that his presumptions tend to be based more on modern printed texts.[116] She considers it important that ancient texts were designed to be heard, because in the Hellenistic world, not only oral speeches, but also written

---

112. Wuellner, "Where Is," 461.

113. Olbricht, "Delivery and Memory," 166; cf. Olbricht, "Classical Rhetorical Criticism," 123.

114. Botha, "Exploring Gesture." However, Botha investigates only the references to gestures in narrative texts (Acts and Gal 2).

115. Dean, "Textured Criticism"; Lee and Scott, *Sound Mapping*.

116. Dean, "Textured Criticism," 82.

texts were influenced by the fact that they were communicated orally. The speaker and the listeners are connected to one another through the sound of speech. For her, the situation of the public presentation and the various reactions of the listeners—that is, the performance event—are important for interpretation.[117] That is the reason why she studies how the Pauline letters are shaped by the sound of syllables and how meaning is thereby generated.[118]

The fact that the oral presentation must be included in rhetorical analysis is a reminder that all rhetoric has an oral basis.[119] It is above all in the investigations into orality that a narrow approach to rhetorical interpretation is overcome. That leads to the third root of the method of performance analysis: orality research.

Orality

In the first half of the twentieth century, Milman Parry (1928, 1930, 1932) and Albert B. Lord (1960) investigated orally performed heroic poems and how they were presented by illiterate Balkan singers in order to better understand the formulaic language and the recurring themes and structures of Homer's poems, and to throw a light on how his epic works were formed.[120] They showed in their research that both Homer's poems and the epics of southern Slavic singers were not the result of the literary work of certain authors but are rooted in a centuries-old poetic tradition and are embedded in an oral cultural setting. The examination of this culture showed that a lot of things that are so natural in the age of printing that they are not even consciously percieved do not apply to the

---

117. Ibid., 81: "If New Testament literature in its first-century rhetorical context was publicly spoken and heard rather than privately written and silently read, each composition's public, oral delivery and auditory reception is essential to its full and faithful interpretation ... Public reception in an auditory mode shaped the composition of every literary work in the Hellenistic world. Literature was known by means of vocal sounds, not by the sight of marks on a page ... But authors certainly crafted their compositions with audience impact in mind, even if they focused their theme, prepared the flow of an argument, and assembled examples and illustrations in advance."

118. Sellin, "Ästhetische Aspekte" works similarly with the sound of speech. Harvey, *Listening* and Harvey, "Orality and its Implications" examines phonetic structures. Cf. also Parunak, "Oral Typesetting" and Wendland, *Finding*, 30, 97–98 and *passim*.

119. Kelber, "Modalities of Communication," 200–202.

120. Parry, *L' épithète traditionelle*; Parry, "Studies in the Epic Technique of Oral Verse-Making," parts 1 and 2.

ancient cultures, which only knew handwritten texts—if they had written language at all. That applies, for example, to the way members of oral cultures read and wrote, to how they treated written texts, to questions of authorship, intertextuality, and the passing on of tradition. The pursuit of these questions has led to the development of the study of oral tradition as its own scientific discipline. While research previously concentrated on the writing as the object of their research, now oral tradition has become a research subject, especially for scholars in the fields of anthropology, cultural studies, the study of ancient cultures, and literary science.[121]

This wave of research on oral traditions was also influenced by, besides the scientific interest, nationalistic movements in the nineteenth and twentieth centuries, which sought their identity in the early traditions of their own cultures.[122] Above all, however, this research was driven by the development of new media for the recording of information: at first sound recordings (Parry and Lord used aluminum cylinders to record the songs of Yugoslavian singers) and film, later electronic recordings. Thus the awareness arose that the medium of writing, which up to then had naturally dominated the transmission of information, was a mode of communication with its own way of functioning.

Just how much knowledge, thinking, and communication do depend on the medium has been clearly demonstrated in particular by Marshall McLuhan (1962), Eric A. Havelock (1963), and Jack Goody and Ian Watt (1968).[123] Havelock took up the theses from Parry and Lord concerning the oral background of Homer's poetry and used it to analyze the complete Greek world. He perceived the invention of alphabetic writing by the Greeks to be the origin of modern culture with its rational thinking, historical consciousness, individuality, democracy, and technological development.[124] Although such a radical thesis has been criticized,[125] it is his merit that the extrinsic conditions surrounding communication

---

121. Boedeker, "Oral-Tradition-Forschung" offers an overview of the American research of oral traditions. Cf. also Vansina, *Oral Tradition*; Assmann, *Kulturelle Gedächtnis*; Assmann et al., *Schrift und Gedächtnis*; also the essays in the journal *Oral Tradition*. Cf. Raible, *Symbolische Formen*; Raible, *Kulturelle Perspektiven*; Raible, *Medienwechsel* on the transition from orality to scribality.

122. Finnegan, "What Is Orality," 131.

123. McLuhan, *Gutenberg Galaxy*; Havelock, *Preface to Plato*; Havelock, *Literate Revolution*; Goody and Watt, "Consequences of Literacy." See also Goody, *Literacy*. A presentation of the history of the research is found in Havelock, *Muse Learns to Write*, 24–29.

124. Cf. also Goody and Watt, "Consequences of Literacy."

125. Cf. Assmann and Assmann, "Einleitung," 1–35; see also ibid., 27–35 for a list of works on orality, literacy, and cultural memory. Cf. also Goetsch, "Übergang."

and the handing down of tradition have become a prominent factor for understanding cultural history. This has shaken the way in which the conditions of our modern society, with the predominance of the written word, have simply been assumed to apply to ancient societies. Research has become more sensitive to the otherness of ancient cultures.

Research into the orally dominated culture of antiquity first worked on identifying the differences compared to our present culture that is dominated by the printed word. It was initially assumed that texts belong either to the oral or the written culture, and that there are significant differences between these cultures. The descriptions of the oral and the written culture where accordingly contrasting. This is also true for Walter Ong, whose influential work *Orality and Literacy: The Technologizing of the Word* (1982) builds on Parry, Lord, and Havelock.[126] For him, the invention of writing changed human thinking more than anything else.[127] He describes the following characteristics of an oral culture in contrast to a literate culture:

- Formulaic and rhythmical language as mnemonic aids
- An additive structure of narration in contrast to a subordinating structure
- More aggregative descriptions (e.g., stereotype epithets) than analytical dissection
- High redundancy
- Conservative and traditionalist way of thinking
- Closely related to the experiences and activities of daily life
- Agonistic in tone
- Empathetic and participatory rather than objective and distanced
- Homeostasis—that which is no longer relevant in the present is lost from memory
- More situational than abstract[128]

The transition from an orally oriented culture to a literary oriented culture appeared to be a progressive development: from simple, characteristically oral forms with repetitions and adjunctive clauses to the

---

126. Ong, *Orality*; cf. also Ong, *Presence*.
127. Ong, *Orality*, 77.
128. Ibid., 31–50; on homoeostasis, cf. Goody and Watt, "Consequences of Literacy," 30–31.

complex sentence structures of written communication. This theoretical line of progression was conceived as advancing up to the development of abstract thinking.

The extreme contrast between orality and scribality—often intermingled with the notion that orality represents a primitive stage—has proven to be an ethnocentric Western preconception.[129] The introduction of writing was not a turning point at which an earlier stage was left behind, but rather set an intensive interaction between written and spoken communication in motion.[130] The peculiarities of oral language were now found in written texts, indeed, even more exaggerated.[131] On the other hand writing opened new possibilities for oral language forms, as seen in the art of rhetoric, which profited from written preparation.[132] In particular, Ruth Finnegan has repeatedly pointed out that there is no "Great Divide" between orality and scribality.[133] Using her own research in Africa and other evidence she demonstrates that certain characteristics of oral composition asserted by Lord and others cannot be regarded as typical.[134] She exposes the notion of a completely different past oral culture as the nostalgia of those living in a modern rationalistic society and argues against a technological determinism in which the discovery of writing must inevitably lead to a cultural revolution. Instead, social structures—who has power over a technology, whom does it benefit—play a significant role in the developing of effects of new communication technologies.[135]

---

129. Assmann and Assmann, "Einleitung," in Havelock, *Schriftlichkeit*, 20; cf. Foley, *How to Read*, 37 assesses that thinking in terms of contrast was not in vain since it first of all created room for the study of oral texts, but now it is time for a more exact examination of the phenomenon in all its variations; cf. also Foley, "Words in Tradition," 169.

130. Cf. Tannen, "Oral/Literate Continuum"; Weissenrieder and Coote, *Interface*. Ong also repeatedly explains the peculiarity of oral culture by pointing to speaking habits still to be found in modern culture and that he calls the residue of oral thinking (e.g., *Orality*, 35, 37, 38, 40, 44, 74).

131. Dewey, "Oral Methods," 33; Fuhrmann, "Mündlichkeit" brings examples from Cicero's published speeches.

132. Quintilian, *Inst*. 10.1.2–3; 10.3.1; Cicero, *De or*. 1.33.152.

133. Finnegan, *Literacy*, 12–14; Finnegan, "What Is Oral Literature," 137–44.

134. Finnegan, "What Is Oral Literature"; Finnegan, "What Is Orality," 141.

135. Finnegan, *Literacy*, 8–12; Finnegan, "What Is Orality," 143–45.

Peter Koch and Wulf Oesterreicher have made a valuable contribution clarifying the relationship between orality and scribality.[136] They systematized the multiplicity of linguistic possibilities by differentiating between the "language concept" and the "medial realization" of linguistic expression. The medial realization of language considers the question of whether it is expressed in speech or writing—whether a particular expression of language is implemented in graphical or phonetic code. This must be distinguished from the language concept, "the ductus and the modality of the utterance, and the varieties of language that are used."[137] The spectrum of possible language concepts stretches from typical spoken language ("language of immediacy," e.g., dialogue, but also personal letters) to typical written language ("language of distance," e.g., administrative regulations, but also academic lectures). In terms of language concept, texts can be situated closer to the oral pole, closer to the written pole, or somewhere in between. The differentiation between medial realization and language concept can overcome the simplistic contrasting schema of orality and scribality, and it is possible to categorize diverse linguistic expressions more precisely, whether they come from early, orally oriented societies or from modern cultures. Pairing the distinction between orality and scribality with the spectrum of language concepts also allows a differentiated apprehension of the "development" of the written language of distance—that is, the emergence of a typical conceptual written language which often only results as the product of a long historical process.[138]

In the last few years John Foley has particularly advanced the research of oral texts. He has established the fact that oral poetry is a very diverse phenomenon occurring throughout the world and from antiquity up into the present time.[139]

Foley suggests differentiating between four categories of oral poetry—without any hierarchy or line of development:

---

136. Koch and Oesterreicher, "Sprache der Nähe"; Koch and Oesterreicher, "Funktionale Aspekte"; Oesterreicher, "Types of Orality."

137. Koch and Oesterreicher, "Funktionale Aspekte," 587 (my translation).

138. Ibid., 589. Cf. Bakker, "How Oral" on an application of this more precise concept to Homer's texts.

139. Foley, *How to Read*, 1–10, 25–26, 34–35, 128–29, 141–45; cf. Finnegan, "How of Literature," 166–68; Middleton, "How to Read."

1. Poetry that is orally composed and performed in front of an audience ("oral performance").

2. Texts intended for presentation to an audience, which were written down beforehand ("voiced texts"). The performance could be done by someone other than the author of the text.

3. Texts from the past that have long ceased to be performed but that still feature traces of their oral composition or performance. Reports of or references to their performance have often survived until today ("voices from the past").

4. Poetry written down for readers but that displays the characteristics of an oral poem ("written oral poems").[140]

Foley names three procedures as methodical repertoire:

1) *Performance theory*: The communicative event is a performance.[141] Listeners are just as involved in it as the presenter.[142] "Performance is part of the meaning,"[143] and the two cannot be separated. Therefore, participation in an event is the key to understanding it. In a written text, only a small part of the performance can be conveyed, so it is important to achieve as much participation as possible: "being there."[144]

2) *Ethnopoetics*: In a performance, attention must be given not only to the word content but also to all the details—for example, the intonation, volume, and tempo of speech; pauses; gestures; position in the room; and much more. Since these elements are not to be found in ancient texts, the focus is placed on the text's structure because close attention to the structure of the text "restores the poetry in them."[145]

3) *Immanent Art*:[146] Foley demonstrates that formulaic language, typical scenes, and repetitive narrative structures so typical of texts from an orally oriented culture are references evoking the tradition. Foley calls this "an *immanent art*: a process of composition and reception in

---

140. Foley, *How to Read*, 39–53.

141. Ibid., 79–94; cf. Finnegan, "How of Literature."

142. Foley, *How to Read*, 138: "Poet and audience are partners in the same process: making and receiving are inextricably linked." Foley, *Immanent Art*, 42–45 establishes a connection to reception aesthetics.

143. Foley, *How to Read*, 164.

144. Ibid., 137: "We must project the 'play' from the 'script' as best as we can, converting the object (back) into an event as far as possible."

145. Ibid., 103; on ethnopoetics, see pp. 95–108.

146. Ibid., 109–24; cf. Foley, *Immanent Art*.

which a simple, concrete part stands for a complex, intangible reality. *Pars pro toto*, as it were."[147] Such formulas metonymically conjure up an imaginary world that is far more comprehensive than what is directly expressed in the text. The choice of linguistic idiosyncrasies ("registers"), the typical conditions for the performance ("performance arena"), and the traditional manner of expression as effective modes of communication ("communicative economy") help the performance to implicitly bring to life a complete universe of tradition.[148] For texts from the past, it is essential to get to know this world of tradition as far as is possible. Foley compares this effort with learning a language, the language of the respective oral poetry.[149]

Research into the relationship of oral and written communication in ancient cultures has brought to light a plethora of important results that have been published both in anthologies[150] and in volumes on individual questions, such as on reading and writing skills in antiquity,[151] on learning to read and write,[152] on the practice of reading or reading aloud,[153] on the role of books and manuscripts,[154] and on the role of memory and oral history.[155]

147. Foley, "Traditional Signs," 63 (italics in the original).

148. Cf. Foley, "Words in Tradition."

149. Foley, *How to Read*, 136, 139.

150. Stolz and Shannon, *Oral Literature*; Foley, *Oral Traditional Literature*; Foley, *Comparative Research*; Tannen, "Oral/Literate Continuum"; Thompson, *Performance*; Vogt-Spira, *Strukturen*; Olson and Torrance, *Literacy and Orality*; Raible, *Symbolische Formen*; Raible, *Kulturelle Perspektiven*; Raible, *Medienwechsel*; Bauman, *Folklore*; Baumann et al., *Homo scribens*; Günther, *Schrift und Schriftlichkeit*; Sellin and Vouga, *Logos und Buchstabe*; Bakker and Kahane, *Written Voices*; Assmann et al., *Schrift und Gedächtnis*; Mackay, *Signs of Orality*; Watson, *Speaking Volumes*; see also the *Oral Tradition* journal.

151. Harris, *Ancient Literacy*; Lentz, *Orality*; Thomas, *Literacy*; Bar-Ilan, "Illiteracy" (for Palestine); Yaghjian, "Ancient Reading"; Hezser, *Jewish Literacy*.

152. Robb, *Literacy*; Snyder, *Teachers*; Morgan, *Literate Education*.

153. Starr, "Reading Aloud"; Saenger, *Space*; Botha, "New Testament Texts"; Johnson, *Readers*; cf. also the discussion about silent and spoken reading: Balogh, "Voces Paginarum"; Hendrickson, "Ancient Reading"; Clark, "Ancient Reading"; Knox, "Silent Reading"; Saenger, "Silent Reading"; Achtemeier, "Omne Verbum Sonat"; Slusser, "Reading Silently"; Gilliard, "More Silent Reading"; Burfeind, "Wen hörte Philippus?"

154. Olson, *World on Paper*; Gamble, *Books and Readers*; Small, *Wax Tablets*; Alexander, "Hellenistic Letter-Forms"; Millard, *Reading and Writing*; Jaffee, *Torah in the Mouth*; Carr, *Writing*.

155. Gerhardsson, *Memory and Manuscript*; Vansina, *Oral Tradition*; Thompson, *Voice*; Assmann, *Kulturelle Gedächtnis*; Byrskog, *Story as History*.

Of course, interpreters of the Bible were always conscious of the fact that prior and parallel to its written transmission, the content had been passed on orally. Especially form criticism has tried to understand the development of the written texts, for example the Gospels, beginning with this oral tradition.[156] As with Parry's Homeric question, form criticism initially concentrated on ascertaining the sources of the written texts and casting a light on the manner in which the texts came to exist. The search for the social setting of the oral communication (*Sitz im Leben*) was also subordinated to this goal.

It was then above all Werner Kelber (1983) who applied the results of orality research to the study of the New Testament in his revolutionary work, building upon the studies of Ong, Havelock, and others.[157] For Kelber, oral and written texts are clearly separate.[158] Accordingly, the different mediums treat information differently: Orality connects the mouth with the ears, scribality connects the eyes with the text.[159]

Kelber sees oral characteristics in the narratives in the fact that life is comprehended in contrasts,[160] that confrontation is more appreciated than harmony,[161] and that tradition is censored and ratified through social interaction with listeners.[162] The Gospel of Mark is a written work and stands in tension with an oral gospel tradition. Mark strives to overcome the oral tradition of his predecessors[163] and to convey the tradition in a new form.[164]

In Paul's letters, Kelber finds a connection between the gospel and the spoken word.[165] He picks up on the ideas of Robert Funk, who in-

---

156. Cf. on this Kelber, "Biblical Hermeneutics," 98.

157. Kelber, *Oral and Written Gospel*, cf. also Kelber, "Narrative"; and Kelber, "Jesus and Tradition"; previously also Lord, *Relationships* on the Synoptics. Cf. the evaluation by Farrell, "Kelber's Breakthrough." For the Old Testament, the following must be mentioned: Niditch, "Oral Tradition"; Person, "Ancient Israelite Scribe"; Miller, *Oral Tradition*; Graham, *Beyond the Written Word* (history-of-religion approach). Culley, "Oral Tradition" offers an overview of the studies on orality in the Old and New Testaments from the end of the nineteenth century up to Werner Kelber.

158. Cf. already Güttgemanns, *Offene Fragen*, 103–4.

159. Kelber, *Oral and Written Gospel*, xv.

160. Ibid., 55.

161. Ibid., 71.

162. Ibid., 92.

163. Ibid., 104.

164. Ibid., 130.

165. Ibid., 141–83.

terprets Paul's travel notes in the sense that the apostle prefers an oral transmission of the message and therefore presents the prospect of a future visit.[166] His own calling, the powerful Word of God, faith that has come from hearing (Rom 10:16–17; 1 Thess 2:13), the contrast between the living word and the written law (2 Cor 3:1–6)—all these things demonstrate that Paul was committed to the *spoken* word. "In Pauline theology the ear triumphs over the eye."[167] Paul's letters are close to oral communication—but at the same time, as written communication they manifest emerging tensions with the purely oral gospel.[168]

Kelber has been criticized for the decisive contrast he sees between the gospel that was passed on orally—the words of Jesus as they were passed on by Peter and the other disciples—and Mark's written version—the rationalized and interpretive report of the life of Jesus.[169] However, he deserves credit for acting upon an important impulse to research the significance of the communication medium in the development of early Christianity and in the interpretation of early Christian texts.

Initially, research on the New Testament concentrated on the transition of the gospel tradition from the oral to the written form. In considering this question, research took up the thread from form criticism, which had also proceeded from the presumption that a previous oral tradition had been written down.[170] The Gospel of Mark stood at the center of interest. Soon, however, in the wake of Kelber and under the influence of literary approaches to the Gospel texts, such as narrative analysis, efforts were no longer made to reconstruct the oral antecedent, but rather

---

166. Funk, *Language, Hermeneutic*, 264–69.

167. Kelber, *Oral and Written Gospel*, 143.

168. Ibid., 172–77, 204–5.

169. Boomershine, "Peter's Denial"; Halverson, "Oral and Written Gospel"; A. Dewey, "Re-Hearing," 113: "Once a new medium has made its cultural appearance, the old medium does not die out, nor does it exist independently of the new; on the contrary there now exists the possibility to use the old in light of the new and vice versa." Cf. also the criticism from Henaut, *Oral Traditions*, 53–74.

170. Cf. Breytenbach, "Problem des Übergangs"; Schröter, *Erinnerung*; previously Güttgemanns, *Offene Fragen*, 69–150. This approach is discussed in Dunn, "Altering" and implemented in Dunn, *Jesus Remembered*, especially 192–254. Gerhardsson, "Secret of Transmission" is critical of Kelber's approach, which was continued by Dunn. Henaut, *Oral Traditions*, 195 considers it impossible to form conclusions about oral traditions from the Gospel texts: "The oral phase of the Jesus tradition is now forever lost." Jaffee, *Torah in the Mouth* examines the relationship between oral and written traditions among Jewish scholars.

the existing texts were themselves investigated as expressions of an oral culture.[171]

The Pauline Epistles have also been studied under the aspect of orality. Thus John Harvey (1998) assumes that the letters achieved their impact through the spoken word. In them he examined parallelism, chiasms, inclusion, refrains, word-chains, inversion, short mnemonic phrases, and other linguistic forms, which are considered typical for the spoken word, and compared them with the forms in the Greco-Roman literature and rhetoric and in the Septuagint.[172]

Casey Wayne Davis (1999) proceeds in a similar way. In his study of the Epistle to the Philippians, he combines rhetorical and linguistic methods with an examination of the oral forms.[173] His interest centers on structures and forms such as chiasms, repetitions, and parallelism, but also on the tone.[174] What is missing in these works is a consideration of the listeners, their interaction with the speaker and among themselves.[175] Thus they remain largely text oriented studies.

Performance Criticism

Research into the oral aspects of ancient cultures has clearly shown that texts were usually read out loud in front of a small or large gathering, thus centering social events. They achieved their rational, emotional, and social effects during a performance situation because of the interaction between the reader/presenter on the one hand and the listeners on the other, and because of the interaction among listeners themselves during the performance.[176] That means the orality aspect is relevant for the

---

171. For example Boomershine, *Story Journey*; Dewey, "Oral Methods"; Dewey, "Mark as Aural Narrative"; Botha, "Mark's Story"; Horsley and Draper, *Whoever Hears You*; Rhoads, *Reading Mark*; and the collections of essays Silberman, ed., *Orality*; Dewey, ed., *Orality*; Horsley et al., eds., *Performing the Gospel*, especially pp. 125–90; Weissenrieder and Coote, eds., *Interface*.

172. Harvey, *Listening*.

173. Davis, *Oral Biblical Criticism*; he reflects on his methods on pp. 55 and 63.

174. Similarly Sellin, "Ästhetische Aspekte."

175. Dabourne, *Purpose* in her study of Rom 1:16—4:25 has an eye on the *effect* on the listeners. But she does not reflect on the *activities* of the listeners.

176. Georgi, *Opponents of Paul*, 113, has already pointed out for the *Synagogue* "that the synagogue ceremony, determined by the duality of Scripture reading and scriptural interpretation, afforded an occasion for lively activity which was nothing short of theatrical." He describes the synagogue service as an attractive performance

understanding of the text. Especially through Foley's influence, the situation of the oral presentation, that is, the performance—not only of the preliterary tradition but also of the written texts—has been taken into account. Reconstructing possible models of the performance situations, identifying the function that handed-down texts fulfilled in the situation, and drawing conclusions for interpreting these texts make up the collective task referred to as *performance criticism*.

Not only did Kelber use orality research to reconstruct the historical origins of the text, but he also already recognized orality's relevance for understanding the text. Thomas L. Boomershine and others have continued along this path and have shown how important it is for understanding ancient texts to bear in mind that they belong to a culture in which oral communication was dominant.[177] They insist that a better understanding of the texts is achieved when one tries to understand them in the context of this performance culture.[178]

David Rhoads (2006) has presented a description of the method of performance criticism[179] for the New Testament.[180] He begins with a

---

even for Gentiles: "The ceremony was thus in reality a performance before an audience, a spiritual theater." Georgi points to the architecture of the synagogue (113) and describes the character of the gatherings as "pneumatic demonstrations" (114). "But since this pneumatic process manifested itself in the ability of the individual charismatics, it thus appeared in a variety of forms and obviously invited a comparison between individual achievements" (114–15).

177. Boomershine, "Peter's Denial"; Boomershine, "Jesus of Nazareth"; Horsley et al., *Performing the Gospel*; J. Dewey, "Textuality"; Loubser, "Orality and Pauline Christology"; Loubser, "Orality and Literacy"; Loubser, "Reconciling"; Hearon, "Implications of Orality"; and the essays in Weissenrieder and Coote, *Interface*.

178. Since the texts were usually read aloud in antiquity, Boomershine, "Peter's Denial," 52–59 suggests reading the texts aloud. The psychological nearness ("sympathetic participation") that thus develops helps the audience achieve an appropriate understanding of the text, since oral communication creates less distance than does silent reading, where one tends to remain distanced and take on an analytical attitude. For example, Boomershine thus reaches the conclusion that the account of Peter's denial in Mark's Gospel should be understood more as the confession of the individual involved and less as a judgment pronounced over him.

179. Cf. the introductory essays in Hearon and Ruge-Jones, eds., *Bible in Ancient and Modern Media*. For the Old Testament cf. Doan and Giles, *Prophets*; Giles and Doan, *Twice Used Songs* and further literature there. Initial considerations also in Hardmeier, *Erzähldiskurs*.

180. Rhoads, "Performance Criticism," and further literature there; cf. Rhoads, "What Is Performance." Rhoads himself (*Reading Mark*, 176–201) has presented the Gospel of Mark and other texts as a performance; before him also Boomershine, "Peter's Denial."

review of the method's origins and a critical discussion of the traditional interpretation. The traditional interpretation, he argues, simply takes for granted that the appropriate way to use New Testament texts corresponds with our modern, print-media-dominated culture, and thus centers on an anachronistic communication medium: print media. He then describes ancient culture as a culture dominated by oral communication. Writing was in use primarily in the upper class but served as an aid for oral presentation; during such an oral presentation a text was usally not read aloud but rather proclaimed from memory. The people experienced the effect of writing in the performance—that is, in an acoustic and social event. Rhoads defines the performance as follows: "any oral telling/retelling of a brief or lengthy tradition—from saying to gospel—in a formal or informal context of a gathered community by trained or untrained performers—on the assumption that every telling was a lively recounting of that tradition."[181] Therefore, performance is the place where the knowledge of the respective social group is passed on and interpreted, and where the interpretation is collectively examined and criticized. Only powerful and memorable speech could make a lasting impression on listeners and anchor the tradition in their memory. Rhoads then outlines the role of the Gospels and the New Testament Epistles in the described culture and comes to the conclusion that the texts were repeatedly presented anew, doubtlessly with smaller and larger deviations, and that it was not through the written texts but rather through these performance events that the Christian message had meaning and was disseminated.

Next Rhoads analyzes seven aspects of the performance event, for which he also draws from his own experiences presenting New Testament texts performed from memory:

1. Performance is an act that includes not only language but all possible modes of articulation with voice and gesture: that is, it represents a holistic event.

2. The content presented is not generated directly by the written words but rather by what the presenter experiences in his body and spirit, and it corresponds to his own momentary situation and that of the audience. Therefore, despite textual preparation, what is presented constitutes a unique composition, a bodily interpretation of the text. Of course, the multitude of performances cannot be reconstructed, but the signals for an appropriate presentation in the various texts

---

181. Rhoads, "Performance Criticism," 119.

deserve attention so that the interpreter can recognize how the individual parts and the complete text develop their effect.

3. The presenter, engaging his or her entire being, embodies the text with its values and perceptions. Listeners/observers do not experience the text without such an embodiment and will only grasp the content if they acknowledge the necessary knowledge, integrity and authority in the presenter.

4. Listeners/observers are an important factor in the performance. They are active and influence the presentation, and do so as a community that quite likely includes very different groups. Within an audience, for each subgroup, given its social position, what is said takes on a different sound in the members' ears.

5. The location and physical context of the performance influence the presentation.

6. In the respective historical and social situation in which the performance takes place (whether characterized by political tension, persecution, poverty) individual details of the text being presented will generate new meanings.

7. In the performance, the text being presented provokes an effect that not only influences ideas, perceptions, and values, but also changes relationships and provokes actions. The listeners are changed. Performance criticism is concerned not only with what the text means but also with the effect it achieves and how that happens.

Next, Rhoads integrates all the existing methodical steps of New Testament exegesis, and some others as well, into performance criticism. Since performance criticism assumes a transition from written communication to oral communication, he argues that this new research method of performance criticism is not only one approach among others, but an altogether new approach to texts that integrates previous methods, profiting from them and at the same time putting them to new uses. Finally, Rhoads contends that New Testament texts should be performed before an audience—as he himself has been doing for many years—since only this experience can provide an understanding for performance analysis of the texts and make a deeper interpretation possible. In closing, Rhoads lists some methodical steps (e.g., analyze the cultural context of the texts, develop a model of the performance event, discern the oral characteristics of the texts, interpret the text in light of the original oral medium, conduct performances before an audience). His concept opens up a perspective for a hitherto little-heeded dimension of text interpretation. However, the concrete methodical steps and control mechanisms must still be worked out in detail.[182] It is also the aim of this study to make a contribution to this project.

Whitney Shiner's book (2003) already takes a step in this direction. He assumes that the people for whom the Gospel of Mark was written did not perceive the meaning of the work in the written text but in the live presentation of the work within a community.[183] In order to reconstruct the performance of Mark's Gospel, he resorts to two methods.[184] First, using references from ancient sources, he infers what would characterize an ideal performance of a text in the culture of those days. Second, he reads references in Mark's Gospel to oral style (e.g., "calling," "a loud voice"), to bodily movements (e.g., "looking around," "pointing"), and to emotions as if they were stage directions for the presenter dramatically performing the narrated event.[185] After providing an introduction to the oral character of first-century culture (chs. 1 and 2), Shiner develops a performance of the Gospel of Mark starting with the presenter's perspective (chs. 3–6). He discusses emotion, performance techniques, and gestures. Shiner then details the listeners' perspective (chs. 7–9). He discusses the listeners' reactions to the performance, the reasons and opportunities for listener applause during the performance, and other listener involvement. With his studies Shiner has set out a way for exploring the performance of early Christian narrative texts.[186]

William D. Shiell (2004) has also studied the performance of the presenter: he examined the Acts of the Apostles.[187] He begins with Greco-Roman culture and its conventions for the presentation of written texts,

---

182. For example, Henaut, *Oral Traditions*, 113–19 criticizes the method of identifying "oral" structures (alliteration, parallelism, chiasms, and so forth) in written texts, since such structures are also found in written texts that do not convey oral tradition.

183. Shiner, *Proclaiming*, 78: "The meaning of any oral performance is found only in that communal context as it is presented by the performer and as it is received by the audience. Delivery is the art of filling the lifeless words on a scroll with fire and life and emotion. Orations may later be studied privately as models of style, but the written oration is a museum piece, deprived of the breath that gives it life and the situation that gives it meaning." On this, also previously Bahn, "Interpretative Reading."

184. Shiner, *Proclaiming*, 3–4.

185. Cf. ibid., 68.

186. Cf. Wire, *Case for Mark*. On rabbinical texts, cf. Jaffee, *Torah in the Mouth*.

187. Shiell, *Reading Acts*.

which he explains with the help of written sources and ancient works of art. Shiell concludes that texts developed their effect by being read out publicly or privately by trained readers. He then evaluates how the conventions for reading aloud could govern the reading of texts among groups of early Christians. Shiell assumes that the readings had their place during meetings in believers' homes, and that reading texts aloud in the home was comparable to reading and performing in Greco-Roman symposia.[188] So the reading of a letter was an important event for the whole church.[189] Using Acts as an example, Shiell shows how the reader shapes the reported speeches and episodes in the text through gestures, facial expressions, and voice modulations. Shiell emphasizes the active role of the listener by reconstructing the role of the presenter from the cultural expectations of the listeners.[190]

Bobby Loubser (2007) has also presented a study about performance criticism of the New Testament texts. His academic work in Africa, an area with many cultures that differ greatly from the traditional cultures of Europe and North America, has made him especially sensitive to this problem. He argues that the New Testament texts should be understood in the framework of the orally dominated manuscript culture of the Greco-Roman world in which they are rooted.[191] He defines the New Testament culture as an "intermediate manuscript (rhetorical) culture" in which, despite the use of writing, the forms of oral thought and style remained intact. Proceeding from a detailed communication model, he first of all establishes how important it is to reflect on the communication medium in order to reach an appropriate understanding of the content it conveys. It is not enough just to study the content of the texts as they exist today, but rather the whole communication process must be considered. In addition to the explicit message that can be encoded in a text, this process also includes nonverbal elements as well as a multifaceted interaction between the sender and the receivers. This whole event is embedded in a complex social system.[192] Loubser—following McLuhan— emphasizes that the communication event is significantly impacted by

188. Ibid., 127–33.
189. Ibid., 127.
190. Ibid., 201.
191. Loubser, *Oral and Manuscript Culture*; preliminary work in Loubser, "Orality and Pauline Christology"; Loubser, "Orality and Literacy."
192. Concerning system theory, Loubser, *Oral and Manuscript Culture*, 26–32 refers to Luhmann and in particular to Bailey, *Sociology*.

the possibilities and limits of the chosen medium. This has often been overlooked in studies of the New Testament texts, because the media being used have not been taken into account.

Loubser's method for media criticism of the New Testament texts comprises the following steps:[193]

1. Putting the texts in the context of their social and cultural world with its predominant communication medium.

2. Examining the texts for explicit and implicit evidence of orality and scribality (references to speaking/listening and writing/reading, but also to seeing).

3. Analyzing the communicative characteristics and functions of the linguistic forms in the text (e.g., formulaic style, repetition, gestures, forceful language like curses or blessings).

4. Analyzing hermeneutical functions of the text (distance from the present-day culture, which makes understanding the text more difficult: e.g., understanding the magical power of the spoken word in ancient cultures, understanding ancient communication relating to individuals or a community, addressing the respective concrete current situation but in a way that is embedded in tradition, taking into account concrete and direct language).

5. Considering ethical and theological conclusions.

These steps are presented as they are applied to Luke 9:51–56.

Loubser then examines New Testament texts (from Luke, Paul, and John) for their openness towards oral performance—whereby the influence of the written medium, which is of course also involved, is somewhat neglected (chs. 4–8). Using the steps mentioned, he discusses the references to oral and written communication in the text[194] as well as the general conventions for ways of thinking and communicating in the surrounding society and culture.[195] This is followed by a reflection on the ethical aspects of interpretation. Concerning the Pauline letters, for

---

193. Loubser, *Oral and Manuscript Culture*, 73 and 76.

194. Ibid., 92, where he finds a prejudice against scribality in Gal 6:11; 2 Cor 2:17; 10:10–11.

195. For example, corporative personality, authority of the written word, orientation on the respective concrete situation and times, relationship between originality and dependence on tradition. It is noteworthy that Shiner, *Proclaiming* proceeds in a similar manner.

which he devotes only little space, Loubser states: "In the Pauline letters writing also mainly served as a mnemonic prop for the performance by the oral reader."[196] That means that many things would not have to be explicitly put into words because the author knew that they would be expressed and embodied by the presenter in his performance. The message was not the written letter but the performance. The letter was a memory aid.[197] Loubser concludes: "The global purpose of the interpreter of the Pauline texts should thus be to reconstruct the performance and audience reception of these texts."[198]

A comprehensive study of the New Testament letter texts has not yet been performed. However, some important work has already been accomplished.[199] Thus James D. Hester has discussed the rhetorical situation for the presentation of the Pauline letters and—taking up Vorster's suggestion and following Searle's speech act theory—urges that attention be given to the active role of the listeners.[200] For him, the rhetorical event is not just about information but rather about something happening through speech. In the process, the meaning of what is said is constructed in interaction with the listeners. The public presentation of the letter in the church is a social event in which one must reckon with the manifold interaction of all the participants. Addressing this, Hester writes: "The particular audiences with which he [Paul] was dealing [in his letters] were complex, in many cases containing factions which had to be treated inventionally differently from one another."[201]

---

196. Loubser, *Oral and Manuscript Culture*, 62. He presumes that the messenger also read the letter out and commented on it. "If therefore, 'Paul' introduces a fellow-worker without stating the reason, we may assume that it has to do with the delivery and performance of the message." Also ibid., 90.

197. Wendland, *Finding*, 44–46, 53–54 contradicts this, placing value on faithfulness to the text in the presentation of the text.

198. Loubser, *Oral and Manuscript Culture*, 63.

199. In his study of Romans 10, A. Dewey, "Re-Hearing" infers from the wording of the text features of the performance of Paul's letter, e.g., p. 119 to Rom 10:15–21: "The very words of Scripture speak to the efforts of people like Paul. Indeed, the person who delivered Paul's letter is indirectly referred to, if one understands the implications of such words coming true in the audience's presence . . . Quite significantly v. 21 would allow the deliverer of the letter an opportunity for a dramatic gesture of open arms." Tsang, "Are We Misreading" briefly discusses the implications of the oral performance of Paul's letters.

200. Hester, "Speaker, Audience."

201. Ibid., 78. Amador, *Academic Constraints*, 68 also considers the differences in the audience: "Often, the composite quality of audiences requires the speaker to

Pieter Botha also emphasizes that the delivery of the letters must be thought of as the presentation of a speech, as a performance. In several essays he has demonstrated that the delivery of a letter is not to be understood as a purely intellectual happening, but rather as a social event with an oral performance.[202] He applies this—though only in a rough outline—to the Letter to the Galatians and points to the authoritative "presence" of Paul through the reader, to the importance of an impressive performance for asserting thoughts and conceptions, and to the gripping, emotional, threatening, and almost magical use of the language (Gal 1:8–9; 3:1).[203]

Rollin A. Ramsaran (2003) examined 1 Cor 15 for signs relating to the letter's performance: for example, register and situation ("performance arena"), metonymic pointers to tradition, the dialogue structure of the chapter, the organization of thought in units suitable for memorizing, and language signals that made listening easier (e.g., keywords, chiasms, instances of parallelism, intensifications). His approach is oriented to the work of Richard A. Horsley and Jonathan A. Draper (1999) on Mark's Gospel, which itself is based on that of Dell Hymes and John Miles Foley.[204]

Gerhard Sellin also writes:

> However, for the purpose of rhetoric, the written works were not only monuments, but also *scores* or screenplays which became a performance in the act of the speech and the discussion . . . they [the Pauline Epistles] were read aloud before the assembly, and thereby performed by a rhetor, i.e., a member of the recipient church who was well-versed in rhetoric. The reader strove to make Paul's "voice" be heard—and the author (Paul)

---

construct an audience in such a way that it does not exclude or insult one or more groups that may compose the empirical audience (those who actually listen)." He describes the various possible reactions of listeners but does not consider how they could mutually influence each other.

202. Botha, "Letter Writing," especially p. 25; and Botha, "Verbal Art." (Botha's papers have been reprinted in Botha, *Orality and Literacy*.) Cf. also Wire, "Performance"; and Ward, "Pauline Voices," especially p. 101: "Texts (such as written gospels or letters) recited or orally composed in Christian worship harkened back to the immediacy of oral discourse. Letters served orality and were thus returned to oral space by way of the public reader."

203. Botha, "Letter Writing," 27–30; following Funk, "Apostolic Parousia" regarding the epistolary parusia.

204. Ramsaran, "From Mind"; Horsley and Draper, *Whoever Hears You*.

had not only entrusted the content of his thoughts to the written characters, but also the whole power of his rhetoric.[205]

The reader, and then Paul's messenger in the subsequent discussion, were of crucial importance for the performance of the letter. Thus a substantial part in the success of the letter Paul sent to Corinth (2 Cor 2:4) must be attributed to Titus's skills.[206]

Finally, Ernst R. Wendland's (2008) work should also be mentioned. He examined four short New Testament letters for their oral effect.[207] His goal is not only to achieve an adequate understanding of the biblical texts but, beyond that, to translate them into modern languages. Since the texts were originally intended to be presented orally and to develop their effect on the listeners by means of that instrument, modern translations should not only do justice to the semantic content but should also be appropriate for the oral medium and have an effect on the modern listener that corresponds to the effect that the original text had. Wendland calls this a "literary functional equivalence (LiFE) translation."[208] After Wendland introduces performance criticism, his analysis of the texts concentrates on identifying traces of orality and defining their rhetorical effect. For this, he mainly uses methods that examine the texts rhetorically and stylistically. Wendland names five methodical steps: 1) genre analysis, 2) analysis of the text structure by examining the "compositional shifts" (change of place, time, person, theme, etc.), 3) analysis of all forms of linguistic or phonetic repetition ("patterned recursion" such as parallelism, inclusio), 4) consideration of the rhetorical intensity and emphasis ("artistic highlighting" through rhetorical questions, exaggeration, irony, metaphor, and interjections, but also through phonetic language structures such as rhythm, assonance, rhyme, and alliteration), and finally 5) a comprehensive rhetorical analysis of the text.[209] This overview of the methods already reveals that Wendland's work is more interested in the phonetic composition and rhetorical effect of the *text*, and not in the *event* of the performance itself. For example, the reaction of the audience

---

205. Sellin, "Ästhetische Aspekte," 411 (my translation; italics in the original).

206. Johnson, "Titus' Tearful Performance"; cf. Mitchell, "New Testament Envoys," 642; Wire, "Performance," 130.

207. Wendland, *Finding*. He examined the following letters: James, 1 John, Philemon, and 1 Peter.

208. Ibid., 259–67; cf. Wendland, *LiFE-style*; and Maxey, *From Orality to Orality*.

209. This outline of the methodical steps is offered in Wendland, *Finding*, 214; on the application to James, see ibid., 70–95, to Philemon, see ibid., 215–58.

is hardly noted—despite previous emphasis on how important the role of the audience is.[210] The role of the presenter appears also to be limited by Wendland to an exact reproduction of the text.[211] Wendland is more concerned with the "proclamation" of the authoritative text and less with the "performance."[212]

The study presented here takes up the diverse suggestions concerning performance criticism and applies them to the Pauline letters. However, the nature of the performance must first be considered. Previous studies have compiled various lists of the most important methodical steps for performance criticism[213] but haven't delivered any criteria by which the working-steps could be evaluated and set into relationship to one another. It is therefore difficult to say if a listing is too comprehensive or if something has been overlooked. It is necessary to have a concept of what a performance really is that is as exact as possible. This concept will help sharpen the eye to find the questions that performance criticism must ask of the text, and to systematize these questions appropriately, and at the same time to help distinguish it from other methods of textual interpretation.

The Essence of Performance

The method of performance criticism that has emerged from rhetoric and orality research assumes that a biblical text, e.g., a letter from Paul, achieves its effect by being read out aloud to an audience. This is in

---

210. For example, Wendland, *Finding*, 16–17.

211. Ibid., 53 (italics in the original): "It seems probable that the conservative Jewish scribal tradition put a much greater emphasis upon the accurate *reproduction* and a precise *reading* (recitation, cantillation, singing) of the biblical text than on its energetic performance before a religious congregation." Page 54: "Indeed, it was presented orally in a communal setting, no doubt often on the basis of the emissary-herald's memory (perhaps aided by a sparse 'note page' of key terms or topics), but the emphasis would still have been upon the writer's message, not the manner in which it was dramatically 'performed,' as if it were a conventional stage production or a secular oration on some current socio-political issue."

212. Ibid., 54–56.

213. Loubser, *Oral and Manuscript Culture*, 73, 76 has initially seven, then five methodical steps; Rhoads, "Performance Criticism," 126–31 lists seven aspects of the performance event, in 173–80 thirteen methods of performance-criticism are named, followed by a series of nine successive methodical steps; Wendland, *Finding*, 214 has five aspects; cf. also the chapters in Shiner, *Proclaiming*, which after an introduction (chs. 1 and 2) reflect seven aspects.

contrast to what is usually the case in our culture, where an individual reader takes in a written text with the eyes and thus comes to an understanding of its meaning. Most of the authors who present the method of performance criticism use this rather inexact and preliminary definition of a performance.[214] In the words of David Rhoads: "These compositions [the New Testament writings] were oral presentations. There was a performer or storyteller. The performances were heard/experienced rather than read. There was a communal audience. There was a physical location and a sociohistorical circumstance that shaped the performance and the reception."[215] Rhoads compares the originally integral role of the oral presentation of the biblical texts with the presentation of musical and theater performances and asks why Bible interpreters analyze the texts without ever having experienced a performance, or without regard to their performance character.[216] He contrasts the oral presentation with the reading of a written text. For him, these represent two very different media for conveying the content of language. Indeed, it was an important impulse in the development of performance criticism to give consideration to orality as the medium of communication used to convey the biblical message.[217] Thomas E. Boomershine, following Marshall McLuhan's assertion that the medium is the message, writes, "Media criticism is based on the recognition of the causal relationship between medium and meaning."[218] However, taking orality into consideration does not yet sufficiently identify what constitutes a performance. In his description of the performance, Rhoads also refers to the audience and the sociocultural situation of the presentation. How are these part of the performance? For this reason we must investigate the nature of a performance.

The studies presented by Richard Bauman have proven to be very influential in this discussion. As an anthropologist, he has examined the

---

214. Cf. the attempt—if somewhat unsystematic—to describe which aspects belong to a performance by Giles and Doan, *Twice Used Songs*, 12–16, 20–23.

215. Rhoads, "Performance Criticism," 118; cf. Rhoads, *Reading Mark*, 177–86.

216. Rhoads, "Performance Criticism," 119. The comparison with music is often found, e.g., in Boomershine, "Peter's Denial," 54; also in Saenger, "Silent Reading," 371: "A written text was essentially a transcription which, like modern musical notation, became an intelligible message only when it was performed orally to others or to oneself." The comparison that in antiquity texts, like music, were assimilated and understood by hearing them read out loud is already found in Hendrickson, "Ancient Reading," 184.

217. For example Boomershine, "Peter's Denial," 49–51.

218. Boomershine, "Peter's Denial," 51; cf. McLuhan, *Understanding Media*, 7.

performance of traditional oral art forms such as heroic epics, eulogies, narratives, proverbs, poetic duels, and religious or ceremonial speeches. He defines *performance* as follows:

> Fundamentally, performance as a mode of spoken verbal communication consists in the assumption of responsibility to an audience for a display of communicative competence ... Performance involves on the part of the performer an assumption of accountability to an audience for the way in which communication is carried out, above and beyond its referential content. From the point of view of the audience, the act of expression on the part of the performer is thus marked as subject to evaluation for the way it is done, for the relative skill and effectiveness of the performer's display of competence. Additionally, it is marked as available for the enhancement of experience, through the present enjoyment of the intrinsic qualities of the act of expression itself.[219]

This definition contains important information for a performance theory. It will serve here as the starting point leading to clarification of what we mean by *performance*. This clarification will then guide us to develop a methodology of performance criticism of the Pauline letters.

Materiality and Corporeality

Bauman defines performance as a special kind of communication. This communication is characterized by the fact that the way it is performed is of foremost importance, above and beyond the content expressed by the language. With this definition Bauman joins John L. Austin, whose work is largely responsible for the important role that the terms "performance" and "performativity" play in the current discussion.[220] Austin differentiates between a "normal" use of speech, which designates or describes something (constative use), and a "performative" use of speech, which does or effectuates something. He illustrates the performative use of language with speech acts such as promising, vowing, appointing, and the like. The verbs thus used express the action that is performed when they are used: that is, the language does not point to the extralinguistic world but rather to itself, to its own execution, through which it changes the

---

219. Bauman, ed., *Verbal Art*, 11; cf. Bauman, "Story," 3.

220. Cf. Carlson, *Performance*, 61–63 on Austin and Searle's concept of performativity.

extralinguistic world. Such statements are judged not as right or wrong but as successful or not.

However, the distinction between the constative and performative uses of language does not mean they are mutually exclusive applications of language. Austin himself gave up this opposition in the course of his deliberations because clear grammatical criteria for differentiating between the two uses could not be found, and because constative statements can also be described as successful or unsuccessful.[221] Instead, Austin differentiates between three aspects of action for all utterances: locution (the production of a statement that conforms to the rules), illocution (an action that is performed by uttering words that express this action), and perlocution (the intended effect on the addressee).[222] Nevertheless, with his examination of performative statements, Austin brought to attention an aspect of language long neglected.

Unlike Austin, Bauman does not focus on the use of language, but rather on those communicative skills as a whole, demonstrated when performing works of language orally before an audience and subject to their judgement. Bauman puts the *manner* of communication—communication techniques or *how* something is said—at the center, not the referential content. Thus for Bauman, as for Austin, the referential or constative function of communication appears to be the complete opposite of performance, as if the content of what is being said is not important for a performance. That is of course not the case, because the performance of oral art or traditional texts also points to extralinguistic entities, and the content can be understood and interpreted. This distinction is therefore not mutually exclusive but serves primarily to emphasize what makes performance something different, namely, an aspect long neglected in dealing with oral communication that was now brought into focus: the medium of communication.[223]

Under the influence of new developments in theatrical arts and inspired in particular by what is known as action art or performance

221. On this, cf. Bohle and König, "Zum Begriff des Performativen," 15–17; Krämer and Stahlhut, "Das Performative als Thema"; Krämer, "Sprache," 333; Krämer, "Was tut Austin."

222. This was the beginning of speech-act theory, which was further developed by Searle, *Speech Acts*.

223. Here performance-research is connected with the renewed interest in orality and the difference between oral and written tradition. For Bauman, however, the medium is not simply the oral language but also the physical presence, the virtuosity, and the overall effectiveness of the presenter.

art, studies of performance theory have continued to reflect upon and generalize conclusions about the contrast between the two aspects of communication: that is, between the symbolic nature of communication and its medial or material nature.[224] Building on Max Herrmann's theater theory, Erika Fischer-Lichte has established that the *human body* is the precondition that constitutes a performance, specifically the physical co-presence of performer and audience.[225] This does not mean that the human body is primarily or even only comprehended as a symbol for a certain *meaning*. This was namely how the task of an actor had been understood since the eighteenth century: the actor was to "embody" a figure as perfectly as possible so that his or her own body would become invisible and disappear behind the role being played. That proved to be an illusion.[226] In contrast to this, modern theater and action art bring to light that which has always been valid for a performance: the human body is directly apprehended in its materiality and *experienced* by the audience. Erika Fischer-Lichte made this comment on a performance by an action artist:

> The corporeality or the materiality of the action clearly dominated over its symbolism . . . In fact it precedes any attempt at an interpretation which goes beyond the self-referentiality of the action. The bodily effect which is triggered by the action appears to have the priority here. The materiality of the action is not transformed into a symbol, it does not disappear behind the symbol, but creates its own effect which is not a result of the meaning ascribed to the symbol.[227]

For Austin, the oral expressions of a *speech act* refer to nothing else but to what they themselves are saying, and in a performance this self-referentiality is found in the *actions* which at first do not express anything else but what they are acting out and thus also refer back to themselves.

Willmar Sauter examines performances primarily in a theater context and comes to a similar conclusion. For him, the "theater event" is

---

224. Cf. Fischer-Lichte, *Ästhetik*, 17–21; Fischer-Lichte, "Theater als Modell," 98–100; Fischer-Lichte and Roselt, "Attraktion," 242–44; Krämer, "Sprache," 345.

225. Fischer-Lichte, "Theater als Modell," 103–4; Fischer-Lichte, *Ästhetik*, 46–57.

226. See Fischer-Lichte, "Performativität," 20–22; Fischer-Lichte, *Ästhetik*, 130–60 on the corporeality of performance and on the change in the perception of "embodiment" in theater brought about by the "performative turn."

227. Fischer-Lichte, *Ästhetik*, 21 (my translation).

also an act of communication.[228] He proposes a three-part scheme for the interaction between the performer and the audience. The first level is the "sensory level" where the performer presents his body and frame of mind in "exhibitory actions" to the audience, and the audience reacts with attention and feelings. That corresponds roughly with Bauman's medial level, or with the corporeal level of Fischer-Lichte. Sauter's second level is the "artistic level" where the performer executes "encoded actions" that demonstrate the artistic abilities of the performer, but that also take the social conventions and the expectations associated with that kind of performance into consideration. This level also involves the medial side of communication but includes what Bauman attempts to take into account with the framing.[229] Sauter's third level is the "symbolic level," where the actions of the performer are—as he calls it—"embodied actions," that is, actions to which a meaning is attributed, both by the performer and by the audience. The three levels of Sauter's concept influence one another, just as the two sides of communication do for Bauman. Although they can be distinguished from each other, they are still experienced simultaneously, albeit with varying intensity. One can experience the performance of an artist and try to understand the meaning of what is being expressed and at the same time pay attention to his or her artistic abilities. But one can also concentrate only on the content of what is being expressed, or admire the artist's performance without paying attention to or understanding the symbolic content of what is being portrayed.

Thus we can say that an important characteristic of performance is that it depends on the physical participation of the performers and of those experiencing the performance—that is, on the ability or inability of the performers,[230] their presence and how well they embody what is being performed; on how the performers and audience are organized in the room, on their temporality and finiteness, and on their breathing, which creates the voice and lets it fade away.[231] The bodies of those taking part in the performance and the things performed with them, that is, the words spoken, the gestures, the movements in the room etc., are not

228. Sauter, *Theatrical Event*, 6–9, 53–61.

229. On this, see below pp. 57–59.

230. Sauter, *Theatrical Event*, 174–86 establishes how crucial the quality of the actors is for the impact of the whole performance. Cf. also p. 4: "If a spectator does not like the actors, the performance becomes 'meaningless.'"

231. On presence, see Fischer-Lichte, *Ästhetik*, 160–75; on spatiality, pp. 187–99; on the voice, pp. 219–26; on temporality, pp. 227–39.

just perceived as symbols bearing meaning—although everything can and usually will also be a symbol—but also as a reality of their own with their own effect. So the thing being performed is not only and sometimes not even primarily a text that must be approached hermeneutically to be understood, but much rather the event itself is of key importance. It is not just about understanding, but also about experiencing.

How does this experiencing happen if the effect of a performance is not only (and often not even primarily) triggered by understanding a *previously* conceived meaning contained in the script or the performed text? It is triggered by bodily feelings.[232] Hearing the voices of the speakers, perceiving gestures and movements as well as sensing smells and not so seldom also contacts—all these are first of all somatic experiences that physically influence the audience. They create a feeling that is not the result of understanding the gestures and sounds, but that arises through mimesis, that is, through mirroring or reproducing what the performers are doing with their bodies. This physical effect is often described using the metaphor of "infection."[233] The postures, tensions and movements of those speaking and acting in front of the audience, or in other words the materiality of their bodies, triggers a corresponding physical reaction in the audience—even if only rudimentary. In a study about public readings of lyrics, Peter Middleton explains this physical reaction using the example of dancing:

> Alongside this conscious activity of semiotic interpretation is another kinesthetic response, equally cognitive, but not linguistic, in which the audience senses the movements of the dancers in terms of their own bodies . . . The watcher dances with the dancer in an imaginative empathy which is not allowed to call the musculature to action . . . Similarly, a sound heard as the voice of another also produces virtual responses throughout the bodies of the audience. When the speaker utters the poem, the listeners also speak it in virtuality.[234]

Thus a further level is opened up in the performance of a text, which goes beyond the process of just interpreting what is being heard for all who are involved. It is the experience of the sounds in their bodily resonance and in the physical knowledge of their production that is triggered in the

---

232. Cf. the discussion of Eugenio Barba's concepts in Carlson, *Performance*, 27.
233. Fischer-Lichte, *Ästhetik*, 54, 138, 162–66.
234. Middleton, "Poetry's oral stage," 240–41.

listeners by the performer. Further physical reactions also result from physically experiencing a performance: for example, spectators or listeners hold their breath, tense their muscles, shiver, cry, or laugh.[235] All these physical reactions lead to an *understanding with the body*—for example anticipating danger or pain, a feeling of vulnerability, excitement or buoyancy—which then prompts *understanding with the mind* through which meaning is grasped. Thus in this process of bodily experiencing, thinking does not precede the physical reaction, but rather follows afterward.[236] In this way, manifold associations and cross-linkages open up new interpretive possibilities.[237] The performance *generates* a broader meaning and does not merely reproduce what is dictated in the script or text.

Of course every communication relies on a medium, and the way that medium is used as material always plays an important role. There is also a consciousness of mediality in written communication that can for example be seen in calligraphy and book art. But previously, the dominant hermeneutic approach has always viewed the manner in which something was presented predominantly as a symbol that had to be interpreted. The widespread use of writing, which indeed cannot encode large parts of the content of oral communication, has helped establish this view as the seemingly normal practice for dealing with oral utterances. Performance theory calls attention to the fact that this is actually a restricted perspective.

Framing through Social Conventions

In the definition quoted above, Bauman describes performance as a special form of communication. It stands out from other forms of communications through certain markers. By means of certain socially defined signals, those present know that they are cast in the role of the audience and must pay attention to and assess the way the communication is done—the aesthetic quality, the performer's abilities and effectivity. John Miles Foley calls the space created by these signals the "performance

---

235. This is particularly evident in acrobatic performances or in physically daring and dangerous feats (like bullfighting), as well as by self-inflicted injuries in performance art.

236. Cf. Schechner, "Magnitudes," 35–36; especially p. 41: "The doing of the action of a feeling is enough to arouse the feeling both in the doer and in the receiver."

237. Cf. Middleton, "Poetry's Oral Stage," 242.

arena."[238] That is the "place" where the performance takes place and where all the participants, the performers and audience, are physically present and attuned to the event.

Bauman borrowed the idea from Erving Goffman that certain social events and actions are demarcated or "framed" by socially defined communication signals. Gregory Bateson has discussed the framing of games and the "keys" that mark the frame. Goffman analyzed this concept with regard to social interaction.[239] For him, the "theater" event is an important example. Institutionalized settings—including such things as spatial markings or settings of time—as well as relationship signals—such as gestures, facial expression, posture and motion—serve to indicate such a frame. Bauman lists a number of markers ("keys") that apply to performances. Foley adopts and discusses these markers, pointing out that they are culture-specific.[240]

In the "performance arena," words are charged with special meaning. Framing creates an interpretive context (Bauman) so that what is said is not simply interpreted according to the common literal meaning and normal conventions. Bauman's strict juxtaposition of content-oriented and performative communication leads him to write: "In artistic performance of this kind, there is something going on in the communicative interchange which says to the auditor, 'interpret what I say in some special sense; do not take it to mean what the words alone, taken literally, would convey.'"[241]

Foley emphasizes the role of tradition, which enriches the words of a performance with meaning.[242] This includes more than just the literal meaning of the words, but rather all the elements of communication employed in the performance. For example, in a performance or even in a speech, the grotesque or an exaggeration is not felt to be inappropriate, and such things are even likely to be expected. More is also possible in the context of a performance than in real life. For example, social conventions about what is acceptable in public are suspended on the stage

---

238. Foley, *How to Read*, 116–17.

239. Bateson, "Theory of Play"; Goffman, *Frame Analysis*; cf. Carlson, *Performance*, 35–36, 45–46.

240. Bauman, *Verbal Art*, 15–24; Foley, *How to Read*, 85–93.

241. Bauman, *Verbal Art*, 9.

242. Foley, *How to Read*, 117–22.

(crimes are enacted in the theater, actors can appear naked on stage, and performance artists injure themselves).[243]

Framing a performance through socially defined markers makes it clear that performance always belongs in a social context.[244] Therefore performance can have quite a different appearance in different cultures and societies. Any study of performance must take this context into account.[245]

Interaction with the Audience and within the Audience

A third element in Bauman's definition of performance is the presence of an audience. The performer takes on the responsibility to the audience for shaping the performance. According to Bauman, the audience is the group of participants who judge the medial quality of the performance. They judge what they see and hear by the way it is shaped and fashioned (the skills and effectivity of the performer). The social convention that marks the frame of the event presses them into this role.

However, this only describes one side of what the audience contributes to the performance. Just like the performers, they are involved in the whole process of the performance. Evidence from antiquity attests to the liveliness of the audience's reactions during theater performances and orations.[246] Thereby it was not only the performer but also individual spectators who called attention to themselves with their actions and were honored by applause or ridiculed by catcalls. Performances took on the character of a folk festival, and this is true for the long history of events from ancient games in honor of the gods to theater and acrobatic performances. It was not until the eighteenth century that theater audiences were relegated to a darkened room from where they were to observe what

---

243. Fischer-Lichte, *Ästhetik*, 11 refers to performance art, which explores the limits of the markers: Should one intervene or not when the performance artist injures herself? Is it valid to behave normally when it would be humane to intervene, or is another behavior appropriate that respects even unusual actions performed by the artist?

244. Cf. ibid., 32.

245. Cf. Sauter, *Theatrical Event*, 9–10. Foley, *How to Read*, 128–30 points out how diverse the oral poetry is that he has examined and therefore redirects the attention from the question of what oral poetry is to the question of how it achieves its effect.

246. Kindermann, *Theaterpublikum*, 22, 24, 129; Korenjak, *Publikum und Redner*, 68–149; Morstein-Marx, *Mass Oratory*, 119–24 describes vigorous audience reactions during political speeches.

was happening on stage as quietly and inconspicuously as possible, as if through a window.[247]

Modern theater and performance arts have now broken open the strict dichotomy between actors and audience that dominated in eighteenth- and nineteenth-century theater, also partly inspired by anthropological research into rituals, where each participant, including the mere spectator, is involved in the whole event, although there are key figures and roles.[248]

Modern performance theory has established that the audience is not only spectator and critic, that is, it is not only engaged in deciphering and interpreting the signs presented to them.[249] The audience reacts to what is being performed, and conversely the actors react to the behavior of the audience.[250] Thus emerges what Erika Fischer-Lichte calls an "autopoietic feedback-loop."[251] This feedback loop includes all those present. The reactions of the members of the audience among themselves also play an important role.[252] Barbara Kirshenblatt-Gimblett describes Chasidic performances of Purim reenactments in the Jewish house of study (*beth midrash*) in Brooklyn. For the spectators there, an important part of the performance is the reaction of the rabbi, who takes a prominent place in front of the provisional stage. Because of the separation of the women's area, many of the women in the audience were able to neither see the rabbi nor follow what was happening on the stage, but rather witnessed the performance through the reaction of those standing closer to the front.[253] It should also be taken into consideration how the reactions of prominent personalities in an audience—usually seated in

---

247. Fischer-Lichte, *Ästhetik*, 59.

248. On theater, see especially Max Reinhardt and Richard Schechner; cf. also Fischer-Lichte, *Ästhetik*, 58–67.

249. Sauter, *Theatrical Event*, 2 emphasizes the contribution of the audience in the generation of meaning: "Here it is important to keep in mind that in the theater the 'message' is not something which is neatly packed and distributed to an anonymous consumer; instead, the meaning of a performance is created by the performers and the spectators together, in a joint act of understanding." Cf. Fischer-Lichte, "Performance," 39.

250. Sauter, *Theatrical Event*, 60–61.

251. Fischer-Lichte, *Ästhetik*, 59–61.

252. Cf. ibid., 54–55 where—following Max Herrmann—she speaks of the audience members mutually "infecting" each other in what they are experiencing.

253. Kirshenblatt-Gimblett, "Performance of Precepts," 114.

visible positions—influence the reactions of the rest of the audience.[254] The interaction of the audience members among themselves and the dependence of the whole performance on the audience's reaction have been exploited from antiquity into modern times by commissioned, sometimes even paid, applauders.[255]

Therefore, the responsibility for what happens does not lie with the performer alone.[256] The staging—that is, the strategies that have been thought out and prepared in order to guide the attention of the spectators and to create an event for them—cannot completely determine how the performance will develop.[257] The staging of a performance can be recognized by the audience or remain unnoticed. If recognized, then the production will also be judged. Recognizing how the performance has been planned and designed does not necessarily impair the experience of the performance.[258]

The physical presence of the audience and the actors makes interaction possible, including the interaction of audience members among themselves. The performance is the result of this interaction. So this view of the performance moves the emphasis away from the performed "piece," which has long stood at the center of attention, to the event itself and to all who are involved in it.

Ephemerality and Emergence through the Autopoietic Feedback-loop

Richard Bauman has pointed out in his definition of performance that it offers an experience that entails enjoying the quality of the act of communication in the very moments it is performed. That implies the event character of performance. What emerges is not something permanent like a work of visual art. The essence of a performance or what the whole

---

254. On antiquity, cf. Kindermann, *Theaterpublikum*, 25–27. Korenjak, *Publikum und Redner*, 149 refers to Philostratus, who reports in the *Vitae sophistarum* how Caracalla influenced the listeners during the speech of the sophist Heliodor, a favorite of the emperor.

255. Kindermann, *Theaterpublikum*, 22 (Greek), 128–29 (Roman); Morstein-Marx, *Mass Oratory*, 132–35; Korenjak, *Publikum und Redner*, 124–27.

256. Cf. Fischer-Lichte, *Ästhetik*, 47–57. She refers to Max Herrmann, who described the theater as "a game of all and for all" (my translation).

257. Cf. ibid., 236–330 on the definition of staging.

258. Ibid., 331–32.

thing is really about actually only exists during the performance. Performance is fleeting.[259] This becomes particularly apparent in modern performance art. Despite being documented in text and pictures or even video recordings, this documentation cannot capture or conserve the performance itself. From a performance perspective, even the presentation of such cultural oral traditions studied by Bauman or of traditional theatrical plays for which written texts exist are not primarily understood as the transmission of a permanent content, but as unrepeatable presentations of the actors' rhetorical and acting skills.

The audience is also intrinsically involved in the uniqueness and ephemerality of a performance. The performer faces the constant challenge of upholding the attention of the audience—against outside influences, against distractions from the audience, and against all forms of fatigue.[260] Everything that happens in the audience causes a reaction, even by the performers. The interaction between all those involved influences the performance event. No performance is the same as another, since the situation of the performers and the unpredictable composition and attitude of the audience are always different.

It is from these unpredictable elements of each performance that its emergent character results. Each time, something unique and special evolves. Performance creates something in the moment of the event that has never existed before and will never exist again.

Erika Fischer-Lichte discusses the emergence of the performance by describing the "autopoietic feedback-loop."[261] Everything that happens in the performance, on both the side of the presenters and the audience, exerts an influence back on the performance itself. That is unavoidable because of the bodily presence of the actors and the spectators. In this manner, new and unexpected situations arise, caused by even the smallest occurrence. This feedback loop is an extended form of the self-referentiality inherent in every performance. And this involves not just the language that points to itself as described by Austin, but the whole event pointing to itself and influencing itself in return.

Using the example of readings by a poet—that is, a performance where a written text is performed by being read out loud so that it comes

---

259. Ibid., 127; Fischer-Lichte, "Performance," 38–39.

260. Cf. Middleton, "Poetry's Oral Stage," 221–22.

261. Fischer-Lichte, *Ästhetik*, 63–82 in the context of the role change between spectators and actors, where the boundary between both these groups is blurred, where all are involved in the event but no single person can control it alone.

very close to how Paul's letters were read—Peter Middleton discusses the situation that in our culture, which is strongly influenced by the written word, an idealistic concept of this act of reading exists, namely, that individuals are confronted with a text under ideal conditions and that the material conditions and limitations such as voice and mood, room and light, as well as interruptions or interaction between the reader and the listeners do not really play a role in the reception process. Such phenomena are seen as imperfections and are ignored as far as possible.[262] However, this overlooks the fact that a public reading, as with an oral discourse, always takes place in a specific space and time and is unavoidably influenced by such concrete manifestations of materiality.[263] What is seen as imperfection during the reading process is in fact part of the act, an important component of the event itself in which the text encounters the real conditions under which, in the end, all communication takes place. Thus it is not irrelevant who is doing the reading. The speaker fills what is being read with living history, bestows it with his or her own measure of creditability, and also links it with his or her own personal relationship to listeners. The voice, emphasis, and gestures of the reader, as well as the atmosphere in the room and the reactions of the listeners, produce a constant commentary accompanying the reading that can even stand in contradiction to the text being presented.

References to Things That Already Exist

A final aspect of performance, only implicit in Bauman's definition, must now be considered. Bauman defines a performance as an event in which the competence and effectiveness with which the act of communication is performed is evaluated by an audience. In order to make such an evaluation, one must be able to make comparisons with something that already exists. Bauman builds on Dell Hymes, who links performance also to tradition when he defines performance as a behavior in which someone "assume[s] a responsibility to an audience and to tradition

---

262. Middleton, "Poetry's Oral Stage," 221–24.

263. Ibid., 221: "Writing and silent reading have helped create assumptions about reading which would not seem so obvious in an oral society, and theorists forget that reading depends on similar conditions to discourse and, like discourse, is always an uncompleted stage in heterogeneous transactions that exceed the moment of encounter, which is itself always taking place in a material space and time."

as they understand it."²⁶⁴ Every performance, although unique, always also points back to previous events. "There is no performance without pre-formance."²⁶⁵

In the performance of texts from an oral tradition like those examined by Bauman, but also of dramatic literature, the performance points to things that already exist in a twofold way. On the one hand, it points to the content of the text or play (script) being performed. Reference to content also takes place in what Foley called Immanent Art, that is, when reference is made to comprehensive traditional elements evoked in the memories of those who are at home in that tradition when a certain formula, keyword, or expression is used.²⁶⁶ The reference to the content of things that already exist corresponds to the constative function of language with which it points to something extralinguistic, to the world outside of language.²⁶⁷ Despite the fact that the traditional texts whose performance Bauman examined do refer to content, he did not include the content aspect in his definition and instead emphasized the medial aspect in order to differentiate performance from the "normal" use of language.

The second kind of referentiality is rooted in the medial aspect of language: a performance refers back to previous performances of the specific text or composition, or to the conventions that have previously applied to performative acts. This is the only way that spectators can evaluate the manner of realization of the communication act. This also includes the aspect that all performances refer to the sociocultural situation of performances—that is, to the frame, markers, and "performance arena" that first make a performance recognizable as such. The fact that a conventional frame makes the performance recognizable is also a reference to something that already exists.²⁶⁸

---

264. Hymes, "Breakthrough," 13, quoted in Carlson, *Performance*, 12.

265. John MacAloon, quoted by Carlson, *Performance*, 12; cf. Schumacher, "Performativität," 386–87.

266. Foley, *How to Read*, 109–24.

267. Jaques Derrida objected to this, arguing that linguistic utterances cannot be based on a primary reality existing outside of language but rather refer back to earlier discourses and are thus, in a certain sense, quotations. On this, cf. Kertscher, "Wittgenstein," 48–52; see also Carlson, *Performance*, 75–76 and the literature mentioned by him on the discussion between Derrida and Searle.

268. Cf. Carlson, *Performance*, 76.

Both "content-related" references to a script and "medium-related" references to previous performances can differ in their intensity. While many performances present a text or a play, experimental theater or modern performance art often forgo the use of a verbal script, even though the plot development is indeed thought through beforehand, as far as the emergent character of the performance allows. The reference to preexisting content is therefore not predetermined in such a performance, but is left—to a certain extent—to the free association of the spectators, who can each ascribe a meaning of their own to what they observe by linking it to their individual knowledge of the world and previous experiences.[269] It is also true that to evaluate the medial aspect of a performance—the physical presence of the artists and their ability to captivate the audience with their actions—the audience at such performances will hardly be able to rely on comparisons with previous performances, but is rather more dependent on their own reactions that are triggered by the event, which of course will always also be influenced by social conventions. If, for example, a performance artist willfully injures herself, this will provoke reactions in the audience that will be determined, on the one hand, by empathy but on the other hand also by moral concepts or social taboos.[270] Therefore, the spectators will also use differing criteria for judging the medial quality of the performance, and these will be constructed based upon previous experiences and cultural knowledge.

Richard Schechner describes the relationship of a performance to things that already exist when he speaks of "restored behavior."[271] According to this concept, performance includes the awareness that predetermined behavior is involved, for example a social role or a role in a play. On the other hand, a performance—whether it is modern performance art or even just traditional theater or the public recitation of an existing text—will never simply be a repetition of what has been handed down.[272] Every performance both consists of what already exists and changes the way things have previously been. The things that are predefined are confronted with the specialness and uniqueness of the people, situation, and atmosphere in each individual performance. Thus the awareness arises that a doubleness is involved: both the predefined behavior and a new

---

269. Fischer-Lichte, *Ästhetik*, 145, 244 writes about a pluralization of possible interpretations; cf. also Fischer-Lichte and Roselt, "Attraktion," 246–47.

270. Cf. Fischer-Lichte, "Performativität," 28–29; Fischer-Lichte, *Ästhetik*, 266.

271. Schechner, *Between Theater*, 35.

272. Carlson, *Performance*, 188; Krämer, "Sprache," 331, 345.

behavior are being acted out at the same time in multifaceted modifications of previous forms.[273] In this way, each performance not only reflects time-honored traditions and established roles but also always contains the potential to undermine or break out of tradition.

The doubleness just described becomes manifest in the actor, who simultaneously presents both his or her own self as a person and the predefined role. The actor is a person, a human being with her own individuality, with his own body and its abilities and limitations, and with her own experiences and desires. The predefined role could be a role in a play or a socially defined professional role such as of a doctor, pastor or police officer, or a provocative role in the actions that stem from the imagination of a performance artist. The actor is conscious of presenting something predefined, and yet she presents it with her own unique self, with his own body and character. This awareness of doubleness also arises when someone compares his or her own behavior with an ideal or a possibility, that is, when a performer observes and evaluates herself or himself and thus becomes his or her own audience.[274]

We have seen above that both the physical characteristics of those involved in the performance and the other media-related conditions play an important role. Thus a performance is first and foremost something experienced and not immediately or only an intellectual understanding of a text or enactment. This experience as absorbed with all the physical senses then in turn leads to an understanding and taps into even more possibilities for interpretation that go beyond the things contained in the piece that has been enacted or the text that has been presented. This raises the question of how the interpretation reached by the experience is related to what the performed text says. In light of the performance, the meaning of the text could be perceived as an abstraction. It is a reduction to the essence. Just as an abstract term (like "circle") describes a multitude of concrete phenomena, but as such an abstraction cannot itself exist (*the* circle does not exist, only concrete manifestations of it), so also must a text be embodied by a concrete person under concrete conditions in order to become visible.[275] The performer embodies the meaning in his or

---

273. Cf. Carlson, *Performance*, 46–47.

274. Ibid., 5.

275. Fischer-Lichte, *Ästhetik*, 256, formulates this trenchantly: "The figure being presented is bound to the specific corporeality of the actor who is producing it. The phenomenal body of the actor, his physical existence in the world, forms the existential foundation for the emergence of the figure. It does not exist beyond this individual

her own special way. He or she adds a new dimension to it that comes through his or her physical presence, not through new text. The framing, that is, the socially prescribed conditions for performances, is also an abstraction. It also does not exist in itself, but only in concrete manifestations of real performances. Thus considering performance it becomes clear that only giving consideration to the text would mean working with a mere abstraction and that important aspects of the inherent reality do not come into view.[276]

Methodology of Performance Criticism

Now that we have determined what constitutes a performance, we can derive from that what is to be understood as performance criticism in this study and the methodological steps it encompasses. We will orient our considerations on the five characteristics of performance that have been identified, beginning with ephemerality and emergence, because they are useful for defining the goal and the limitations of the method discussed here. We will then turn to the sociocultural context (frame), because by studying the societal situation something like an ideal for specific performances in a specific time and culture can be identified. This ideal can then be consulted for reconstructing a *possible* performance of the texts in question. After some fundamental considerations concerning how performance criticism should deal with a written text and how performance elements could leave their mark in a written text, we will discuss the methods that can be used to draw conclusions based on the text about materiality, audience-relatedness, and referentiality in the performance of that text.[277]

---

body. That means that when an actor depicts a character, he does not reproduce something which is predetermined somewhere else—in the script of the play—but rather creates something completely new, something unique which can only exist through his own individual corporeality" (my translation). Cf. Fischer-Lichte, "Theater als Modell," 107–8.

276. Here performance research overlaps with reader-response criticism as developed by Wolfgang Iser and others. There it has also been established that the text does not contain everything that accounts for its meaning, but that the reader also contributes to the generation of the text's meaning. In contrast to performance, the interaction of multiple people, that is, the autopoietic feedback-loop, does not occur while reading. On reader-response criticism, cf. Warning, *Rezeptionsästhetik*; Iser, *Akt des Lesens*; Körtner, *Inspirierte Leser*.

277. Cf. the method presented by Shiner, *Proclaiming*, 3–4. Examining the sociocultural context ("frame") of the performance corresponds approximately to his first

Objective and Limitations of the Method
—Ephemerality and Emergence

Performance criticism of the New Testament texts assumes that these texts are designed for and evidence of the event of their performance before an audience. "Even when oral poetry survives only in manuscript, the imperative remains: we must project the 'play' from the 'script' as best we can, converting the object (back) into an event as far as possible."[278] What John Foley says here concerning oral poetry is similarly true for the letters and also the narrative texts of the New Testament. It is necessary and also possible to conceive of them as vestiges of performances. Thus we will do more justice to the texts, because they were written in such a way as to develop their effect in an oral performance.

However, the task that Foley calls for of reconverting literary compositions that we have in the form of written objects back into living events encounters the problem that every performance is something transient and ephemeral. Performances from the past cannot be reconstructed in the full sense of the word, just as future performances will ultimately always remain inaccessible. As demonstrated above, it belongs to the nature of a performance that something emerges which has never existed before and then irrevocably disappears. A well-founded performance criticism must face this fact, reflecting upon and respecting the limitations of the method.

It is therefore the task of performance criticism to develop, as far as possible, a *heuristic evaluation model* of the performance of a text. It will construct *a possible and probable* performance, attempting to capture what was typical of the event in order to understand an event such as the reception of a letter from Paul, which is assumed in the text. Consequently, performance criticism means *reflecting on* the performance based on a historical text that itself was an important part of the original performance. Analysis and reflection serve to clarify what was experienced in that performance. Performance criticism thus involves an *intellectual* examination of both the corporeal manifestation and the content of what is said in the text. It is about analyzing the event and its effect on the listeners. This is an intellectual process that can be expressed in language.

---

methodological step. Examining the traces of performance in the text is included in part in his second step.

278. Foley, *How to Read*, 137.

Understanding the event is not the same as experiencing the event itself. What Erika Fischer-Lichte has said concerning contemplating performances in general is also true for engaging in performance criticism: it helps to understand, but at the same time also causes a change. When contemplating a performance, something experienced more at the gut level of feelings and impulses must be translated to a level of conscious language and thus, to a certain extent, becomes detached from the actual experience.

> Thus language as a specific medium has at its disposal only its own unique materiality, and as a specific system of symbols also only its own unique rules. When these are used or followed as the basis for a description [of a performance], the process of writing takes on a life of its own; it develops its own dynamics which can bring it within a certain proximity of the remembered perceptions, but at the same time of necessity lead away from them. Every linguistic description, every interpretation, in short: every attempt to understand a performance after the event contributes to the production of a text which follows its own rules . . . The attempt to understand a performance thus generates a text as an independent entity which now itself needs to be understood.[279]

How would this kind of contemplation benefit the interpretation of New Testament texts? The benefits are twofold. First, such contemplation brings into focus the fact that these are texts that do not correspond to our culture, which is dominated by written communication. The interpreter becomes aware that an interpretation that sees the linguistic expressions only as references to extralinguistic realities and therefore takes into account only the constative function of language while overlooking the performative function is only working with an abstraction and thus comprehends only part of what happened through the linguistic utterance. Widespread focus on the author is also not appropriate, because the author (and later his text) cannot control everything that happens in the performance.[280] Through performance criticism, the perspective is opened up to include the medial quality of communication (materiality

---

279. Fischer-Lichte, *Ästhetik*, 280 (my translation).

280. Ibid., 80–81, speaks of "uncontrollability" and emphasizes "that the process of the performance always executes itself as a self-creation . . . self-creation means that all who are involved produce it together, but that it cannot be completely planned, controlled and in this sense produced by any one person, that it completely escapes the controlling power of any one of them" (my translation).

and corporeality, aesthetics), the social context (framing), the interaction with the audience, and the diverse referencing structures. In this way, new aspects of *content* are also tapped into, and meanings and effects that otherwise would have remained hidden become visible.[281]

And second, the task of understanding a text with the help of performance critcism is a process that points forward to a future situation where the text will again become an event, perhaps in a sermon, or to some other occasion when the text becomes the center of collective attention in a group. Performance criticism does not itself produce a re-performance of the New Testament texts. It is, however, a necessary step in that direction, because a deeper understanding of their performance can be fruitful in creating a new corporeal articulation of the communication through these texts. Researchers such as Thomas E. Boomershine, David Rhoads, and Whitney Shiner, who themselves engage in such performances, have repeatedly pointed out how impressive such an event is, and how personally *experiencing* and *shaping* a performance of text is important for understanding the text.[282]

Conventions of Letter Reception— Framing the Performance of a Letter

The socially conventionalized framing is an important characteristic of performance. For performance criticism this means that besides the other aspects of the nonlinguistic context of a biblical text—questions concerning social organization, culture, economic conditions, law, religion, and so forth—the special conditions of the *performance* must also be examined. On the one hand, these include the conventions for dealing with written texts, for publication of written material, and for reception of their content. On the other hand, these include the social conditions and norms for delivery and above all for presentation of a text.[283]

---

281. Maassen, "Text und Performanz," 294–95 illustrates this using the example of the oral implementation of a text: "Orality, the use of voice, is an effect of the text's performance; it gives the text added semantic value" (my translation). Cf. also Middleton, "Poetry's Oral stage," 218.

282. For example Shiner, *Proclaiming*, 6–8; Rhoads, *Reading Mark*, 176–201; Boomershine, "Biblical Storytelling."

283. Cf. Horsley and Draper, *Whoever Hears You*, 160.

Dealing with Written Texts

The performance of New Testament texts and particularly the Pauline letters is rooted in the conditions under which texts were used in Greco-Roman culture. Important research has been done on this.[284] Orality and scribality existed in a tension-filled relationship mutually influencing each other.[285] Although writing was widespread and used in a great number of ways, the society was nevertheless predominantly characterized by oral communication.[286] Writing was laborious and expensive.[287] Oral communication was preferred and considered to be more reliable.[288] If reading and writing abilities were necessary, specialists were available for these tasks. For most people the ability to read and write was not necessary.[289] One could even be educated in literary and cultural matters without being able to read oneself.[290]

Writing was understood less as a system of symbols for direct communication and more as a system for encoding the spoken word.[291] Thus it was normal that written texts were read out loud and that they only then were thought to have achieved what the original communicator in-

---

284. On this, cf. Botha, "Greco-Roman Literacy"; J. Dewey, "Textuality," 39-47; Shiell, *Reading Acts*, 9-136; Loubser, *Oral and Manuscript Culture*, 55-72; on Rome, see Woolf, "Literacy or Literacies"; on Greece, see Lentz, *Orality*; on Palestine, see Hezser, *Jewish Literacy*; on the Old Testament Israel, see Niditch, *Oral World*.

285. Finnegan, *Literacy*, 12-14, 172, 175; cf. Foley, *How to Read*, 66-69. On the use of books and the interaction of spoken and written communication, cf. Gamble, *Books and Readers*, 28-32; cf. also Goldhill, "Anecdote," 98; Habinek, "Situating Literacy."

286. Ong, *Presence*, 22-87; Downing, *Doing Things*, 75-83. Knoop, "Zum Verhältnis von geschriebener und gesprochener Sprache," 222 demonstrates that it wasn't until the nineteenth century that the spoken word lost its powerful effect and the written word took over primacy in language.

287. Harris, *Ancient Literacy*, 193-96; cf. Hezser, *Jewish Literacy*, 132-33.

288. Alexander, "Living Voice."

289. J. Dewey, "Textuality," 41.

290. Cf. the discussion of ancient sources by J. Dewey, "Textuality," 45-46; Downing, *Doing Things*, 29-40.

291. Lentz, *Orality*, 63-65; Thomas, *Literacy*, 91. According to Knoop, "Zum Verhältnis von geschriebener und gesprochener Sprache," 221-22, there was no independent style of written language until the modern age: "All writing is only assistance for intonation and therefore potentially spoken language, that is, to be presented by speaking or reading out loud. In this respect spoken language is *the* language that can be recorded in writing" (my translation, emphasis in the original). On ancient education in general, see Bonner, *Education*; Lentz, *Orality*, 46-70; Harris, *Ancient Literacy*, 233-48; Shiell, *Reading Acts*, 14-29; Vegge, *Paulus*.

tended.²⁹² The information encoded in the written medium often worked together with the components of language that could only transported orally (voice, loudness, speed) and with nonverbal signals (e.g., pointing gestures, position in the room).²⁹³

Conventions of Letter Reception

The framework for the delivery of letters—that is, the social conventions characterizing such an event—is especially important for performance criticism of the New Testament letters. Performance criticism will therefore give consideration to the customary signals that marked the letter-reception event and their effect on the mindset of and the expectations placed on all those involved.

The framing of a performance causes the spoken words to be received differently than they would have been not spoken within this frame.²⁹⁴ What would this mean for particular passages in the letter—for example those expressing modesty (1 Cor 2:1–4; Phlm 9), voicing a desire for nearness (Rom 1:9–12), or announcing travel plans (2 Cor 13:1; Phlm 22)?²⁹⁵ Because this study is concerned with how Paul's letters achieved their effects upon the recipients, the conventions linked with the situation upon the *reception* by and *reading* of the letters to the recipients are particularly relevant.²⁹⁶

---

292. Achtemeier, "Omne Verbum Sonat" and the literature mentioned above in footnote 153 on p. 37 in the discussion of silent and spoken reading; Lefèvre, "Römische Literatur."

293. Using legal documents, Hibbitts, "Coming to Our Senses" has demonstrated that in cultures where the written word played a less dominant role than today (he calls them "performance cultures") all the physical senses were used in order to communicate rights and obligations. Section 3.4: "Ultimately, the meaning of significant cultural and legal messages resides less in the individual components of communication (although these must be recognized) than in their synthesis, performance."

294. Alexander, "Hellenistic Letter-Forms," compares the Epistle to the Philippians with letters that were only concerned with fostering fellowship and had no other content; cf. Koskenniemi, *Studien*, 107, who speaks of *Verbindungsbriefe* ("letters of bonding"). The words that Cicero wrote to Atticus (*Att.* 9.10.1): "I have nothing that I could write," have their place within the framework of written communication and would not be spoken outside this framework; a similar situation is found in *Att.* 8.14.1.

295. On travel plans, cf. Funk, "Apostolic Parousia"; Mullins, "Visit Talk"; Schnider and Stenger, *Studien*, 92–107.

296. By contrast cf. Richards, *Paul and First-Century Letter*, who examines the conventions at the *creation* of a letter.

Theory of Performance Criticism 73

M. Luther Stirewalt has argued convincingly that Paul's letters can be compared to the official administrative letters from rulers or public officials.[297] It would follow from this that a socially established procedure existed for the receipt and reception of Paul's letters, comprising the following steps:[298]

1) The letter was transported. As a rule, those bearing his letters were messengers sent by Paul.[299] Or he entrusted his letter to church members who were about to undertake a journey (e.g., Phoebe, Rom 16:1). This corresponds with the usual practice for sending letters.[300]

2) The letter was delivered, that is, it was handed over to the recipient or a representative of the recipient group. The handing over of the letter is explicitly mentioned in Acts 15:30, and this took place *before* it was read out loud and subsequently discussed. This procedure appears to be part of the usual protocol. In this way, the responsibility for the letter was transferred to the recipient group. This situation is presupposed in 1 Thess 5:27, where the recipients are charged with having the letter read to the group. This was therefore the responsibility of the recipient or the recipient group, not the messenger. The delivery of a letter calls to mind how Demetrius compared a letter to a gift in *De elocutione* (224).

3) The recipient commissioned someone to read the letter out loud (cf. 1 Tim 4:13). Since the letter was placed in the hands of the recipient, it is unlikely that the courier would have been the one to read the letter, as has often been suggested,[301] for then the recipient would have had to return it to the courier. The messenger would also have had to point to himself or herself when reading the section of the letter recommending

---

297. Stirewalt, *Paul*, 5–8, 13–18; see also the overview of relevant research above on pp. 14–15; cf. also Schnider and Stenger, *Studien*, 91.

298. Stirewalt, *Paul*, 6 only names "official presentation, public reading, and oral reports." Tsang, "Are We Misreading," 16 additionally names the convening of the meeting in which the letter is to be presented.

299. For example Timothy (1 Cor 4:17), Titus (2 Cor 2:12–13; 8:16–24), Tychicus (Col 4:7–9), Epaphroditus (Phil 2:25–30) and Onesimus (Phlm). Cf. Mitchell, "New Testament Envoys."

300. Riepl, *Nachrichtenwesen*, 241–44; Epp, "New Testament Papyrus Manuscripts"; Llewelyn, "Sending Letters"; Llewelyn, "Directions"; Hezser, *Jewish Literacy*, 265; Wagner, "Bote," 2–4.

301. For example, Botha, "Verbal Art," 419; Cox, "Reading," 81, 90; Ramsaran, "From Mind," 10–11, 29; Shiell, *Reading Acts*, 32–33; Richards, *Paul and First-Century Letter*, 181, 202; Wendland, *Finding*, 16. The rationale given for this has often been that Paul's messenger would have had exact knowledge of how the letter was to be presented.

him or her as a messenger to the recipient. Peter Head has studied the papyrus letters in which the letter carrier is mentioned. It was never the task of the messenger to read the letter, and the ability to read and write was never a prerequisite for serving as a messenger.[302]

The public reading of a letter required the ability to convert the visible characters back into audible speech. There were not many who had the ability to do that.[303] Knowledge of reading and writing was found primarily among members of the upper class, and literacy was considered to be a status symbol.[304] For them, writing was a means of retaining their control and power—for example through administrative letters, reports, inscriptions, propaganda, and other things.[305] In addition, the specialists that the upper class needed to perform these tasks, such as public officials and slaves trained in clerical duties, were also literate.[306]

Even if someone was able to read, it did not mean that he had the necessary skills to present a letter publicly.[307] For this reason it would have been only a small group of people[308] who were repeatedly commissioned to read written documents publicly. This eventually developed

---

302. Head, "Named Letter-Carriers." On ancient Semitic letters, cf. Meier, *Messenger*, 194–95.

303. See Harris, *Ancient Literacy* on the prevalence of the ability to read and write in the Roman Empire. He estimates that it was about 15 percent for the male population in towns (p. 329) and markedly less in the country and among women. His results have been widely accepted, e.g., Botha, "Greco-Roman Literacy," 199. On Greek culture, cf. Thomas, *Literacy*. Bar-Ilan, "Illiteracy"; Niditch, *Oral World*, 39–59; and Hezser, *Jewish Literacy*, 27–38 assume low levels of reading and writing ability in Palestine. Klauck, *Ancient Letters*, 55–56 and Gamble, *Books and Readers*, 7 assume a somewhat greater prevalence.

304. Harris, *Ancient Literacy*, 248, 250; Botha, "Greco-Roman Literacy," 205–6.

305. J. Dewey, "Textuality," 40–41. Thomas, *Literacy*, 21 quotes Lévi-Strauss, *Tristes Tropiques*, 393: "The primary function of writing, as a means of communication, is to facilitate the enslavement of human beings." On writing and power, cf. the articles in Bowman and Woolf, *Literacy*.

306. Cf. Habinek, "Situating Literacy," 122; on slaves as lectors, cf. Shiell, *Reading Acts*, 31–33.

307. Cf. Plinius minor, *Ep.* 9.34, where he as a highly educated nobleman confesses that he cannot read aloud very well.

308. Cox, "Reading," 81 suspects that in a small church it would have been only one or two people; cf J. Dewey, "Textuality," 50. Since women were less literate than men (cf. Harris, *Ancient Literacy*, 239–40, 253; for Italy 259, 263–64; for the Western provinces 271; for Roman Egypt 279–80) and therefore were less likely assigned to present Paul's letters, I will use only the male form for the presenter.

into the office of the lector.³⁰⁹ In Christian churches, these people would have belonged to the households of those few members from the somewhat wealthier and better-educated classes.

4) The one commissioned to perform the reading prepared himself by working through the letter and rehearsing it. It was necessary to be familiar with the text in order to be able to present it. *Scriptio continua* and few or no recognizable optical signals structuring the text made it difficult to present a document spontaneously.³¹⁰ Writing was above all conserved orality.³¹¹ The meaning of the text became accessible to the reader only after it was transmuted into sound.³¹² Thus, a person who was supposed to read a text aloud publicly had to first read it aloud for himself or have someone read it to him in order to know how to shape the oral performance. Harry Y. Gamble writes:

> The initial reading of any text was inevitably experimental because it had to be decided, partly in retrospect, which of the possible construals of *scriptio continua* best rendered the sense. If public reading were not to be halting, tentative, or misleading, those decoding judgments had to be made in advance through rehearsals of the text.³¹³

5) A meeting was convened. As was usual for official letters, Paul's letters were addressed to groups. The reception of such a letter was a public event. When one of the groups came together, the opportunity presented itself to have the letter read out loud to all of them. This would

---

309. On the lector, cf. Shiell, *Reading Acts*.

310. Achtemeier, "*Omne Verbum Sonat*," 17 points to Petronius, *Satyrikon* 75, where Trimalchio praises a slave because he can read (aloud) *directly* from the page, that is, without analyzing the text beforehand for himself. Cf. also Bahn, "Interpretative Reading," 433; Saenger, "Silent Reading," 370-71; Achtemeier, "*Omne Verbum Sonat*," 10; Starr, "Reading Aloud," 343; Hezser, *Jewish Literacy*, 451, 463; Tsang, "Are We Misreading," 212.

311. Thomas, *Literacy*, 91; Dean, "Grammar of Sound"; cf. Lentz, *Orality*, 63-64 with reference to Plutarch, *De musica*, 1131d.

312. Cf. above the comparison with music on p. 51, footnote 216; similarly Small, *Wax Tablets*, 23 with reference to Svenbro, "Phrasikleia," 236.

313. Gamble, *Books and Readers*, 205. Cf. also J. Dewey, "Textuality," 51; Hezser, *Jewish Literacy*, 452; Stirewalt, *Paul*, 17; Vegge, *Paulus*, 115; Wendland, *Finding*, 9. Aristotle, *Rhet*. 3.5.6 discusses the difficulty of properly recognizing which words belong together during the presentation. Irenaeus points out in *Haer*. 3.7.1 that the meaning of a text will be properly understood when the "correct" places for breathing are observed, even though they are not discernable in the text; cf. Gamble, *Books and Readers*, 229.

have generally been at the regular meetings of the church (cf. 1 Tim 4:13; Rev 1:3), which took place in the evening together with a communal meal and subsequent fellowship with proclamation and discussion.[314]

6) Those participating in the meeting took their places. The order of seating was often socially organized. That was true for the theater on a larger scale, but also for the small symposium. Groups that belonged together sat together.[315] Places of honor were situated in plain view.[316] The benches were arranged either in a half circle or in rows running along three or even four walls of the room. This seating order encouraged a lively interaction between all those in attendance.[317] "The theater is in this respect exemplary for many other showplaces of ancient rhetoric: As we shall see, the spectators sat mostly on steps and in a half circle (or open rectangle), and open-air performances were more the rule than the exception."[318] In the odeon or in the bouleuterion, the seating was also arranged in a half circle or in concentric rows along the walls.[319] The oldest synagogues display rows of seats along two, three, or four walls.[320] Carsten Claussen draws this conclusion: "The visitors to the

---

314. Cf. Wick, *Gottesdienste*.

315. Cf. Luke 14:8; Jas 2:2. Theissen, "Soziale Integration," 297 argues that it would be difficult to envision that according to 1 Cor 11:21 some in Corinth could be satiated and drunk while others did not have enough if the wealthy were not "probably in a separate room from the others and are lying at their own table" (my translation). On the seating order in the theater, cf. Kindermann, *Theaterpublikum*, 132: "'In this way, the whole theater offered an orderly transparent picture of the Roman population, organized according to political structure' (T. Bollinger) and social status" (my translation); cf. also 126, 128, 187, on Athens, 20, 24.

316. A Roman law from 68 BCE reserved the first fourteen rows behind the orchestra (of a temporary theater) for the knightly nobility; until then, these had been designated only for the senatorial nobility; Beacham, *Roman Theatre*, 67. The audience reacted not only to what was happening on the stage but also to the socialites who were present; Beacham, *Roman Theatre*, 133, 149, 169.

317. On internal communication within the audience, cf. Korenjak, *Publikum und Redner*, 147-49.

318. Ibid., 30 (my translation).

319. Ibid., 29-30: "whereas the different sectors of the audience certainly could have each other in view and communicate with one another both optically and acoustically... What's more, out in the open air and during daylight hours there is no way of darkening the audience area to separate the listeners from each other and to focus their attention on a lighted stage—a circumstance that further facilitates the effects of group dynamics" (my translation).

320. Cf. Claussen, *Versammlung*, 169 (Gamla), 172 (Masada), 175 (Herodium), 184 (Modi'in), 192 (Delos); 207 (Dura Europos). Cf. Strange, "Ancient Texts," 32-35,

synagogue all face each other due to the seating around the perimeter. This architectural characteristic could possibly imply that the discussion among the visitors to the synagogue played a large role."[321] A symposium could take the shape of three klinai or couches forming an open rectangle (triclinium) or several couches in a half circle. There were also meeting houses with lounges for reclining along three of the four walls.[322] That means that the listeners could all see one another and that they mutually exerted influence and control over one another.

7) The messenger was greeted publicly, and the letter was brought forward. In some cases, the messenger would give an initial oral report before the reading of the letter.[323] That in some letters the recommendation of the messenger comes before the actual information and is given a lot of space seems to support this.[324] In any case, the messenger always had the responsibility of being a witness at the reading of the letter and reporting back to the sender about the immediate reactions of the audience.[325]

8) The letter was read out loud.[326] This presentation corresponded to ancient orations. Sculptures of orators show the speaker holding the text either open or rolled up in his left hand.[327] The rolled-up text served as a symbol for the source of the recitation, not as an immediate aid for the delivery of the speech. Usually it was recited from memory.[328] Even when the text was read from an open document, the performance was more like a text recital than a reading.[329] The presentation of the letter was based on the customs of public speaking. Vocal expression, gestures, and personal bearing were similar to what listeners were accustomed to from

---

who compares the architecture of synagogues with that of bouleuterions.

321. Claussen, *Versammlung*, 177 (my translation).

322. Cf. Klinghardt, *Gemeinschaftsmahl*, 62–83. On the seating order in Qumran and in the Sanhedrin, cf. Gerhardsson, *Memory and Manuscript*, 245–47.

323. Meier, *Messenger*, 131–245; Stirewalt, *Paul*, 8.

324. According to Stirewalt, *Paul*, 9 the letter was originally subordinate to the oral message.

325. 1 Clem 63:3; 65:1.

326. Cf. Riepl, *Nachrichtenwesen*, 371–74.

327. Cf. Aldrete, *Gestures*, 46.

328. Quintilian, *Inst.* 1.11.14; cf. also Olbricht, "Delivery and Memory."

329. Cf. Sonkowsky, "Aspect of Delivery" concerning the presentation of written texts in Aristotle's rhetoric. Quintilian, *Inst.* 10.7.31–32 allows only an occasional glance at the prepared text, and pleads in general for memorizing the speech.

speeches, recitations, and drama.[330] In the Roman period, orators learned from actors how a speech should be presented.[331]

By being read publicly, the letter was brought to the attention of the actual recipients, which for Paul's letters are the members of a church or a group of churches.[332] The spoken reading made the authority of the sender audible; the reader embodied the presence of the sender.[333] The typical forms of oral language written into the letter strengthen the authority of the sender because they demonstrate his competence in influencing the public through the spoken word.[334] It can be assumed that the audience showed a lively reaction even while the letter was still being read.[335]

9) The letter was discussed in the meeting. The messenger answered questions or explained parts of the letter. In this way the oral and the written messages became combined.[336] The messenger had the authority

---

330. Cf. Shiell, *Reading Acts*, 34-101; Ward, "Pauline Voices," 99-101, who evaluates Quintilian for recitation among Christians.

331. Cf. Quintilian, *Inst.* 11.2.33. Beacham, *Roman Theatre*, 156: "a symbiosis in which theatrical performance drew upon the style and sentiments informing political oratory, while in turn politicians looked to the theatre as a platform both for impressive display and for mass communication and manipulation of popular feeling. Aesopus even gave Cicero lessons in elocution." Bonner, *Education*, 224 points to Plinius minor, *Ep.* 5.19.3, who praises his reader Zosimus because he had the quality of a comic actor. However, Quintilian warns in *Inst.* 1.8.2; 1.11.6-12; 2.10.13; 11.3.4; 11.3.57 about play-acting when presenting texts or modulating the voice too much. Cf. also Aldrete, *Gestures*, 67-73.

332. Holland, "Frightening"; cf. Schnider and Stenger, *Studien*, 123: "so the commission to greet and kiss are, from a pragmatic textual perspective, a sort of signal to commence publication" (my translation). This is also the intention of the directions for reading (1 Thess 5:27; Col 4:16), on this, see Oestreich, "Leseanweisungen."

333. Stirewalt, *Studies*, 5; Holland, "Frightening," 9-15.

334. Cf. Fuhrmann, "Mündlichkeit," 56 who points out that the traces of orality in a written speech also served to demonstrate that the author possessed the authority and competence to bring about a particular decision by his own oral presentation before the people or before the court. "The speaker would have robbed himself of his own authority if he had come up with the idea of turning his speech into an edifice of lofty ideas disconnected from time and space" (my translation).

335. On the audience's reaction, cf. Korenjak, *Publikum und Redner*, 68-95.

336. Eph 6:21-22; Col 4:7-8. Sykutris, "Epistolographie," 200; Doty, *Letters*, 45-46; Reck, *Kommunikation*, 204-5; Hezser, *Jewish Literacy*, 263; Richards, *Paul and First-Century Letter*, 171-209, 182-85, 201-4. Riepl, *Nachrichtenwesen*, 374 describes "the custom of giving him [the envoy] oral instructions and explanations" (my translation). On this, cf. Head, "Named Letter-Carriers," 288-91, 294-97 with textual examples from papyrus letters.

to speak in the name of the sender.[337] His legitimation was established by a section of the letter recommending the messenger to the recipients.[338] Usually the recommendation came at the end of the letter—that is, just before the messenger took the stage.[339] In those cases where the actual message was only delivered orally, the letter served primarily to legitimize the messenger and to confirm the oral message.[340] Accordingly, in such cases the recommendation of the envoy can be found at the beginning of the letter or can even be the main content of the letter (cf. Acts 15:25–29).

10) Finally, a reply was prepared (cf. 1 Clem 63:3; 65:1), or the letter was passed on (Col 4:16). The messenger was dismissed. Often the messenger would also deliver the reply.[341]

Fundamental Considerations concerning Text Analysis in Performance Criticism

Before discussing the specific methodical steps of performance criticism that serve to uncover evidence of performance in the texts available to us, we must first consider some fundamental methodological questions.

The Text as a Whole

Methodologically, the starting point for performance criticism is the traditional text as it exists today. Therefore the text is considered as a whole. It can be assumed that the letters from Paul, which are the subject of this study, were read out in their entirety in front of a church assembly. None of the letters is so long that it could not be heard in its entirety because of its size. That means that the effect of the text would first be achieved by its overall impression. The listeners would not have been able to remember and analyze the wording and every linguistic detail, and they most likely would not even have understood everything. In contrast to what is normal when working with the written text today, the listeners could not halt

---

337. Mitchell, "New Testament Envoys," 649–50.

338. On recommendations in letters, cf. Keyes, "Greek Letter"; Kim, *Form and Structure*.

339. For example, Rom 16:1–2; 1 Cor 16:10–11; Col 4:7–9. On this, cf. Venetz, "Stephanas," 15–19.

340. Cf. Lehmann, "Brief oder Botschafter?" 91–94 on two Lachish-Ostraca; Hezser, *Jewish Literacy*, 277 on a letter from Bar Kochba.

341. Cf. Josephus, *Ant.* 11.8.3; 13.5.8; 13.9.2; Meier, *Messenger*, 230–44.

the reception of the text and take time for reflection. They could not jump back to remote previous passages in order to make comparisons—unless parallel statements were clearly emphasized so as to function as opening and closing parentheses. Listeners were also not able to look ahead in the development of the text to where it might be leading them and thus to grasp the text by considering the end—at least not when experiencing the performance for the first time, and also only in a limited sense when listening again, because each performance is always unique and compels listeners to become fully immersed in each specific moment of a performance.[342] When the text is understood from the overall impression gained through the complete performance, there is less danger that speculations over questions of detail will lead to results completely estranged from the text.[343]

Performance Is Woven into the Fabric of the Text

How can a possible and probable performance be reconstructed for texts only available in written form? Foley calls such texts "voices from the past" and compares them to potsherds dug up by an archaeologist, which bear witness to past cultures.[344] He finds indications in the text that mark the media heritage: that is, they point to the original performance.[345] Performance criticism will give heed to these vestiges contained in the text. Irmgard Maassen, who has examined texts from the early modern age for their performativity, has called these traces "performative text strategies." She points out that these strategies are not some kind of supplemental features found to be prevalent to a greater or lesser degree, but that the performance is woven into the very fabric of the text itself:

---

342. It is another aspect that the text can frustrate or correct specific expectations and concepts which it had created upon reception of earlier parts. Such frustrations create the awareness that the previous understanding was only preliminary, that a deeper understanding is possible. The recipient is invited to go back to the start and experience the text anew with the understanding gained during the first performance.

343. Cf. e.g., below on pp. 196–97 the different interpretations of 1 Cor 12:3.

344. Foley, *How to Read*, 45–50. He speaks of "textual shards" (p. 45) and expressly includes parts of the New Testament in his categories "Voices from the Past" (p. 46 and 50).

345. Foley, *How to Read*, 48: "Research has isolated key features, somewhat different for each tradition and genre of course, that mark a poem's media heritage. These features are the residue of oral performance; they constitute 'what's left' when an oral poem is reduced to a text."

> Performance in the text describes the performative text strategies in the medium of the text itself, which serve the simulation of presence, authenticity, corporeality, sensuousness, and eventfulness, that is, in the real sense of the word, the performative structures of the text ... But in this context, performance in the text does not mean ... the search for remnants of performative practices, e.g., for traces of orality, in the historically more modern medium of written text in the sense of a linear development concept. Such traces are not understood as witnesses to older, 'more authentic' forms of performative cultural practice which have somehow been preserved in the text by mere coincidence and are all that remain of the actual object under examination. The assumption is much rather that these traces of performativity have been consciously laid, that they represent a textual strategy that serves the intended enactment of orality and authenticity.[346]

The texts are written for performance, as a playscript is written for the stage and is not narrated like a novel; as a sermon is fashioned for oral delivery and therefore does not correspond to an essay in language and approach. Robert P. Sonkowsky has demonstrated for ancient texts that the characteristics of the presentation were already taken into consideration during the preparation of the speech—often in writing:

> On the basis of the evidence pertaining to theory, however, this conclusion may be advanced, that in the Aristotelian tradition, which includes the Theophrastan and the Ciceronian, the techniques of delivery are not merely something that is added in a superficial way after the process of literary composition has been completed, but something that is vitally involved in the very labors of composition anticipating the public presentation.[347]

Following Foley, Horsley and Draper also emphasize that texts alluding to an oral performance are written in an "oral register," that is, in a form of speech that makes it possible to reconstruct the performance.[348]

---

346. Maassen, "Text und Performanz," 291 (my translation). Maassen names performative strategies written into the text like "dialog form, the simulation of corporeality, sensuousness and presence by linguistic means, control of focus of attention, fictive authentications, self-fashioning and recipient fashioning, playful creation and undermining of social roles: the potential for creative reinterpretation in the act of iterating social and cultural 'scripts'" (my translation).

347. Sonkowsky, "Aspect of Delivery," 273.

348. Horsley and Draper, *Whoever Hears You*, 184.

It is the task of performance criticism to recognize and evaluate these performative text strategies.[349]

However, it must be kept in mind that texts can be impacted by performativity to varying degrees. It is not a question of either/or concerning the performative strategy of written texts, but rather of gradual differences. Texts can be arranged on a scale ranging from such texts as theater scripts or songs—which can of course also be read silently—to texts such as scientific treatises—which can also be presented orally as lectures.[350] Although the Pauline letters were fashioned in accordance with the customs of their times for oral presentation, their reception history shows that they were also able to achieve an effect as texts that are read silently. Accordingly, performance criticism does not intend to replace all previous exegetical methods, but rather to complement them in such a way that an important aspect of the New Testament texts no longer remains ignored.

Text Analysis and the Materiality of Performance

We have seen that the materiality of communication is very important for performance. The manner something is communicated is perceived with its own unique significance. The mediality of communication produces an effect and generates meaning. In oral communication, this aspect is mainly in the corporeality of all those taking part in the performance, both performers and audience. Performance criticism will therefore give special attention to the elements of mediality and corporeality in the text.[351] It will not just evaluate these elements as carriers of yet-to-be-interpreted content. They will much rather be taken into account as trigger-

---

349. This corresponds only in part to the method of Shiner, *Proclaiming*, 4, who applies the descriptions of and references to the characters' use of voice, gestures, and movements in narrative texts as instructions for the speaker. These descriptions do not necessarily give the text a performative quality but have their function on the level of the written medium, since it cannot directly reproduce elements of the performance and must therefore describe them to make them explicit. It is a different case with the search for "applause markers" in Shiner, *Proclaiming* (p. 158), which represent an element of the performance that is written into the text as described by Maassen.

350. In the appendix to her article, Maassen, "Text und Performanz," 302 presents an informative list of text strategies, prepared by Manfred Pfister, which can aid in establishing the degree of performativity of a text. Cf. also the comprehensive and helpful list of attributes of oral language in Wendland, *Finding*, 25–30.

351. Cf. Rhoads, "Performance Criticism," 128.

ing their very own effect, which can strengthen, weaken, or modify the understanding of the text's content that must be grasped intellectually. Here we will present four aspects of materiality and corporeality while making no claim to completeness.

Text as Oral Event

The performance of the texts was an oral event. The corporeality of the performance manifested itself and developed its effect through audible language, that is, in the experience of the breathing and voice of the presenter and the acoustical resonance in the bodies of the listeners. For this reason, performance criticism will attempt to return the text to the oral medium. For this, special attention must be given to those features which make the medium of oral language visible in the written text. These are mainly linguistic figures related to hearing—for example, sounds and sequence of sounds, alliteration, assonance, rhyme, rhythm, pauses, and intonation.[352] Sound and rhythm can be recognized in a text when one reads "with the ears."[353] On the other hand, intonation is not encoded in written language. It is also hardly possible to indicate pauses in the ancient form of writing (*scriptio continua*). But by reading out loud, places can be recognized where pauses appear to be meaningful and necessary.[354] In this respect, features that structure the text are of help, such as all forms of repetition, especially parallelism and chiasms, as well as transitions concerning addressees, topics, and the narrative (the characters, the place, and the time).[355]

Mnemonic Aids

Oral language is more dependent on memory than written language for both the speaker and the listener. Accordingly, linguistic forms that correspond to memorization and help listeners retain what is heard will occur

---

352. On this, cf. the works of Dean, "Grammar of Sound"; Jeal, "Melody, Imagery and Memory," 6–12; and Sellin, "Ästhetische Aspekte."

353. Weiss, "Beiträge," 166 (my translation).

354. Cf. the closing signals in Rom 12:9–21 cited by Sellin, "Ästhetische Aspekte," 421, which would cause one to expect a pause in speech.

355. On the lively oral formation and presentation of texts from Roman historians, cf. Gärtner, "Gesten in der Darstellung," who evaluates the change of subject, change of narrative manner, change of the presenter's mental location, and also excurses and other "disturbances" in the line of thought as signs of orality.

more frequently in texts designed for oral performance. These include all forms of repetition, especially parallelism, framing, and chiasms. Using texts from Homer, Stephen Nimis has shown that framing and chiasms have arisen out of oral language.[356] Repetitions are also important for retention. As a special form of repetition, parallelism serves (among other things) to help anchor proverbial sayings in memory (for example, 1 Cor 12:26; 15:42–44; 2 Cor 3:6b; 9:6).

Corporeality

The references in the texts concerning the corporeality of the performer and of the audience are of particular importance for performance criticism. After all, it is through the body that a performance becomes an experience, that is, an event in which physical mimesis generates meaning that goes beyond semantic understanding. References to the corporeality of the author are evident in the Pauline letters: for example, to his voice (Gal 4:20), his tears (Phil 3:18; cf. 2 Cor 2:4), his age (Phlm 9), his bodily health (2 Cor 12:7; poss. Gal 4:13–15; 6:17) or general weakness (1 Cor 2:3; 2 Cor 4:10; 11:30; 12:5–10; Gal 4:13), his physical ailment (Col 1:24; 2 Cor 11:23–30), and how he treats his body (1 Cor 7:24–27; Phil 4:11–13).[357] Paul thematizes his physical presence or absence (1 Cor 5:3; 2 Cor 10:10–11; 13:10; Phil 1:27; 2:12; Col 2:5) and even his death (2 Cor 5:6–8; Phil 1:20–24). When listeners hear these passages, they become aware of the corporeality of the author. If, for example, the age of the presenter corresponds with what Paul says about himself in the Letter to Philemon (Phlm 9)—for example when an elderly church member presented the letter—then the reader would not only verbalize the apostle's thoughts, but he would also embody him visibly in front of the congregation. On the other hand, if the letter was read by a young person, then the contrast between the reader's condition and Paul's described condition experienced by the listeners would stir up their imagination even more and heighten their awareness of Paul's condition.[358]

---

356. Nimis, "Ring-Composition." On chiasms in the Pauline letters, cf. e.g., Harvey, *Listening*; Harvey, "Orality and Its Implications"; Murphy-O'Connor, *Paul the Letter-Writer*, 86–95; Heil, "Chiastic Structure."

357. On the significance of physical appearance in rhetorical performance, cf. Gleason, *Making Men*; Larson, "Paul's Masculinity."

358. Cf. Fischer-Lichte, *Ästhetik*, 146–50 on the effect of performances by actors with a frail habitus or the casting of women in male roles.

It is not only the corporeality of the author but also the physical condition of the listeners that is thematized when Paul mentions the strength of the recipient in contrast to his own weakness (1 Cor 4:10–13; indirectly in Gal 4:15). Such references stimulate the awareness of the corporeality of both the presenter and the listeners and unleash an effect that goes beyond the mere semantic meaning of the words.

There is a similar effect when Paul notes that he is shedding tears as he writes (Phil 3:18). With this statement he makes the listeners aware of the difference between his state of mind and that of the presenter, who very probably would not burst into tears at that point. Paul mentioning his tone of voice in Gal 4:20 has the same effect. It is precisely because Paul does *not* expect the presenter to speak with a changed tone of voice at this point that he mentions how his own performance would sound. The perception that the sender himself is quasi-present through the medium of the orally presented letter (cf. 1 Cor 5:3; Col 2:5) is interrupted.[359] In this way, awareness of the medium being used to communicate the message is brought to conscious awareness.

Gestures are also a part of the corporality of performance.[360] Pointing, especially, would correspond to statements in the text. When the text points to a particular person present, the presenter would support this with hand movements and his glances, and would thereby direct the eyes of the listeners accordingly (e.g., Rom 14:3). The presenter of a letter might similarly direct attention to the letter's envoy while recommending him or her (e.g., Rom 16:1).

The method of deducing the gestures and posture of the speaker from what is said in the text has the disadvantage that gestures that treat ironically or question statements in the text are difficult to discover. In Gal 5:10 Paul speaks vaguely about those who have confused the church with their demands for circumcision. In contrast to the vague statements, if the reader would consciously look towards certain people whom he knows to be representatives of this position, he could achieve a special

---

359. On this, cf. Holland, "Frightening," 9–18. He demonstrates that Paul conceives the performance of his letters in such a way as if he himself is the one speaking the words he has written and affecting the recipients through the reader. On letters as a substitute for personal presence, cf. Thraede, *Grundzüge*, 39–47; and Stirewalt, *Studies*, 86. Betz, *Galatians*, 24, 236 interprets Gal 4:20 as a sign that Paul is aware of the deficits of written in comparison to oral communication. He does not see the possibility that it could be a deliberate element of the performance that brings the medium of communication (letter and reader) into conscious awareness.

360. Cf. Botha, "Exploring Gesture"; Aldrete, *Gestures*.

effect perceptible to all those present. Such a strategy could only be plausibly supported from the text if it could be shown that irony is being used consistently throughout the letter.[361]

Performative Space

A further aspect of the materiality of performance is the "performative space" in which the performance takes place.[362] That does not simply mean the concrete room (that is, the building or the place where the actors and spectators gather) but rather the space that organizes and structures the performance—without completely predetermining it, however—by way of both its characteristics and the things that happen in it. The arrangement and movement-in-space of those involved in the performance will always turn out differently depending on the place of the performance, and yet a certain basic structure will still be realized to a greater or lesser extent. This performative space is also written into the text.

Although there are no explicit directions in the text as to how the presenter should position himself or how he should move, the conventions for oration and the structure of the text do allow inferences to be made. During the performance the speaker would stand in a special position in the room. He would take the center of attention facing the various groups in the audience. The position in space taken by the person presenting a letter from Paul at the meeting would symbolize the position which Paul claimed for himself in the church: a special role opposite all the church members with their different groupings and interests. This is something performance criticism must take into consideration.

Whether in a larger setting (theater or forum), indoors (odeon, bouleuterion, synagogue), or in a more informal setting (triclinium), the speaker not only had the listeners directly in front of him, but they also more or less surrounded him on three or sometimes even four sides.[363] This made it necessary for the speaker to continuously change his posture and turn his gaze in different directions in order to give attention to all parts of the audience. Because the audience was often seated according to social order and, in general, persons who felt they belonged together

---

361. Cf. Nanos, *Irony*. On Paul's rhetorical strategy of obfuscating, cf. Given, *Paul's True Rhetoric*; on irony in Paul's texts about God, cf. Holland, *Divine Irony*.

362. Cf. Fischer-Lichte, "Theater als Modell," 100–102; Fischer-Lichte, *Ästhetik*, 187–209.

363. On rooms and rhetorical practice, cf. Korenjak, *Publikum und Redner*, 30–33.

also sat together, the speaker would turn to individual segments among the listeners in accordance with whom the content was addressing. Performance criticism calls attention to the positioning of those involved in the performance, thus enabling a more differentiated reading of the text we have before us.

When one of Paul's letters addresses particular groups in the church, as in, for example, the First Letter to the Corinthians (1 Cor 1:12; 7:1, 8), or if Paul speaks separately to church leaders and ordinary church members (1 Thess 5:12–14), then we can assume that attention was also turned physically towards them when being addressed. This physical turning can also leave an impact in the text. Thus in Phil 4:2 Paul formulates, Εὐοδίαν παρακαλῶ καὶ Συντύχην παρακαλῶ. The repetition of the word παρακαλῶ would be unnecessary in written language. However, because speaking to each of the named persons was coupled with a physical turning towards them, this is not an unnecessary duplication, but rather a signal for the respective individual address. It takes time for a presenter to physically shift his gaze. The repetition of the word provides this time and practically provokes the corresponding bodily movement. If groups are being addressed that are in opposition to one another, then this can also be expressed in the text in parallel antithetic structures (e.g., Rom 14:3). Parallelism can serve, not only as an aid for memory, but also as visible representation for the groups in the audience that are assumed or constructed by the author. But also in cases where Paul does not turn to certain groups in a letter, where he ignores them or avoids a confrontation with them, this textual strategy will be reflected in the physical posture of the presenter and where he looks. Thus we see that quite different strategies for performance can be found written into a text.

The performative space and therefore the materiality of a performance also include what the presenter and audience have in mind when they see the place of the performance. This is more than just what meets the eye: with Martin Korenjak one could call it "the symbolic character of each place, i.e., the sum of the associations which are tied to it and which are normally determined by its customary usage."[364] If, for example, one

---

364. Ibid., 28 (my translation). An example is found in Cicero, *Deiot*. 6, where he complains that he has to speak in a private house and points out how the speech would be influenced by the public venue—with a view of the Roman curia and the forum. On orators in Rome, cf. Aldrete, *Gestures*, 19–34; Morstein-Marx, *Mass Oratory*, 25–60 (situation in the forum), 79–82, 92–107 (statues in public spaces). Cf. also Rhoads, "Performance Criticism," 129–30.

came together in a place for cultic fellowship like a Mithraeum, then anything said would have a different effect on the participants than in a building used for teaching. If the Christian church met at a place of teaching (cf. the meeting place at Ephesus according to Acts 19:9), then communicative characteristics could be expected, such as one's invocation of personal authority (Gal 1), an appeal to authoritative tradition (1 Cor 11:23–25; 15:3–6), an authoritarian ending of a discussion (1 Cor 11:16; 14:36–38), doctrinal argumentation, and diatribal style.[365] Evidence of doctrinal discussion is often found in the Pauline letters, both from Paul in his argumentation and from the addressees in their doctrinal disputes as reflected in the letter. The fact that the letters also contain liturgical elements[366] indicates a room where doctrinal discussions and liturgy were both at home—perhaps an allusion to the synagogue as an important tradition in the background of early Christian gatherings.

Another frequent element of the Pauline letters is language relating to the family.[367] The church members are called brothers and sisters, fatherly authority (1 Cor 4:14–15; 1 Thess 2:11–12) and motherly care (1 Cor 3:2; 1 Thess 2:7) are used as illustrations, the church's relationship to God is defined as that of a child (Gal 4:4–7), and the internal growth of the church members is compared with the maturation of a person (1 Cor 13:11). Such a manner of speaking would come quite naturally when the church was meeting in the sphere of a family—that is, in a house church. The symbolic character of each respective performative space contributes to the plausibility of the corresponding customary use of language.[368] It is also the task of the performance criticism to take this into consideration.

---

365. On the background of diatribe in teaching, cf. Stowers, *Diatribe*, 48–78; Schmeller, *Diatribe*; Campbell, "Determining the Gospel," 325–27.

366. Prayer reports (e.g., Phil 1:4), blessings (e.g., Rom 15:13; 1 Thess 3:11–13; 5:23), hymns (e.g., Phil 2:6–11), praise of God (e.g., Rom 11:33–36), liturgical formulas (e.g., 1 Cor 16:22).

367. Cf. Birge, *Language of Belonging*.

368. The expression in 2 Cor 10:7 τὰ κατὰ πρόσωπον βλέπετε, which is difficult to interpret, could point to something which Paul knows is in the room but which we do not know of today.

Text Analysis and the Role of the Audience in the Performance

Performance criticism of biblical texts must always keep in view all those involved in the event. In that way the focus on the interpretation of the work in hand and its author—a consequence of the dominating position of the written medium—are overtaken by an examination of the *event*, just as Hester has called for concerning the New Testament letters.[369] This event is constituted by the interaction between presenter and audience and the interaction of the audience members among themselves.[370] Performance criticism of letter texts will therefore consider all evidence that refers to the role of the audience as recipients of the letter or that allows conclusions as to their actions during the performance.

The text assumes there is an audience, and we find double evidence of this: on the one hand, when the listeners are addressed directly, and on the other hand, when the text presupposes or consciously provokes a reaction from the audience.

Addressing the Audience

Whereas listeners are seldom addressed directly in narrative texts,[371] listeners are addressed very frequently in the texts of the New Testament letters, in accordance with the genre. For performance criticism, the *way* the recipients are addressed plays an important role. It is important to distinguish whether an individual person (e.g., Col 4:17) is addressed, or whether certain groups (e.g., Gal 6:6) are addressed, which can be done directly or quite often indirectly. Performance criticism also takes careful consideration of the salutation of the Letter to Philemon (Phlm 1–2), where just as in the closing remarks not only Philemon, but also his coworkers and house church are addressed. As a rule, the form of address also expresses how Paul relates to the ones being addressed, such as with the benevolence of the frequently used ἀδελφοί, but also with the consternation of Ὦ ἀνόητοι Γαλάται (Gal 3:1). The one reading the letter

---

369. Hester, "Speaker, Audience."
370. Cf. Rhoads, "Performance Criticism," 128–29.
371. For example, when the reader is addressed in Mark 13:14 or the testimony in John 19:35.

aloud would adjust his voice and tone to the emotional content of the thoughts in the respective letter.[372]

Attention must also be given to *allusions* to the persons or groups who are present, whether by citing their words or opinion (e.g., 1 Cor 10:23), or by referring to their lifestyle (Rom 14:2; 1 Cor 5:1).[373] Consideration must also be given to cases where an expected address is *missing*, because intentionally ignoring some people would have a distinct effect on the whole audience. Missing addresses are especially important when they concern opponents of Paul. Performance criticism of the Pauline letters must take into account that representatives of the opinions and actions that Paul rejected or was fighting against would be present when his letters were performed—for example, representatives of those in the Galatian churches demanding that circumcision should be compulsory.

Interaction within the Audience

By directly addressing the recipient groups or alluding to them, the text mirrors the structure of the audience (e.g., Phil 1:2: church, overseers, and deacons). For example, opposition in the audience can be recognized by the parallel structures in the text as described above, which are linked with shifting attention to the various groups in the audience. Beyond that, performance criticism examines how the manner in which the audience is addressed or alluded to induces reactions within the audience that *change* the relationship of the individual groups to one another: conflicts can be fueled or tensions reduced through the performance.[374] Therefore performance criticism views the New Testament letters not only as carriers of information but also as events which shape the relationships between those involved while they are happening and thus also exert an influence that impacts life outside the performance. When Paul admonishes the recipients in his letters, then that is not just some advice about what the recipients should do in the *future*, but the way the admonition happens makes it an event in itself in which something happens within

---

372. Thus, for example, there is the question as to whether 1 Cor 13 should sound warm ("love") or more polemical (whether the language of men or angels, without love, everything is but "rattling metal").

373. Kindermann, *Theaterpublikum*, 25 points to the fact that in comedies the citizens in the places of honor were richly endowed with innuendos.

374. Cf. Rhoads, "Performance Criticism," 129.

the audience *during* the performance.³⁷⁵ This special kind of dynamics in a performance becomes apparent with the help of performance criticism.

In addition to uncovering the relationship dynamics of the people and groups within the audience, performance criticism examines other audience reactions presupposed in the text or provoked during its presentation, such as laughter, indignation, dismay, enthusiasm, sadness, and scorn. The fact that audience reactions were very lively in ancient times has been widely established.³⁷⁶ Approval or disapproval were expressed with loud shouts (cf. Acts 19:32) or repeated acclamations (cf. Acts 19:34).

Citing Quintilian and others, Whitney Shiner expects that signals can be found in Mark's Gospel that would have been understood by the audience as invitations to applaud ("applause lines").³⁷⁷ These are primarily sentences at the end of a passage, which summarize what has been said in a succinct manner and correspond to what the audience believes to be right.³⁷⁸ One can also find succinct statements in Paul's letters.³⁷⁹ However, such sentences would not always have enthused the whole audience, but often would have found agreement in only one group. Thus majorities and minorities within the audience would become visible, perhaps created during the performance, because the opinions in the audience could be manipulated by controlling applause.³⁸⁰ In this sense, the anticipated reaction of the audience can be part of the letter's strategy.

Evaluation by the Audience

An important characteristic of performance is the role of the audience in evaluating the aesthetic quality of the medial realization—for example the competence of the performer. It is about *how* something is presented,

---

375. Cf. ibid., 130–31.

376. Cf. Aldrete, *Gestures*, 33, 77; on Christian gatherings, cf. Shiner, *Proclaiming*, 147–49; on the danger of an angry audience, cf. Morstein-Marx, *Mass Oratory*, 165–66.

377. Shiner, *Proclaiming*, 153–70.

378. Korenjak, *Publikum und Redner*, 131.

379. For example, Rom 3:26; 4:25; 1 Cor 9:22; on this, cf. Holloway, "Paul's Pointed Prose."

380. Cf. Shiner, *Proclaiming*, 144 with reference to Plutarch, *De recta ratione audiendi* 41c, where he warns against becoming too uncritical of a speech under the influence of a speaker's impressive appearance and the fervent acclamations of the audience during a performance; cf. also Morstein-Marx, *Mass Oratory*, 14–20, 119–43.

that is, the aesthetic components of what is happening. Not only was an ancient audience's acclaim or criticism won by content-related aspects of a presentation; audience reaction was particularly strong in response to successful or inept use of lingusitic and dramatic skills. Thus it was often the case that the audience celebrated a clever expression or a masterly performance, but also loudly criticized false intonation or clumsy phrasing.[381] For example, sentences at the end of speech sections not only were summaries of content but were also opportunities to demonstrate oratorical competence and to solicit applause for the quality of the performance.[382] Performance criticism will examine a text for all the evidence that presupposes or indicates the evaluative role of the audience.

The aesthetic aspects of language and presentation are the first examples of such evidence that should be mentioned. The author of a letter and the presenter would both know that they would be evaluated by the audience. They would both be motivated to give a good performance. The characteristics of oral language such as rhythm and pauses; phonetic structures like alliteration, assonance, and rhyme; and formal structures such as parallelisms and chiasms all contributed to the audible aesthetic appeal of a performance and were subject to audience appraisal. The author would not only work carefully on the linguistic form, but would also anticipate the performance situation and make appropriate use of how listeners are addressed, comparisons, the social roles of those attending, references to the time and place of the performance, historical allusions, emotions and relationship to the listeners. The presenter would also prepare himself carefully and bring the linguistic subtleties to bear in an appropriate manner. He would also demonstrate his commitment by putting all his effort into the use of the modulation of his voice and bodily movements.

The awareness of being subject to the audience's assessment would also lead the author of a text intended for performance to distinguish himself from other authors and their performances, and to place himself in the best light. Performance always also meant competition.[383] The Corinthians' evaluation of Paul's personal presentation and the performance of his letters is given particular consideration in 2 Cor 10:11. Paul refers to this assessment even though he was seen as inferior to his rivals

---

381. Korenjak, *Publikum und Redner*, 140.

382. Morstein-Marx, *Mass Oratory*, 138 brings an example from Cicero.

383. Cf. Bahn, "Interpretative Reading," 436; Thomas, *Literacy*, 108; Pogoloff, *Logos and Sophia*, 173–96; Winter, *Philo*, 126–32.

by many Corinthians, and he promises a strong appearance in person should it be necessary. Even though Paul presents his ethos at the beginning of a letter (2 Cor 4:2; 1 Thess 2:1–8) and distances himself from false preachers (Phil 1:15–17; Gal 6:12–14; 2 Cor 11:12–15), underlines his honest intentions (2 Cor 1:12—2:4; Gal 1:10), and defends his reasons for not using sophistic means of persuasion (1 Cor 2:1; 1 Thess 2:3–7), plays down his rhetorical abilities while at the same time demonstrating his mastery of the art of rhetoric (1 Cor 2:1–5; 1 Thess 2:1–12),[384] he does not necessarily do so to defend himself against concrete accusations; it is much more often a sign of the fact that he is aware of the evaluative role of the audience and is submitting himself to their judgment. Paul's polemic against other preachers (1 Thess 2:5) is like an invitation to the listeners to express their praise for his performance and that of his representative declaiming his message before them. The discussion of his performance in comparison to that of Apollos (1 Cor 3:4—4:5) also reveals the rhetorical rivalry between them and directly addresses the Corinthian audience's evaluative function (1 Cor 4:3). And when Paul reminds his listeners of their previous positive assessments, he is challenging them to again make a positive evaluation, this time of the performance of his letter.[385]

In this context it is important to recall the fact that Paul calls attention to his corporeality in his letters. By mentioning his bonds (Phil 1:13; Phlm 9; Col 4:3, 18; Eph 6:20), his age (Phlm 9), his change of tone (Gal 4:20), or his tears (Phil 3:18), he creates an *alienation effect* during the performance. Since the presenter would not have the described characteristics himself—he would not be in bonds, would not be crying, would perhaps still be young, would not change his tone, at least not as Paul would do it—the audience would become aware that they were experiencing a performance, not the real presence of Paul. Before this, they might have recognized Paul's manner of expression in what was being said, might have felt that they had been transported into Paul's presence—that is, they might have been experiencing the presentation as if Paul had been speaking to them himself. But now they would be wrenched out of this illusion, they would become conscious of the fact that they were only experiencing a performance of Paul's communication, and that they are an audience. At the same time, the consciousness of the discrepancy between the content of what was being said and the

---

384. On this widespread practice, cf. Andersen, "How Good."

385. Gal 4:13–20; 1 Thess 1:5; 2:1–2, 9–12; 2 Thess 2:5; 3:7; on the reminder concerning the effect of Paul's earlier appearances, cf. Holland, "Frightening," 7–9.

corporeality experienced would animate them to evaluate the quality of the performance. Because this evaluation is such an integral part of what makes up a performance, this discrepancy would remind the listeners of their role as an active audience.

Text Analysis and References to What Already Exists

The final characteristic of a performance that must be considered is how connections are established with things that already exist. These references may concern content (for example indicating that the performance being presented to the audience is based on an existing script) or concern mediality (for example, establishing a connection with previous or future performances). Both kinds of references leave traces that can be found in the text.

References to Content

The fact that the *content* of a performance comes from an existing script is reflected in the text of the New Testament letters where they have self-referential elements. When Paul makes reference in his letter to the writing itself,[386] then the presenter could call attention to the manuscript in his hand by holding it up or pointing to it. The same would apply to the reading of the passages in which Paul points out that the postscript of the letter is written by his own hand, which the listeners would be unable to see during the presentation (Gal 6:11; Phlm 19).

Performance criticism will also take into consideration the places where traditional elements are evoked by the use of formulaic language (Immanent Art) as described by Foley. As is typical for oral poetry, simple phrases and characteristic wording stand *pars pro toto* for complex concepts that are part of the prevailing tradition of those who are at home in the performance. Such phrases that should be examined in Paul's letters would include, for example, ἐν Χριστῷ ['Ιησοῦ] (e.g., Rom 6:11, 23; 8:1–2; 9:1; 12:5; 15:7; 16:3 and many more) or also διὰ Χριστῷ (e.g., 2 Cor 1:5; 3:4; 5:18). The formulaic function of this phrase can also be recognized by the fact that it is used as a closing signal (Rom 5:21;

---

386. Rom 15:15; 1 Cor 4:14; 9:15; 14:37; 2 Cor 1:13; 13:10; Gal 1:20; Phlm 21; cf. Eph 3:3. On Paul's references to his own written communication, cf. Holland, "Frightening."

6:23; 7:25; 8:29). Further references to tradition would be the formulaic use of εὐαγγέλιον[387] or χάρις θεοῦ[388] and many other phrases. Until now, these phrases have only been examined for their theological significance and not as formulaic phrases of an oral performance.

References to Mediality

Medial references are found in the performance of letters in those places where they look back to earlier or forward to coming performances.

Fundamentally, every presentation of an administrative letter points to *previous* performances in the sense that it invokes a known social institution. When an author thematizes himself as writer of the letter, this refers to predefined behavior or social role, namely the role of the author of an administrative letter. This also indirectly defines the role of the recipients: they are subject to his power. For example, Paul "stages" himself as apostle and church founder and relegates those listening to the performance of his letter to the role of those who are his "children" (1 Cor 4:15; 1 Thess 2:11–12; Phlm 10, 19) or his "construction" (1 Cor 3:10). In a very similar way, the letters from Ignatius "stage" the bishop's authority. In each performance of the letter, the social roles that are written into the text will be confronted with the concrete attributes of the reader (his age, the strength of his voice, his personal gift of leadership, his own authority in the church) and also the respective church's specific situation. Performance criticism cannot reconstruct the specific conditions of individual performances of a letter but will consider to what extent the text is suited to strengthen the reader's personal role and authority. If, for example, Polycarp as the bishop of Smyrna were to present the letter from Ignatius that was addressed to himself, or also if one of his subordinates with appropriate reading skills were to undertake the task, then the episcopal authority expressed in the letter would overlap with that of Polycarp and thus strengthen it. That would also be the case for later performances of the letter in which another bishop would undertake the role of the recipient in the same way. By contrast, the performance of the Letter to

---

387. Also with formulaic extensions such as e.g., τοῦ Χριστοῦ (1 Cor 12:9; 2 Cor 2:12; 9:13; 10:14; Gal 1:7; 1 Thess 3:2), τοῦ θεοῦ (2 Cor 11:7; 1 Thess 2:2; 2:8, 9), or τοῦ υἱοῦ αὐτοῦ (Rom 1:9).

388. 1 Cor 1:4; 3:10; 15:10; 2 Cor 1:12; 6:1; 8:1; 9:14; Gal 2:21; Col 1:6; 1 Thess 1:12; also extended with ἡ δοθεῖσα (Rom 12:3, 6; 15:15; 1 Cor 1:4; 3:10) or ἐν ᾗ ἑστήκαμεν (Rom 5:2); cf. also the use in the salutatory and closing greetings of the letters.

Philemon would be completely different. If Philemon—or in later performances another church leader—were to present the letter himself or have one of his subordinates do it, then the authority of the presenter would not be strengthened by but rather subjected to Paul's authority, and thus his status would be shifted closer to that of the listening congregation.

But it is also the case that any particular letter—if it has already been read multiple times before—points back to the previous times it has been presented, often specifically to its "debut performance," that is, to the situation when the letter was read for the first time to the original recipient. An interesting and quite complex example is the allusion in Clement's first letter to the First Letter from Paul to the Corinthians (1 Clem 47:1–4). The instructions to take Paul's letter into the hand (ἀναλάβετε τὴν ἐπιστολὴν τοῦ μακαρίου Παύλου τοῦ ἀποστόλου) indicate that the letter was available for a repeated presentation and indeed also thus used—after all it is assumed here, about forty years after the first reading, that the Corinthians are familiar with the content of this Pauline letter. At the same time, an allusion is also made to the "debut performance" by referring to the divisions in the church back at that time. Clement's first letter therefore consciously draws on the performance of an apostolic letter—both of later performances and the original one—and thus assumes for itself the preexisting role of an authoritative letter in arbitrating strife.

Beyond that, *future* performances may also already be presupposed in a text, for example in the instructions for reading that are found in Paul's letters (1 Thess 5:27, Col 4:16) and also in letters in general. The closing part of the Syrian Baruch-Apocalypse is made up of a fictional letter from Baruch to the nine-and-a-half tribes of Israel. It contains the admonishment to repeatedly present the letter: "When therefore you receive this my epistle, read it in your congregations with care. And meditate thereon, above all on the days of your fasts" (2 Bar 86:1–2).[389] The instructions assume that in the synagogues at the time in which this Jewish document was written[390] authoritative letters where read repeatedly. Paul's churches could have treated the apostle's letters in a similar way.

The fact that according to 1 Cor 1:2 the First Letter to the Corinthians was not directed to the Corinthian church alone, but to all the saints "who in every place call on the name of our Lord Jesus Christ"

---

389. On the reading instructions in syrBar 86:1–2, cf. Oestreich, "Leseanweisungen," 242.

390. At the beginning of the second century CE, according to Klijn, "Syrische Baruch Apokalypse," 107.

also implies the repeated performance of the letter.[391] According to 1 Thess 4:18, the words being read were to help grieving church members comfort each other. Glenn S. Holland concludes from this that the letter was to be presented and that the listeners to Paul's words also repeated them out loud.[392] Performance criticism will give consideration to all this evidence.

---

391. If this extension of the list of addressees is not a subsequent generalization, then it can be concluded that Paul expected a widespread distribution of his letters. On the generalization of the list of addressees upon the publication of a collection of Paul's letters, cf. Schmithals, "Zur Abfassung," 189; Trobisch, *Paulusbriefsammlung*, 80–83, 107.

392. Holland, "Frightening," 5.

2

Influencing Audience Interaction by Use of Letters

The following text studies investigate the letters of Paul and other authors, applying the methods of performance criticism. An important aspect of this approach is the consideration given to the role of the audience. We will first examine the general communication process from the perspective of audience interaction during the public reading of Paul's letters.

Addressing a Divided Audience

Paul's Audience Listening to His Letters Was not United

The audience takes an active part in the formation of the performance. They influence the presenter through their bodily presence and their reactions to the reading. However, the listeners not only influence the reader but also interact among themselves and react collectively. The interaction in the audience will be livelier and stronger the more inhomogeneous their composition is or the more divisive the content of the reading tends to be.

Paul's letters contain much evidence indicating that there were differences and divisions in his churches. The question of the relationship between believers of Jewish and non-Jewish origin is a subject throughout Paul's Epistle to the Romans (Rom 1:16–17; Rom 4; Rom 9–11). At the end in chapters 14 and 15 a specific controversy is openly addressed:

the Christians in Rome condemn and despise one another because they have different attitudes concerning certain dietary laws.[1] Most commentators understand these passages as Paul's reaction to a real controversy among the believers in Rome.[2] These tensions probably stemmed from the observation of Jewish laws. By way of background, Jewish Christians returning to Rome after the edict of Claudius had been repealed found that the house churches were dominated by Gentile Christians who had distanced themselves from Jewish customs for political reasons.[3] This thesis has been substantiated in detail by Wolfgang Wiefel and Peter Lampe[4] and has achieved widespread scholarly recognition.[5] A spatial separation, that is, the fact that believers did not meet at a central gathering but in several larger private homes could have contributed to allegations and misunderstandings.[6]

In the First Epistle to the Corinthians, schisms (σχίσματα) are expressly mentioned twice (1:10-12; 11:18). Gerd Theissen writes: "The Corinthian church is characterized by an inner social stratification: a small but influential upper-class group of Christians dominates a larger group from the lower social classes."[7] Paul had been informed of the conflicts through the people of Cloe's household (1:10-11). Paul had also had a missive from the church in which he was asked to state his position concerning several questions. These questions also reveal differing opinions

1. Reasoner, *Strong*, 1-23 and Gäckle, *Die Starken*, 21-30 provide a good overview of the various interpretations of "the weak" and "the strong" in Rom 14-15.

2. Whether Paul addresses a real problem in these chapters or is just expressing fundamental principles—as assumed for example in Karris, "Rom 14:1—15:13"—has often been discussed. Reasoner, *Strong*, 24-44 and Gäckle, *Die Starken*, 323-27 present literature surveys on this question. Cf. also the essays in Donfried, *Romans Debate*.

3. Michel, *Römer*, 7-9.

4. Wiefel, "Jüdische Gemeinschaft"; Lampe, *Stadtrömischen Christen*.

5. Stuhlmacher, "Abfassungszweck," 186; Haacker, "Römerbrief als Friedensmemorandum," 38; Moiser, "Rethinking," 576-77; Crafton, "Paul's Rhetorical Vision," 320-25; Jewett, "Ecumenical Theology," 93; Gäckle, *Die Starken*, 291-300, 329-30; cf. previously Marxsen, *Einleitung*, 91-93; Wilckens, "Abfassungszweck," 120; Wilckens, *Römer* 1:36-39; and also Bartsch, "Empfänger," 82-84, 86-87, for whom there was as yet no "church" (composed of heathens and Jews) in Rome. Thorsteinsson, *Paul's Interlocutor*, 92-97 rejects this and identifies the receivers of the Epistle to the Romans as only Christians with non-Jewish backgrounds.

6. Gäckle, *Die Starken*, 305-8; cf. Jewett, "Ecumenical Theology," 94-96.

7. Theissen, "Soziale Schichtung," 231 (my translation); cf. Meeks, *First Urban Christians*; Stegemann and Stegemann, *Urchristliche Sozialgeschichte*, 253-55 relativize "upper-class": well-to-do, but not upper class.

in the church (for example, about eating meat offered to idols [chs. 8–10] or the importance of certain spiritual gifts [chs. 12–14]). Some were using their gift of speaking in tongues to win recognition and honor in the church. Theissen has also examined the problems concerning the Lord's Supper in 1 Cor 11 and has concluded that two opposing parties also differ in their social composition: those who were μὴ ἔχοντες and those who have brought their own food (ἴδιον δεῖπνον).[8] Diverging opinions in marriage questions were obviously also an issue (ch. 7), although they cannot so easily be assigned to two opposing factions. The fact alone that Paul received his information from two different channels can be interpreted as an indication of the complexity of social structures.[9] This information was given orally through slaves or freedmen from Cloe's household[10] and in writing, probably authored by official representatives of the church, who would be expected to be from a somewhat higher-class background.[11] From the perspective of the messengers using oral communication, the situation in the church had to do with specific individuals (Paul, Apollos, Peter), whereas from the perspective of the written communication, it was based on facts. Margaret Mitchell has endeavored to interpret the First Letter to the Corinthians according to a single basic message: an admonition to unity.[12] It is certainly correct that the topic of unity cannot confined solely to the first chapters. Charles K. Robertson has published a study following a systemic approach that sees the controversy as that of a young church seeking its own identity.[13]

Paul's Second Letter to the Corinthians features no further references to the controversies he dealt with in his first letter. Nevertheless, his second letter certainly witnesses to continued dissention in the church there. The crisis that emerged in the relationship between Paul and the church because of the "superapostles" (most probably Jewish Christian

---

8. Theissen, "Soziale Integration." Theissen (p. 294) establishes that the ἕκαστος in 1 Cor 11:21 should not be overtaxed since there are those who do not have their own meal at all. Obviously Paul is speaking here to specific people in the Corinthian church.

9. Theissen, "Starken," 286-87; Theissen, "Soziale Integration," 309-11.

10. Theissen, "Soziale Schichtung," 254-55.

11. The fact that Paul speaks of a σχίσμα is based in both 1 Cor 1:11 and 11:18 on oral information that he receives with caution in 1:18. Cf. Theissen, "Starken," 286; Theissen, "Soziale Integration," 310.

12. Mitchell, *Paul and the Rhetoric*.

13. Robertson, *Conflict in Corinth*.

traveling apostles)[14] had consequences for the local church. This was dramatically demonstrated during Paul's short visit to Corinth (coming from Ephesus in about 54 CE). A church member had attacked Paul in an insulting and unjust manner (2 Cor 7:12), apparently questioning his office as an apostle. The church did not take Paul's side. Despite his conciliar tone in 2 Cor 2:5–11, Paul makes a qualification (v. 5): "But if any has caused sorrow, he has caused sorrow not to me, but in some degree—in order not to say too much (ἵνα μὴ ἐπιβαρῶ)—to all of you."[15] This qualification shows that Paul could not assume that the Corinthians had a unanimous position. There were still differences of opinion among the church members.

The problems Paul speaks of in the Letter to the Galatians and that are often assumed to have come from outside the Galatian churches[16] obviously left their mark. In Gal 5:15, Paul uses drastic words to warn of the destructive effects of controversy in the church. He certainly had reasons for making this statement.[17]

It cannot be taken for granted that churches without controversies needing arbitration or differences to be overcome were therefore homogenous. Although the tone of the Epistle to the Philippians is friendly

---

14. Cf. Georgi, *Opponents of Paul*; Wolff, *Zweiter Korinther*, 5–8. On questions of method, cf. Sumney, *Identifying*.

15. Wolff, *Zweiter Korinther*, 44 interprets μὴ ἐπιβαρῶ in 2 Cor 2:5 as a qualitative limitation—"only to a certain degree"—because he sees a contradiction to the πάντας ὑμᾶς which immediately follows. But this "contradiction" is unproblematic in lively speech (my translation).

16. On the opponents in Galatia, cf. Rohde, *Galater*, 14–21; on the method, cf. Barclay, "Mirror-Reading." Schewe, *Galater*, 16–59 and Elmer, *Paul, Jerusalem*, 3–26 give an overview. See below pp. 230–35 for the conclusions arrived at in this question by way of performance criticism.

17. Witherington, *Grace*, 384: "that Paul believes that factious bickering and disputes are already probably happening in the Galatians congregations." Also Schlier, *Galater*, 246; Bruce, *Galatians*, 242; Barclay, *Obeying*, 71; Schewe, *Galater*, 110. However, Mussner, *Galaterbrief*, 373–74; Betz, *Galatians*, 273; and Becker, *Galater*, 87 see no real background; Vouga, *Galater*, 131 is undecided. Schewe, *Galater*, 108–10 provides a survey of the literature. This text, Gal 5:15, has lead Lütgert, *Gesetz und Geist*, 9 to the conclusion that Paul was having to deal with two opposing fronts in Galatia: the Judaizers and the libertines. Schewe, *Galater*, 108–16 on the other hand has convincingly argued that the controversy among the believers in Galatia "was a manifestation of the *one* theological crisis that is connected with legalism and circumcision." She concludes: "The harm done to the church is much more an *inevitable manifestation* of the conviction that the Torah must be observed" (p. 110 and 113; my translation, italics original).

throughout, the unity theme still plays an important role in the letter (1:27—2:11), and a specific conflict between two coworkers of high-standing is addressed (4:2–3).[18] In Phil 1:15–18, Paul speaks of rivalry among missionaries in his own personal environment and certainly does so with an eye to situation in Philippi. His generous treatment of those who challenge his authority becomes a model for how to resolve problems in Philippi. That might explain the prominent mention of those carrying responsibility in the church in the letter's introduction (σὺν ἐπισκόποις καὶ διακόνοις).

According to the First Epistle to the Thessalonians, the relationship of Paul to this church appears to have been a very positive one. There doesn't appear to have been any disunity in the church, though brotherly love is still mentioned in the prayer requests (3:12) and in Paul's concluding admonitions (4:9–10).[19] However, Paul also speaks in this epistle of different groups. He names those who work for the church and who are in positions of leadership (the κοπιῶντες and the προϊστάμενοι, 5:12), probably church members who have become leaders because of their social status.[20] On the other hand, there are also the "unruly" (ἄτακτοι), the "fainthearted" (ὀλιγόψυχοι), and the "weak" (ἀσθενεῖς) in the church (5:14). Because we find such differentiations in this epistle, we must assume that the listeners here are not all alike, even though there is no obvious quarrel to be observed in the church.

The above survey shows that differences in the churches and the groups that may have formed as a result must be evaluated very differently. One might agree with Theissen, who outlines social differentiations in the Corinthian church. One could also refer to these cliques as religious groups. In any case, Paul used religious arguments (for example, concerning the weak in the Corinthian and Roman churches), although these conflicts certainly also had other components. Cultural differences also played a role insofar as Paul differentiated between Greeks and

---

18. Cf. Holloway, *Consolation*, 47–48: The discord is a result of the discouragement in Philippi, which was primarily a result of Paul's arrest. For details on this, cf. Peterlin, *Philippians*; he discusses on pp. 61–62 the opinions of those who do not see discord in Philippi.

19. Cf. however Friedrich, "Erster Thessalonicher," 251, who assumes there were differences of opinion; cf. also Masson, *Thessalonicians*, 73, 79.

20. There would have been social differences, although the church was generally poor (2 Cor 8:2 about Macedonia) and Paul had twice received money from Philippi (Phil 4:16). The members were probably craftsmen, wageworkers, and small traders (Phil 4:11), as Haufe surmises: *Thessalonicher*, 11.

barbarians and the wise and the foolish (Rom 1:14). Groups could also form along ethnic lines, as Esler shows in his study of the Epistle to the Romans.[21] The fact that it was necessary to overcome ethnic barriers in order to achieve church unity is shown in Rom 15:7–12 and Gal 3:28. Often several aspects would have worked together in the formation of a group. Church leaders were often of higher social status; they opened their homes as patrons and hosts, and as the heads of the households exercised leadership functions at the same time. Religious and ethnic factors would have worked together in the formation of groups because ethnic origin (e.g., being Jewish) often also determined the religious practice (whereas there were also non-Jews who adhered to Jewish religious customs).

This does not mean that there was always rivalry between the different groups within a congregation. Not all groups had disputes with each other. There were also different groups that could be addressed separately in peaceful churches such as in Thessaloniki.

The Speaker Adapts to a Mixed Audience

It is not uncommon for a speaker in a performance to be confronted with a diverse audience, sometimes even with strong contrasts. It is his job to adapt to that fact and address the specific interests of the various listeners and groups.[22] This is especially important in court, where the audience comprises both the opposing faction, one's own party and also the judge. All have to be won over. The speaker must keep in mind that the groups will each understand his words differently.[23] This is also the case in deliberative rhetoric where differing viewpoints on the matter under consideration will cause different reactions and even divisions among the audience.[24]

---

21. Esler, *Conflict and Identity*; cf. Walters, *Ethnic Issues*.

22. Cf. the different interests of the age groups in Aristotle, *Rhet.* 2.12–17.

23. Fuhrmann, "Mündlichkeit," 58 refers to Cicero's speech *Pro Milone*, in which the speaker comments on the various groups among the listeners. Cf. Cicero, *Pro Flacco* 66: "Sic submissa voce agam tantum ut iudices audiant; neque enim desunt qui istos in me atque in optimum quemque incitent; quos ego, quo id facilius faciant, non adiuvabo." Cicero subdues his voice so that the many Jews attending would not be able to hear what he is saying to the judge, since they are trying to influence the case. It concerned Flaccus's prohibition of the payment of temple taxes from Asia to Jerusalem.

24. Korenjak, *Publikum und Redner*, 147–49 uses examples from Sophist speeches to illustrate the communication among the members of the audience, which also contains elements of group building and rivalry.

The same is true in a letter event. It was clear to Paul that the listeners at the presentation of his letters would have different backgrounds and differing opinions.[25] That is why he differentiates in his argumentation and how he speaks to specific listeners. In addressing the listeners, he touches on their ethnic heritage or religious backgrounds (e.g., Rom 11:13 ὑμῖν δὲ λέγω τοῖς ἔθνεσιν), and refers to their behavior (e.g., 1 Cor 11:21) or conceptions (1 Cor 15:12). He also turns his attention to specific groups in his audience without explicitly addressing them, such as by broaching the issue of certain behaviors, opinions, or typical responsibilities. Quoting a group's own slogan (e.g., 1 Cor 10:23a) or summarizing their thoughts or questions succinctly has the same effect. Generally, when Paul addresses a certain individual, he aims at a whole group (e.g., Phil 4:2–3). When one person was addressed, there would always be others who felt spoken to. In the case of higher-status addressees, these others would be dependents such as family members, slaves, or coworkers, while for others it would be the like-minded, members of the same home church, or those of the same social standing, who would react with solidarity.

In some cases, a speaker would employ a parallel construction addressing certain groups of listeners. In this parallel construction, two opinions are contrasted: for example, the weak and the strong are contrasted in Corinth and in Rome (1 Cor 8:7–12; Rom 14:1–4). There were certainly those positioned in between or without any definite opinion or having no interest in the debate. By using these contrasts, the apostle reduced the debate to just two sides, which he then treated alternately—with the presenter emphasizing each through body movements. To be more exact, there are three positions, since the apostle positioned himself in an independent, mediating role between the other two positions. These positions would be reflected physically in the room if the reader was in the center and the members of the respective opposing parties sat together.

Setting up such a parallel construction, Paul either agrees with the group he is addressing or corrects it, commends or admonishes it. He makes it clear to them and at the same time to all the others present what his position is in relationship to them. This would be physically expressed through the one performing, who by reading the epistle becomes Paul's representative. By modulating his voice, the reader could transmit the emotional content of the letter to the group. Gestures and stance could

---

25. On conflicts in early Christian churches, cf. the conflict-theory approach in Heiligenthal, "Methodische Erwägungen."

help indicate who was being addressed, and often it would only thus become clear. The performer could physically face those being spoken to and possibly move a step towards them. He could look straight at them, his facial expression emphasizing praise or criticism. By using hand gestures, he could also identify and focus attention on the addressees.

The addressees would answer by being especially attentive, looking directly at the reader and smiling, nodding, looking skeptical or antagonistic, or even calling out or protesting, depending on the content. The physical acts were an integral part of the performance that made it an event that encompassed more than just understanding the predefined contents.

Since the audience was not a unified entity and groups of listeners with different viewpoints were being addressed, we cannot simply assume that Paul meant to address and confront each listener in the same way such as in the sense of this simple communications model:

Paul ⟶ Epistle text ⟶ Audience

We must rather expect that certain portions of his letter (arguments, hints, quotes, requests, admonitions) are being addressed to specific listeners or groups among the listeners. This model traces the simplest case:

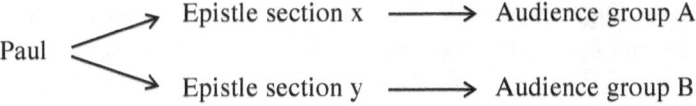

This has already been taken into consideration by many commentators for quite some time.[26] According to Gerd Theissen, Paul's remarks in

---

26. Ellis, "Paul and His Co-Workers," 449 establishes that Paul directly addresses different persons and groups in his letters, even though they are not necessarily specifically mentioned at the beginning of the letter. He cites as examples Rom 7:1; 11:13; 14; 1 Cor 11:20–22; Phil 4:2–3. According to Ellis, portions of the letter are addressed specifically to Paul's local coworkers. Schreiber, *Gemeinde in Korinth* applies the theories of group dynamics to the Corinthian church. He does expect that the individual groups in Corinth would have reacted differently to Paul's letter, but he does not consider the effect it would have had on the church as a whole and does not investigate whether this was the effect Paul intended. Stirewalt, *Paul*, 13 emphasizes that "Paul's letters are addressed to whole ecclesiae or to house churches even when he is dealing with one-to-one relationships (Phil 4:1–2; Phlm; cf. Col 4:17) or with factions within a community (1 Cor 3)." An example of disregarding the fact that a specific person or

1 Cor 11:17-22 and his statement "Do you not have houses in which to eat and drink?" (v. 22) are directed to those who are better off, not to the μὴ ἔχοντες. Theissen also assumes that in 1 Cor 6, Paul is addressing those rich enough to be able to afford litigation in the heathen courts, despite the fact that he uses the simple form of address, the second-person plural, in verse 4. In the same way, "in 1 Cor 9:3, Paul is defending himself only from a few: τοῖς ἐμὲ ἀνακρίνουσιν." Those would have been people of authority in Corinth, protagonists acting on behalf of other missionaries and belonging to the upper classes.[27] The basic proposition of Philip F. Esler's sociohistorical interpretation of the Epistle to the Romans is that there are tensions between the Christian believers in Rome since some had Jewish backgrounds while others were from non-Jewish backgrounds. Paul's concern was to reduce the conflicts by strengthening the common identity in Christ. Corresponding to his approach, Esler paid very close attention to which group was being addressed in a particular section of the letter.[28]

Groups in the Audience Influence Each Other

Most commentators who suggest that specific sections of Paul's epistles are meant for particular addressees treat the text as verbal information to the addressee without paying attention to the public reading. But the public reading of the epistle is a community event. In this situation, the listeners not being specifically targeted at any one time also hear what is

---

group is being addressed can be found in Holtz, *Erster Thessalonicher*, 250: Because Paul spoke of all the church members admonishing each other in 1 Thess 5:11, and because ἀδελφοί coupled with παρακαλεῖν, e.g., in 4:1 (compare brethren in 4:13; 5:1) refers to the whole church, he concludes (following Best, *Thessalonians*, 229) that 5:14 also addresses the whole church. See also below the section on this text, especially pp. 212-15.

27. Theissen, "Soziale Schichtung," 257-58 (my translation); cf. Theissen, "Starken," 286 on 1 Cor 8-10: "It is interesting that Paul's remarks are almost exclusively addressed to the powerful. Almost all texts using the second person are directed at them; compare for example: 'But take care that this liberty of yours does not somehow become a stumbling block to the weak' (1 Cor 8:9; compare 8:10-11; 10:15, 31)" (my translation).

28. Esler, *Conflict and Identity*, 119 argues again, concluding from Rom 1:5-6, 13 that Paul had written the Epistle to the Romans for Gentile Christians only. His argument is that it is unthinkable that Paul would have ignored the Jewish Christians present at the reading of the letter and thus shamed them.

being said.²⁹ Paul must always take into account that whatever he says about or to specific listeners will also be heard and commented upon by the others present and so also will trigger reactions from them.

Neither Paul as the writer nor the one reading can expect the listeners to show a uniform reaction. Where some might applaud, others might jeer. Things that would convince and enthuse some listeners might leave others indifferent, and still others might be angered. If Paul anticipated the situation of the church assembly when writing the letter as the tradition of good letter writing did, then he also would have formed the letter correspondingly.

When, as Theissen suggests, Paul addresses his criticisms to the wealthy in 1 Cor 6 because they were publicly litigating against one another in the courts, then the poor and the slaves in the church heard it also. Wouldn't they then reflect on their own relationship to the rich? Perhaps some had been drummed together to accompany the respective persons to court as supporters in order to lend emphasis to the case of a specific party.³⁰ Wouldn't the public reading of Paul's letter relativize the high-handed, "judgmental" authority of the upper classes toward the lower classes?

The Epistle to Philemon is not only addressed to the wealthy owner of the slave Onesimus but also to his house church, as can be seen in the opening address and the blessing at the end of the letter (vv. 2 and 25). M. Luther Stirewalt is right when he writes: "It is clear that in this letter the singular address to Philemon takes place in a corporate liturgical setting."³¹ The same is true for the instructions to the two women in Phil 4:2–3³² or for the instructions to Archippus in Col 4:17. Upon hearing Paul's instructions to the individual, the whole church shares the responsibility of helping the individual carry them out.

---

29. Witherington, *Conflict*, 36: "Each letter includes, therefore, what Paul is willing for an entire congregation to hear, or at least overhear where he singles out a member or group in the congregation." Cf. also A. Dewey, "Re-Hearing," 112: "Thus the appearance of opposing parties (as happens quite often in Paul's letters) would have a divisive effect, since there is a competition for acoustic space."

30. Theissen, "Soziale Schichtung," 258.

31. Stirewalt, *Paul*, 17. Cf. p. 15: "Individual messages in a letter require the attention of an assembly."

32. Cf. ibid., 18: "Reconciliation between the two women is to be undertaken immediately in the congregational setting, and the companion (Syzygos) who is presiding and reading the letter must initiate the effort."

What is the effect when the whole house church hears what Paul is negotiating with Philemon concerning Onesimus? Whose side would the other slaves and the commoners take? Wouldn't Philemon be exposed to pressure from the congregation? Would not his authority be called into question? These are some of the many questions that arise if the Pauline epistles are not just read as information to specific addressees but as evidence of oral performances experienced by diverse groups of listeners.

Paul would therefore not only be addressing various groups through the performance of written letters, but by addressing one group he would at the same time be indirectly influencing other groups of listeners. This influence was not just unavoidable because everyone always heard everything, even when not being directly addressed. We can assume that Paul consciously sought to influence listeners not being addressed in his communication strategy. When directly addressing a certain group, he would at the same time have had an eye on the effect that his words would have, or that he would like them to have, on other listeners.

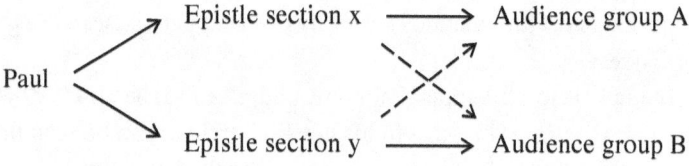

The Speaker Influences the Interaction within the Audience

When Paul addressed only a specific part of his audience, that group was distinguished in a way that all those present could hear. In this situation, the others would react in their own ways. They would also position themselves with respect to those being addressed, either looking up to or down on them, expressing solidarity with them or distancing themselves from them. If the apostle quoted certain listeners or put concise statements into their mouths in order to characterize their views, that would trigger strong reactions in *all* the listeners. Depending on their own convictions, these reactions would signal either approval or rejection. Such quotes not only directed attention to intellectual positions; they also physically directed the eyes of the listeners toward certain persons in attendance, elevating them or marginalizing them, thereby shaping how the groups related to each other.

We can assume that the group being addressed could be identified in the room. Generally it would have been recognized by its verbal or non-verbal reaction to the performer. In addition, seating in ancient times was often socially organized, so that we can assume that the people belonging together also sat together. Therefore the interaction in the audience was not just on an intellectual level, but also in physical terms through glances, movements or exclamations. The way seating was arranged also encouraged interaction among audience members since they could see one another's reactions.

By specifically addressing parts of the audience, Paul triggered reactions not only in those addressed but also *between* the groups of listeners:

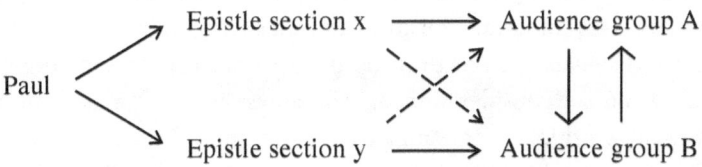

This even happened around questions that factually concern only a specific group, as in the case of the well-to-do church members and civil courts. Reactions of separate groups were even more pronounced when they were confronted about their attitudes toward other groups, as in Rom 14–15.

That addressing separate groups within a single audience was common in antiquity and can therefore also be expected of Paul is shown in two of Paul's public appearances recorded by Luke in the Acts of the Apostles. The reactions of diverse listener groups are found in Acts 17. Paul was speaking in Athens to two groups of philosophers: Stoics and Epicureans. As can be expected due to their separate philosophical conceptions, the groups reacted contrarily: one group—the Epicureans—considered Paul to be a babbler, while the Stoics presumed Paul was speaking about a new God (v. 18).[33] The speech that followed at the Areopagus also provoked divergent reactions. When Paul spoke of the divine judge who would judge human actions after the resurrection of the dead (v. 31), one

---

33. Cf. Neyrey, "Acts 17," who, however, does not examine Luke's record from the viewpoint of a performance but rather focuses on the stereotypes by which the opposing groups were known.

group—probably Epicureans—reacted with derision, whereas others—probably adherents of the Stoic perspective—showed interest and wanted to hear more: some of them even became believers (v. 32).

Luke's account of Paul's defense before the Sanhedrin in Acts 23:6–10 shows that Paul could deliberately use differences to divide his listeners. Paul causes tumult by speaking of the resurrection of the dead, knowing that his listeners were at odds on this subject. Paul's performance causes such turmoil among the audience that the meeting has to be ended.

Performance Criticism Understands the Public Reading of a Letter as an Activity

Performance criticism views the public reading of a letter as an (oral and performative) activity and not just as transfer of information. It is an activity with a specific goal. The goal can be a specific interaction between groups of listeners such as drawing the groups closer to each other, or fostering mutual consideration or willingness to make a compromise. Performance criticism of Paul's letters asks how Paul addresses and reaches the different groups. Above all, it investigates the effects the message could be expected to have had on the various listeners and listening groups. These effects help to draw conclusions about how performance could have taken place. David Rhoads formulates it thus:

> At the same time, a single audience may have comprised people from diverse social locations . . . So when we interpret a text as an oral composition, we are not necessarily dealing with an ideal hearer or a homogeneous audience but with multiple hearers in a communal audience . . . The performance of a composition might divide an audience. Paul may have composed letters designed to generate division with an assembled audience, as, for example, when he wanted to exclude the Judaizers from Galatia (Gal 1:6–9). Paul may also have composed letters to foster unity among people from very different social locations, particularly, for example, in Corinth and Rome. Imagine how Paul composed and then had someone perform the Corinthian correspondence so as to retain the attention and increase the commitment of the rich and the poor, the strong and the weak, and people with diverse theological/ethical perspectives . . . Imagining all these different letters being performed to gathered audiences that included both (or several) parties in a conflict helps to sharpen

our understanding of what was at stake and what might have happened as a result of the performance.[34]

Donald Hans Liebert was one of the first to address this problem specifically in a short study on what he called the "group letters." According to his definition, these are letters addressed to more than one recipient. He defines the *function* of group letters as follows: "The group letter genre is an orally delivered communication to a diverse but intimate group of people who will be hearing the reading in each other's presence." The effect is a changed interaction between the listeners.[35] Liebert points to the Letter to Philemon, which Paul also addressed "to Apphia our sister, and to Archippus our fellow soldier, and to the church in your house" (Phlm 2). "Paul was saying good things about Philemon in the presence of other people, and he wanted them to know how he felt about him. Paul wrote with the expectation that the people addressed in his letter would be interacting with each other as they heard this words."[36] Then Liebert deals with Paul's First Letter to the Corinthians, a church with groups having differing opinions and preferences: "If he had written to them as individuals, the letter could easily have been interpreted as support for one faction against another faction. Paul made a wise choice. The best way to write to friends who disagree is to write to them in a group letter, especially if you want them to adjust the way they look at each other."[37] Paul utilizes the letter event: "He wants each to overhear his communication to the other. The group letter is an ideal vehicle for encouraging reconciliation."[38]

The aspect that Rhoads considers mandatory and that Liebert rudimentarily discusses is an important concern in performance criticism, which we will investigate more thoroughly in the following text studies.

---

34. Rhoads, "Performance Criticism," 129; cf. Botha, "Greco-Roman Literacy," 211: "The 'political' side of Paul's letters has received little attention, how he uses writing to control and influence others and to promote a (probably) minoritarian viewpoint."

35. Liebert, "Apostolic Form of Writing," 437; Liebert also has this: "The uniqueness of intimate letters to more than one person is that the people who are addressed can be directed to orient their action to each other, and not just to the one who wrote the letter . . . The author intends to adjust the relationships between the people in the audience" (ibid.).

36. Ibid., 434.

37. Ibid., 438. He then uses 1 Cor 8–10 as an example and investigates the use of letters to various addressees in the ancient church.

38. Ibid., 435.

Singling out Individual Listeners

Three-group Situations according to Simmel

The reading aloud of Paul's letters to the church assembly could be understood as an interaction between two parties: between the reader and the audience. The first party would be represented by the person reading the letter. This person would be chosen for this task because of his education, because he was a church leader or because of his close relationship to Paul. The reader does not stand alone but represents a group. He is not only Paul's representative, but also represents Paul's coworkers and supporters who are often mentioned in the letters as cosenders. In Samuel Byrskog's opinion, Paul's letters were not produced by a single person, but by a group who had discussed the letter together, edited several draft versions and finally took common responsibility for the letter.[39] The second party in the letter reading event is the group of listeners, the assembled believers to whom the letter is read.

The interaction between the reader and the audience was an essential part of every performance. Those listening to Paul's letters reacted to what was being read and also to the way it was read. Their reactions could show approval or rejection, delight or displeasure, enthusiasm or indifference. With their reaction they in turn influenced the reading, because the reader adjusted his declamation—intonation and tempo, and accentuation and emotional engagement—to the mood of his hearers. This mutual influencing creates the unpredictable and uncontrollable aspect of a performance.

The situation in a performance changes considerably when the reader singles out one particular person in the audience. That can happen, for example, by him turning to someone and perhaps even addressing him or her directly by name. Phil 4:2 is an example of this. There Paul has a special admonition for the two women—Euodia and Syntyche. But the person being singled out must not necessarily be mentioned specifically by name. In 1 Cor 5:1 Paul mentions a man who has married his father's wife. Since Paul has been pre-informed by members of the Corinthian church—probably some of Chloe's people (1 Cor 1:11)—we can assume that everyone in the congregation knew whom he was talking about. Although not provable it is probable that this man was also present. At any rate, Paul would have had to expect it.

---

39. Byrskog, "Co-Senders," 230–50, especially 249–50; cf. Stirewalt, *Paul*, 10.

Addressing a single person or a small group in the audience changes the performance from a two-party situation into an interaction involving three parties. The reader divides the audience into the group being addressed—even when it is only one person—and another group which is not being addressed at the moment but overhears what is said. In his sociology (first published in 1908), Georg Simmel investigates the change from a two-group situation to a three-group situation. He sees this change as a big step to a new relational quality, a much more fundamental change than by the transition from a three-group situation to four or more groups.[40]

In a two-group situation, each group relates totally and exclusively to the other group, both groups being dependent on one another. The relationship between them can develop to great harmony, but also to fierce animosity. In contrast, in a situation with three or more groups there is always someone who can mediate when there are tensions but also someone who impedes too much intimacy.

According to Simmel, a three-group situation can have three basic forms.[41] First, one group can mediate between the two other groups. Second, one group is the *tertius gaudens*—that is, one party profits from the rivalry between the other two. He calls the third characteristic *divide et impera* which in a two-group situation one party deliberately splits the other by activating schismatic forces in order to dominate or otherwise win an advantage (Graphic 1).[42]

---

40. Simmel, *Soziologie*, 114–24.
41. See also Sofsky and Paris, *Figurationen*, 248–379 on group situations.
42. Simmel's three characteristics are found in Simmel, *Soziologie*, 125–50.

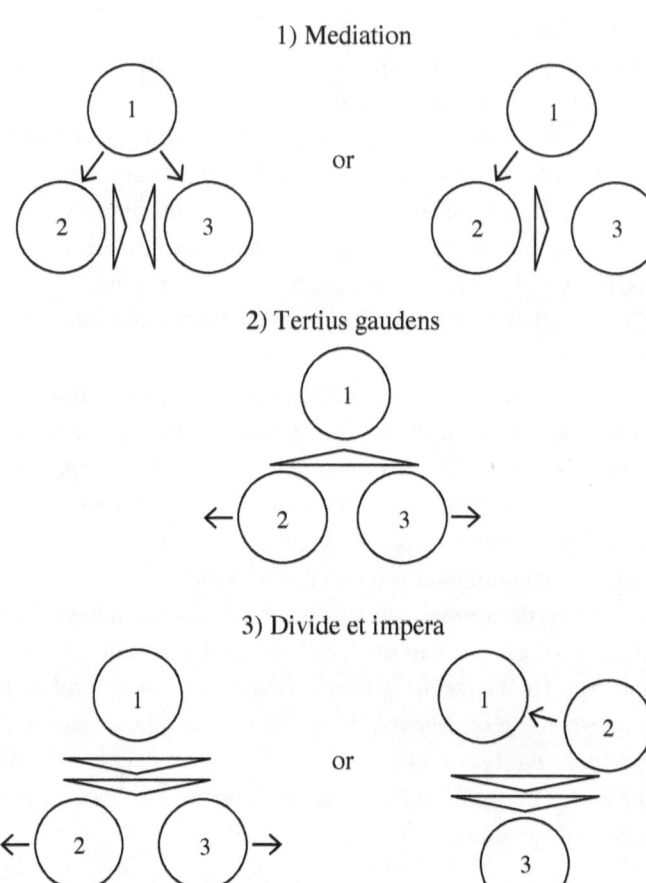

Graphic 1: Simmel's Three-group Constellations

What Simmel describes is exactly what happens at a performance like a speech or a public reading of a letter when the reader singles out and addresses a solitary person or small group. Later in this study of the Pauline letters, the dynamics of the interaction between the three groups involved triggered by such a strategy on the part of the reader will be investigated and comparisons will be made to other documents. In this chapter we will confine ourselves to the cases where a single person or a few individuals are being addressed.

We need to remember that in the ancient world the couch or seating arrangement where the performance took place encouraged interaction not only between the reader and his listeners but also between individuals or groups in the audience. Whether in the theater, the odeon, the bouleuterion, or the synagogue, and also in dining or assembly rooms of a society or association, or in private houses, the benches or couches were arranged along three or four walls, in a circle or half circle, so that the listeners could see the reactions of the other listeners.

Recommendation of Individuals

Phoebe (Romans 16:1–2)

The first case is Paul's recommendation of people who delivered letters. The section of the letter recommending the messenger is part of the message and would have been read in front of the whole congregation. For example, Paul recommends Phoebe, the leader of the Cenchreaen church (Rom 16:1–2), at the end of the Letter to the Romans. Since Phoebe had brought the letter to Rome, she was certainly present when her name was read out during the performance of the letter. The reader probably turned and looked at her as he read her name out, and perhaps he specified her by a movement of his hand. At this moment the attention of the audience would have been diverted from the reader, who was standing in some prominent place. All would have turned to the recommended person. Phoebe would thus be singled out from among the listeners and become, so to speak, a third party. This change in social relationships would be reflected in the glances and attitudes of those present. Corresponding to the first of the three typical constellations of Simmel's three-group situation, Paul's recommendation of Phoebe would have the effect of mediation by one party between the two others (Graphic 2). Paul introduced Phoebe as his messenger to the Roman Christian house churches using his apostolic authority and his role as the sender of the letter. Messenger recommendation was an important function of ancient letters. We find examples in Phil 2:25–30 (Epaphroditus); 2 Cor 16:10–11 (Timothy); Col 4:7–9; Eph 6:21–22 (Tychicus); and Pol. *Phil.* 14 (Crescens).[43]

---

43. Cf. Keyes, "Greek Letter"; Kim, *Form and Structure*; Reck, *Kommunikation*, on letters of recommendation.

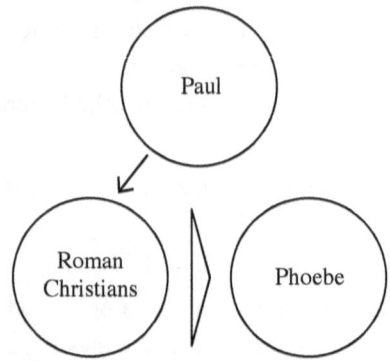

Graphic 2: Recommendation of individuals

Claudius Ephebus, Valerius Bito, and Fortunatus (1 Clement 63:3; 65:1)

A somewhat different situation presents itself in Clement's first letter. Written at the end of the first century CE to the church in Corinth, the letter aimed to reinstate deposed bishops. Three people, the messengers from Rome who had brought the letter, are recommended at the end of the letter event as being faithful, wise, and without reproach (1 Clem 63:3). They are also mentioned by name: Claudius Ephebus, Valerius Bito and Fortunatus (1 Clem 65:1).[44] The relationship between the sending group (represented by the reader) and the receiving group (the Corinthian congregation) changes from a two-group situation to a three-group situation. The recommended messengers are distinguished from the rest of the audience, making them a third group. They would now have the full attention of all the hearers. What are the characteristics of the relational structure thus created? Superficially we have the mediation situation. But there is more to it than that. Here we have another of the three typical forms of Simmel's three-group situation, namely, the one he calls *divide et impera*. The reader, representing those sending the letter and standing as counterpart to the listeners, divides the audience into two groups. Then the reader allies himself with the newly created group, with the messengers. He calls them the witnesses between the Roman church and the Corinthians (1 Clem 63:3: οἵτινες μάρτυρες ἔσονται μεταξὺ ὑμῶν

---

44. Cf. Schmitt, *Paroikie*, 17–20 on the messengers from the Roman church.

καὶ ἡμῶν). They are on the side of the Romans and would report on the Corinthians' reactions to the letter. The reader and the messengers from Rome form thereby two groups facing a third that they dominate. Although the Corinthian Christians constitute the majority in the audience, they are nevertheless, in Simmel's terms, the weaker party, forming only one of three groups.

We can assume that this three-group situation also became visible in the room during the performance. The Roman messengers, being distinguished guests, probably sat or lay together in a prominent position. When reading their names the reader likely turned to face them and connected with them through gaze and gestures, possibly even moving a step in the direction of the honored visitors, forming an alliance with them. Thus the social structure created by the letter performance pressured the Corinthian Christians into following whatever the letter expected of them.[45]

Criticism of Individuals

First Clement 57:1

A further example of the three-group situation is found in Clement's first letter, where he addresses those who caused the deposing of the bishops.[46] They are referred to several times in the letter. They are described as rash and self-confident (1:1), proud, seditious (14:1), and hypocritical (15:1). They are repeatedly spoken of as a small group (e.g., 47:6 ἓν ἢ δύο πρόσωπα). At the end of the letter they are ultimately spoken to directly (57:1): "You therefore, who laid the foundation of the sedition" (Ὑμεῖς οὖν οἱ τὴν καταβολὴν τῆς στάσεως ποιήσαντες). Here again we see the strategy which Simmel calls *divide et impera*. The reader as representative of the sender divides the audience and invites the majority to side with him against those few who have been causing the problems in Corinth. At one point he even incites the listeners to look directly at the accused: "But now consider [literally: observe] who they are who have perverted you!" (47:5: νυνὶ δὲ κατανοήσατε τίνες ὑμᾶς διέστρεψαν). This would surely have

---

45. The letter in Acts 15:23 appears to aim for a similar effect. The first and longest part of the letter is the recommendation of the messengers, who together with the writer (represented by the reader) form two groups facing the third group, the recipients.

46. See the comprehensive study of this letter's performance below in chapter 4, pp. 259–74.

been a hostile stare. These people were important members of the church, otherwise their revolt against the earlier authorities would not have been successful. Certainly they would have been seated in prominent places during the reading. The letter's strategy is to create a hostile atmosphere between those in the back rows and the leading personalities. This prepares the way to carry out sanctions against those who have caused the problems: their banishment (ch. 54). It would have probably been impossible to achieve this goal without the *divide et impera* strategy of the performance.

First Corinthians 5:1–5

Paul follows a similar strategy in 1 Cor 5:1–5, where he urges the church to disfellowship a member who had married his father's wife, probably his stepmother. Marriage to one's own stepmother is explicitly forbidden in Jewish law (Lev 18:8). Roman law saw such a marriage as incest (*stuprum*), which was punishable by banishment and the forfeit of all property.[47] If Andrew D. Clarke is right, then the guilty person was a prominent member of the Corinthian church.[48] The reason for the union with his father's wife could have been financial.[49] Or the woman could have been a slave. Taking her would then not have been a punishable offense according to Roman law. The fact that the church did not react as Paul had expected could have been due to the church member's high social standing.[50] Paul singles this person out from the audience by way of the performance and accuses him of behaving worse than unbelievers. Thus Paul causes a division among his listeners and summons the majority of church members to side with him in the conflict (Graphic 3).[51]

---

47. Gaius, *Institutiones*, I 63 (approx. 160 CE); Cicero, *Pro Cluentio* 14–15 (union of mother-in-law with son-in-law); cf. Gardner, *Women*, 125–27.

48. Clarke, *Leadership*, 77–88.

49. Ibid., 80–85: The dowry was not returned to the father when a marriage ended, but remained with the wife until she remarried. Wives who were childless could secure their inheritance by remarrying and having children.

50. Ibid., 79: "It may be that in 1 Corinthians 5 there is a situation . . . where the honour of a leading figure is defended, rather than justice pursued." Cf. also pp. 84–85.

51. The strategy in 1 Cor 6 is very similar, where Paul reacts to Corinthian church members taking each other to court.

Influencing Audience Interaction by Use of Letters 119

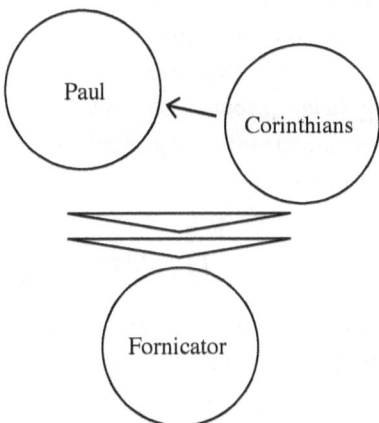

Graphic 3: Criticism of individuals

Cicero: *De Lege agraria*

We can see that the strategy we have been considering was a common rhetorical method when we study Cicero's speeches.[52] Cicero often addressed his opponents by naming them explicitly in order to get the audience on his side and to cause hostility against certain persons. One example is his second oration against the *lex agraria*, a draft bill put forward by Publius Servilius Rullus, a Roman tribune of the people, in 63 BCE. In order to prevent the law, Cicero explained to the Roman populace the law's disadvantages and accused those supporting the bill of following selfish motives. Cicero addresses Rullus directly in four places.[53] He accuses him of hypocrisy, because he and his friends pretend to act in the interests of Roman farmers and veterans without their own land. He accuses them of drafting the bill purely for their own financial advantage. Since the new law would give a ten-man council sweeping powers, Cicero accuses the bill's drafters of planning to replace the old order with a new power structure centred in Capua (2.74).

In his speech Cicero uses προσωποιία, a form of speech putting fitting words into someone's mouth (speech-in-character).[54] He asks Rullus

---

52. I thank Stephan Gäbel for his contribution to the study of Cicero's speeches.
53. Cicero, *Agr.* 2.22, 31, 63–64, 66–67.
54. Theon, *Prog.* 8; cf. Standhartinger, *Studien*, 37–38.

a question and then immediately puts an answer in his mouth. In this way Cicero acts out a supposed questioning of Rullus in front of the audience (2.66–67). Of course, this puts Rullus in an impossible position. Cicero, in pursuance of the *divide et impera* strategy in a three-group situation, singles out his opponent in front of all and at the same time draws the rest of the audience over to his side.

Cicero: *Pro Lege Manilia* 37

It is clear from his speech about Pompey's military command that Cicero was quite conscious of what effect his strategy would have. He insinuates that certain military commanders were using monies meant for the war effort for their own private purposes. He says:

> Your murmurs show, O Romans, that you recognise, in my description, men who have done these things. But I name no one, so that no one can be angry with me, without making confession beforehand of his own malpractices.

Cicero reminds his audience of corrupt commanders without giving any names. The audience's reaction clearly shows that they have taken Cicero's side against the commanders.

Another example is the following statement in Cicero's speech against the *lex agraria* (2.63–64):

> I am not accustomed, O Romans, to speak of men with unnecessary harshness unless I am provoked. I wish it were possible for those men to be named by me without speaking ill of them, who hope to be themselves appointed decemvirs; and you should quickly see what sort of men they are to whom you have committed the power of selling and buying everything. But, that which I have made up my mind that I ought not to say, yet you can still form an idea of in your minds.[55]

---

55. Cicero, *Leg. Man.* 37: "Vestra admurmuratio facit, Quirites, ut agnoscere videamini qui haec fecerint; ego autem nomino neminem; qua re irasci mihi nemo poterit nisi qui ante de se voluerit confiteri." *Agr.* 2.63–64: "Non consuevi homines appellare asperius, Quirites, nisi lacessitus. vellem fieri posset ut a me sine contumelia nominarentur ei qui se xviros sperant futuros; iam videretis quibus hominibus omnium rerum et vendendarum et emendarum potestatem permitteretis. sed quod ego nondum statuo mihi esse dicendum, vos tamen id potestis cum animis vestris cogitare." Translations in C. D. Yonge, *Orations*.

Cicero does not name anyone except Rullus. But his suggestion that people could be named has the effect of publicly compromising those under suspicion. Cicero allies himself with the audience against the persons he is considering.

Supporting Specific Individuals

2 Corinthians 2:5–11

In 2 Cor 2:5–11, Paul singles out a certain individual from the Corinthian church without specifically naming the person. Through the reading of the letter Paul states publicly that he had forgiven the person and that the church should also forgive him. Paul refers to an incident that happened during his short visit to Corinth. Someone, presumably a highly respected member of the church, had insulted Paul, and the church had not intervened (2 Cor 7:12). The conflict had been resolved through a letter (2 Cor 2:9; 7:8: "letter of tears") and Titus's visit (2 Cor 7:6–7, 13–15). The church had disciplined the person (2 Cor 2:6), thereby showing that they had repaired their relationship with Paul. If the punishment had not been exclusion from the church but rather a form of demotion or censure, then it is highly probable that this church member would have been present at the reading of what we know of as 2 Corinthians.[56]

Why did Paul point this church member out? What happened when the attention of the listeners was directed to this person? Hans-Josef Klauck explains it as follows: "The polarity between the apostle ('I') and the church ('you') is expanded through a third relationship ('someone'). This 'someone' remains anonymous, which nevertheless does not mean that it was not immediately clear to everybody exactly whom he was talking about."[57] It appears at first glance as if Paul is mediating between the repentant offender and the church. Considered superficially, his object is to end the punishment. The church member should not become overwhelmed with grief. The church is exhorted to forgive and return the member to his full rights (2 Cor 2:7–8). However, we must ask ourselves, was this exhortation necessary? Was the church in danger of overdo-

---

56. Klauck, *Korintherbrief*, 157 assumes that the punishment would have been exclusion from the church for a period of time. But Wolff, *Zweiter Korinther*, 42, 44 points out in his translation that ἱκανόν in v. 6 indicates that more drastic measures would have been possible: "Ausreichend (ist) für solch einen die Strafe, die von der Mehrzahl (unter euch ausgeführt wurde)."

57. Klauck, *Korintherbrief*, 156 (my translation).

ing the miscreant's punishment?⁵⁸ Paul himself admits that not all the members had supported the punishment (v. 6).⁵⁹ Apparently, this member had supporters in the church. So it's clear that mediation could not be Paul's primary intention. Beyond that, Paul continues, "What I have forgiven, *if I have forgiven anything . . .*" (v. 10: εἴ τι κεχάρισμαι). After all the difficulties that even necessitated Titus's intervention, Paul now sounds as if he is not sure that there had been anything to be forgiven at all. Paul is obviously playing the situation down.⁶⁰ Besides, it is conspicuous how often Paul speaks of himself in this section: about whether he is attacked or not (v. 5), about his letter to the Corinthians as a test of their "obedience" (v. 9), about his forgiving (v. 10). The solemn παρακαλῶ ὑμᾶς (v. 8) is a strong expression of his self-assurance. After explaining why the punishment should not go on, Paul admonishes the church *expressis verbis*, which was quite unnecessary, given that the previous sentence already had the sense of an imperative.

These observations suggest that Paul is really concerned with his *own* standing in the church. He divides the listeners into two parts: on the one side the majority that he is addressing and on the other side the miscreant and—we might add—his party. In this way he has the opportunity to demonstrate his apostolic authority and his relationship to the church, both of which are leading issues in the whole letter. Paul poses as one who is willing to take a step backward, to forgive and to overcome discord. He plays down the insult. But he does it without losing face. He presents himself as one who loves the miscreant more than the church loves him. He demonstrates his apostolic authority by explicitly admonishing the church (v. 8). And in harmony with his main concern of showing his authority, he speaks of the earlier letter as having been a test of their obedience (v. 9).

In this section of Paul's letter we have an example of the third characteristic of Simmel's three-group constellation, which he calls *tertius gaudens*. The third party profits from the existing division between the other two. Paul directs attention to the church member who has been punished and implies that the church was divided on this measure, that the listeners were therefore disunited. But indirectly he is addressing the

---

58. As according to Wolff, *Zweiter Korinther*, 44.

59. ἡ ἐπιτιμία αὕτη ἡ ὑπὸ τῶν πλειόνων: "the punishment [inflicted] by the majority [of you]."

60. Klauck, *Korintherbrief*, 158.

entire church, because in this way he can present himself in a positive light and underline his apostolic authority (Graphic 4).

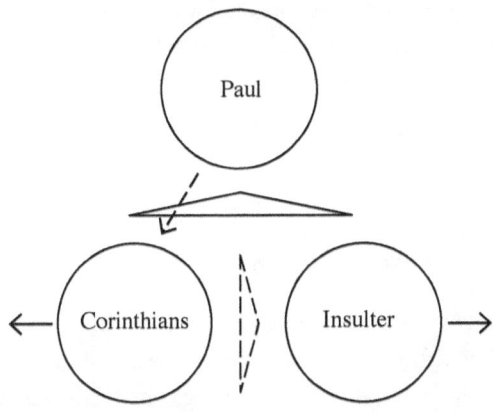

Graphic 4: Supporting individuals

Cicero: *Pro Lege Manilia* 69

We find a parallel to this strategy in Cicero's *Pro Lege Manilia*. At the end of his speech Cicero directly addresses C. Manilius, the one who had introduced the draft law that would give Pompey the military command against Mithridates, the king of Pontos in Asia, and Tigranes, the Armenian king. Cicero praises Manilius's initiative, exhorts him to remain true to his convictions, and finally assures him of his full support.[61] In reality there was no real opposition to this law.[62] Cicero's assurance that he would stand with Manilius was actually unnecessary. But Cicero singles him out of the listening masses and announces his support to the ears of the whole populace because this furthers his *own* ends. This speech was Cicero's first political speech. It was his chance to present himself to the people. By turning to Manilius and offering him his full support, Cicero had the opportunity to speak about his own abilities and advantages: his zeal (*studium*); his wisdom (*consilium*); his industriousness (*labor*) and his ability (*ingenium*); his power as praetor; his reputation for authority (*auctoritas*), fidelity (*fides*), and steadfastness (*constantia*); and also his

---

61. Cicero, *Man.* 69.
62. Fuhrmann, ed., in Cicero, *Sämtliche Reden*, 1:328.

selflessness and singular purpose of furthering the welfare of the state. Although Cicero addresses Manilius, he is actually speaking to the people in general in this part of his speech and is probably also trying to impress Pompey. He can present himself as the ideal statesman without appearing arrogant or presumptuous. The three-party constellation gives him as the speaker an advantage over the position of both Manilius, whom he is addressing, and the people.

Admonitions for Individual People

Euodia, Syntyche, Gnesios Syzygos (Philippians 4:2–3)

Paul creates a very complex situation through his Letter to the Philippians where he addresses Euodia and Syntyche (Phil 4:2–3). He singles out both of these women in the meeting where his letter is being read out: "I urge Euodia and I urge Syntyche to live in harmony in the Lord." (Εὐοδίαν παρακαλῶ καὶ Συντύχην παρακαλῶ τὸ αὐτὸ φρονεῖν ἐν κυρίῳ.) As shown above,[63] the performance is recognizable by the repetition of the finite verb.[64] In a normal sentence with two subjects, it is not necessary to repeat the predicate. If the author wants each subject to have its own predicate, he would modify the predicate or use a verbal synonym for reasons of style. In this case, however, the verb is repeated, creating a kind of parallelism. When Paul dictated the letter, he probably pictured the situation of the performance in his mind's eye, imagining how the reader would first turn to Euodia and then to Syntyche, admonishing both women individually, one after the other, using the same words—but without addressing them directly.

They obviously were quarrelling and were being called to reconciliation. This is followed by an address to a γνήσιος σύζυγος (genuine companion), telling him to help the women end their dispute. It is not clear who the companion is, one of Paul's local coworkers or perhaps, as Antonio Piras suggests, Paul's own wife.[65]

---

63. Cf. above the section on performative space, pp. 86–87.

64. Cf. Lohmeyer, *Philipper, Kolosser, Philemon*, 165: "The double use of the verb 'admonish' evokes a picture of an arbitral court where both parties are called upon to compromise" (my translation).

65. Piras, "γνήσιε σύζυγε." Hájek, "Comments on Philippians 4:3" ponders as to whether it could be Luke.

This section creates a three-party situation. The σύζυγος is the mediator between the two women. But this three-party situation is itself again part of a larger three-party constellation, which also includes the reader, representing Paul, and the rest of those listening. In other words: Paul has written the Letter to the Philippians in such a way that during the performance the listeners would be divided into the three protagonists on the one side and the observing remnant on the other. The audience's attention is directed to the three protagonists, who make up the inner circle of the constellation as a whole. If we apply Georg Simmel's differentiation of the various three-party situations, then we have a mediation situation in the inner circle. But what is the role of the congregation, which has also heard the admonitions to the two women and their mediator? Here we have a further example of the *divide et impera* constellation. The reader singles out a small group within the audience—made up of the two women and their mediator—and calls them to take certain action. Paul himself (in the person of the reader) and the rest of the audience unite in the role of observers. On the one hand, the little group sees itself confronted by the authoritative apostle and his coworkers, who are represented by the reader; and on the other hand the small group stands in full view of the church majority. A small group is confronted by two larger ones. Thus, Paul uses a strategy that builds up pressure on the little group during the performance, especially on Euodia and Syntyche. The quarrel between the women and the efforts made to reconcile them become a public issue.

The addressed companion is also put under pressure. He is publicly assigned with the task of mediation, and it will be obvious to everyone if he is successful in reconciling the two women or not (Graphic 5).

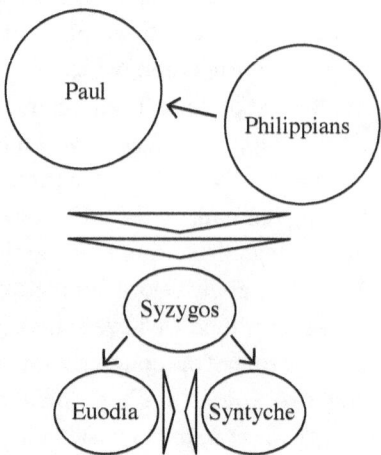

Graphic 5: Admonitions for individuals (Phil 4:2–3)

Paul's strategy also has an effect on the church members looking on. Since they are witnesses to the admonition, they will also be witnesses to the results of Paul's intervention. It will be difficult if not impossible for them to remain indifferent and claim to have no knowledge of the problem. They are part of the process and have a control function.

The pressure on the three people in the inner group is alleviated by the apostle's words of praise. The mediator has been publicly honored since he has been entrusted with the difficult task of achieving reconciliation. Listeners probably looked at him in admiration. Euodia and Syntyche have been praised for their earlier achievements: "who have shared my struggle in the cause of the gospel" (4:3). This praise suggests that the women were leading personalities in the church. The praise for the women was surely spoken in the direction of the mediator. But at the same time such praise from Paul helps all those listening to view the women with acknowledgement. The positive retrospective increases the expectation that the conflict will be resolved.

Another effect of Paul's strategy must be mentioned: strengthening cohesion in the whole church. A feeling of community is created when all members participate in the church's affairs. This is evidenced for the congregation during the performance, which steers the attention of those present to an internal affair. So the outer circle of observers becomes involved with the inner circle made up of a few of their brothers and sisters.

Archippus (Colossians 4:17)

Another case of an individual being singled out of the listening group is the admonition for Archippus in Col 4:17.[66] He is addressed with the imperative, "Take heed to the ministry which you have received in the Lord, that you may fulfill it." It is not clear what the task was, but it must have been so important that it justified a formal assignment in the name of the κύριος. This assignment was probably given in the presence of the whole church. Archippus is also mentioned in the opening of the Letter to Philemon (v. 2). He was obviously an important member of the house churches in Colossae.

The message to Archippus again involves the whole church. The one reading the letter out loud does not speak directly to Archippus, but rather tells the listeners to pass the admonition on to him (εἴπατε Ἀρχίππῳ). This does not mean that Archippus was not present at the public reading. It much rather makes the listeners participants in the act of admonishing Archippus, and this to a greater degree than in the assignment given to Syzygos in the Letter to the Philippians. The performer does not just have the majority of the audience as observers on his side in this matter; rather he involves the audience as collective partners and coworkers in the admonition.[67] Of course this procedure puts a lot of pressure on Archippus to fulfil expectations. On the other hand, the responsibility for Archippus fulfilling the task is thus also laid to great extent on the shoulders of the church members (Graphic 6).

---

66. It is irrelevant whether this letter was written by Paul or under his authority by one of his closest coworkers (cf. Dunn, *Epistles*, 38), or, as many believe, if it was written later by one of Paul's students (e.g., Pokorný, *Kolosser*, 2–17). In any case, Archippus's admonition demonstrates that this form of direct address was a well-known practice of Paul's.

67. We find a similar strategy in the list of greetings at the end of the Epistle to the Romans. Paul does not send the greetings to the listed persons and house churches directly (ἀσπάζομαι) but rather asks the church to pass the greetings on (ἀσπάσασθε). In this way he lets the recipients have a part in giving the greetings: he involves them in the act, which is good way of strengthening their associations with one another. Cf. also Stuhlmacher, *Römer*, 220.

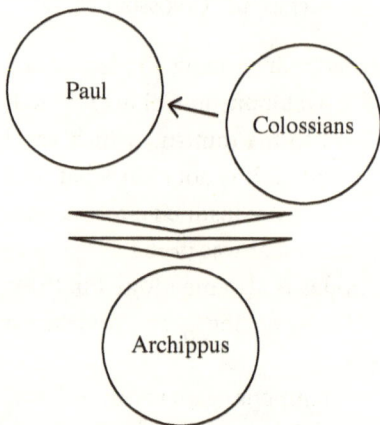

Graphic 6: Admonitions for individuals (Col 4:17)

James D. G. Dunn writes: "That the whole community (all the recipients) have the responsibility of recalling Archippus to his task (particularly if he was a member of an important household in the community) conforms to Paul's concept of mutual responsibility and shared authority within the community, to which all, including the more important members, are to be subject."[68] Here too the common task has a strong bonding effect. Dunn's conclusion that Paul's request indicates that "Archippus seems to have been unwilling or unable (for some reason) to carry [his task] through"[69] overlooks the possibility that the admonition was not primarily included in the letter out of concern for Archippus or his failure, but for the sake of the church and its unity.

Letters to Individuals Read in Front of the Church Assembly

Paul to Philemon

To close this section we consider two early Christian letters that not only contain sections singling out or directly addressing individuals but that specifically address an individual while nevertheless presupposing a larger group of listeners. It has been established that Paul's Letter to Philemon despite the personal subject matter is actually for the house church

---

68. Dunn, *Epistles*, 288.
69. Ibid.

and its leading personalities.[70] The letter's recipients are Philemon, who is called a beloved [brother] and fellow worker; Apphia, who is designated as a sister; Archippus, a fellow soldier (Ἀρχίππῳ τῷ συστρατιώτῃ ἡμῶν); and the church in Philemon's house. The usual greeting formula χάρις ὑμῖν καὶ εἰρήνη is in the plural form. The whole body of the letter is then in the singular form and addresses Philemon. But at the end (v. 22), when Paul announces that he will soon be coming, the whole church is involved: ὅτι διὰ τῶν προσευχῶν ὑμῶν χαρισθήσομαι ὑμῖν.[71] The final blessing is again in the plural: Ἡ χάρις τοῦ κυρίου Ἰησοῦ Χριστοῦ μετὰ τοῦ πνεύματος ὑμῶν.[72] The plural forms at the letter's beginning and end attest its public character.[73]

The letter is concerned with Philemon's reaction to the return of his runaway slave Onesimus, who in the meantime has become a Christian through Paul's ministry.[74] The references to the house church show that Paul intended for the members to hear the letter together with Philemon and the other persons named.[75] This means that Philemon could

---

70. Cf. for example Wickert, "Philemonbrief"; Winter, "Philemon," 1–2; Dunn, *Epistles*, 313; Frilingos, "'For my Child, Onesimus,'" 99; Fitzmyer, *Philemon*, 81. Witherington, *Philemon*, 54 stresses the fact that it is not a private letter. Neither is it addressed to Philemon's family members, even if Apphia was his wife and Archippus his son, as Witherington and many others have conjectured. However, Apphia's and Archippus' relationship to Philemon is unclear, because the persons named in the letter's heading are all characterized by their relationship to Paul and to the church (συνεργός, ἀδελφή, and συστρατιώτης), not by their relationship to Philemon. L. Hartman, "On Reading Others' Letters," 173 sees it differently and understands the Letter to Philemon as a private letter.

71. With the second-person plural: "that through your prayers I will be given to you."

72. Again with the second-person plural: "The grace of the Lord Jesus Christ be with your spirit."

73. O'Brien, *Colossians, Philemon*, 267–68, 273 differs, presuming that the other names were only mentioned out of politeness and that the letter was not read out publicly.

74. Winter, "Philemon," 3 has a different opinion: "Onesimus was with Paul in prison because the former had been *sent* by the congregation in Colossae" (italics original). Lampe, "Keine Sklavenflucht" suggests that Onesimus came to Paul because he was looking for an *amicus domini*, someone who would negotiate for him and speak for him. Derrett, "Function of Philemon"; and Nordling, "Onesimus fugitivus" defend the traditional view.

75. Cf. Dunn, *Epistles*, 313; Fitzmeyer, *Philemon*, 81; Stirewalt, *Paul*, 92; also Frilingos, "'For My Child, Onesimus,'" 99: "The first reading of the epistle takes place within the public space of the *domus*." Seen differently in Arzt-Grabner, *Philemon*, 115.

not deal with Onesimus in private.[76] Whatever Philemon would decide in respect to his slave, his decision would undoubtedly effect his honor status among the church members.[77] He had to treat the issue according to the Christian principles taught by Paul if he did not want to lose face with the members of his house church.

We have again a situation when a listener group is divided deliberately. The one performing the letter as Paul intended singles out Philemon from the audience and directs him to accept Onesimus, who is also present. The speaker acts as a mediator between Philemon and Onesimus (v. 17).[78] But this three-party constellation is only the inner circle of the letter event. The three parties are surrounded by another three-group constellation, including first the reader, who represents Paul and his fellow workers;[79] second, the church and its prominent members such as Apphia and Archippus; and third, Philemon. The constellation of this outer circle fits the description of Simmel's *divide et impera*. Paul pulls Apphia, Archippus and the church members to his side, thus pressuring Philemon (Graphic 7). "The eyes of his church will be on him, watching how he responds to Paul's appeal."[80]

---

76. Lohse, *Kolosser, Philemon*, 268; Stuhlmacher, *Philemon*, 31; Murphy-O'Connor, *Paul the Letter-Writer*, 53; Bieberstein, "Disrupting," 111–12; Witherington, *Philemon*, 55. According to Binder, *Philemon*, 45, the house church was a *camera caritatis*, a place of trust, where the relationship between Philemon and Onesimus could be discussed. However the house church appears to have been more of a public setting.

77. Dunn, *Epistles*, 306; Frilingos, "'For My Child, Onesimus,'" 99–100.

78. Cf. Stirewalt, *Paul*, 93. On a somewhat different triangle relationship, see Frilingos, "'For My Child, Onesimus,'" 103.

79. Timotheus as coauthor (v. 1) and those sending greetings (vv. 23–24); cf. Petersen, *Rediscovering Paul*, 100.

80. Witherington, *Philemon*, 56; especially Petersen, *Rediscovering Paul*, 263. It is particularly Petersen who has elaborated on the public side of the Epistle to Philemon, e.g., 99–101, 265, 268–69, 288–89, 298. Cf. also Lyons, "Paul's Confrontation," 127: "Philemon and the community of believers that gather at his house are given the opportunity to ratify this re-valuation within their social setting, thereby becoming ancillary agents in the process." Dunn, *Epistles*, 313: "The assumption is that the letter would be read openly at a meeting of the house church . . . Of course, this was a not altogether subtle way of bringing pressure on Philemon, but the very fact that it could be done indicates that Philemon was likely to recognize the church's right to take an interest in and even advise on the internal affairs of his own household."

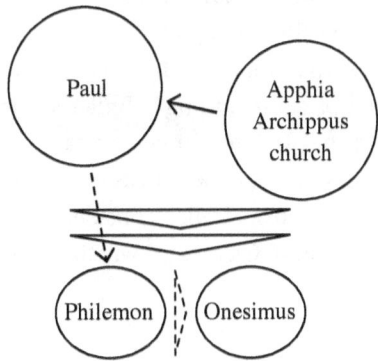

Graphic 7: Letters to individuals (Phlm)

Paul expects more from the outer three-party constellation than he does from the inner one, not only the reconciliation between Philemon and Onesimus, but—most probably[81]—that Philemon will free his slave so that he can then serve Paul (vv. 13–14, 21). Petersen writes:

> Because Paul has made a public issue of the case, he will also have to react publicly to any failure by Philemon to respond as he should. Although the apostle never specifies what administrative consequences might follow from Philemon's disobedience, he does specify a time and a place for a public reckoning should that prove necessary. Given both the case and the issue it poses, Paul's reference to his coming to visit Philemon at his house/church in the near future (v. 22) again only thinly veils sentiments . . . That Paul's visit could turn out to be the occasion for administrative action cannot have escaped the notice of anyone who was party to his letter.[82]

The announcement of his visit is the point in the letter where Paul returns to using the plural, whereas the main part was formulated in the singular.

Of course Paul must reckon with the possibility of the listeners taking sides with Philemon. He is after all their brother, a friend of relatively

---

81. Cf. Lee and Scott, *Sound Mapping*, 233–34.

82. Petersen, *Rediscovering Paul*, 267; cf. Lohse, *Kolosser, Philemon*, 287; Stuhlmacher, *Philemon*, 54; Bieberstein, "Disrupting," 114. Binder, *Philemon*, 66 does not understand Paul's announced visit as meaning that he will be controlling Philemon's treatment of Onesimus, but rather as meaning that he wants them to have a part in the joy of his own release. Cf. also Nordling, *Philemon*, 290–92.

high social standing and the church's host.[83] If the church gets the impression that Paul is expecting too much of Philemon, then they could turn against the apostle. That might be the reason why Paul uses arguments, and pleads instead of commanding.[84] Philemon is invited to act of his own free will (vv. 8, 9, 14). Since Philemon can thus save face in the eyes of the watching church, that makes it easier for them to side with Paul.[85] We already observed above similar consideration given to the public's mood in the First Letter of Clement,[86] which we will be expanding upon below.[87]

Ignatius to Polycarp

Ignatius's letter to Polycarp[88] begins with the usual preamble naming the sender and the recipient. The letter is addressed to Polycarp, bishop of the church of the Smyrnaeans. The first five chapters are all written in the singular and contain a collection of admonitions designed to encourage Polycarp in his work for the church. The sixth chapter suddenly changes from the singular to the plural: Τῷ ἐπισκόπῳ προσέχετε ἵνα καὶ ὁ θεὸς ὑμῖν.[89] The reader, after exhorting the bishop, now turns to the church members who have apparently been there from the start.[90] At first, chapter 6 is about the relationship between the church and the bishop. Soon admonitions follow concerning the relationships between church members: they must work together (συγκοπιᾶτε ἀλλήλοις), have patience with

---

83. Petersen, *Rediscovering Paul*, 100; Witherington, *Philemon*, 56: "There may also be the effect of putting pressure on the community in regard to their Christian commitment so that they will not simply side with Philemon, who is their friend and high status host."

84. Petersen, *Rediscovering Paul*, 300–301 emphasizes that Paul is testing Philemon and the church to see whether they recognize his authority as an apostle to send them directives from outside. At the same time Paul's authority is tested, because it will damage his own apostolic authority both in Philemon's household and with all who hear of the case if Philemon and his house church do not follow his admonitions.

85. Dunn, *Epistles*, 324; Frilingos, "'For My Child, Onesimus,'" 103–4.

86. See above pp. 117–18.

87. See below pp. 271–72, concerning Gal 4:29–30 p. 252.

88. This letter from the former bishop of Antioch in Syria was written in Troas during the Trajan period, in about 107 CE, after Ignatius had met Polycarp as he stopped in Smyrna on his way to martyrdom in Rome. Cf. Schoedel, *Briefe des Ignatius*, 26–28.

89. "Give heed to the bishop that God may also give heed to you."

90. Schoedel, *Briefe des Ignatius*, 425 interprets the change as Ignatius's strategy to influence the church through the bishop.

one another (μακροθυμήσατε οὖν μετ' ἀλλήλων ἐν πραότητι, ὡς ὁ θεὸς μεθ' ὑμῶν), and fight the battle for God faithfully and with perseverance. After referring to a prayer of the church of Smyrna, by which God had brought the return of peace to the church in Antioch in Syria, Ignatius returns to the singular and addresses Polycarp again personally (Ign. *Pol.* 7:2). Polycarp is to call an assembly together that is to send a messenger to Antioch (compare the same concern in Ign. *Smyrn.* 11). Then follows another section in the plural in which the journey to Antioch is presented as an assignment for the whole church (7:3): "This work is both God's and yours (ὑμῶν), when you complete it (ἀπαρτίσητε). For I believe in the grace of God that you are ready (ὅτι ἕτοιμοί ἐστε) to do the good deeds which are proper for God. I exhort you (ὑμᾶς) by no more than these few lines, for I recognise your fervour for the truth (ὑμῶν τὸ σύντονον τῆς ἀληθείας)."[91]

Then Ignatius again addresses Polycarp in the singular, instructing him to also direct other churches to send messengers, or at least a letter, to Antioch in Syria (8:1). After various greetings, the letter's concluding wishes (8:3) are again in the plural and include the whole church.

Ignatius's letter, despite the address being in the singular (Πολυκάρπῳ), is not a private letter, but is rather designed to be read publicly.[92] The audience includes not just the bishop but also the church in Smyrna. The church also hears the first five chapters of what Ignatius writes to the bishop: how he first praises him for his steadfastness, and then admonishes him and gives him instructions as to how he should conduct his duties. Some of what is said would have pleased to the church members: "Suffer all men in love" (1:2). "Let not the widows be neglected" (4:1). "Do not be haughty to slaves, either men or women" (4:3). But in general, Polycarp is exhorted to ensure correct behavior in the church: to foster unity; to correct deviants; to end strange teachings; and to encourage subservience to the bishop, frequent meetings, and correct marital behavior. Although these exhortations are directed to the bishop, they are in truth issued in strong support of his office and in affirmation of his au-

91. Translation by Lake.

92. Paulsen, *Briefe des Ingatius*, 105 explains the change as being due to the influence of traditional church exhortation. The fact that Ignatius addresses the whole church in Ign. *Pol.* 6:1 "does not justify literature-critical operations, but can be explained by the general traditionalism of the material which Ign used." Paulsen evaluates as almost an oversight the change in the address from Polycarp to the church: "With 6, Ign falls into a parenesis to the believers and then gets back to the real recipient of the letter in 7:2" (my translations).

thority. These chapters are intended for the ears of his church. The church is being told indirectly to lead a Christian life as Ignatius understands it. When the reader turns to the church members in chapter 6, they are admonished directly to engage in exactly the behaviors that Ignatius has exhorted the bishop to ensure among them: subservience and unity and faithfulness in the fight for God.

What is the letter's strategy? Right from the start the listeners are divided into two groups, as they were in the Letter to Philemon. One group includes the leader of the church; the other group comprises the crowd. The reader first addresses the bishop, and since the admonishment is public, he has the church members, formally, as witnesses on his side. It appears that the bishop is put under public pressure to follow the writer's directions. But in contrast to the Letter to Philemon, this letter is not concerned with the leader's personal affairs, but rather with the conduct of the church. That means that what is said to Polycarp is indirect exhortation to the church. These exhortations are then intensified when the reader directly addresses the church in chapter 6.

Was this admonition for Polycarp necessary? Did he need Ignatius's public support? Did it help him, or did it undermine his authority by awakening the impression in his church that Polycarp was not up to the task? What is the purpose of this strategy? The situation appears to correspond to what Simmel calls *tertius gaudens*. By dividing the audience right at the beginning of the reading of the letter, specifically along the already existing boundaries between the leader and his followers, Ignatius wins the advantage of a position superior to all others.[93] By admonishing Polycarp he demonstrates in front of all his own superiority. And he strengthens this claim by exhorting the church members to be subservient and behave as Christians should. That is similar to what Paul does in 2 Cor 2 and to what Cicero does in *Pro Lege Manilia* 69: the performer strengthens his own position by singling out one of the listeners and thereby dividing the audience (Graphic 8).

---

93. Schoedel, *Briefe des Ignatius*, 42–44 discusses Ignatius's expressions of self-degradation and interprets them as a sign of his search for identity. They appear to me to be more of a rhetorical means of compensating for his high claims to authority.

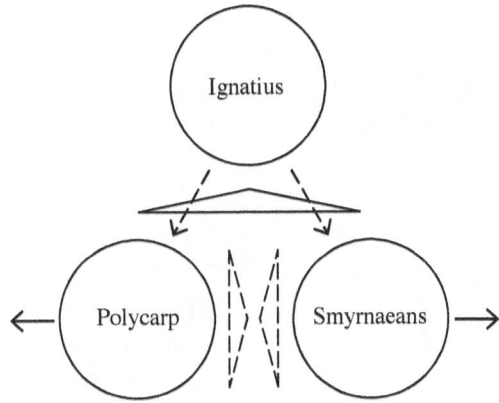

Graphic 8: Letters to individuals (Ign. *Pol.*)

Dividing the church from the bishop and first indirectly and then directly admonishing the church is balanced out by statements that call on Polycarp to deal patiently and understandingly with the church (1:2; 2:1; 4:1, 3). Ignatius does not side totally with Polycarp, but also has an eye out for the interests of the church members. Ultimately he divides the listeners only to point them back to each other: the bishop to the church in their needs, and the church to their bishop in obedience.

We can understand the rhetorical strategy used in this letter if we understand Ignatius's purpose for writing it. He uses his advantage gained in the first six chapters in order to demand a particular commitment from the Christians in Smyrna for his home church in Syria. He wants an emissary equipped with full authorization to travel to Antioch to support the church there (cf. Ign. *Phld.* 10; Ign. *Smyrn.* 11).[94] He wants other churches to join in this service. This request is directed alternately to the bishop and to the church. Chapters 7 and 8 therefore continue to divide the audience, but at the same time to unite the bishop and the church together in this particular task. Dividing the audience gives Ignatius the superiority he needs to ensure that his demand is carried out. The mutual esteem and consideration practiced between the church in Smyrna and their bishop is the precondition that makes it possible for them to fulfill his request.

---

94. Ibid., 435 assumes that Ignatius wanted to strengthen his own rehabilitation with his critics in Antioch.

Conclusions

Using Simmel's social theory of the change from a two-party constellation to a three-party constellation, we have studied different letter events when the performer has singled out individuals in the audience and addressed them directly or indirectly. This strategy has shown itself to be effective in three ways. First, the writer/reader can mediate between the individuals and the rest of the audience—for example, by recommending a messenger and letter carrier (mediator). Second, the writer/reader can put pressure on an individual or group by allying himself with the rest of the audience (*divide et impera*). And third, the writer/reader can profit from dividing the audience by using the situation to inconspicuously promote his own image or to demonstrate his superiority in a subtle way (*tertius gaudens*). Taking these strategies for dealing with the audience into consideration helps us to understand the rhetorical strength of a letter. These rhetorical strategies are discernible especially if we view letters as "written remains" of a public performance.

Focusing on the Reader as Communication's Medium

The essence of a performance includes not only communication of referential content but also simultaneous experience of the medial side of that communication.[95] What is said points not only to a reality outside of language, but at the same time to the current ongoing act of language use. According to Richard Bauman, the reader assumes the responsibility for the way the communication is performed, and the audience has the task of evaluating the competence and effectiveness of the performance.[96] Modern performance studies[97] have clearly shown that the human body is an essential element of every performance. The physical copresence of the reader and the listeners constitutes the performance, initiating a process that makes each performance—through the autopoietic feedback-loop—a unique event.[98]

---

95. See what has been said above on pp. 52–54 about the definition of a performance.

96. Bauman, *Verbal Art*, 7–11.

97. Fischer-Lichte and Roselt, "Attraktion"; Fischer-Lichte, "Performativität"; Fischer-Lichte, *Ästhetik*; Carlson, *Performance*.

98. Fischer-Lichte, *Ästhetik*, 46–57.

There can be no spoken language without someone producing the acoustic utterances and the other communication signals with his or her body. These include the characteristics and idiosyncrasies of the individual physique; the abilities and limitations of the performer; the physical presence; his or her existence in time; movements, breath, and voice; and especially the performer's personal history, which can be seen and experienced in his or her body. There can also be no performance without audience reaction, which is also communicated by means of the bodies in the "performance arena." At first, everything that belongs to the medial side of the performance event is independent of the meaning of the text or piece being presented. The process of experiencing the medial side of the communication generates its own effects, which arise, not through cognition, but rather through bodily experience and physiological mirroring. These effects can harmonize with and support the referential content of the presentation or contrast with it and cause tension. At any case, what is being presented gains additional meaning through the experience of the material and medial aspects of the performance.

Performance criticism will therefore pay special heed to the text elements that direct attention to the medial aspects of the performance. They remind the audience of their basic role in every performance, namely, to evaluate the ability of the performer, the effectiveness of the communication, and the aesthetic quality of the event. For performance criticism of the Pauline letters, this means that an interpretation must search for clues in the text capable of calling attention to the presenter as performance medium and thereby triggering an effect in the audience.[99] Above all, this could be references that bring the physical body of the reader into the focus of the audience. As far as we know, no such study has as yet been undertaken. Here we will investigate selected passages from three of Paul's letters.

Philemon 8–9

The first text that we—again—turn to is the Letter to Philemon. This letter from Paul was written to a wealthy leader of the house church in Colossae with the object of reconciling him with his runaway slave, Onesimus.[100] Who would have been the reader to present this letter? Perhaps

---

99. Cf. Rhoads, "Performance Criticism," 128.

100. On the discussion, cf. Wolter, *Kolosser, Philemon,* 228–32; Hübner, *Philemon, Kolosser, Epheser,* 33–35; Wengst, *Philemon,* 30–39; Witherington, *Philemon,* 68–73.

it was a member of Philemon's household who had enough education and was able to read the letter to the assembled members of the house church. Perhaps Philemon had invested in the education of a young slave, as was customary, so that he could perform the various reading and writing functions in his home and business. In this case, the reader may have been quite young. Or Philemon had a secretary, a tried and trusted man of mature age. Or there was someone in the house church who was well-educated and undertook the duties of a lector.

Of course, the oral presentation of a letter involved more than just pronouncing the words that the sender had written. *Scriptio continua* and other writing conventions of the Hellenistic era and the expectations of the listeners as to how the text should be presented demanded careful preparation by the one who was to present the text. Writing was encoded and preserved orality. The reader first had to work through the text for himself, find the right word and sentence partitions, and then read the text out aloud for himself in order to understand it. Then he had to decide where and how he was to place emphasis, and how he could design the performance so that the listeners would experience the reading as if Paul were standing before them.

During the performance, the reader would come to the main part of the letter and say (vv. 8–9), "Therefore, though I have enough confidence in Christ to order you to do what is proper, yet for love's sake I rather appeal to you—since I am such a person as Paul, the aged, and now also a prisoner of Christ Jesus." How would these words affect the listeners when they were spoken? If the reader was a young slave, he would speak with a youthful voice: τοιοῦτος ὢν ὡς Παῦλος πρεσβύτης.[101]

Had Onesmus gone to Paul to ask for his aid (according to Lampe, "Keine Sklavenflucht," 135–37; Lampe, "Philemon," 206; Dunn, *Epistles*, 304–5), or was he a vagabond (Arzt-Grabner, *Philemon*, 101–8) or—rather unlikely—a delegate sent to Paul from the church (Winter, "Methodological Observations"; contrast Nordling, "Onesimus fugitivus" and Nordling, "Some Matters")? The answer to this question does not influence the performance strategy presented here.

101. Stuhlmacher, *Philemon*, 37–38 and O'Brien, *Colossians, Philemon*, 290 interpret πρεσβύτης as "envoy" ("ambassador"). They understand it as a reference to Paul's apostolic authority. Likewise Petersen, *Rediscovering Paul*, 126–28, who sees a structural analogy between v. 9 and v. 11 (τόν ποτέ σοι ἄχρηστον νυνὶ δὲ καὶ σοὶ καὶ ἐμοὶ εὔχρηστον), therefore understanding the word pair πρεσβύτης and δέσμιος as *a contrast* and therefore assuming that πρεσβύτης has a meaning that brings authority to expression. This is not convincing, since in v. 11 the contrast is expressed on the one hand through ποτέ and νυνὶ δέ and on the other hand through ἄχρηστος and εὔχρηστος, but in v. 9 there is nothing to signal a contrast. Petersen points additionally to 2 Cor 5:20

Would there not be an open contradiction between what was being said and the one saying it?

On the other hand, how much more poignant would it be for the listeners if they heard the words νυνὶ δὲ καὶ δέσμιος Χριστοῦ Ἰησου being spoken by an older secretary, a slave or a freedman, whose lifelong dependence on a rich landowner—his "captivity" as it were—was apparent in his own physical appearance?[102] Paul's self-description as captive could gain particular significance through the body and voice of the performer. It would, however, create much more tension if a wealthy and well-educated member of the house church spoke these words. In any case, it could only be his *own* voice, his *own* body carrying the marks of his *own* life story, which the reader would lend to Paul for the duration of the performance of his letter.

As soon as Paul refers in the letter to his own body, the listeners would experience either that the message of the text gained additional force through the body of the performer or that the contrast between the sender's body and the reader's body would cause tension.[103] At any

---

(cf. Eph 6:20) where just as in Philm 9 παρακαλῶ is used, but there Paul uses the verb πρεσβεύω and not the noun πρεσβύτης. Nordling, *Philemon*, 230; Nordling, "Gospel in Philemon," 77 interprets this as follows: by using πρεσβύτης, Paul points to both his age (49 to 56 years old) *and* his role as ambassador (πρεσβευτής). Similarly Binder, *Philemon*, 54, for whom the word πρεσβύτης, as used here, appears to resonate with the meaning of "representative" and "envoy." Lohse, *Kolosser, Philemon*, 277 and Lampe, "Philemon," 216 justify their interpretation as "old man" with the argument that his authority is precisely what Paul does *not* want to emphasize in this particular sentence. Similarly, see Lee and Scott, *Sound Mapping*, 230. This argument is not refuted by the fact that Paul in general makes his authority as an apostle clearly recognizable in the Letter to Philemon, according to Petersen, *Rediscovering Paul*, 188. But (contrary to Witherington, *Philemon*, 67) it is also not just a case of trying to arouse sympathy. The reference to age certainly implies a claim to respect, just as the reference does to being a prisoner for Christ. On this, see Wolter, *Kolosser, Philemon*, 259–61; Dunn, *Epistles*, 322, 327; Lampe, "Philemon," 216; Wengst, *Philemon*, 59.

102. Petersen, *Rediscovering Paul*, 127 sees an expression of humility in the reference to captivity; cf. Lyons, "Paul's Confrontation," 127–28. However, Ignatius of Antioch understands his chains to be a distinction and calls them "spiritual pearls" (Ign. *Eph.* 11:2; cf. Pol. *Phil.* 1:1). So this self-description appears to imply a claim for respect. It is, however, not based on the *apostolic office* but on *personal ethos*. The personal ethos is also in view in the references to captivity in Phil 1:7, 13, 17 (cf. Col 4:3, 18; Eph 3:1; 4:1; 6:20; 2 Tim 1:8, 16).

103. Expositors have not paid attention to this aspect of the text because they treat the letter anachronistically as a personal message for Philemon that he would read silently for himself. Binder, *Philemon*, 54: "Everything that the apostle here refers to about himself is 'incidental.' He is not trying to impress, neither with his being old nor

rate, the goal of the writer would be to steer audience attention toward the body of the reader of the letter. Thus the medium of communication would become visible.[104]

The attention to the reader would disrupt the illusion that Paul was, so to speak, present in the congregation. The listeners' interpretation of the content of the words and their attention to the medial side of the communication would move apart. The effect would vary depending on the social standing of the listener. A slave in Philemon's household would react differently than a freeborn person, a more mature person differently than a young person. In any case, in this moment the listeners would become aware that they are an audience and are experiencing a performance.

When the medial side of the performance moves to the forefront, it has a distancing and alienating effect on the audience. Normally the effect of Paul's letter on the listeners would depend on how well and with what commitment the performer carries out his task.[105] The better the reader embodies Paul, the stronger the effect of the performance would be on the listeners. The listeners would identify themselves so strongly with the performance that they would experience Paul as if he were present.

However, Paul's referring to his body reminds the listeners that Paul is *not* himself present. With this reminder of Paul's body, the illusion is destroyed, and listeners are left at a critical distance. They are no longer simply experiencing performance; they are no longer simply mirroring the feelings suggested by the performance. The experience of such

---

with the statement about being robbed of his freedom" (my translation).

104. This effect seems to be supported by Paul's mentioning his name in Phlm 8. (On the mentioning of names with ὡς cf. Arzt-Grabner, *Philemon*, 201.) Paul also uses his name in 2 Cor 10:1 and 1 Thess 2:18. In both cases the context is also the body, namely, the apostle's physical presence or absence. Col 1:23–24 also speaks of the body, namely, the apostle's suffering. This suggests that mentioning the name would also awaken awareness of the medial aspect of the communication. This could also apply to Gal 5:2 and Eph 3:1, where the apostle's name is mentioned in connection with the authority of his speeches and judgements. Here the name could make the audience aware that the words they are hearing in the performance cannot be separated from the person of the apostle. The case is somewhat different in Phlm 19, where by writing his own name Paul guarantees that he will fulfill a legally binding commitment to repay Philemon for expenses related to Onesimus. Cf. Wolter, *Kolosser, Philemon*, 276; Dunn, *Epistles*, 339–40; Lampe, "Philemon," 225; Arzt-Grabner, *Philemon*, 240–46.

105. An example is the strong effect of the masterly performance of Paul's letter of tears in Corinth. Cf. Johnson, "Titus' Tearful Performance," who assumes, however, that Titus was the reader.

alienation calls on them to take responsibility for their actions and reactions themselves, and that at various levels.

First of all, the audience is stimulated to assess the quality of the performance. Evaluating the reader's ability—that is, his presence in the room, the aesthetic quality of the reading, and the effectiveness of his communication—is an important element of what it means to be an audience. This includes evaluating the coherence of the message content and the medial aspect of the performance. The church in Philemon's house becomes conscious of how well the reader is able to represent Paul and where he reaches the limits of his own corporeality.

This leads to the second point: every reading is an interpretation. While the church members evaluate the presentation, because they have been reminded that Paul is not himself speaking, their dependence on the performer's interpretation of the letter is lessened. The ability to judge the coherence in the performance requires them to first have their own interpretation of Paul's words. As long as the listeners are captivated by the performance, they will receive the letter the way it is understood and presented by the reader. As soon as they are aware that they are experiencing a performance they are expected to evaluate, they will need their own interpretation. The focus on the medial aspect of the performance has a kind of "democratization effect." The responsibility for interpreting Paul's letter is not carried by the reader alone but is transferred to the entire listening church.

This democratization effect could have been of crucial importance during the reading of the Letter to Philemon. There were substantial differences in social standing between Philemon, his relatives on the one side, and his slaves and dependents on the other. There may have been some other (relatively) wealthy persons in the church, and there were certainly other poor people and slaves.[106] In the assembled church, the reader acts on behalf of Philemon and at that moment is part of the socially superior group, even if he is in actuality a slave. He is offering the ruler's interpretation. Through Paul's strategy of mentioning his body, this interpretation must then face the evaluation of the whole assembly.

---

106. Concerning the question of slaves in the Pauline churches, O'Brien, *Colossians, Philemon*, 270 writes: "the terms 'slave' and 'master' are transcended. . . . finally it is of no ultimate significance to him [Onesimus] as a Christian as to whether he is slave or free." On the social hierarchies, cf. Petersen, *Rediscovering Paul*, 89–199, who considers the social pressure on Philemon (pp. 99–100) but does not take into account social differences among the listening members.

The *church*, the majority of whose members are very probably from the lower social classes, is encouraged to form its own judgement.

Paul's dependency on the interpretation of his letter by the reader would also be reduced by the reference to his own body. The reader could have been influenced by Philemon prior to the performance in the church assembly. After all, Philemon had been the first to receive the letter and could have tried to ensure that the one assigned to read the letter would present it in a way that would benefit his own interests. However, Paul made sure that the performance would be clearly recognized as such and that it would be evaluated. The letter's interpretation would be subject to the assessment of all those listening.

There is a third level to this strategy of Paul's in which the audience is led to take responsibility for their own actions. It concerns the future status of Onesimus. Should he remain a slave in Philemon's household, or should he now, after his conversion through Paul and his return to Colossae, be regarded as a brother in Christ?[107] This was not just a question that Philemon had to answer. The letter, whose main body was addressed to Philemon, was read to the assembled house church. Philemon's decision as to what should happen with Onesimus therefore became a public issue.[108] The whole church was challenged to make a decision in the matter.[109]

Paul's strategy of creating awareness of the medial aspect of the performance brings to mind Bertolt Brecht's "epic theater." According to the ideal in traditional theater, the actor dedicates his voice, his mimicry and gestures—that is, his whole body—to the role he is playing. He embodies it. The audience is drawn into the world being depicted; they identify themselves with the characters in the theater script who are being brought to life before their eyes. In Aristotle's classic theory of drama (*Poet.* 6), this awakens "sympathy and fear" in the audience (ἔλεος καὶ φόβος) and has a cathartic effect. In contrast to this traditional type of theater,[110] Brecht uses various technics in his "epic theater" in order to

---

107. Cf. Petersen, *Rediscovering Paul*, 96–97.

108. Ibid., 99; cf. Nordling, *Philemon*, 176; Nordling, "Philemon in Context," 300, 304.

109. Petersen, *Rediscovering Paul*, 100: "The return of the house-master's slave as a born-again brother requires that the rest of the community renegotiate its relation with *each* of them" (italics original). Cf. Stuhlmacher, *Philemon*, 31.

110. Cf. how Brecht diverges from the Aristotelian dramaturgy in Brecht, "Über experimentelles Theater," 415–18.

destroy the audience's illusions.¹¹¹ Above all, the actors play their roles with an inner detachment, they consciously act *in front of* the audience as if to display the role without advocating it themselves.¹¹² That means the actors are always recognizable as mediums in their roles.¹¹³ Brecht called the effect the "Verfremdungseffekt" or the "V-Effekt" (the alienation effect or estrangement).¹¹⁴ The audience should not empathize with the characters being presented, nor should they identify themselves with them, but they should rather distance themselves and critically appraise the presented relationships between the characters. Brecht wanted the audience to be consciously aware that they were watching a play.

The goal of "epic theater" is to activate the audience. According to Brecht, the purpose of the theater should not be to present the "normal" or the "all too human," that which is true at all times, but rather to show what is time-bound and socially conditioned so that it is subject to change and also must be changed.¹¹⁵ The audience should not think,

111. For example, an announcer or a narrator appears, a choir comments, the actors speak directly to the audience, there are written titles for the scenes or projections extending the associative scope of the enactment, a sparse scenic design is used that is more like a commentary than an illustration, and finally the music comments on or stands in contrast to the play instead of giving emotional support. In this way the illusion of the stage is interrupted time and again.

112. Brecht, "Vergnügungstheater," 63: "The actors also executed an incomplete transformation and held their distance to the figure being depicted, yes even provoking criticism" (my translation). Cf. also Brecht, "Verfremdungseffekte"; Brecht, "Neue Technik."

113. Brecht, "Kleines Organon," 153–54: "The fact that the actor appears on the stage as two different persons, as Laughton [the actor] and as Galileo [the character], that the presenting Laughton does not disappear behind the presented Galileo—which has given this style of acting the name 'epic'—in the end, this means nothing more than that the real, the profane process is no longer being disguised—Laughton is really on the stage showing his understanding of Galileo" (my translation).

114. Brecht, "Über experimentelles Theater," 418: "To alienate an event or a character one must primarily remove the self-evident, the known, the obvious and create astonishment and curiosity about it or him" (my translation). Brecht, "Strassenszene," 100: "The demonstrator, by paying special attention to his movements, doing them very carefully, probably slowed down, achieves the V-effect [alienation effect]; that is he defamiliarizes the small subprocess and raises it in its importance, making it remarkable.... [The performer] interrupts his imitation with explanations as often as he sees fit. The choirs, the epic theater's projected documents, the turning-directly-to-the-audience by the actors are basically nothing else" (my translation).

115. Cf. Brecht, "Neue Technik," 113; Brecht, "Aus einem Brief," 284; Brecht, "Über experimentelles Theater," 418–19.

"things will always be this way,"[116] but should maintain a critical distance to what is enacted in order to be able to evaluate what is happening on the stage and reflect on alternatives to what is being presented.[117] In this way Brecht wanted to urge the audience to take actions that would change social realities.[118]

1 Corinthians 5:3

It is no accident that Paul uses the alienation effect in his letters at such places where the church to which the letter is directed is expected to make a decision. That is also the case in the First Letter to the Corinthians, our second example. In 1 Cor 5:3–5 Paul refers to his physical absence, though being present in spirit:

> For I, on my part, though absent in body but present in spirit, have already judged him who has so committed this, as though I were present. In the name of our Lord Jesus, when you are assembled, and I with you in spirit, with the power of our Lord Jesus, I have decided to deliver such a one to Satan for the destruction of his flesh, so that his spirit may be saved in the day of the Lord Jesus.

That the presence-and-absence motif in letters is typical has often been established.[119] Above all Heikki Koskenniemi and Klaus Thraede

---

116. Brecht, "Vergnügungstheater," 63–64: "The dramatic-theater spectator says: Yes, that is what I have always felt.—That is how I am.—That is to be expected.—That will always be so.—The plight of this person appals me, because he has no way out.—That is true art: everything comes so naturally.—I shed tears with those that cry, I laugh with those that laugh" (my translation).

"The epic-theater spectator says: This I would never have thought.—One shouldn't do that.—That is so conspicuous, hard to believe.—It must stop.—The plight of this person appals me, because there would be a way out after all.—That is true art: there is nothing to be taken for granted.—I laugh over those in tears, I cry about those that are laughing" (my translation).

117. Brecht, "Kleines Organon," 166: "The events should not be allowed to follow each other imperceptibly, but rather one should be able to come in between and make a judgement" (my translation).

118. According to Brecht, "Kleines Organon," 144, the purpose of the V-effect is "to portray the world in such a way that it becomes treatable" (my translation).

119. See Koskennienni, *Studien*, 35–47 for a focus on the mental presence of the friend. See especially Thraede, *Grundzüge*, 39–47 and *passim*. See also White, *Light*; Klauck, *Ancient Letters*, 159–61; Holland, "Frightening." See above in the introduction pp. 8–10 on this motif in the letter genre.

have pointed out this motif in its various forms, as being typical of friendship letters. The friendship letter is described therefore as being a *medium* to help bridge the separation and evoke the spiritual presence of the friend. Commenting on 1 Cor 5:3, Thraede notes, "It is the letter itself which in reality mediates the παρουσία of the apostle and in the real sense of the word 'represents him.' . . . It is very important for him that he himself is present in the moment that the church reads the letter because the letter acts in his stead." In other words, "it should be emphasized that the 'as-if-presence' really happens *in* the letter."[120] The common ἀπὼν-παρὼν-motif interrupts the purely content-centered exchange and the communication itself becomes the topic. With the formula ἀπὼν τῷ σώματι παρὼν δὲ τῷ πνεύματι, the impact of the letter is reflected on as the impact of a *medium*. On the one hand, a letter can make the spatial separation more bearable[121] and express and strengthen the affinity (φιλοφρόνησις) between writer and recipient;[122] on the other hand, the letter can make one painfully aware of how limited written communication really is.[123]

The experience of the quasi-presence happens through recognizing the friend in the letter. Cicero writes to Cassius (*Fam.* 15.16.1) that he virtually sees his friend before his eyes.[124] This experience presupposes a *medial evaluation* of the letter. The better the writer manages to manifest his personality in the letter, the stronger the recipient will feel the quasi-presence of his correspondent. This is why Demetrius requires that the character of the writer should be recognizable in his letter.[125]

From the aspect of a performance before an audience, which is typical for an apostolic letter, the ἀπὼν-παρὼν-motif fulfils the same function as the referral to the corporeality of the sender.[126] It turns the attention

---

120. Thraede, *Grundzüge*, 99 (my translation, italics in the original). Cf. Schnider and Stenger, *Studien*, 92-107.

121. Cf. the examples of Cicero's letters in Thraede, *Grundzüge*, 39-47.

122. Cf. the first letter type, the τύπος φιλικός, in Ps.-Demetrius, *Formae epistolicae*.

123. On this, see below on pp. 148-49 the interpretation of Gal 4:20.

124. "ut quasi coram adesse videare"; cf. Thraede, *Grundzüge*, 43. Cf. Seneca, *Ep.* 40.1: "Nam quo uno modo potes, te mihi ostendis." ("For you are revealing your real self to me in the only way you can" [translation in Malherbe, *Ancient Epistolary*, 29].)

125. Demetrius, *Eloc.* 227. Cf. Koskenniemi, *Studien*, 40; on the letter as "picture of the soul," cf. Thraede, *Grundzüge*, 23-24.

126. Holland, "Frightening," 11 on 1 Cor 5:3-5: "Performance of the letter . . . invokes and makes real his personal presence, allowing him to be active among the members of the congregation . . . How could Paul do this? Only through the performance

to the medial side of the performance. The reader, who embodies Paul with all means available to him, must admit, when he reads this passage, that he is *not* Paul: ἀπὼν τῷ σώματι. He embodies Paul, lends him his voice and gestures, but at the same time presents a different body, namely, his own and not Paul's. This causes an alienation effect, which points the listeners to their role as an audience, to their responsibility to evaluate the quality of the performance. At the same time, the listeners are encouraged to take a stance on the πορνεία issue. Paul, immediately after the ἀπὼν-παρὼν motif, demands a decision from the church, namely, the decision to expel the church member living with his father's wife.[127]

Probably the expulsion concerns the exclusion of a church member of higher social status, from whom the church may possibly be profiting.[128] For this reason it was very important that Paul encouraged the normal church members to form their own opinions. The alienation-effect activates the listeners to make their own judgements.

Galatians 4:13–20; 6:17

A third text example, which is also the most interesting one in this connection, is Gal 4:13–20. We find here not only a sentence that points to Paul's body, thereby creating a distancing effect, but several statements that destroy the illusion of Paul's presence in the performance.

First of all, Paul reminds the Galatians of the time when he first worked in their area (vv. 13–14).[129] It appears that Paul had not intended to stay in Galatia, but physical infirmity (ἀσθένεια τῆς σαρκός) had forced him to remain there.[130] He used this time to preach the gospel. His illness must have been visible, afflicting either his head, hands, or feet. He must have been a repulsive sight, for Paul testifies that the Galatians would have been willing—if it were possible—to give him their own eyes (v. 15). εἰ δυνατόν implies that giving their eyes is not to be understood

---

of his letter by a reader/performer who speaks (and so here also acts) in Paul's name and persona."

127. Action is also involved in connection with the ἀπὼν-παρὼν-motif in Phil 1:17 and 2:12.

128. Chow, *Patronage*, 130–39.

129. Cf. the references to the ethic of friendship in Becker, *Galater*, 68; Betz, *Galatians*, 221–25 and *passim*.

130. Differently Becker, *Galater*, 68.

metaphorically.¹³¹ James D. G. Dunn concludes that it must have been an illness affecting the eyes.¹³² Paul's sickness and his resulting offensive physical appearance impaired Paul's ethos, and counteracted his rhetorical effectiveness.¹³³ The Galatians could have felt revulsion and spit at his feet,¹³⁴ but they resisted this temptation and welcomed him as God's messenger.

The listeners would have been transported into the past and reminded of the apostle's appearance at that time when this passage was read out in the Galatian churches. The actual appearance of the various readers would most likely have contrasted strongly to Paul's appearance at the recollected time: it is hardly probable that one of them would have had signs of an acute illness such as inflamed and watering eyes. Paul, by mentioning τὴν ἀσθένειαν τῆς σαρκός, begins to distance the listeners from the illusion that they are listening to the apostle himself. So they are reminded that they are taking part in a performance event. This would lead listeners to reflect on the quality of the performance. While being invited to compare the physical condition of the reader with their memories of the physical impression Paul had given as he stayed with them, the Galatian listeners are at the same time being called to assess whether the reader's ethos corresponds to Paul's ethos, whether he shows the same passion, whether his intonation has the same urgency that Paul's would have if Paul himself were speaking.

In Gal 4:18 we again find the motif of physical absence that in 1 Cor 5:3 had drawn attention to the medial aspects of the performance: πάντοτε καὶ μὴ μόνον ἐν τῷ παρεῖναί με πρὸς ὑμᾶς. This statement also makes the listeners realize that the voice they are hearing does not belong to Paul himself. Here again the alienation effect is evident, challenging the listeners to make their own assessment of the quality of the performance and at the same time to assess the appropriateness of the reader's interpretation and finally to consider the question being pursued in the letter.

There follows the exclamation in verse 19: τέκνα μου, οὓς πάλιν ὠδίνω μέχρις οὗ μορφωθῇ Χριστὸς ἐν ὑμῖν. The body is again spoken of. Paul compares himself to a woman in labor bringing a child into the

---

131. Ibid., 69.

132. Dunn, *Galatians*, 236; cf. Mussner, *Galaterbrief*, 309.

133. Witherington, *Grace*, 309.

134. It can be left open whether or not the spitting resulted from fear of the evil eye. Cf. ibid., 201–3.

world.¹³⁵ Since, however, Paul does not refer this time to his real body but is speaking metaphorically, the reader would have expressed this sentence very dramatically in order to appropriately present the apostle's own pain. However, the alienation effect in the previous sentence causes the audience to listen critically.

Verse 20 ultimately makes it completely impossible for the reader to physically represent the apostle: ἤθελον δὲ παρεῖναι πρὸς ὑμᾶς ἄρτι. The reader, who with his own voice and body creates the presence of the apostle, who expresses Paul's thoughts and feelings as authentically as possible, must now speak the words: I wish I could be present with you now.¹³⁶ The reader who is representing Paul in the performance thus acknowledges that he is not Paul. The illusion is destroyed. The listeners no longer hear Paul's voice but have become aware of the medium of the letter event. We are again confronted with the ἀπὼν-παρὼν-motif as letter topos, which causes an alienation effect.¹³⁷

This is intensified in the sentence that follows: ἤθελον δὲ . . . ἀλλάξαι τὴν φωνήν μου.¹³⁸ Paul refers to his real voice, the voice he produces with his own body.¹³⁹ What should the reader do at this point? Should he change his voice? Paul says that he would like do that himself, but *cannot*. Should the reader *not* change his voice? Would that not be inappropriate when one is representing someone who is appalled and perplexed? And

---

135. Cf. Gaventa, "Maternity of Paul."

136. Wilhelmi, "ἀλλάξαι τὴν φωνήν" has shown the difficulties in this verse and lists various possible interpretations. He recognizes correctly that v. 20 offers two statements in the irrealis mood. However his interpretation that Paul wished he could speak so loudly that he could be heard in Galatia is not plausible. Wilhelmi also does not give consideration to the performance situation in which the expression of such unreality would only become meaningful.

137. Cf. Mullins, "Visit Talk"; Betz, *Galatians*, 236 on motifs of longing in letters.

138. "I could wish . . . to change my tone."

139. This sentence has been variously interpreted: generally, the letter's oral performance has not been a consideration, but the interpreters rather assume that Paul is contrasting written with vocal communication. Betz, *Galatians*, 236 interprets thus: "to be translated as 'exchange my voice,' i.e., for the letter." Similarly Mussner, *Galaterbrief*, 314; Bruce, *Galatians*, 213; Becker, *Galater*, 70. Probably likewise Rohde, *Galater*, 190–91, who explains that the concern is "not the sound of the voice" but rather that Paul "if personally present in Galatia would be able to find the right tone of voice, that is, depending on the situation, he would either speak as a friend or speak harshly with them" (my translation). Witherington, *Grace*, 316 differs from this: for him the statement is not a question of presence but indeed of the tone of voice and refers to ancient rhetoric. Schlier, *Galater*, 215 thinks that Paul would like to speak "in 'angels' tongues,' in the heavenly language" (my translation). This idea has not found acceptance.

if he tries to change his voice, in what way should he change it?[140] Paul does not give the reader any help. Whatever the reader does, the listeners will be aware that he is not speaking as Paul would. This completely destroys the listeners' illusion that they are hearing Paul. Their attention is directed to the medium, to the reader. Paul is lamenting the limits of the written medium. The letter here, in contrast to in 1 Cor 5:3 and other letter literature, does not create a quasi-presence. On the contrary, the letter event is an occasion for Paul to long even more to be personally present, and a way for listeners to perceive the limitations of the performance.

When the attention here is directed to the medium, it is not the *written* medium, not the letter as object.[141] It is the *performative* medium, namely, the letter *event* that comes into focus of awareness.[142]

A final reference to Paul's body is to be found in Gal 6:17: ἐγὼ γὰρ τὰ στίγματα τοῦ Ἰησοῦ ἐν τῷ σώματί μου βαστάζω. What are "the marks of Jesus"? The most plausible interpretation is that they are Paul's scars from mistreatment endured because of his mission.[143] Paul speaks of this persecution in Gal 5:11 and distances himself from those who have sought to avoid persecution (6:12).

Once again the apostle's reference to his body brings about an alienation effect. By emphasizing ἐγώ, Paul distances himself from those who

---

140. Cf. Becker, *Galater*, 70 for his considerations on this point.

141. As for example in Seneca, *Ep.* 40.1: "quanto iucundiores sunt litterae, quae vera amici absentis vestigia, veras notas adferunt? Nam quod in conspectu dulcissimum est, id amici manus epistulae inpressa praestat, agnoscere." ("How much more pleasant is a letter, which brings us real traces, real evidences, of an absent friend? For that which is sweetest when we meet face to face is afforded by the impress of a friend's hand upon his letter—recognition" [translation in Malherbe, *Ancient Epistolary*, 29]).

142. Betz, *Galatians*, 24, because he does not have the performance in view, remains focused on the written medium: "The letter is a necessary substitute for such an oral exchange. By necessity, therefore, the letter is reductive. The letter represents its author, yet cannot act and react as its author might in person. Thus the sender expresses himself *in absentia* and without the full range of communicative devices which an oral conversation can provide . . . If one looks at the letter from the point of view of its function, i.e., from the rhetorical point of view, this substitution is indeed a poor one. Since it is simply a lifeless piece of paper, it eliminates one of the most important weapons of the rhetorician, the oral delivery. The actual delivery of the speech includes a whole range of weapons relating to modulation of voice and to gestures, all of which a letter makes impossible. In his remarks Paul is fully aware of these disadvantages, as shown in 4:18–20."

143. For example, Schlier, *Galater*, 285; Rohde, *Galater*, 279–80; Witherington, *Grace*, 454; Becker, *Galater*, 103. Mussner, *Galaterbrief*, 418–20 lists various interpretations.

are requiring circumcision in order to avoid persecution (6:12). "In this way, Paul consciously highlights his own person,"[144] creating a contrast to the one reading the letter in his place. The mention of his physical στίγματα finally separates him completely from the one doing the reading. Paul would have made a gesture indicating his scars at this point. The reader cannot do that. He must speak Paul's words without living them out in his own body. This would make the imperfection of his embodiment visible.

Why does Paul repeatedly refer to his body in the Letter to the Galatians? What could be his reasons for repeatedly creating awareness of the medial aspect of the letter event? Perhaps Paul is unsure whether the various readers of his letter in Galatia will meet his expectations for an appropriate performance. The author of a playscript is dependent on the actors who enact his work before an audience. Paul the author was dependent on the one reading out the letter. There is no doubt that the performance is built on how the reader understands the contents of the letter in his preparation for the public reading. Every performance is at the same time an interpretation.

Paul could not know who would be responsible for this task in the various Galatian churches. He had to expect that some performers might be on his opponents' side.[145] Could they not compromise Paul's message by the way they presented it? Would not the letter's effect be weakened by emphases in the wrong places, by a critical gesture or a fundamentally impassive attitude during the performance? It is therefore plausible that Paul did not want to be completely dependent on the readers. By referring to his own body and the alienation it created, he challenged the listeners to judge for themselves whether the performance was appropriate or not. The listeners should themselves imagine how Paul's voice would sound, which words he would emphasize, what he was trying to put across. The interpretation is therefore not be left to the readers or to those responsible for appointing them. The *whole* church is called to take a critical stance toward the performance and is charged with the responsibility of interpreting Paul's letter.

This responsibility ultimately encourages the listeners to also find their own position on the issue presented in the letter itself. The Letter to the Galatians deals with the problem of the call by some of Paul's

---

144. Mussner, *Galaterbrief*, 418 (my translation).

145. See below pp. 230–35 on the Letter to the Galatians on the fact that Paul's opponents where part of the churches.

opponents who remain unnamed to require circumcision of Gentile believers. A decision has to be made. It appears that some wealthy and therefore prominent church members were advocating for the validity of the law, such people who could recommend themselves as benefactors (4:17), who valued social honor and had something to lose (6:12–13).[146] Paul would have to expect that precisely these people would be responsible for the preparation of the performance in some of the churches. Through their social standing they would have had a higher education (including the ability to read), and probably also had dependents in their households with reading skills. In order to suppress their influence, Paul strengthened the church members' autonomy with his strategy.

To summarize, we can say that Paul, through diverse direct and indirect references to his own real body (to his age, to illness, to his voice, to his tears and scars) or his physical absence was able to disrupt the illusion of his presence during performances of his letters. Such disruptions created critical distance between listeners and the performance. This alienation effect directed audience attention to the medial aspect of the performance. This had a threefold effect. First, listeners were directed to evaluate how well the performance was executed, to enjoy or criticize the abilities and competence of the reader (the typical role and responsibility of every audience). Second, Paul's disruption strategy reduced the audience's dependence on the reader and the reader's interpretation for understanding the letter. Through his disruption strategy, Paul reminded listeners of their own responsibility to interpret his letter for themselves. And third, calling his audience to evaluate the performances of his letters and their interpretations also put listeners in a position to take their own stand about its content. Paul's performance strategy prepared the audience to make a decision about how to receive his message.

---

146. On these texts, see below pp. 255–56.

3

Strategies in Letter Writing to Achieve Reconciliation

The last chapter showed that the performance of a letter could elicit differing reactions in an audience. How this was achieved will now be examined in detail in some longer passages from Paul's letters. In this chapter we will consider how the letter event might have brought about reconciliation between contrarily thinking and even hostile groups in the church. This happened not just through understanding the letter's content but also through interaction between audience members during the reading. It is neither the instructions nor the admonitions alone that caused listeners to turn to each other in a positive manner, but rather the performance itself stimulated this reaction. The letter's content and the letter reading as a medial event complement and confirm each other. By calling our attention to this process, performance criticism also contributes to a better understanding of the letter's content.

Controversy in Rome over Diet (Romans 14:1—15:13)[1]

Context and Limits of the Pericope

Rom 14:1—15:13 is the last and longest unit in the section of the Letter to the Romans in which Paul addresses the practical consequences of his

---

1. An earlier, more rhetorically oriented study of this passage was published 1999 in Oestreich, "Argumentation."

gospel. After *general* admonitions on a harmonious church life in Rom 12:3—13:14 (against pride, 12:3; the motif of the body as topos of unity, 12:4-5;[2] brotherly love, 12:9-10; mutual concern and hospitality, 12:13; unity, 12:16; harmony, 12:18; against vengeance, 12:19-21; against political revolt, 13:1-7; love as life's fundamental principle, 13:8-10), Paul begins in Rom 14:1 with *concrete* directions for the Christians in Rome, namely, an admonition to mutual acceptance despite differing opinions.

Where does this pericope end? The phrase τὸν ἀσθενοῦντα in Rom 14:1 is taken up again in Rom 15:1 with τὰ ἀσθενήματα, and the imperative προσλαμβάνεσθε is repeated in Rom 15:7. This suggests that Rom 15:1-7 deal with the same theme and are also part of the pericope. Heil has interpreted the twofold usage of προσλαμβάνειν as the frame, and Rom 15:7 as the conclusion of the section.[3] However, Rom 15:8 is not a new beginning but rather another argument supporting mutual acceptance—now extended to include the contrasting categories of Jews/non-Jews[4]—which is supported by biblical quotes and closes with a prayer wish. The pericope closes therefore with Rom 15:13.[5]

We accept the unity of the passage. Separation hypotheses have not established themselves.[6] In our analysis of the passage it will be shown that there is an inner cohesion and that it has a meaningful form.[7]

Structure

The passage begins with a series of parallel statements (14:2, 5, 6), injunctions (v. 3), and questions (v. 10). Paul talks repeatedly and alternately about two different groups of Roman Christians or addresses them

---

2. Cf. Mitchell, *Paul and the Rhetoric*, 157-63.

3. Heil, *Ablehnung der Speisegebote*, 243.

4. Cf. Haacker, "Römerbrief als Friedensmemorandum," 32 on this contrast as the main concern of the first section of the Letter to the Romans.

5. Nygren, *Römerbrief*, 313; Michel, *Römer*, 296; Schmidt, *Römer*, 237; Käsemann, *Römer*, 352; Wilckens, *Römer*, 1:21; 3:80; Meeks, "Judgment"; Stuhlmacher, *Römer*, 195-207 and many others treat Rom 14:1—15:13 as a unit.

6. Schmithals, *Römerbrief*, 25-29, 489, 512-13 assumes that the Letter to the Romans is compiled from originally two letters. One consisted of Rom 1-11 and 15:8-13. The other contained Rom 12:1—15:7 and 16:21-23. On this, see Wilckens, *Römer*, 1: 27-29; 3:104-5.

7. The textual tradition that moves the doxology from Rom 16:25-27 to 14:23 certainly has liturgical roots and is secondary, cf. Wilckens, *Römer*, 1:22-23.

directly.[8] He reaches a first conclusion with the christological statements in verse 9, which apply to all Roman Christians in common.

After that, verse 10 picks up the admonitions from verse 3 again: do not judge, do not despise. Then Paul substantiates each admonition separately and extensively. After each conclusion he adds a Scripture quote (14:11 and 15:3), which is then applied to the listeners' situation (14:12-13a and 15:4). So we have again a parallelism—first forbidding listeners to be judgmental in verse 10c to 13a with the conclusion: "Therefore let us not judge one another anymore." After a skillful transition (v. 13b) Paul then addresses his directive to the other group[9] in 13c not to be an obstacle to a brother. This section closes with Rom 15:1-4.[10]

There follows a third part, framed by two "prayer-wishes" for unity and peace, which are intended for everyone (15:5-6 and 13).[11] Verse 7 picks up again on προσλαμβάνειν from Rom 14:1. Now the directive to accept one another is justified christologically and supported by quotes from the Scriptures (vv. 8-12). This section addresses all the listeners together. The division is overcome. Only the justification in verses 8-9 has again a parallel structure.

The passage's structure can be depicted as follows:[12]

---

8. Wilckens, *Römer*, 3:109, 115 considers them to be individuals rather than groups; also Moiser, "Rethinking," 578.

9. Jewett, *Romans*, 857 differs, seeing larger parts of this section as directed to all listeners.

10. Cf. Moo, *Romans*, 865, 867. On the other hand, Wilckens, *Römer*, 3:80; Gäckle, *Die Starken*, 389 and many others separate Rom 14:23 from 15:1. But those addressed in Rom 15:1 do not change, and the thoughts continue without interruption: the members of the group being addressed are to follow Christ's example and use their strength (recognized with a beatitude in Rom 14:22) to carry the weak. It is in Rom 15:5 that for the first time the strong are obviously no longer being addressed, but rather the whole church.

11. Together with Gäckle, *Die Starken*, 391 and many others one could presume that the "prayer-wish" for both groups in Rom 15:5-6 ends the long section that has been addressing the strong. But Rom 15:7 continues the train of thought, drawing a logical conclusion (διό) from v. 6 and with δόξα again picks up the keyword δοξάζειν from v. 6.

12. Ibid., 389 must be rejected when he writes, "there is a clear line of thought in the four sections 14:1-12, 13-23; 15:1-6 and 7-13, but a skillfully crafted overall structure in the text cannot be discerned" (my translation).

Introduction (14:1)	Admonitions for both groups: προσλαμβάνεσθε
Section 1 (14:2–9)	
14:2–6	Parallel structures—two groups alternately being admonished to respect each other
14:7–9	Both groups jointly are given the underlying christological principle, also arranged in *parallelismus membrorum*
Section 2 (14:10—15:4)	
14:10ab	Parallelism (recourse to v. 3)—the behavior of both groups successively critically questioned
14:10c–13a	Explanation for the first group
14:10c	Argument
14:11	Scripture quotation
14:12–13a	Application of the Scripture quotation
14:13b	Transition (play on the various meanings of the word κρίνειν)
14:13c–15:4	Explanation for the second group (in two parts)
14:13c–18	Arguments, part 1
14:19	General summary
14:20—15:1	Arguments, part 2
15:2	General summary
15:3	Scripture quotation
15:4	Application of the Scripture quotation
Conclusion (15:5–13)	
15:5–6	"Prayer-wish" for both groups
15:7	Admonitions for both groups: προσλαμβάνεσθε (recourse to v. 1)
15:8–9	Reason for praising God (in parallelism), for each group separately
15:10–12	Scriptural quotes for joint praise
15:13	"Prayer-wish" for both groups

Parallelism is an important structural element of the pericope.[13] The whole section is dominated by the juxtaposition of the two groups pre-

---

13. Meeks, "Judgment," 291 speaks of a "pattern of reciprocity"; cf. Weiss, "Beiträge," 245.

sented in Rom 14:12. In the first part we repeatedly find parallel-structured statements, although not always of the same length, which initially address the two groups alternately. This section ends with a christological statement, which, although it is for both groups, has a parallel structure (14:7–9). In the second section there is a question in parallel form posed to both groups, followed by admonishing sections—one for each group. In the third section, Rom 15:8–9, we again find a parallel structure. An overview of the numerous parallelisms in this section reveals the following form, wherein the two groups are designated as A and B:

Section 1 (14:2–9)			
14:2		AB	Parallelism
14:3–4		AB+	Parallelism with an explanation added to the second injunction
14:5		AB	Parallelism
14:6a		A(B)	Parallelism (elliptic: later text traditions add the second line)
14:6b		AB	Parallelism
14:7			Parallelism (vv. 7–9 apply to both groups)
14:8			Parallelism
14:8c–9			Summary
Section 2 (14:10—15:4)			
14:10ab		AB	Parallelism (recourse to v. 3)
14:10c–13a		A	Explanation A
14:13c—15:4		B	Explanation B (in two parts: distinctly longer)
Conclusion (15:5–13)			
15:5–7			"Prayer-wish" (τὸ αὐτὸ φρονεῖν ἐν ἀλλήλοις) and admonition for all (προσλαμβάνεσθε ἀλλήλους)
15:8–9		AB	Parallelism (partly elliptic)
15:10–13			Scripture quotes and "prayer-wish" for all (χαρὰ καὶ εἰρήνη)

The frequent parallelism in this section can be understood as a "performative text strategy"[14] indicating that the text was designed to be read out before a disunited audience. On the one hand, this kind of

---

14. Maassen, "Text und Performanz," 291.

parallelism can presuppose differences between groups in the audience. This appears to be the case in Rom 14:1—15:13, which speaks of mutual criticism or contempt as a situation that must be overcome. On the other hand, the performance of a text that assumes differences can itself create divisions in the audience. Any latent tensions in the audience might then be brought into awareness, or the many groups and personal interests present in the audience could be bundled into two opposing camps. This second scenario could also be significant for Rom 14:1—15:13, since among the believers in Rome there were certainly not only those who had clearly positioned themselves in the conflict, but also others who were either vacillating or indifferent.[15]

The constant switching between one group and the other in the first section, the intensive attention to both groups in the second part, and the common address to both groups in the third section all reflect the linguistic journey that the listeners take during the presentation: from the division of the believers into two groups to the shaping of a new togetherness. This does not mean that the diversity must be abandoned, as the final parallelism in Rom 15:8-9 reminds us: despite the different reasons for praising God, the hymn can be sung in unity.[16] The parallelism lends to the converging perspective of the diverging viewpoints a linguistic form.

Verse-by-verse Interpretation

Romans 14:1

Paul begins with the injunction Τὸν δὲ ἀσθενοῦντα τῇ πίστει προσλαμβάνεσθε, μὴ εἰς διακρίσεις διαλογισμῶν.[17] Who is being addressed and should accept the weak in faith? This is not obvious. There are two possibilities.

1) It is usually accepted[18] that Paul in using the designation "weak" takes up a common expression, albeit a discriminatory one, used by

---

15. Cf. Minear, *Obedience of Faith*, 8–15.

16. Jewett, *Romans*, 885; cf. Jewett, "Ecumenical Theology."

17. "Now accept the one who is weak in faith, but not for the purpose of passing judgment on his opinions."

18. Cf. e.g., Michel, *Römer*, 296, 298; Schmidt, *Römer*, 227; Minear, *Obedience of Faith*, 8, 10; Wilckens, *Römer*, 3:87, 111; Schmithals, *Römerbrief*, 495; Jewett, *Romans*, 834.

those in Rome with no scruples about eating meat to label those who, for reasons of faith, only eat vegetables.[19] The "strong" are usually considered to be Gentile Christians and the "weak" to be Jewish Christians. Since the last mentioned would not have designated themselves in a derogatory manner, the injunction in verse 1 can only be directed at those using the discriminatory term.[20]

This interpretation has problems, however: Paul in verse 3 denounces the contempt with which some of the Roman Christians receive the others. If Paul used of the descriptor "weak" with such a disparaging significance, then he would himself be continuing the contempt he is taking position against. What chance would he then have of being heard by the "strong"? Could his call to accept the "weak" be taken seriously if he himself were using a contemptuous formulation?[21] And would he not thus close the ears of the "weak" because he had taken sides with the others?

2) It is also possible that the designation "weak in faith" does not borrow the discriminatory language of the letter's recipients in Rome, but that it was Paul's own formulation.[22] This is supported by the following points:

a) In connection with the question in the Corinthian church about meat offered to the idols, Paul had explained the behavior of some church members in a way understandable to others: that some had a weak conscience (1 Cor 8:7). After that he spoke in an abbreviated way of the "weak." Thus Paul had a history of using this designation, and it could be that he now used it again.[23]

---

19. Wilckens, *Römer*, 3:81 also thinks "eating vegetables" is a discriminatory designation used by the "strong."

20. Thus e.g., Bartsch, "Empfänger," 85.

21. Schmithals, *Römerbrief*, 496-97 recognizes this problem and circumvents it by assuming that at the time of receiving the presumed "Rome B" letter there were only "strong followers of Paul" in Rome. He ignores the fact that Paul addresses clear admonishments to those abstaining (494). It is also unclear how a controversy could escalate in a uniform church to which Jewish Christians were simply asking for membership. Byrne, *Romans*, 405 recognizes the problem as well. Jewett, *Romans*, 834-36 argues that Paul uses the terminology used by the "strong" in order to take a position against the disparaging attitude it expresses and to end the humiliating status of the "weak."

22. This view is now supported, with good reasons, by Gäckle, *Die Starken*, 444-49; cf. also Sampley, "Weak," 46-48, who, however, disputes the existence of two stable groups.

23. Cf. Schneider, *Schwachen*, 130, 132-33. Wilckens, *Römer*, 3:87 presumes a

b) When the "weak" are first mentioned in Rom 14:1, an explanation is included: τῇ πίστει. However, this explanation is not as detailed as in 1 Cor 8:7, where Paul introduces the terminus for the Corinthians.[24] Nevertheless this would be unnecessary if Paul chose to adopt a common Roman speech convention.

c) Paul explains in Rom 14:2 whom he sees as the "weak": those who eat vegetables. This explanation would be unnecessary if he was using terminology common to Roman Christians.

d) The corresponding designation "strong" is found for the first and only time in Rom 15:1. (It is completely absent in 1 Cor 8.) If this were common language, then it would be to be expected that "the strong," or a similar designation for those who have no scruples about eating meat, would already have been mentioned in Rom 14:2.

e) In addition, in Rom 15:1 the contrast is expressed using different wording than in Rom 14:2: οἱ δυνατοί and οἱ ἀδύνατοι instead of οἱ ἀσθενοῦντες. This change likely reflects terminology chosen by Paul and not an expression in common use.

f) Most important, it is not to be assumed that Paul's term "weak" has a pejorative meaning. Although the terms ἀσθενοῦντες and ἀδύνατοι were usually used for lower or inferior social classes, and often in a deprecatory sense,[25] Paul uses them when he wants to elevate the status of people. In 1 Cor 8:7 Paul solicits understanding for the brothers by referring to their past and their weak consciences. He wants to relieve them of accusations and disparagement. In 1 Cor 12:22 Paul argues using the image of the weakest members of the body (μέλη τοῦ σώματος ἀσθενέστερα), taking for granted that they are not disrespected but instead are given special attention. In Gal 6:2 Paul demands from his readers that they carry each

---

dependence of the language in Rome on that in Corinth, since a coincidental development of the same terminology would otherwise be difficult to explain. However, he considers the term "weak" to be discriminatory and asserts that it was brought to Rome by church members from Corinth who considered themselves to be freed from the law.

24. There, those not knowing that the eating of meat offered to the gods is irrelevant, have a weak *conscience*. Here it is not the weakness of conscience but the weakness of *faith*. There are, however, many similarities. See the comparisons made by Schneider, *Schwachen*, 58–67 and especially Gäckle, *Die Starken*, 438–44; cf. also Meeks, "Judgment," 293.

25. On this, cf. Theissen, "Starken"; Reasoner, *Strong*, 45–63 and the comments in Jewett, *Romans*, 834–36, 876–78; in contrast, Gäckle, *Die Starken*, 376 does not see a social background for Paul's designations.

other's burdens (τὰ βάρη βαστάζετε). It is Paul's express concern in this connection that a brother who may be guilty of some error is not looked down upon, and that no one boasts because of him (cf. v. 1 and v. 3). Therefore, this carrying of one another's burden does *not* have a derogatory connotation here but instead is intended to arouse sympathy and compassion.[26] Paul formulates it similarly in Rom 15:1: We who are able should bear the weaknesses of the ones who are not able (τὰ ἀσθενήματα βαστάζειν). The message here is about sympathy and helpfulness. This features no derogatory tone. Jesus, who cared for the weak (Rom 5:6; 15:7), sets the standard for helpfulness. Additionally, by applying the command in Lev 19:14 that forbids putting stumbling blocks in the way of a stranger (perhaps, that is, the blind), Paul also "presumes that the 'weak' have a certain need for protection."[27] That means, if Paul is not speaking in a derogatory manner about weaknesses (ἀσθενήματα), then it can be assumed that the reference to the "weak in faith" in Rom 14:1 is not meant disparagingly. It is more likely a well-meaning description.[28] This understanding does not present the problem of Paul himself doing what he denounces among the Roman Christians—showing contempt for the "weak."

If the term "weak" was not a term in common use by the Roman believers to denote a certain group of the church members and, therefore, if it was not immediately clear to the audience whom Paul means by the ἀσθενῶν (and who would be the strong), then those receiving the letter and hearing the call to accept the "weak" would all be able to identify themselves with the "strong." Thus Paul would initially ensure that each listener felt he or she is being spoken to.[29] By using this wording, Paul first invites all Roman Christians to see their fellow Christians in a new light and to start treating them appropriately: they are not stubbornly stuck in the past or underdeveloped and subject to God's condemnation; rather they are valuable fellow Christians in need of love and help.

26. Keck, *Romans*, 349 also points this out; cf. Gäckle, *Die Starken*, 415.

27. Michel, *Römer*, 308 (my translation).

28. Cf. Godet, *Römer*, 266: "This expression is somewhat more considerate" (my translation). Perhaps it comes from the educational system, as Haacker, "Römerbrief als Friedensmemorandum," 38, n. 35 suggests, in the sense of "beginner" in contrast to the "advanced student." However, Haacker, like many others, believes that the expression is borrowed from the language used by the "strong." Cf. Luther, *Römerbrief*, 464, who speaks about the normal weakness of a young boy.

29. Sampley, "Weak," 47–48.

What is the issue addressed by the admonition to accept the "weak" in faith? It is directly followed by an explanation: church members should not quarrel over opinions.[30] Paul assumes that the Roman Christians were trying to convert each other to their respectively held conceptions. Apparently everyone was convinced he or she was in the right. Paul says right at the start, before taking any kind of position on the point under debate, that the questions being debated are of secondary importance. Listeners would have understood the word διαλογισμοί as downplaying the significance of their disputed opinions. They themselves would not have called them "speculations" or "scruples."[31] By using the plural, Paul additionally downplays their significance, making it clear that it is not a question of "*the* truth," but rather of a multitude of human speculations. The dispute over opinions is relativized. The relationship of the church members to one another is shown to be more important than the question of facts; "law" and "truth" are less important than love and unity. Paul opens a new perspective on their situation and invites them to act accordingly.[32]

How would the Roman Christians have received this argument? In a controversy one tries to justify oneself and find allies. What Paul does is to downplay the zeal of *both* sides in propagating their own "truth." The representatives of *both* concepts would have reacted skeptically to Paul's words. On the other hand, Paul's use of the word προσλαμβάνειν brings a new thought into the controversy, which has its own appeal. Every controversy causes distress; disharmony makes the church unattractive for believers and nonbelievers: a "war of words" is a tiring burden. Paul's exhortations open up a way to overcome the dispute, without one position triumphing over the other. They should accept one another unconditionally and not make their fellowship—specifically their table fellowship[33]—dependent on whether the others have the "right" understanding or not.

The symbolic character of the performative space should also be noted here. The first reading of the letter—as well as subsequent readings—was performed during the meeting of believers. The direct form of address in the passage (Rom 14:4, 10, 15, 20-22) shows that

---

30. μὴ εἰς διακρίσεις διαλογισμῶν: without [entering] into disputes about opinions.

31. Cf. Schmidt, *Römer*, 227.

32. Crafton, "Paul's Rhetorical Vision," 337: "new [rhetorical] vision of life in the body of Christ."

33. Michel, *Römer*, 298-99.

representatives of both groups were present.³⁴ The place where this happened was likely one of the larger home churches. A regular part of their meetings was a common meal.³⁵ Therefore the performance took place at a location more fitting than any other to create a family atmosphere, foster fellowship and hospitality, and serve as a venue for the communal meal. The term προσλαμβάνεσθαι, which Paul uses to tell the Roman believers what they should do, can, concretely, mean "hospitality" (2 Macc 10:15; Acts 18:26; 28:2; cf. for λαμβάνειν John 13:20; 2 John 10). This means that during the performance, the surroundings would have given the listeners a vivid illustration of what was expected of them. The presenter might even have gestured towards the room where their common meal had taken place. It would be a contradiction in itself to sit together with someone in the same house and perhaps share a meal without accepting and welcoming him or her. In this manner, the symbolism of the performative space would reinforce what was said in the performance.

Romans 14:2

Verse 2 has a parallel structure and describes the situation: there were differences of opinion among the Roman Christians concerning what could be eaten.

A	ὃς μὲν πιστεύει φαγεῖν πάντα,
B	ὁ δὲ ἀσθενῶν λάχανα ἐσθίει.³⁶
A	One person has faith that he may eat all things,
B	but he who is weak eats vegetables [only].

---

34. The separation could not have been as absolute as Minear suggests (*Obedience of Faith*, 7)—with no common church services, no common meals, no collective feasts—because otherwise the discussions (14:1) and attempts to influence one another (which are assumed by what is said in 14:15, 20, 23) would not have been possible. This argues against Jewett's suggestion, *Romans*, 835-36, 840 that it was a controversy about the admission to the communal meal.

35. Klinghardt, *Gemeinschaftsmahl*, 271-95; Smit, "Symposium"; Taussig, *In the Beginning*, 21-54.

36. Jewett, *Romans*, 837-38 hears a tone of mockery in the lapidary and exaggerated form of expression used ("all" and "vegetables"). "The rhetorical effect of placing these parameters so far beyond the likely, actual behavior of groups in Rome is to enable each group to smile and feel included in the subsequent argument" (p. 838). More

It probably concerned questions in connection to the provisions of the *Jewish* law,[37] because Paul uses the keyword κοινός in Rom 14:14, not used anywhere else by him, which is typically used for Jewish dietary regulations.[38] In addition Paul introduces in Rom 15:8–12 the contrast between Jews and Gentiles in his treatment of controversies in Rome, a contrast that has been seen throughout the letter.[39] Paul generalizes on the dietary questions and points to the fundamental issue, a question of faith (v. 1: τὸν δὲ ἀσθενοῦντα τῇ πίστει). This is an indication that Paul sees the specific controversies in Rome as symptoms of the general problem of coexistence between Jews and Gentiles in one church.[40] However, there may also have been Gentile Christians among those following the Jewish laws, just as there were Jewish Christians—like Aquila and Prisca (16:3)—among those of the more liberal persuasion.[41] Obviously, Paul

---

likely than the reaction of the listeners as conjectured by Jewett is that they would have felt that their convictions were not being taken seriously. If, however, the background of the wording was the derisive language used by *both* groups in Rome themselves, in order to defame the opposing group, then the listeners would have clearly recognized his sarcasm when Paul uses their words. In this way he would show how absurd he considers the controversy to be from both perspectives. The listeners would have been disquieted.

37. Thus the majority of interpreters, cf. Wilckens, *Römer*, 3:79, 112–13; Meeks, "Judgment," 292; Schneider, *Schwachen*, 126; Moo, *Romans*, 828–31; Gäckle, *Die Starken*, 361. Shogren, "Kingdom," 248–51 demonstrates that by abstaining from certain foods, the Jews could be expressing their fundamental rejection of the Gentile dominion ("conscientious hero").

38. Schneider, *Schwachen*, 121; Byrne, *Romans*, 404–5; Gäckle, *Die Starken*, 369–70.

39. Why didn't Paul describe the contrasts right from the beginning as ethnic tensions? Why does he at first avoid all references to Jewish regulations? Apparently, he does not want the normal ethnic differences to intensify the religious differences. Cf. Oestreich, "Ethnische und religöse Spannungen," 202–3; Keck, *Romans*, 335; also similarly Gäckle, *Die Starken*, 377–78, 398.

40. Crafton, "Paul's Rhetorical Vision," 331–32: Paul theologizes the problem of the Romans, in order to show where it fits in his vision of all peoples praising God together; cf. Wilckens, *Römer*, 3:107.

41. Cf. Stuhlmacher, *Römer*, 195; Reid, "Paul's Rhetoric," 137; also Brown, "Not Jewish Christianity." Crafton, "Paul's Rhetorical Vision," 336–37 suggests that the people described by Paul are caricatures or typical characters. It could be that certain individuals particularly stood out. Karris, "Rom 14:1—15:13," 170, following Rauer, *Die "Schwachen" in Korinth*, 88, 95, also speaks of individuals. He contests that there were two confronting parties in Rome (Karris, "Rom 14:1—15:13," 158–59) and contends that Paul did not have in mind a specific situation in the Roman church, but is making a general call to unity motivated by his experience in the Corinthian church (p. 164).

summarizes the variety of opinions and the differing intensity with which these were championed, reducing them to two groups. The question of which laws were actually being debated can be left open here, because they have no direct relevance for the objectives of this study.[42]

The parallelism, which Paul begins in verse 2 and which characterizes the whole section, is very important for understanding his argument. It is an expression of Paul's will to treat both sides in the same manner.[43] He does not take sides with one of the two disputing parties, but he takes a third position separate from the others.[44] Paul uses the same number of words and approximately the same length sentence for both sides. The fact that Paul keeps the same distance from both positions serves his goal of fostering peace among the believers. In this way he invites the Roman Christians to also step back and be more objective concerning the differences of opinion. He intends to break open the hardened fronts. At the same time, the parallelism is an important strategy for Paul in reconciling the quarreling parties: his use of parallelism makes it possible for him to alternately address the one side and then the other.

The objectivity and the descriptive distance with which Paul introduces the two positions as well as his alternation when addressing the two groups is mirrored in the performative space by the reader. As was usual in a performance, the reader stood in a position where he could be seen by the audience, and the audience often sat in a half circle. He could address both sides by moving his body and turning his gaze toward them, and if all members of the parties were not sitting together, he could indicate the sides symbolically through hand gestures. Through the arrangement of the persons in the room and the reader's gestures, the content of the written text being read became visible.

Can it be justified to say that both sides are being *addressed* alternately in verse 2? Doesn't vese 2 simply offer a description of both standpoints? It should be noted that only in verse 2—that is, after his admonition in verse 1 to accept the "weak"—does Paul identify who he is

---

42. For discussions of the various possibilities, see Schmithals, *Römerbrief*, 490–93; Schneider, *Schwachen*, 68–115; Reasoner, *Strong*, 102–38; Gäckle, *Die Starken*, 337–61.

43. Cf. Gäckle, *Die Starken*, 387.

44. In Rom 1:11–12, we can see that Paul found it somewhat problematic to take such a stance in a church he was not yet familiar with, because there he positioned himself *under* the Roman Christians again after having first quite naturally taken a position *before* them as the giver. Cf. also the change of position in Rom 15:14–15 and 15:30.

calling the "weak." He had left this open at first. Paul achieves two things by placing the clarification after the admonition. On the one hand, the emotional appeal in verse 1 to give support and show empathy is more strongly applied to those who have freed themselves from the Jewish regulations. But this becomes clear only in retrospect. Now they know that the admonition in verse 1 was meant for them. They receive correction for their *behavior*. Such an explanation that sheds new light on the foregoing statement and opens up new aspects for the listeners has the effect of refreshing in the memory what has already been said and giving it new force.

On the other hand, Paul shows, if only implicitly, what he himself thinks about the matters under debate (explicitly then in 14:14). He criticizes the cause of the "weak" side (having already downgraded its importance). They receive a correction of their *understanding*. Thus, verse 2 in connection with verse 1 contains both an objectively descriptive parallelism and a corrective parallelism, which Paul indeed applies alternately to both groups.

Romans 14:3–4

The following verses continue in the same vein. Verse 3 contains two parallel admonitions, one for each of the disputing parties.

A	ὁ ἐσθίων τὸν μὴ ἐσθίοντα μὴ ἐξουθενείτω,
B	ὁ δὲ μὴ ἐσθίων τὸν ἐσθίοντα μὴ κρινέτω.
A	The one who eats is not to regard with contempt the one who does not eat,
B	and the one who does not eat is not to judge the one who eats.

Again perfect parallelism is used. The difference in the beginning of the two sentences lies only in the position of the negation μὴ. That forces the presenter to clearly distinguish the two sentences from each other and to emphasize the μὴ. This makes the parallelism even clearer. The two differing verbs at the end of the sentences, that is, in positions of emphasis, are in the third-person imperative, that is, not addressing any individual directly. But they have been chosen to specifically fit the typical behavior of each of the groups so that there can be no doubt as to who is meant.

First, the eaters are admonished not to treat the abstainers with contempt.[45] The term "weak," with its emotional connotations, is not repeated. Paul returns to a more objective designation: "he who does not eat." Apparently the eaters feel themselves superior. They ridicule the abstainers and treat them with contempt. They hear that Paul does not condone their behavior. At the same time the abstainers hear Paul speaking up for them. He admonishes the one group (the eaters) while at the same time speaking up for the other one (the abstainers).

It follows the admonition that the abstainers should not judge the eaters. This group meets the eaters' derision by condemning the eating of meat, as verses 3c–4 suggest, probably in view of God's final judgment. Again Paul speaks positively about one group (the eaters) while directly criticizing the other one (the abstainers).

According to the usual protocol for the reception of official letters to a group, it is likely that the reader was a Roman Christian. That means he would have known exactly who was being spoken to. It would have taken much self-discipline for the reader *not* to look toward each respective group being addressed when he read the parallel sentences, even just to see what their reactions to the admonitions would be. And since the groups were situated so that they could see each other—that is, on three sides of the room, in a half-circle, or on one or more triclinia[46]—the audience, with their glances, would also have sought out those whom Paul was addressing with each of his parallel imperatives. They too would have known the most prominent representatives of the groups juxtaposed in Paul's parallelism.

The performance is therefore embedded in the text in the sense that it influences where the presenter and the audience would direct their gazes. Only a minority of the audience would be neutral in the dispute about what to eat or what not to eat and so would, so to speak, look from a distance at one group and then the other. The majority of the audience would feel that they belonged to one of the two groups in question and would watch the other group when it was mentioned. That means that the representatives of the disputing groups would be looking at each other.

---

45. In the following the group of Roman Christians who were convinced that they could eat everything will be called the "eaters." The group who avoided certain food, whom Paul calls the "weak," will be called the "abstainers." These designations draw on the respective characteristic behaviors as mentioned by Paul in v. 2. The widely used designations "strong" and "weak" will be avoided here since *for us* they include a judgmental element which, in my opinion, was not intended by Paul.

46. Cf. Klinghardt, *Gemeinschaftsmahl*, 62–97 on rooms and seating arrangements.

Paul was admonishing them not to look negatively upon one another. The performance initiated interaction between the groups.

The two exhortations are not the same length. The second has an additional thought (v. 3c)[47] and is then complemented by the illustration about the servant of another (v. 4). God has accepted the eaters. The judgment proclaimed over the eaters by the abstainers apparently referred to whether one would stand or fall in the final judgment. We can deduce that abstainers had questioned God's acceptance of the eaters. But Paul is certain that God's acceptance is founded solely on what God does and not on human observance of the law—a central theme of the Letter to the Romans. As we have already seen in verse 1, Paul again puts the disputed question into perspective. Whether one can eat or not, this is an opinion that in the end is irrelevant. This brings, for the first time, an eschatological aspect into the passage.

With the supplement in verses 3c–4, Paul again speaks in favor of the group that he is not momentarily addressing. He says to the abstainers, God has accepted the eaters.[48] The performance not only directs their attention to the eaters but also instructs the abstainers to see the eaters in a positive light. This corresponds to the positive way the eaters should view the abstainers, namely, as those in need of consideration for their weakness. The interaction between the groups involved initiated by the performance helps them to view each other positively: with respect and with the certainty that God has accepted the other group.

In verse 4, Paul brings in a new argument. He introduces it with the metaphor of another man's household slave who is responsible solely to his or her own master. It is quite possible that there were servants present at the meeting, perhaps also owners of house slaves. This makes the metaphor especially relevant.

What function does this metaphor presented in the style of a diatribe have? Paul uses it to separate the disputing groups. The verdict that the abstainers pronounced over the eaters, perhaps also the attempt to convince them of the correctness of their own practice, presupposes that the church members belong together, that the church only has *one* common Lord, and that therefore only a *uniform* practice can be the right practice. Paul contradicts this: each individual stands alone before his or

---

47. Stuhlmacher, *Römer*, 198 falsely says that the supplement refers to "the brother whose faith is still weak" (my translation).

48. Nygren, *Römerbrief*, 316; Michel, *Römer*, 300; Schmidt, *Römer*, 228; contrary to Meeks, "Judgment," 295, who thinks that both the "strong" and the "weak" are being addressed here, as does Schmithals, *Römerbrief*, 498.

her Lord, he says. Just how important this argument is for Paul is shown by the fact that he returns to it in verse 12 and also in verse 22. Paul's argument concerning another man's servant separates the listeners from each other. To unify the diverse members and opinions within the church is no longer specifically the concern of the church. It is the *Lord* who joins together the diverse actions of his servants and makes a whole out of the diversity. Thus the diversity under which the church is suffering has its place "in the Lord" and can therefore be endured on earth.[49]

Why does Paul introduce this argument with a verbal image? Metaphors give a new structure to the experience and knowledge of those realities being addressed. A metaphor superimposes the structure of the image's reality (here the slaves of different households) atop the discussed reality (the relation of the church members). Paul's metaphor teaches the Roman Christians to see themselves as if they were a gathering of house slaves who have differing responsibilities and duties, perhaps meeting at the market. There it would be normal that the servant of one master would have nothing to do with the servant of another master. This way of viewing themselves (as more distanced from one another) gains plausibility through the metaphor taken from the listeners' social environment. If Paul had introduced this argument without using a metaphor, he would probably garnered protests for what he said.

Paul's metaphor has a mediating function. It prevents a hard clash between the original view and the metaphorically introduced one. It separates contrasting perceptions of an issue from each other by raising a completely different issue and pushing that issue between the contrasting perceptions of the previous one. By using a metaphor, Paul implements in the linguistic sphere what he does logically with the content of his arguments: he separates opposites from one another in order to make peaceful cooperation possible.[50] At the same time, the metaphor mediates between the speaker and the listeners. Direct language confronts the listeners with criticism; metaphorical language invites listeners to apply the criticism hidden in metaphor to themselves.[51]

---

49. Cf. Meeks, *Origin*, 216–17.

50. Gestrich, "Sprache der Versöhnung," 504: "The [metaphorical] transfer lies in the utilization of yet uncontaminated or unencumbered configurations on the great carpet of language, which are therefore more 'able to take the load of meaning' at the present moment" (my translation). Cf. also Gestrich on the reconciling and peacemaking functions of speech in general.

51. Cf. Sampley, "Weak," 45.

The strength of a metaphor depends on how convincing the postulated analogy is. Would the Roman Christians have accepted the meeting of unrelated slaves as an analogy for the company of believers? Paul's argumentat would have met resistance from those who not only wanted to be accepted without changing their standpoint and conduct, but who also desired to be proved right and to convince the others. Paul would have been listened to by those who were tired of the disputes and had suffered under the discrimination of the respective opponents.

Just as he had at the end of verse 3, so in verse 4 Paul again verifies that God will accept the eaters and their actions (σταθήσεται). The judgment of the eaters over the abstainers will be overcome and averted by the greater judgment of God. Paul does not argue about the question of what is right, but he uses an argument from authority: God has the last word. Paul does not speak here of the fact that he is of the same opinion as the eaters, doubtless in order to preserve his distanced position and in order not to abandon his objectivity.

Romans 14:5

Verse 5 brings into play a new difference in Christian behavior: the observance of special days. Again it is not completely clear what the dispute was about: the weekly Sabbath, Jewish feasts, fasting times, or (heathen) bad days?[52] In the context of the observance of dietary laws it is probable that it was about days of fasting.[53] Since this study concerns the performance of the letter, this question can be left open.

The verse is very similar in form to the parallelism in verse 2.

A	ὃς μὲν [γὰρ] κρίνει ἡμέραν παρ' ἡμέραν,
B	ὃς δὲ κρίνει πᾶσαν ἡμέραν·
C	ἕκαστος ἐν τῷ ἰδίῳ νοΐ πληροφορείσθω.
A	One person regards one day above another,
B	another regards every day [alike].
C	Each person must be fully convinced in his own mind.

---

52. For a discussion, see Gäckle, *Die Starken*, 351–59.

53. Cf. Dederen, "On Esteeming"; Karris, "Rom 14:1—15:13," 77; Reasoner, *Strong*, 158, who remains undecided. Some think it was about Sabbath observance—for example Stuhlmacher, *Römer*, 198; Sampley, "Weak," 48; Weiss, "Paul and the Judging"; Gäckle, *Die Starken*, 358–59, 361. For a discussion, cf. Dederen, "On Esteeming"; Reasoner, *Strong*, 146–58; Gäckle, *Die Starken*, 351–59.

However there are three differences. First, the groups are referred to in the opposite order. Those observing dietary laws are referred to last in verse 2; those obeying the rules about days are referred to first in verse 5. Second, there is no explicit or implicit assessment or admonition here as is in verses 1–2. There is no emotional appeal to one of the sides, and no standpoint is being indirectly criticized. Third, Paul adds a last statement which summarizes both of the positions he has mentioned: Each person must be fully convinced in his own mind.

Especially because of the last two differences, it is—in contrast to the previous discussion on the question of eating meat—impossible to associate positions on observing particular days with specific Roman Christians.[54] So in making this statement Paul's objective is not, as has been widely assumed, to pinpoint another dispute among the Roman Christians. Perhaps the observance of days was not an acute problem in Rome. Why does Paul mention it at all? He wants to say, there are even more problems one could dispute,[55] but one really shouldn't. In this way Paul shows that the acute problems in Rome can be seen in a broader perspective—a perspective that allows disputing parties to step back. What we see here is a generalization, an abstraction. Sampley evaluates the generalization and concludes that it is a rhetorical device to free the disputing parties from their deadlocked opinions and to invite them to gain a more objective perspective.[56]

This interpretation is underlined by the afterthought in verse 5c. For the first time in the passage Paul summarizes two parallel statements, one addressed to each of the conflicting sides, with a third statement valid for both sides. The linguistic form used here reveals the strategy behind the argument: the opposing positions are named and resolved in the superordinate statement. The positions are unmasked as personal convictions and put into perspective. At first Paul demonstrates that this is possible using a question not under dispute in Rome. He can reckon

---

54. Many commentators take it for granted that it was the abstainers who were also observing feast days. Paul does not specify that, as Sampley, "Weak," 41, 46 has rightly observed.

55. And which are disputed in other places; cf. Gal 4:10, where Paul reacts differently, and Col 2:16.

56. Sampley, "Weak," 42; cf. Cicero, *Or. Brut.* 14.45–46, where he instructs the orator to "always turn off the controversy, as much as possible, from particular persons and times, (for we may argue more at liberty concerning general topics than about circumstances) in such a manner that what is proved to be true *universally*, may necessarily appear to be so in all *subordinate* cases" (translation: E. Jones).

with agreement concerning a *theoretically possible* controversy over the observance of feast days and thus can prepare the way for agreement in the *current* controversy over dietary questions.

Romans 14:6

This verse has a bridging function: it leads from the observation of feast days, which Paul had introduced, back to the controversial questions of diet. The verse has three lines: the first line has two parts, and the other two lines have three parts each.

A	ὁ φρονῶν τὴν ἡμέραν	κυρίῳ φρονεῖ·	
B	—		
A	καὶ ὁ ἐσθίων	κυρίῳ ἐσθίει,	εὐχαριστεῖ γὰρ τῷ θεῷ·
B	καὶ ὁ μὴ ἐσθίων	κυρίῳ οὐκ ἐσθίει	καὶ εὐχαριστεῖ τῷ θεῷ.
A	He who observes the day,	observes [it] for the Lord,	
B	—		
A	and he who eats,	does so for the Lord,	for he gives thanks to God;
B	and he who eats not,	for the Lord he does not eat,	and gives thanks to God.

The exact parallelism of the last two lines leads one—only after first listening to the complete verse, however—to expect a corresponding parallel in the first line. Such an addition is indeed found in some later manuscripts. It is, however, clearly secondary. Why didn't Paul formulate a parallelism in the first line? It appears that he is in a hurry to return to the dietary question. In a sense, he leaves the theme of the observance of days apparently prematurely, before finishing the parallelism. This observation confirms once again the assumption that the observance of certain days was not a point of contention in Rome and was only brought into the argument as a generalization. After gleaning agreement that there was no cause to quarrel over certain days, Paul returns to the question of eating meat, which is under dispute in Rome, in order to achieve reconciliation in this matter by the same strategy.

It can be seen in the form of the two lines in verse 6b–c that Paul is building on the argument in verse 5. So in verse 6, as in verse 5a–b, the two standpoints are named without being judged: "whoever eats . . ." and "whoever abstains . . ." A statement is added for each standpoint that is the same for both: κυρίῳ. This addition corresponds to the statement in verse 5c, which is also valid for both standpoints.

In contrast to verse 5c, the statement in verse 6 that is valid for both groups has an explanatory extension: "for he gives thanks to God." This explanation refers to the prayer of thanksgiving, which, according to Jewish and also Christian custom, was offered before meals. Here that which is valid for both groups is, in contrast to the very general formulation in verse 5c, concretely tied to day-to-day living. Here again it is helpful to take a look at the space in which the performance took place: if the letter was being presented in the symposium part of the gathering of believers, the traces left by the common meal would still have been visible in the room. The fact that all had given thanks for the meal would still be alive in everybody's memory.

Each practice is brought into connection with the Lord. As in verses 3c-4 (and in the Letter to the Romans as a whole) the Christian's behavior is not measured by whether they comply with the law's ordinances or not, but rather by their relationship with the Lord. Paul values each behavior positively. Each person can know that he or she is accepted, because his or her motives have been judged positively. Nobody's faith or relationship to the Lord is called into question. In this way Paul does what he expects the Roman Christians to do: to not judge others and to not treat them with contempt.

The concrete expression of the relationship to the Lord—the thanks given to God—shows that Paul is thinking from the perspective of the eaters. The reason for the thanks given to God is somewhat theoretical for the abstainers, because it would make more sense to give thanks for something that one eats than for something one does not eat. Paul endeavors to be as objective as possible in his arguments, not to side with either of the parties. That is the reason for the formulation's strict parallelism. However, his personal convictions can be seen repeatedly, if only indirectly. Abstainers in particular would have noticed that Paul was trying to be objective, even though he did not agree with their opinion. This would have added credibility to his argument.

Romans 14:7–9

These verses present a passage that cannot be assigned to either of the contending parties but is meant for both (οὐδεὶς γὰρ ἡμῶν). At the same time, these arguments form the conclusion of the first part of Paul's argumentation. In this way Paul, as he has already shown in verse 5 with an uncontroversial example, leads the two parties form differences to commonalities.

Despite this, these verses also have a consistent parallel structure. Verse 7 introduces a new contrast: life and death.[57] It is hard to imagine a sharper contrast. Verse 8 formulates things very similarly to verse 6: in each line the verb is repeated, with the qualification "to the Lord." The τῷ κυρίῳ takes up again the thought from verse 6 and the metaphor of the servant from verse 4,[58] and brings everything together in Christ.

This clearly reveals Paul's strategy. The sharp contrast—life and death—is connected by Christ, he is the Lord of all (cf. 1 Thess 5:10).[59] The easier is deduced from the more difficult: if Christ can connect even such opposites as life and death, how much more can he reconcile the differences between the Roman Christians.[60] "The behaviors so important to the two groups (vv. 5–6) now appear small and insignificant in contrast to Jesus Christ's fundamental sovereignty over the life of each individual."[61] At the same time, Paul can—as in verse 5—proceed on the assumption that the overcoming of this contrast in Christ is not a point of contention among the letter's recipients.[62] This is additionally backed up by the christological statement in verse 9: Christ is the Lord of the living and the dead, because he died and lives again. In this way Paul ultimately bases his argument on the heart of the Christian creed (cf. 1 Cor 15:3–4). In so doing Paul presumes that each of the disputants belongs to Christ.[63]

Verses 7–9 compose the first climax of the performance.

---

57. Schmithals, *Römerbrief*, 500 believes it is only mentioned due to tradition and is not motivated by the current context; cf. also p. 502.

58. Gäckle, *Die Starken*, 413.

59. On how Paul thinks in antitheses, cf. Weiss, "Beiträge," 175–81.

60. Cf. Luther, *Römerbrief*, 482.

61. Michel, *Römer*, 303 (my translation); cf. Jewett, *Romans*, 849.

62. Contrary to Schmidt, *Römer*, 229 who hears a hidden imperative in vv. 7–8.

63. This would contradict the interpretation from Nanos, *Mystery*, 154–57 that the "weak" are Jews from outside the Christian community.

7a	First parallel	οὐδεὶς γὰρ ἡμῶν ἑαυτῷ ζῇ
b	(9/10 syllables)	καὶ οὐδεὶς ἑαυτῷ ἀποθνῄσκει·
8a	Second parallel	ἐάν τε γὰρ ζῶμεν, τῷ κυρίῳ ζῶμεν,
b	(12/17 syllables)	ἐάν τε ἀποθνῄσκωμεν, τῷ κυρίῳ ἀποθνῄσκομεν.
c	Third parallel	ἐάν τε οὖν ζῶμεν,
d	(6/8 syllables)	ἐάν τε ἀποθνῄσκωμεν,
e	Conclusion	τοῦ κυρίου ἐσμέν.
9a	Aphorism	εἰς τοῦτο γὰρ Χριστὸς ἀπέθανεν καὶ ἔζησεν,
b		ἵνα καὶ νεκρῶν καὶ ζώντων κυριεύσῃ.
7a	First parallel	For not one of us lives for himself,
b		and not one dies for himself;
8a	Second parallel	for if we live, we live for the Lord,
b		or if we die, we die for the Lord;
c	Third parallel	therefore whether we live
d		or [whether we] die,
e	Conclusion	we are the Lord's.
9a	Aphorism	For to this end Christ died and lived again,
b		that He might be Lord both of the dead and of the living.

The language becomes hymnic.[64] The fourfold repetition of ἐάν τε lends the statement a certain forcefulness. The verb endings are identical and form an end rhyme. The sentences from verses 7 and 8 have a parallel structure and change repeatedly between ζῇ/ζῶμεν and ἀποθνῄσκει/ἀποθνῄσκομεν. The second parallelism is extended in length by respectively adding τῷ κυρίῳ. The third parallel is then shorter and moves toward the brief conclusion: τοῦ κυρίου ἐσμέν. It is followed in verse 9 by a maxim that summarizes the death and resurrection of Jesus in a creed-like form. Using the words νεκρῶν καὶ ζώντων it picks up once again on the contrast in verses 7 and 8 and closes with κυριεύσῃ, that is, with the root which has dominated the argument since verse 4.

That is poetic language. The presenter would have continually intensified the volume and expression in his voice. The parallel lines give the words a pulsating rhythm, which alternates between two extremes: life and

---

64. Michel, *Römer*, 303 thinks of a baptismal confession; Gäckle, *Die Starken*, 412 of phrasing that has been crafted in advance; Schlier, *Römerbrief*, 409 of a spontaneous hymn to Christ by Paul. It is quite thinkable that Paul lapses into poetic language while dictating.

death. The presenter would have spontaneously supported this rhythm by moving his hand back and forth. As the lines shorten in the third parallelism (v. 8c and d), hand movements would have accelerated until finally underlining the concluding words (v. 8e). The audience would have been carried away by such growing intensity in the speech—if it was performed well. It was not uncommon for the audience to become enthusiastic over masterly presentation and beautiful use of language. Performance indeed always included an evaluation of the medial aspect of language, that is, of the manner of the presentation. If the presenter succeeded in gaining approval for the form of the language, then this approval prepared the way for acceptance of the content. The following sentence (v. 9)—perhaps after a short pause—utilized the poetical momentum of the language to relate content. It is an aphorism, a weighty, succinctly worded sentence that aptly summarizes a comprehensive truth. Aphoristic sentences often gave the audience the opportunity to react with applause.[65] The presenter, inspired by the poetic form of the previous lines, emphatically intoned the truth of the aphorism and then paused. The audience understood this indirect invitation to react, and so applauded. Some of them likely called out, repeating parts of the speech: τοῦ κυρίου ἐσμέν. Others called out the early Christian creed hinted at in the aphorism: Χριστὸς κύριος. Who among those present could have resisted the beauty of the language? Who would have wanted to contradict the aphorism? Of course, we do not know whether the performance happened exactly like that. It is not the goal of performance criticism to determine that. The main concern is to reconstruct a possible and probable performance.

Romans 14:10a–b

After the applause died away, it was followed by a contrast that could not have been keener. The audience had just been united in their appreciation of the speaker, and then it found itself being sharply attacked, again with two parallel sentences (v. 10).

A	Σὺ δὲ τί κρίνεις τὸν ἀδελφόν σου;
B	ἢ καὶ σὺ τί ἐξουθενεῖς τὸν ἀδελφόν σου;
A	But you, why do you judge your brother?
B	Or you again, why do you regard your brother with contempt?

---

65. Korenjak, *Publikum und Redner*, 131; Shiner, *Proclaiming*, 154–57.

The two groups characterized in verse 2 are here addressed directly. Paul moves between addressees from one sentence to the other, without making the switch recognizable in the form of address. Both cases use an emphatic σύ, although it refers to different people in each sentence.[66] Such a procedure fits well in a situation of orality, where one can imagine the two questions each being connected to a physical turning of the body and pointing gestures.[67] That would be even more plausible if the representatives of each position were sitting grouped together. That is quite conceivable, since besides the religious aspects, the controversial concepts had also a social or ethnic component.[68] It was common to have an established seating order according to social affiliation.[69] Even if the opponents sat mixed together in the audience, the speaker could fix his eye on a representative of each of the groups. As in verse 3, the gaze of the groups in the audience is directed toward one another.

This time the representatives of both groups are directly accused of the wrongful behavior already described in verse 3: if you agreed to what has just been said, how could you judge or despise the brethren? If it is true that Christ is Lord over the greatest conceivable contrast, then the differences among the Roman Christians should not lead to mutual alienation. Once again, each side is admonished not to disdain the other. What is new is that the judged or the despised are called brethren. Here again there is an intensification.

How would the representatives of the different perceptions react to this way of speaking? What those on the one side would experience as criticism of their behavior would be greeted by the other side as a confirmation of their position. The strict parallelism again demonstrates the

---

66. The emphasized address with "you" is reminiscent of a diatribe style; here, however, it does not have the function, as in the diatribe, of introducing an *imaginary* opponent for the didactical dispute (cf. Bultmann, *Stil der paulinischen Predigt*, 10–11; Stowers, *Diatribe*, 79–118; somewhat differently Schmeller, *Diatribe*, 22–24) but turns rather to the *real* participants in the church congregation where Paul's letter is being read out.

67. As Moo rightly observes in *Romans*, 846.

68. Cf. Walters, *Ethnic Issues*; Oestreich, "Ethnische und religiöse Spannungen"; especially Esler, *Conflict and Identity*, 40–76 on ethnic identity; 339–56 on Rom 14:1—15:13.

69. On seating order, see above on pp. 76–77. Social placement also mentioned in Meeks, *First Urban Christians*, 30. Stegemann and Stegemann, *Urchristliche Sozialgeschichte*, 244 refer as comparison to the fixed seating order at club meals "in so far they confirm the internal group roles and status positions" (my translation).

neutrality and distance of the speaker from both groups. He does not take a side but wishes to speak to both sides.

Romans 14:10c–13a

After the two parallel questions in verse 10, there follows in verses 10c–13a an argument directed at the abstainers that takes up the first critical question found in verse 10a. Although Paul speaks of a judgment for all in verses 10c–13a using the inclusive *we*-form, these verses are still addressed to those who are judging others (cf. v. 3b). Because of the use of the *we*-form, the abstainers would not see themselves alone exposed to public criticism, and the address would lose some of its sharpness. This would make it easier for abstainers to accept the criticism.

After that, what follows is a second section, Rom 14:13b—15:4, again with the *we*-form—directed at the eaters and corresponding to the second question found in verse 10b. The respective change of addressee is not actually explicitly expressed in words. The performer would have expressed the change by directing his gaze and turning his body toward the new addressee.

The content of the first section (vv. 10c–13a) includes an allusion to the teaching of the last judgment, according to which each person must stand for himself or herself before the judge. (This eschatological perspective was already found in verses 3c–4.) Human judgments have no justification (cf. 1 Cor 4:5). The decision whether someone is saved or not must be left to God. Apparently some Christians in Rome had questioned whether their fellow Christians were accepted by God because of dietary questions. Paul, by criticizing this judgmentalness, admonishes the one group (the abstainers) and takes sides with the other group (the eaters).

Paul's argument (v. 11) is strengthened by the short Scripture quotation from Isa 45:23: "As I live, says the Lord, every knee shall bow to me, and every tongue shall give praise to God." This text belongs to oldest inventory of the primitive church's scriptural interpretation and serves to confess Jesus as judge of the world; such a confession is central to the primitive church's christological hymn in Phil 2:6–11. Thus Paul reverts to traditional beliefs recognized by all.

The text in Isaiah is also interesting because the Gentiles, in the context of Isa 45, are also invited to Israel's salvation (vv. 20 and 22). The quotation with its terse formulation ἐμοὶ κάμψει πᾶν γόνυ καὶ πᾶσα γλῶσσα ἐξομολογήσεται is therefore a formulaic recourse to familiar tradition. The presence of this formulaic recollection of earlier tradition signals far more complexity than the spoken words alone would indicate (*pars pro toto*). According to Foley, the formulaic use of tradition is a typical feature of oral performance.[70] It can be presumed that the listeners to the performance were at home in this tradition and aware of the original context for the quoted passage. With this quotation we can hear the implicit theme of the tensions in Rome: the relationship between Jews and Gentiles, which is explicitly expressed in Rom 15:8–12 and is Paul's concern throughout the Letter to the Romans. Verse 12 closes with a maxim, which is brought to bear against the abstainers as a universal truth: "So then each one of us will give an account of himself to God."

Romans 14:13

Hardly noticeably[71] and by using a skillful play-on-words[72] with the meaning of κρίνειν, Paul is able to lead over from one group to the other in verse 13. The admonition in 13a not to judge closes the topic of verses 10c–12, which was addressed to the *abstainers*. However, the *we*-form (κρίνωμεν) and especially the ἀλλήλους signal that now the eaters are also included.[73] On the other hand, Paul returns to the verb κρίνειν in verse 13b, which up to now had belonged to the dominating word field, but he uses it with a changed meaning and function: it becomes an introductory imperative (κρίνατε) for the following passage, which describes the typical misconduct of the *eaters*: "to put an obstacle or a stumbling block in a brother's way" (τιθέναι πρόσκομμα τῷ ἀδελφῷ ἢ σκάνδαλον). So Paul turns to the eaters in verse 13c.[74]

It is good rhetorical style to have flowing transitions with no hard breaks.[75] This adept and gradual change of emphasis from one group to the other becomes especially clear when one realizes that representatives of both groups were present at the same time among the listeners and that the presenter would have spoken verse 13b while turning to face the group of eaters.

70. Foley, "Traditional Signs," 63.

71. The transitional function, from v. 13 to a new section, has often gone unnoticed. Cf. however Schmithals, *Römerbrief*, 494.

72. Cf. Godet, *Römer*, 273; Byrne, *Romans*, 415; Moo, *Romans*, 851.

73. Cf. Stuhlmacher, *Römer*, 201.

74. Cf. Schmithals, *Römerbrief*, 503.

75. Classen, "Paulus," 31.

Romans 14:14

With the following explanation, which is directed to the eaters (Rom 14:14—15:4), Paul takes up the second line of verse 10 and gives a lengthy justification of why he considers their behavior to be inappropriate. He begins by saying that they are basically right (v. 14a, as also vv. 20, 22).[76] They would have expressed vigorous agreement. Paul's statement at first signals understanding for and agreement with those whom he intends to admonish. By first stating his agreement with them, Paul makes them willing to listen to him. It is conspicuous that he does not use such a *captatio benevolentiae* when admonishing the abstainers. It is also conspicuous that the section for the eaters is much longer than the one for the abstainers. There is a simple reason for this: Paul expects more from the eaters. Not only should they change their *attitude* toward their brothers (no longer judging, no longer condemning), but they should also change their *behavior* and abstain from the foods in question.

How would the abstainers have reacted, now that Paul *expressis verbis* and with emphasis (οἶδα καὶ πέπεισμαι) is agreeing with the eaters? Has he not thus given up the objectivity that up to this point had secured the attention of both parties? With the abstainers in mind, Paul adds, "but to him who thinks anything to be unclean, to him it is unclean" (v. 14b). This statement gives the abstainers the right to live according to their own understanding. Paul repeats this in verse 20 "All things indeed are clean, but they are evil for the man who eats because of offense [of his brothers]." And in verse 23 he calls it sin if the abstainers, against their convictions, eat meat. Paul is in a sense, agreeing with both groups.[77] At least he ensures that his agreeing with the eaters does not lead to a disparagement of the abstainers. Rather Paul's agreement with the eaters becomes a model for the eaters, who themselves should show understanding for the abstainers.

Romans 14:15–19

After the performance has repeatedly turned each group's attention to the other in a positive way, Paul, in his admonitions to the eaters in verse 15, picks up the word "brothers" from verse 10 and expects a περιπατεῖν

---

76. By using the word κοινός he indicates what the dietary question was about: the Jewish laws concerning the purity of foods or sacrificial meat as in 1 Cor 8–10.

77. Cf. Minear, *Obedience of Faith*, 19.

κατὰ ἀγάπην. Love is of greater value than knowledge of whether foods are clean or unclean.[78] Building on an old creedal formulation (1 Cor 15:3: Χριστὸς ἀπέτανεν ὑπὲρ κτλ.), that is, on traditional wording (a method very typical of oral discourses), Paul summarizes the value of the brethren with the formula ὑπὲρ οὗ Χριστὸς ἀπέθανεν. This formula conjures up Christ's all-inclusive act of salvation before the eyes of the Christian listeners, on which the following arguments are then oriented (Rom 15:3–9).

A further argument for mutual love and acceptance rests on Paul's fear, expressed in verse 16, that "the good" might be maligned. Paul implies that should they continue to malign each other, the disputing parties might get a bad reputation among the wider public.[79] Verse 18 expresses the same thought positively: by achieving a good togetherness, the Roman Christians will merit recognition from God and humans—unbelievers included.[80] The fact that this argument is being used in the passage addressing the eaters shows that this group had a higher social status, lived more in the public eye, and therefore was more anxious about public recognition.

Verse 17 is a maxim, formulated in antithetical parallelism.

A	οὐ γάρ ἐστιν ἡ βασιλεία τοῦ θεοῦ βρῶσις καὶ πόσις
B	ἀλλὰ δικαιοσύνη καὶ εἰρήνη καὶ χαρὰ ἐν πνεύματι ἁγίῳ·
A	For the kingdom of God is not eating and drinking,
B	but righteousness and peace and joy in the Holy Spirit.

The terms referring to God, the formulations ἡ βασιλεία τοῦ θεοῦ and ἐν πνεύματι ἁγίῳ, form the outer chiastic elements, and the human actions the inner elements (βρῶσις καὶ πόσις and δικαιοσύνη καὶ εἰρήνη καὶ χαρά). The listing signals the comprehensive scope of the statement. Such proverbial sentences play an important role in oral discourse and are very convincing for listeners. The speaker expresses a value judgment in a form that postulates general validity—that is to say, the long-held

---

78. Cf. the argumentation in 1 Cor 8:1, which also contrasts love and knowledge.

79. Schmithals, *Römerbrief*, 505; differently Moo, *Romans*, 855: The eaters' freedom gives them a bad reputation with the abstainers.

80. Michel, *Römer*, 308; and Wilckens, *Römer*, 3:92 interpret the slandering in 1 Cor 10:30 as negative speaking by the "strong" church members, not by outsiders.

and widely recognized wisdom of the respective society or group.[81] On the one hand, listeners feel involved in the judgment because the traditional wisdom is also their own wisdom; on the other hand, listeners are invited to adopt the poetically expressed wisdom for themselves by repeating the maxim, which has been worded in a form easy to memorize. Indeed it was quite common for listeners to repeat out loud the speaker's distinctive sentences.[82]

The generality of such sentences in Paul's argument should not lead us to think that they are directed at all listeners, as if at this point Paul has stopped addressing the eaters. To conclude this would be to fail to recognize the function of the maxims: they achieve their effect precisely because they are used to apply a general truth to a *specific* situation—which is of course known to the listeners and therefore does not need to be explicitly mentioned—and thus to decide the issue.[83] Broadening a statement to be valid for all those present would weaken its effect in the discourse.

The terms δικαιοσύνη καὶ εἰρήνη καὶ χαρά are relational expressions.[84] Just as in verses 3–9 Paul has already shown that the relationship to the Lord is crucial, here the relationship to the brothers becomes important. The disputed question is awarded less importance in light of the greater good—namely, the relationships to the Lord and to the brothers.[85]

Verse 19 closes provisionally with an injunction corresponding formally to verse 13a, the conclusion of the former passage (*we*-form, adhortatory subjunctive). It is the positive counterpart to what was rejected in verse 13c: instead of πρόσκομμα τῷ ἀδελφῷ ἢ σκάνδαλον, now εἰρήνη καὶ οἰκοδομὴ εἰς ἀλλήλους.[86]

The abstainers would have enjoyed hearing the admonitions to the eaters. The statements in verses 17–19, however, are so generally worded

---

81. Foley, *How to Read*, 125: "True proverbs . . . are the instructional medium par excellence of oral tradition." Cf. Ong, *Orality*, 34–35.

82. Korenjak, *Publikum und Redner*, 132; cf. also Acts 19:34.

83. Ong, *Orality*, 35.

84. Smit, "Symposium" has shown that they can describe the ideal symposium.

85. Verse 16: ὑμῶν τὸ ἀγαθόν. The good is the βασιλεία τοῦ θεοῦ, which exists in the relationship to the Lord and thereby also to the brothers. Cf. Michel, *Römer*, 308: "for the sake of the insignificant 'eating'" (my translation).

86. Old textual witnesses contain the indicative form διώκομεν. Stuhlmacher, *Römer*, 201 decides for the indicative form and takes v. 19 as the beginning of the following section vv. 19–23.

that they could also be applied to them. Self-confidence is not appropriate (cf. Gal 6:1).

Romans 14:20–23

In verses 15–19, Paul uses very general terms ("love," "righteousness," "peace," "acceptable to God and approved by men"). He is more explicit in the second section of his admonitions to the eaters (Rom 14:20—15:4). While otherwise calling for a change of attitudes (not judging, not despising, mutually accepting), Paul here demands deeds (not eating). Only here towards the eaters is Paul so specific.

For this purpose Paul starts anew. Many elements of his argument are repeated: the imperative (v. 15b; v. 20a); downplaying the importance of the disputed question in favor of greater values, namely, the works of God (v. 17; v. 20); agreeing in principle with the position of the eaters (v. 14a; v. 20b); conceding the relative rights of the abstainers (v. 14b; v. 20c); and pointing out the advantages of recommended behavior (v. 18; v. 21: καλόν). New is the injunction to abstain. It is not enough for Paul that eaters stop despising the abstainers. He expects them to abstain from what is actually allowed, for the sake of their brothers. He develops this to a basic tenet by introducing a new example, wine drinking, and implies that there are also other examples (v. 21: μηδὲ ἐν ᾧ ὁ ἀδελφός σου προσκόπτει). Probably the question of whether wine was allowed was not an acute problem in Rome,[87] since this is the only reference to it. As he had in verse 5, Paul here generalizes in order to make the fundamental nature of his answer clear and to help the Roman Christians see their dispute in a larger context.[88]

The performance of this section also creates a positive outlook in those being addressed (the eaters) toward the other group (the abstainers). It would be a sin if the abstainers ate that which they believed was forbidden.[89] The abstainers' problem is made clear: their doubts would

---

87. Cf. Schmithals, *Römerbrief*, 490; Gäckle, *Die Starken*, 404, 419; the cautious discussion in Wilckens, *Römer*, 3:110; see, by contrast, Stuhlmacher, *Römer*, 195.

88. Sampley, "Weak," 49.

89. Verse 23. This verse ends with an aphorism: πᾶν δὲ ὃ οὐκ ἐκ πίστεως ἁμαρτία ἐστίν. The validity of this comprehensive statement has been questioned. It is typical for maxims, which comprehensively express a valid truth that they give no regard to the fact that maxims may also exist which state the opposite truth, as can be seen in many traditional oral proverbs. The effectiveness of the aphorism used here is also linked to the specific situation to which it is applied. Moo, *Romans*, 864 rightly emphasizes, that

cause their own downfall should they be forced to eat the meat in question. Thus the view of the abstainers is given more esteem in the eyes of the eaters. The words of blessing for the one who has found certainty awakens the eaters' sympathy for those with deep-seated doubts.[90] Here we have emotional influencing, such as we found in the descriptor "weak."[91]

Romans 15:1

There follows an appeal to the strength of the eaters. They are the δυνατοί. This characterization provides the eaters with a strong incentive to do what is being asked. As was implied above, this designation is not intended to disparage the ἀδύνατοι. It is the selfless superiority of the adult over the child, the teacher over the pupil, the healthy over the sick with his or her weaknesses (ἀσθενήματα) that is called for here (reminiscent of Isa 53:4). Exercising such selfless superiority is an obligation and is at the same time an honor.[92] Strength is abused if it is only used for personal advantage; it obligates to help the neighbor (vv. 1b-2).[93] At the same time, Paul again signals togetherness with the ones being addressed by using the *we*-form. "[Paul] himself joins the rank of the 'strong' and helps them to follow the difficult path of sacrifice and love."[94]

---

this statement is brought against the eaters, who are inducing the abstainers to act, not by faith, but because of social pressure.

90. Schmidt, *Römer*, 235.

91. A possible objection from the eaters—cf. Nygren, *Römerbrief*, 319—is picked up by Paul in v. 22a (on the reading without ἥν see Schmidt, *Römer*, 235): what is the purpose of faith if it is not allowed to be lived out? Paul's answer, according to Stuhlmacher, *Römer*, 203, could be understood as meaning that everyone is free to live out his convictions in his own home but must show consideration for others when in the church assembly. However, Paul's wording corresponds to what he said to the abstainers in vv. 4 and 12: each person is alone accountable for himself or herself before his Lord. No one should try to force his or her own convictions on others.

92. Paul knows that this superiority can also be abused and can lead to boasting. Cf. Gal 6:1 where Paul also appeals to the strength of the church members, but subsequently warns against self-confident arrogance and argues against κενοδοξία in the whole passage.

93. On the concept of obligation in Rom 15:1, cf. Jewett, *Romans*, 876; on obligation in Romans 14-15, cf. Reasoner, *Strong*, 187-99.

94. Michel, *Römer*, 316 (my translation).

Romans 15:2–4

In verse 2, Paul continues to address the eaters and advances a basic principle. However, he does it, as in Rom 14:19, in such a general form (ἕκαστος) that both parties can feel they are being spoken to. There follows the reference to the example of Christ, the authority accepted by all. Jesus Christ too had not sought his own advantage. Finally Paul brings—as with the admonition for the abstainers in Rom 14:11—a scriptural quote. The quotation from Ps 69:9 belongs, as does the quotation from Isa 45:23, to the repertoire of the early Christian christological Scripture interpretation and shows Jesus as the Righteous One, who as a substitute took the abuse which was actually meant for God.[95] Again we must assume that this quotation metonymically opens up a whole horizon of tradition for the listeners. Thus the δυνατοί in Rome should bear the burdens of others.

Verse 4 reinforces the Scripture quotation by pointing out that Scripture serves to foster hope. This is an allusion to the hope of the eschatological liberation from all burdens. So Paul shows that sacrificing one's own freedom is not a temporary measure until the abstainers have changed their opinions, but indeed is a fundamental attitude. The eschatological hope (as already in Rom 14:4, 10–12) therefore becomes an argument.[96] Here Paul is anticipating a thought that comes to fruition in verses 8–12: the eschatological expectation of Jews and Gentiles joined together in praising God.

Romans 15:5–6 and 13

The final section, Rom 15:5–13, begins and ends with general statements applying to both groups; so it is similar to the conclusion of the first part in Rom 14:7–9. It is Paul's prayer that God may give, and his charge to the Roman Christians that they may live out, what he is concerned with in the whole passage: harmony and mutual acceptance (vv. 5, 7), joy and peace (v. 13, cf. Rom 14:17). The wording is particularly euphonious:

---

95. The model of the suffering righteous one in Ps 69 is used to interpret the suffering of Jesus, cf. Matt 27:34; Heb 11:26. This includes the reference to the temple in Ps 69:9 that is quoted in John 2:17.

96. Schmidt, *Römer*, 238; Käsemann, *Römer*, 370.

v. 6	ἵνα ὁμοθυμαδὸν ἐν ἑνὶ στόματι δοξάζητε τὸν θεὸν — Assonance with the vowel o.
	End formulation: τὸν θεὸν καὶ πατέρα τοῦ κυρίου ἡμῶν Ἰησοῦ Χριστοῦ.[97]
v. 13	ὁ δὲ θεὸς τῆς ἐλπίδος — Rhythm and end rhyme.
	πληρώσαι ὑμᾶς πάσης χαρᾶς καὶ εἰρήνης — Assonance of the vowel a in turn with the long e.
	ἐν τῷ πιστεύειν, εἰς τὸ περισσεύειν — Rhythm and end rhyme.
	End formulation: ἐν δυνάμει πνεύματος ἁγίου.

The "prayer-wishes" at the beginning and the end of this section are Paul's rhetorical means to induce the Roman Christians to behave as he wishes. They point to the fact that peace is only possible in God. If the Christians in Rome heed Paul's appeal, then they partake in a divine work. He wants those receiving the letter to know that they will not be fulfilling *Paul's* will when they do what he has written, but rather *God's* will. Both "prayers," like the quotations, are arguments from authority: they make it difficult for those being admonished to rebel against the presenter. Paul takes himself—and the one reading the letter out—rhetorically "out of the line of fire." It would be much easier for listeners to decide against Paul than to reject God himself or the Scriptures.

At the same time the prayers form a hymnic-liturgical conclusion[98] to the whole section Rom 14:1—15:13. Thus Paul ends the passage with πάθος, as he often does in the Epistle to the Romans (e.g., 8:32–39; 11:33–36; 15:33).

Romans 15:7

The "prayer-wishes" frame three ideas: first, the recapitulative injunction to mutual acceptance, this time directed to both groups together (v. 7 ἀλλήλους)[99] and with δόξα τοῦ θεοῦ given as the purpose; second, parallel statements about what God has done for the Jews and Gentiles (vv. 8–9a); and third, a series of scriptural quotations (vv. 9b–12). It is

---

97. Cf. Jewett, *Romans*, 875.
98. Michel, *Römer*, 320.
99. Heil, *Ablehnung der Speisegebote*, 265; by contrast Byrne, *Romans*, 428–29; Thorsteinsson, *Paul's Interlocutor*, 119 also sees only the Gentile Christians as being addressed in Rom 15:7. For him, the implicit recipients of the Letter to the Romans are the Gentile Christians. The Jews are only mentioned as a background.

manifoldly recognizable in these remarks that Paul is coming to the end of his argument: he refers back to the beginning of the section using προσλαμβάνεσθε; he takes up again the frequently cited example of Christ; he repeats the verb δοξάζειν that was used in verse 6; and he ends up addressing both groups together.

Romans 15:8–9a

Paul begins with λέγω γάρ. Paul had already formulated his own convictions very emphatically using the first-person singular in Rom 14:14: οἶδα καὶ πέπεισμαι ἐν κυρίῳ Ἰησοῦ. But this time the language is self-referential: that means the verb expresses what the speaker is doing (in what Austin calls "performative language"). This formulation brings the medial aspect of the performance into the consciousness of the listeners, since the presenter becomes visible as someone who does something. Initially, it is *he himself* who is doing what he says (λέγω) in front of the physically present audience with his own voice, with the strength of his own breath. The audience has two options. They can direct their attention to the referential content of what is being said, and in effect thereby hear Paul speaking. Or they can attend to the fact that someone else is speaking, not the one who had originally uttered the words λέγω γάρ—when the letter was dictated. The greater the differences are between the presenter and the letter writer as the Roman listeners imagine or know him to be, the stronger the probability is that the listeners will experience the materiality of the performance (Fischer-Lichte). On the one hand, this would have the effect that Paul would no longer be completely embodied by the speaker, but rather that he as the letter's author would effectively step out from behind the speaker and thus into the awareness of the listeners as a separate personality. Although many in Rome did not know him, he creates himself as a distinct reality of his own in the listeners' imaginations through the performative language λέγω γάρ. On the other hand, given Paul's performative language and the distance it creates between Paul the letter writer and the local performer, listeners would experience their own presence and role in the performance and would be prompted to judge the quality of the presenter's performance.

Another parallelism appears in verses 8–9a. However, the parallelism is not exact.[100] In the first line, which concerns the Jews (v. 8), Paul

---

100. On the discussion of syntax difficulties, cf. Wagner, "Christ, Servant of Jew"; Lambrecht, "Syntactical and Logical Remarks."

leaves out the thought that what God has done for the Jews should lead to his being praised. This thought was mentioned in both of the preceding verses and is at first not repeated. In the second line, which concerns the Gentiles (v. 9), praising God is again referred to, but the precondition for praise is omitted, namely, that Christ has also become a servant to the Gentiles.[101] Paul takes for granted that his listeners will deduce the missing thoughts from the context.

Both these verses are worded in a very distanced manner. Whom are they addressing? As we have seen, when addressing a specific group, Paul speaks positively about the other group. Verse 8 speaks about God's saving work for the Jews. But the message in verse 8 is addressed to the Gentiles in order to raise their estimation of the Jews (cf. Rom 11:13-24). Conversely, verse 9 is addressed to the Jews, encouraging them to accept the Gentiles. Together they should praise God in such a way that each group would have "a specific reason for and part in the liturgical service of the church."[102] The fullness of praise to God is therefore only possible together.

Romans 15:9b-12

Next comes a series of scriptural quotes. All the texts speak about the Gentiles, and each quote has a verb that expresses praise to God (ψάλλειν, ἐξομολογεῖσθαι, εὐφραίνεσθαι, αἰνεῖν, ἐπαινεῖν, ἐλπίζειν). Thus they complement the second line of the parallelism (v. 9a), clearly distinguishing it from the first. These quotations serve to explain the reason for God's showing mercy to the Gentiles through the recognized authority of the Scriptures (the Torah, Prophets, and Writings). To which of the listeners is this argument directed? Admittedly the Gentile

---

101. With Wilckens, *Römer*, 3:106, I understand v. 9a in dependence on λέγω γὰρ and parallel to v. 8. So also e.g., Sass, "Röm 15,7-13," 516; Byrne, *Romans*, 431; Haacker, *Römer*, 297; Lambrecht, "Syntactical and Logical Remarks," 259-60; Gäckle, *Die Starken*, 428-29; by contrast see Schmidt, *Römer*, 240; Käsemann, *Römer*, 372; Keck, "Christology"; Moo, *Romans*, 876-77. Lohse, *Römer*, 387 suggests τὰ δὲ ἔθνη as second accusative besides ὑμᾶς to be attached to ὁ Χριστὸς προσελάβετο in v. 7b. However, that would mean that the Gentiles are being spoken *about*, as if they in contrast to those addressed as "you" were not present. Wagner, "Christ, Servant of Jew and Gentile" offers another explanation of the sentence structure, in which Christ is the subject doing the praising in v. 9 and not the Gentiles. A united praising of God, as in the prayer in v. 6 and as appears in the quotation in v. 10, as well as the praising done by the Gentiles, mentioned in vv. 11-12, would then not be included in the perspective of vv. 8-9.

102. Michel, *Römer*, 322 (my translation).

Christians also acknowledged the authority of the Scriptures and were familiar with them from the readings in the church services, particularly since many of them were God-fearers or came into the Christian church from the environment of the Jewish synagogues.[103] The scriptural quotes could have fuctioned to reassure Gentile Christians of their acceptance by God. However, of Rom 14:1—15:13 is not about justifying one's own acceptance by God, but is rather a call to accept the other group. Thus the scriptural quotations underline the injunction to the Jews in verse 9: Just as God has accepted the Gentiles as attested throughout the Scriptures, so should the Jews also accept their fellow Christians coming from among the Gentiles.[104] However, the second quotation, from Gen 32:43, promises praise from the Gentiles in the midst of Israel, so that this quotation underlines in a very special way the fact that Jews and Gentiles belong together.

The scriptural quotations have an eschatological thrust: they show the goal God wishes to achieve with the plan of salvation.[105] All nations will praise God *together*. The δόξα of God is the goal, as it is throughout the Letter to the Romans (Rom 1:23; 3:23; 5:2; 8:18, 21; 9:23).[106] The Roman Christians can see themselves in the light of this goal and thus recognize their duty—mutual acceptance—and help to realize this goal through their own lives.[107]

Both the prayers and the scriptural quotations in the last section required intensified, hymnic diction from the presenter. All the listeners would have been drawn into praise and prayer at the end of the passage. In this manner the letter's performance would fulfill what the content says and demands. The language is performative in that it points to itself—that is, in that it does what it says.

Summary

Throughout the whole performance of this passage there is the strategy of alternatingly addressing one group in the presence of the other to encourage them to view the other group positively, which is documented

103. Stuhlmacher, "Abfassungszweck," 188.

104. Cf. Moiser, "Rethinking," 579; as directed to the whole church, Wilckens, *Römer*, 3:104–5.

105. Wilckens, *Römer*, 3:104.

106. Cf. Käsemann, *Römer*, 88–89.

107. Crafton, "Paul's Rhetorical Vision," 337.

in the linguistic parallelism. The speaker joins in solidarity with the respective group not being addressed at that moment. Directly addressing the respective group is a rebuke or a command; indirectly addressing the other group is an appreciation of, a joining in solidarity with them (14:14 and 14:20, 23). Paul's addressing the groups alternately in the letter is a form used in oral communication and presupposes an oral performance. Paul writes as he would preach if he were in Rome.[108]

At first it is natural that one side would feel confirmed and supported when the other side is being criticized. This happens, for example, through the words κρίνειν and ἐξουθενεῖν, which have negative connotations (14:3 and 10). Then, however, each party is shown that the other one is valuable. "Instead of siding with one party against the other, Paul alternately defends each side against the attacks of the other."[109] He defends the other side (14:3, 6), awakens understanding for the relative legitimacy of each position (14:20b, 23), points out that each has already been accepted by Christ (14:3c, 4c) or refers to God's eschatological goal (15:9–12), and speaks of the other being a "brother" in Christ (14:10, 13, 15).

The parallel sections are not always symmetrical.[110] Rom 14:3c–4 is a supplement to verse 3b, so that the abstainers are more sharply criticized than the eaters. The parallelism in Rom 15:8–12 is also unsymmetrical, because Paul adds a list of scriptural quotations to Paul's message for the abstainers, explaining the reason for God's dealings with the Gentiles, while quotations explaining God's dealing with the Jews is missing (in contrast to Rom 3:3–4 [Ps 51:4]; Rom 11:29 [Num 23:19]). This asymmetry to the disadvantage of the abstainers—Paul admonishes them more emphatically and clearly distances himself from their point of view—is relativized by the fact that the admonition for the eaters (14:13b—15:4) is considerably more extensive than the admonition for the abstainers (14:10c–13a). Admittedly, the eaters do receive a clear signal of understanding and recognition of their strength—which is also an asymmetry to the disadvantage of the abstainers. But Paul is so specific towards the

---

108. Weiss, "Beiträge," 166; Bultmann, *Stil der paulinischen Predigt*, 3, 72, 74; Jervell, "Brief nach Jerusalem," 71.

109. Nygren, *Römerbrief*, 316 (my translation); cf. Gestrich, "Sprache der Versöhnung," 500: reconciliation, "this καταλλαγή unites and pacifies the respective hostile counterpart in such a fashion *that neither side must give itself up in the mediating reconciliation process*" (my translation, italics original).

110. Rom 14:6 is asymmetrical only in form, because here a link has been left out. Rom 15:8–9 is also incomplete.

eaters that he demands that they abstain from foods that are actually allowed, so as not to be a hindrance to their brethren. Paul expects far more from those whose opinions he shares than from the others.

The parallelism used so often in this passage is well suited to relativize the differences since it demonstrates that the opposing opinions could be seen in connection with each other. After all, parallelism is a linguistic strategy that places contrasting statements directly next to each other, enabling them to be viewed together. Although the speaker uses the first-person plural to address each group separately, in order to join in solidarity with each respective side, and although Paul even reveals that his position is that of the eaters (14:14, 20), Paul still maintains a certain balance through the complex parallel structure of the text. The speaker retains his position of distance and superiority, making it possible for him to influence both sides.[111] Listeners are invited to identify themselves with the speaker. It is his position, his ethos that they should adopt. They should view the dispute from a neutral position, in a certain sense from a detached viewpoint. This was hardly possible up till then, because in their own eyes there could only be an either-or. The performance opens a new and distanced viewpoint on the dispute and can in this way help to improve the togetherness. Therefore the effect of the public reading of the letter is to prompt an interaction between the groups within the audience. As a result, the relationship between the two groups changes positively during the performance.

Again and again and especially toward the end of the passage, the antithetic parallels are complemented with a closing statement, explanation, or injunction that applies to all (Rom 14:5, 6, 7-9; 15:5-7, 13). This form of speech underlines once again the integrative purpose of the speaker. The differences are depicted using parallelism and then brought together in a new element that applies to all.

Instituting Friendship
(Plato, *Sixth Letter*)

We will consider two nonbiblical letters before returning to the study of Paul's letters. It will become clear that the performance strategy we have

---

111. Cf. Wilckens, *Römer*, 3:100.

been considering in Rom 14:1—15:13 is no isolated case. A parallel from Plato's letters is especially helpful in this respect.[112]

Plato's sixth letter,[113] from about 350 BCE,[114] is addressed to three people: to Hermeias, the ruler in Assos, and to two of Plato's students, Erastos and Coriscos, who, originally from Assos, had left the academy and returned home. Plato's goal is to join the Platonic students and the ruler in friendship. So we also have a letter here where the recipients can be divided into two groups that are to be brought together: the ruler and the two students of Plato.

Plato begins by revealing the purpose of the letter: the friendship of the parties being addressed will advantage both sides. A god had bestowed good fortune on them (6.322c: θεῶν τις ὑμῖν τύχην ἀγαθήν . . . παρασκευάζειν) since they live close together as neighbors and thus could be of great usefulness to one another when needed (ὥστε ἀλλήλους εἰς τὰ μέγιστα ὠφελεῖν).

Then Plato describes the advantages for Hermeias, if he should accept the Platonic students' friendship (6.322d): "For Hermeias will find in his multitude of horses or of other military equipment, or even in the gaining of gold itself, no greater source of power for all purposes than in the gaining of steadfast friends possessed of a sound character" (φίλων βεβαίων τε καὶ ἦθος ἐχόντων ὑγιές).[115] With these words, Plato first (μὲν) turns to Hermeias, without directly addressing him. He shows him the advantages of friendship with his students by speaking positively of them.

There follows (δὲ) a much longer passage (6.322d-e) in which Plato shows the advantages that Erastos and Coriscos would have from the friendship: they have good theoretical knowledge but have no experience in dealing with bad people. This section praises Hermeias (6.322e): "Hermeias, on the other hand, seems to me . . . to possess this practical ability both by nature and also through the skill bred of experience" (ταύτην δ' αὐτὴν δύναμιν Ἑρμείας μοι φαίνεται φύσει τε . . . καὶ τέχνῃ δι' ἐμπειρίας

---

112. Suggested in Mitchell, *Paul and the Rhetoric*, 236, n. 283. She also refers to Plato's eighth letter (354a-e), where Plato first announces his strategy to address both sides as a referee, then addresses each side successively, and finally makes an appeal to all of them.

113. Authentic according to Probst, *Paulus und der Brief*, 65.

114. On the dating of Plato's letters, cf. Hackforth, *Authorship of the Plantonic Epistles*.

115. Text according to Eigler, *Werke*, 362-65; translation in Bury, *Plato in Twelve Volumes*.

εἰληφέναι). The passage does not address Plato's students directly, but it is intended for them, and the praising of Hermeias is for their benefit. The greater length of the passage may have come about because Plato felt compelled to explain existing deficits of his students in order to avoid leaving a negative impression of his academy. They have no knowledge of the evil in the world because they have spent a large part of their lives in the company of Plato and his friends, who are "men of moderation and free of vice" (6.322e).

Both passages are so configured that each party receives a description of the advantages of the other. This is similar to the Letter to the Romans, where Paul speaks to one group, giving a positive characterization of the other. However, in Plato's epistle there is no antagonism to be overcome between the parties.

Just as in Romans 14, the first section of Plato's sixth letter, which does not directly address the recipients, is followed by a second part using the direct form of address. Plato first turns again to Hermeias (6.323a: σοὶ μέν, Ἑρμεία): "I counsel you to hold fast to these men by every righteous means (ἔχεσθαι δὴ . . . τούτων τῶν ἀνδρῶν) and regard this as a duty of no secondary importance." He speaks again positively of Erastos and Coriscos: "that you will not easily discover more trustworthy characters (ἀξιοπιστότερα) than these your neighbors." Plato underlines this positive testimony using three verbs (φημὶ καὶ μηνύω καὶ μαρτυρῶ), that is, with great emphasis.

Then there is another change of addressee: Coriscos and Erastos are spoken to (Κορίσκῳ δὲ καὶ Ἐράστῳ πάλιν) and advised to hold fast to Hermeias and to forge a bond of friendship (φιλίας συμπλοκήν) with him. Here Hermeias is only indirectly spoken of positively; that is, he is recommended as a friend.

So we have four sections, directed alternatingly to the one side and then the other, each time with positive statements about the side not being addressed. The pattern is the same as that found in Romans 14.

Plato, after speaking to each party successively, closes the letter by speaking to them collectively. He assumes the role of one who in cases of disagreement has the necessary distance to mediate. He invites them to write to him (δεῦρο παρ' ἐμὲ καὶ τοὺς ἐμοὺς πέμπετε μομφῆς κατήγορον ἐπιστολήν) if difficulties arise (6.323b: ἂν δέ τις ὑμῶν ἄρα ταύτην πῃ λύειν δοκῇ) so that with an answering letter he can heal the bonds of friendship (συμφῦσαι καὶ συνδῆσαι πάλιν εἰς τὴν προϋπάρχουσαν φιλότητά τε καὶ κοινωνίαν).

At the end of the letter Plato makes reference to the situation of the reading of the letter (6.323c): "All three of you must read this letter, all together if possible (ταύτην τὴν ἐπιστολὴν πάντας ὑμᾶς τρεῖς ὄντας ἀναγνῶναι χρή), or if not, by twos; and as often as you possibly can, read it in common, and use it as a form of covenant and a binding law" (χρῆσθαι συνθήκῃ καὶ νόμῳ κυρίῳ). Reading together presupposes reading aloud, so that it is as if Plato is also present through the voice of the reader.[116] He sits, so to speak, opposite both parties and is so able to reinstate and strengthen the friendship time and again.

In the letter, where Plato speaks of the advantages for his students through Hermeias, he describes himself as an old man (6.322d: καίπερ γέρων ὤν). Whichever one of the three recipients it is who reads the letter out to the others, the still-young students of Plato or the ruler, there will always be a contradiction between what is being read out and the physical body of the presenter. The medium of the performance comes into view in the difference between the performer and the sender. In this way, Plato creates an awareness of himself as the third party in the discourse.

Establishing Peace after Unrest (Claudius to the Alexandrians)

The goal of bringing disputing parties peacefully together by means of a letter is also to be found in the letter from Emperor Claudius to the Alexandrians (41 CE). After massive disturbances in the city between the Greek and the Jewish populace in Caligula's time and after Caligula's murder, delegates from the Greek and Jewish communities appealed to Emperor Claudius.[117] The emperor sent a letter to Alexandria, which was read out publicly—as the Egyptian prefect L. Aemilius Rectus reports (lines 1–11)—and subsequently publicized in written form by the prefect. It is significant and conforms to the protocol for official letters, that the reading and publishing of the letter was the responsibility of the official receiving the letter, not the emissaries sent by the emperor who had delivered the letter. Probably the letter would have been read out at a public place or market square in the city, possibly being presented from a pulpit (βῆμα) frequently used for that purpose. Representatives of both groups would have been present.

---

116. On the reading instruction, cf. Oestreich, "Leseanweisungen," 239.
117. On the background, cf. White, *Light*, 131–33; Klauck, *Ancient Letters*, 84–86.

First, the emperor successively admonishes both sides, each with about the same number of lines (16 and 12 lines), to keep the peace. To the Greeks he says (lines 73–88):

> As to who should be held responsible for the disorder and sedition against the Jews or, rather, if the truth be told, the war, although your ambassadors, and especially Dionysios son of Theon, argued forcefully, notwithstanding, I have not desired to make a detailed examination (of the hostility), but I have stored up within me an immutable hostility against those who renewed the conflict. Simply stated, if you do not lay to rest this destructive and obstinate hostility against one another, I shall be forced to show what a benevolent ruler can become when turned to (inflict) justified wrath. Wherefore, still even now, I entreat you that, on the one hand, the Alexandrians [διόπερ ἔτι καὶ νῦν διαμαρτύρομε εἶνα Ἀλεξανδρεῖς μὲν . . .] behave gently and kindly towards the Jews, who have inhabited the same city for many years . . .[118]

There follows a change of the ones being addressed, which the presenter would have emphasized through the direction of his gaze and his posture. To the Jews he says (lines 88–100),

> On the other hand, I order the Jews (Ἰουδέοις δὲ ἄντικρυς κελεύωι), unreservedly, not to waste effort seeking more than what they formerly had, nor for the future to send two embassies as if they lived in two (separate) cities, a thing which was never done before, nor to force their way in to contests (presided over by) the gymnasiarchoi and the kosmetai. . . . Otherwise, I will take vengeance against them in every respect, just as though they were a widespread plague infecting the whole inhabited world.

In the last section of the letter both sides are called to cease fighting (lines 100–104): "(But) if you both (Alexandrians and Jews) forsake such things and are willing to live with gentleness and kindness toward one another, I, for my part, will have the greatest consideration for the city."

In this letter we see, too, that two groups are being addressed successively (again with μὲν . . . δὲ), and that also each time in the presence of the other group. Here also, after separate addresses to each group, there follows a section for both of them, as we also found in the Letter to the Romans. Here, however, the emperor does not try to awake understanding in each of the disputing parties for the other group. He

---

118. Text and English translation in White, *Light*, 133–37.

does not speak to one group positively about the other as is the case with Paul and Plato. However, he does refuse to lay the blame for the unrest on the other side as each delgation claims he should.[119] The Greek delegation had urged the emperor to investigate the most recent altercations, since the last wave of unrest in the conflict had been caused by the Jews. The emperor refused categorically to do this (line 76). The Jewish delegation—there had probably even been two Jewish delegations (lines 90–91)[120]—had most likely pointed out that at the beginning of the fighting, in the time of Caligula, it had been started by the Greeks. The emperor, by refusing to investigate which party was guilty, avoided confirming acknowledging to the one group the badness of the other. This strategy also served to appease both sides.

Above all, Claudius relied on his authority by threatening each side with his wrath if the unrest continued, but also promising both sides his favor if they would live together in peacefulness and friendliness (ἐὰν . . . ἀμφότεροι μετὰ πραότητος καὶ φιλανθροπείας τῆς πρὸς ἀλλήλους ζῆν ἐθελήσητε). The emperor quite clearly uses his distanced and superior position to intervene in the dispute and to end it. The presenter would have underlined this through a superior demeanor.

Tensions in Corinth Due to Spiritual Gifts (1 Corinthians 12:3)

Problems in 1 Corinthians 12:3

The First Letter to the Corinthians also had the purpose of relieving tensions in the church. Chapters 12 to 14 are concerned with problems arising out of differences in dealing with various spiritual gifts. What 1 Cor 12:3 means has been especially puzzling for interpreters. It will now be shown how taking the performance into consideration can help in understanding the text.

Paul begins 1 Cor 12:3 with an emphatic διὸ γνωρίζω ὑμῖν, which on the one hand presents the following as a conclusion drawn from what had previously been said (v. 2), and on the other hand lends weight to the statements that follow.[121] Two negatively worded parallel sentences

---

119. Klauck, *Ancient Letters*, 95–96.

120. For a discussion of the two delegations, see White, *Light*, 132–33.

121. Holtz, "Kennzeichen des Geistes," 370: a "solemnly emphatic decision of significant character on a debatable issue" (my translation). Maly, "Regel," 86: "solemn

follow, which bring a certain stereotypical way of speaking in connection with the Holy Spirit.

A	οὐδεὶς ἐν πνεύματι θεοῦ λαλῶν λέγει· Ἀνάθεμα Ἰησοῦς,
B	οὐδεὶς δύναται εἰπεῖν· Κύριος Ἰησοῦς, εἰ μὴ ἐν πνεύματι ἁγίῳ.
A	No one speaking by the Spirit of God says, "Jesus is accursed";
B	and no one can say, "Jesus is Lord" except by the Holy Spirit.

That this text belongs to Paul's more difficult statements can be seen by the large number of proposed interpretations. Anthony Thiselton lists no fewer than twelve interpretations of this verse.[122]

The cursing of Jesus, especially, has raised questions. Is it thinkable that someone in the Corinthian church had cursed Jesus? And should it have happened, is it not self-evident that such an utterance could not come about by the agency of the Holy Spirit? Isn't Paul's emphatic statement that no one would curse Jesus when speaking in the Spirit simply stating the obvious?[123] If there had been a cursing of Jesus in Corinth, why did Paul treat such a shocking occurrence so casually, why with just this one sentence?[124] Or was the curse directed at Jesus not meant negatively but instead as the believer's recognition of God's actions in Jesus, who according to Gal 3:13 was cursed for our sakes?[125] But why, then, would such a statement be denoted as not coming from the Spirit?

The many interpretations of this difficult verse[126] can be divided into two main groups, depending on whether it is assumed that the cursing of Jesus really happened or not.[127] A real cursing of Jesus could have been

introduction" (my translation).

122. Thiselton, *First Corinthians*, 918-24. Vos, "Rätsel," 251 calls this verse a puzzle.

123. Holtz, "Kennzeichen des Geistes," 370.

124. Thus the question raised by Maly, "Regel," 92; Holtz, "Kennzeichen des Geistes," 371; and Vos, "Rätsel," 255.

125. Thus van Unnik, "Jesus"; Witherington, *Conflict*, 256 also debates a positive meaning of ἀνάθεμα, namely "votive offering."

126. Textual corruption as a solution for this question will not be discussed here. For example, according to Albright and Mann, "Two Texts," 273, Paul is quoting an Aramaic liturgical responsorium: Ἀνὰ ἀθὲ μαρὰν ἀθὰ Ἰησοῦς. ("I am coming. Come, our Lord Jesus!") Consequently, the original text would have read: "No one, who is speaking, says: 'I'm coming. Come, our Lord!' except through the Holy Spirit."

127. Synopses of previous interpretation attempts are found in Schrage, *Erste Brief an die Korinther*, 114-17; Thiselton, *First Corinthians*, 918-24; and Wolff, *Erster*

pronounced in the synagogue, that is, outside the church assembly,[128] or the cursing could have been suggested to Jewish Christians there.[129] Or it could have happened during a persecution situation.[130] A connection between the cursing and ecstasy has also been suggested.[131] An influential hypothesis has come from Walter Schmithals, proposing that Jewish gnostics had cursed the earthly Jesus since they rejected his coming in the flesh (1 John 4:2).[132] If on the other hand there was no real cursing of Jesus, then Paul could have been contrasting two opposing confessions as the criteria for differentiating between the spirits in the charismatic diversity in Corinth or—more fundamentally—as criteria for basic life orientation (Traugott Holtz).[133] That would make the curse a purely rhetorical construction from Paul.[134]

First Corinthians 12:3 as propositio

Performance criticism presumes that in this passage we have the written remains of a dynamic event. We can therefore only come close to understanding the true meaning of the text when taking into consideration the event created by its reading in its entirety, indeed, only by endeavoring to experience it ourselves. Important aspects of 1 Cor 12:3 include the context, that is 1 Cor 12–14,[135] as well as the performance situation and the social context in which it is embedded.

Korinther, 285–87.

128. For example, Schlatter, *Paulus*, 333.

129. For example, Derrett, "Cursing Jesus."

130. Cullmann, *Christologie*, 225–27.

131. Barrett, *First Corinthians*, 280. Mehat, "L'enseignement"; and Forbes, "Early Christian Inspired Speech" disagree.

132. Schmithals, *Gnosis*, 117–22; Brox, "ΑΝΑΘΕΜΑ"; Dunn, *Jesus and the Spirit*, 234–35; Pearson, "Did the Gnostics Curse" already argued against this. Thiselton, *First Corinthians*, 923 proposes this had been the exclamation offered by a group in Corinth that had a one-sided understanding of Jesus (cf. 1 Cor 15:12).

133. Cf. Maly, "Regel"; Holtz, "Kennzeichen des Geistes." Schmithals, *Gnosis*, 117 believes the opposite could be possible, that Paul was using the Κύριος Ἰησοῦς to represent a contrast to the real exclamation of a curse.

134. For example, Schrage, *Erste Brief an die Korinther*, 116–17; Wolff, *Erster Korinther*, 286.

135. The importance of the context has been especially noted by Vos, "Rätsel." Holtz, "Kennzeichen des Geistes," 372 also points to the context in the expectation "that 12:2-3 contains a very general characterization of what—according to Paul's

The text in 1 Cor 12:3 is part of the introduction to the section encompassing chapters 12–14, where the apostle is probably reacting to an inquiry from the Corinthians. Throughout the passage, Paul deals with problems that have arisen because the Corinthians disagreed about the use and merit of certain spiritual gifts.

In verse 1 Paul introduces the new theme (περὶ δὲ τῶν πνευματικῶν), addresses his listeners (ἀδελφοί), and makes his own role as teacher clear (οὐ θέλω ὑμᾶς ἀγνοεῖν).

In the next verse he reminds his listeners of the time when they were heathens. Whatever Paul really meant with this sentence, it is clear that it is important for him to consider this as a thing of the past.[136] He is therefore speaking to the believers in the Corinthian church who have left this behind them.

This raises the first question: how did *Jewish* Christians in Corinth, without such a background, react to this? Was the dispute about the working of the Spirit primarily a dispute among the Gentile Christians? Or did the Jewish Christians belong to those practicing *prophetic* speech? Be that as it may, Paul placed some of those present in the position of observers.

Paul forms an emphatic (γνωρίζω ὑμῖν) conclusion (διὸ) in verse 3 from what has been said in verse 2. So the plausibility of an explanation of verse 3 depends on whether the connection with verse 2 and the logic of the conclusion are adequately explained.[137]

The fact that Paul comes to a conclusion after a few introductory remarks, although the treatment of the underlying question of the working of the Spirit only follows later, leads to the assumption that the striking statements in verse 3 function to introduce Paul's thesis. Accordingly, this verse has been considered rhetorically as a *proposito*.[138]

That means that in verse 3 a central statement summarizing the whole passage on the working of the Spirit (chs. 12–14) is to be expected.

---

judgment—is the essence of the spiritual" (my translation). Cf. also Bassler, "Curse." Smit, "Argument and Genre," 212–14 also considers the rhetorical context, when he defines 1 Cor 12:1–3 as *exordium* with *insinuatio*.

136. It is usually surmised that this involves ecstatic phenomena in service of the gods. Paige, "Pagan Pompe" suspects a procession for the gods. On the discussion, see Thiselton, *First Corinthians*, 911–16.

137. For example, it remains unclear in Vos, "Rätsel" to what extent v. 3 is a conclusion from v. 2.

138. Standaert, "Analyse rhétorique," 30–31; Vos, "Rätsel," 268.

So this excludes interpretations according to which Paul, in verse 3, is addressing a theme not continued in the following passages.

For the first hearers of the letter, the *proposito* would have clearly delineated the apostle's concern. That is the function of such an introductory thesis, namely, to prepare the listeners for what they can expect from the following speech and how they should understand the following arguments. Since modern readers have obvious difficulties with verse 3, the opposite procedure is expedient—that is, using all the apostle's statements in the passage as a help to understand the *proposito*.

Parallelism of 1 Corinthians 12:3 and 12–27

Paul's goal in 1 Corinthians 12–14 is to help the church suffering from divisions and tensions find unity.[139] After treating this goal in relationship to other factors, Paul now concerns himself with the situation that the diversity of spiritual gifts in the Corinthian church has led to rivalry, confusion, and mutual contempt.

The apostle emphasizes with three parallel sentences in 1 Cor 12:4–6 that despite the differences, the charismata all have a common origin, which he characterizes as a trinity of Spirit, Kyrios, and God, thereby cleverly establishing a divine unity in diversity. The diverse gifts display unity not only in source but also in purpose, since they are for the benefit of all (v. 7: πρὸς τὸ συμφέρον). There follows a list of the diverse gifts, which all emanate from the same Spirit (vv. 8–11).

The issue of the unity of the diverse workings of the Spirit is made clear by the conventional metaphor of the body (vv. 12–27).[140] What is often neglected in this respect is the fact that Paul picks up thoughts and structures that had already been used in the introduction. They can be summarized in five points.

1) Just as Paul reminded the listeners of their heathen past in verse 2, so verse 13 contains a *retrospective view*, speaking about how the previous ethnic and social differences were relativized through baptism.

2) Not only the past change from unbelief to belief is mentioned, but also the *working of the Spirit* in their lives when this change happened called to mind (v. 3: ἐν πνεύματι θεοῦ, ἐν πνεύματι ἁγίῳ; v. 13: ἐν ἑνὶ πνεύματι).

---

139. On this, see in particular Mitchell, *Paul and the Rhetoric*.
140. On this metaphor, cf. ibid., 157–63.

3) In verse 3, Paul quotes and comments on two short confessions in the form of nominal sentences, which possibly could be repeated by the audience or perhaps had been spoken by others: Ἀνάθεμα Ἰησοῦς and Κύριος Ἰησοῦς. Such *quotations* are also found in verses 15–16 and 21.

4) The argument in which the quoted statements are to be found is twice worded as a negation in verse 3: "*no one* speaking . . ." and "*no one* can say . . ." The argument in verses 15–22 is also a negation. What is said by the foot and the ear and also by the eye and the head is refused as unjustified. Verses 15–22 present an energetic rebuttal of false thinking and judgment (v. 22: ἀλλὰ πολλῷ μᾶλλον), just as verse 3 does.

5) The structure of verse 3 is characterized by two short sentences parallel in form. They are usually understood as an instance of antithetical *parallelism*.[141] The hallmark of antithetical parallelism is two opposing or contrasting statements serving to emphasize *one* specific thought. An antithetic structure, although far more elaborate, is also found in verses 15–21. First, feet and ears are quoted in parallel wording: "Because I am not a hand/eye, I am not a part of the body" (vv. 15–16). A general section follows without dialogue, explaining why the statements quoted are not appropriate, and emphasizing that the various members are essential parts of the same body (vv. 17–20). Verse 21 starts anew, again with two parallel quotations, this time from eye and head: "I have no need of you." Again a passage follows with a fundamental argument, rebutting the quotations and explaining why all members of the body are necessary, especially those parts that often are thought to be less important (vv. 22–24). There are thus two sections that stand antithetically opposed insofar as that the speakers being quoted have contrasting positions in the social ranking of the church. First, the despised members declare their inferiority and question their position as members of the body. Then the distinguished members proudly express their independence.

The conclusion of the body illustration is the statement that there should not be division in the body but that its members should unite in caring for one another and take an active interest in each other (vv. 25–26). Paul then departs from the image of the body and applies the resulting lesson to the church and its diverse gifts (vv. 27–30). All this results in the following structure:

---

141. Vos, "Rätsel," 256–58 disagrees.

Introduction	v. 14	Introducing the body illustration
Section 1		
1.1		Statements from the despised
1.1.1	v. 15	Foot
1.1.2	v. 16	Ear
1.2	vv. 17–20	Paul: all members belong to the body
Section 2		
2.1		Statements from the distinguished
2.1.1	v. 21a	Eye
2.1.2	v. 21b	Head
2.2	vv. 22–24	Paul: all members are needed
End	vv. 25–27	Applying the image of the body

Tensions among the Corinthians

The parallel structure of this section leads performance critics to make conclusions about the addressees in the Corinthian church. The performance with its opposing quotations points to two groups among the listeners, who are in tension with one another. At the same time the differing positions among the listeners are reduced to two, a two-party situation is created among the listeners. The quotations from the inferior and superior body parts are the means used to refer to the groups. Each person present at the performance would know who was meant by the references to the foot, the ear, the eye, and the head. Since the characterizations of both groups included aspects of their status (μέλη τοῦ σώματος ἀσθενέστερα . . . ἀτιμότερα), and since people of the same status often sat together in the church meeting, it is quite possible that the members of the groups sat together, and that the presenter turned to them or made gestures in their direction to indicate them.

The foot and the ear, less eminent members of the body, are quoted in statements that express their lowly status and even question whether they belong to the body of Christ. Apparently Paul had certain people in mind who did not possess spectacular gifts of the Spirit. Although it put them in an inferior position,[142] they had nevertheless adopted for them-

---

142. Martin, *Corinthian Body*, 88–96 points to "esoteric speech" as a status symbol

selves a typically high estimation of the gifts of the Spirit and of speaking in tongues; they, like others in the Corinthian church, felt that the ones who have such gifts deserved honor.[143] It is important to note the emotion of discouragement and low self-esteem that tinged such statements, which the performer would have conveyed vocally.

Paul tells these church members with low self-esteem that each member is a part of the body and is needed, no matter how important or insignificant the manifestation of the Spirit may be in him or her.

When the letter was read out to the church, the members having a higher status, because they possessed special gifts, would naturally be listening too. Their looking down on those whose gifts appear to be less important would be indirectly corrected. But it is also implicitly stated, that there is no reason why glossolalia or any other working of the Spirit should be banned from the church.

The presenter would then turn to those in the church who felt that they were important. He tells them explicitly, using Paul's words, that the apparently unimportant members should not be looked down upon; in fact, even these deserve special care and attention. The lowly members hear that too and know that Paul accepts them and has a high regard for them.

The apostle, in this passage, therefore speaks specifically to the various groups in the church, aiming for mutual acceptance. Each side in the audience should look favorably on the others, and that would be literally true during the performance.

Chapter 13 follows, showing that it is love that actually creates the bond of unity. Only through love can the various gifts be of value to the church (vv. 1–3). Paul turns here to the desire for status in the church (οὐθέν εἰμι), which is expressed in the importance attached to different gifts, as the illustration of the body has made clear. Paul relativizes the importance of all the workings of the Spirit, particularly of speaking in the language of angels (glossolalia) and prophecy. Love, however, is not tied to certain workings of the Spirit, with which some Corinthians sought to bolster their status. Chapter 13 therefore develops the theme of chapter 12 further in the sense that those who could demonstrate

---

and to the hierarchical order implied by the illustration of the body.

143. Shiner, *Proclaiming*, 171 and 178 points out that, during the performance, what happens in the fictive world of the story—that would be here the imaginary speech of the body members—also happens in the social world of the audience. The listeners find themselves in the story.

impressive workings of the Spirit—represented in the illustration of the body by the eyes, hands, and head—are contrasted with the more valuable and decisive factor of love.

At the same time, chapter 13 introduces a *new* thought, which is then explained more thoroughly in chapter 14. Glossolalia and prophecy, two outstanding workings of the Spirit, are named in verses 1–2 and verses 8–9; knowledge is also mentioned in each reference. It would appear that glossolalia and prophecy—the latter characterized by an increase in knowledge—are two workings of the Spirit that the apostle had special reason to single out. That is done in chapter 14, where Paul ascribes prophecy greater importance—again in connection with knowledge (v. 6)—because, in contrast to glossolalia, it is understandable and can serve to edify others (14:2–14). From a performance point of view, it becomes clear that chapter 13 has a hitherto largely overlooked *bridging* function. While in chapter 12 the contrast is between those exhibiting spiritual gifts and those who cannot, in chapter 14 the contrast is between other groups, namely, those speaking in tongues and the prophets. This shift in contrast occurs in chapter 13.

Therefore, in chapter 14, the apostle is no longer criticizing the disregard for believers with few or no spiritual gifts. In chapter 14 he mediates a *hierarchical dispute* between the groups practicing glossolalia and prophecy. Now those who are excluded from the two disputing groups because they apparently have no spiritual gifts are in a (comfortable) position as observers.[144]

In the hierarchical dispute, Paul allocates the more spectacular gift to a lower rank and gives prophecy a higher position by pointing out its understandability that leads to an increase in knowledge. However, Paul is careful not to completely ban glossolalia from the church (14:5, 15, 18–19). Each gift has its justification and is welcome in the church—if it fulfills certain conditions.

These conditions are listed at the end of the chapter. Paul gives specific instructions regulating how those speaking in tongues or prophesying should behave (14:27–33). He again addresses the representatives of two groups one after another, each time with the other group listening. By setting out the directions using a parallel structure (limiting the number of speakers in vv. 27 and 29, σιγάτω in vv. 28 and 30), he makes

---

[144]. If Paul speaks to the Gentile Christians in 1 Cor 12:2, because speaking in tongues was especially practiced by them, it could be that he now includes the Jewish Christians. Perhaps the prophets were especially prevalent among them.

sure that both groups have the same rights. The parallel structure can be depicted as follows:

Introduction	v. 26	Diversity in the church service, admonition to orderliness
Section 1	vv. 27–28	Direction for those speaking in tongues
1.1	v. 27a	Number: two or three
1.2	v. 27b	One after another
1.3	vv. 27c–28	Keeping silent if there is no interpreter present
Section 2	vv. 29–32	Directions for those prophesying
2.1	v. 29	Number: two or three
2.2	v. 30	Silence, when another begins to prophesy
2.3	vv. 31–32	One after another
End	v. 33	Principle behind all instructions: God is a God of peace

It can be deduced from the two sections with parallelism in chapters 12 and 14 that Paul divides the letter's recipients into different groups. On the one hand, there are the πνευματικοί, who present the workings of the Holy Spirit in order to enhance their own status in the church. They themselves are divided into two rival groups: the prophets and those who speak in tongues. On the other hand, there are those believers who are looked down upon by the πνευματικοί because they cannot exhibit such gifts.[145]

Finally Paul comes to his concluding remarks, first addressing the prophets and the (other) spiritually gifted (those who speak in tongues?) and pointing out that he himself is speaking with divine authority (vv. 37–38). Allen Rhea Hunt points out the sarcasm in this verse.[146] Those with spiritual gifts, especially those who spoke in tongues and prophesied, who had just been admonished by Paul, could prove their spiritual

---

145. Wire, *Corinthian Women*, 140–43 interprets the contrast between the prophets and those who speak in tongues in 1 Corinthians 14 as Paul's *goal* and not as an *existing* contrast among the Corinthians. She argues that prophecy and ecstatic prayer belonged together for the female prophets in Corinth, but Paul wanted to reduce speaking in tongues and curtail the amount of speaking in general in order to create more room for reflection. However, if individual women in Corinth combined both prophecy and speaking in tongues (and other gifts) in one person, thus manifesting a lively diversity of speech in the church, then Paul could not expect a negative answer to his questions in 1 Cor 12:29–30.

146. Cf. Hunt, *Inspired Body*, 136–39.

competence by acknowledging the admonition as inspired by the Spirit. The performer would have expressed the sarcasm through tone of voice and intonation. This would have inevitably put smiles on the faces of those described as having no or lesser gifts.

Two short parallel instructions follow, directed successively at each of the rival Spirit-filled groups; the instructions read to one group validate the gift of the rival group (v. 39). To those who speak in tongues Paul says, Seek to prophesy. To the prophets he says, Do not forbid speaking in tongues. The conclusion is an admonition to all: All things should be done decently and in order (v. 40). What we find in verses 39–40 corresponds to a way of speaking that we have already observed many times, with which Paul seeks to reconcile different opinions by giving an admonishment for each group that upholds the value of the other group. Also the final admonition directed to both sides fits into this scheme.[147]

Just as we have found that 1 Cor 12:4-27 contains parallels to 1 Cor 12:1-3, which is the introduction to the whole section, we also find that the conclusion of chapter 14 also corresponds in two points to the beginning of chapter 12, in that apostolic authority is emphasized (12:1 and 14:37-38) and then two parallel statements are presented (12:3 and 14:39).

Reconciliation of Opposites in 1 Corinthians 12:3

From the above consideration of the context, we can now draw conclusions for a better understanding of 1 Cor 12:3. Since the whole passage is concerned with fostering unity among the various groups in the Corinthian church, this intention must also be postulated for the *proposito* in 1 Cor 12:3.[148] This excludes those interpretations that see in this verse a criterion for distinguishing between spirits or between a true confession in word and deed and a false one. Such a criterion would have the purpose of delineating borders, whereas the apostle is much rather endeavoring to break them down. Also all interpretations that see this as a curse for-

---

147. See what has been said above on pp. 165-66 and pp. 171-73 about Rom 14:3 and 6-9.

148. So rightly Vos, "Rätsel," 260. Cf. Mitchell, *Paul and the Rhetoric*, 267-68: "In 12:3 Paul relativizes all claims to greater or less spiritual attainment because of ecstatic gifts by saying that every Christian is indeed a spiritual person, because every Christian who makes the common acclamation Κύριος Ἰησοῦς (cf. 8:6) shows that he or she is possessed by the Holy Spirit."

mula used outside the church do not fit the context, which is concerned with internal issues of status and rivalries in the church. There is also no mention of a persecution situation. Neither does the problem of a false (Walter Schmithals) or an inadequate (Willem van Unnik) understanding of Christ appear anywhere in the context.

After having shown that Paul is addressing opposing groups in the church in both chapters 12 and 14 through parallel sections of his letter, we can expect that the parallel statements in 1 Cor 12:3 have the same purpose. To one group in the Corinthian church Paul says that no one speaking in the Spirit curses Jesus. To another group he says that no one confesses Jesus as Lord who does not have the Holy Spirit. And because as the apostle is seeking to create a balance between the groups throughout the whole passage—on the one hand by recognizing the status of both groups in the church (all are members of the body; glossolalia and prophecy both belong in the church), and on the other hand by also correcting both sides—we can therefore also assume that 1 Cor 12:3 has the same purpose. Thus interpretations of 1 Cor 12:3 that would place the cursing of and the confessing of Jesus outside this context and do not consider that they belong together and are used as mutually complementing arguments can be eliminated.

In the *proposito*, the apostle formulates on the one hand what those speaking in the Spirit do *not* say, and on the other hand that which *cannot* be said without the Spirit: that is, he formulates each statement negatively. This manner of speaking returns in 1 Cor 12:15–21, where the apostle corrects two false assumptions among the Corinthians: the inferiority of those who cannot demonstrate impressive workings of the Spirit, and the proud self-satisfaction of those who can.[149]

What is the false way of thinking Paul is correcting in 1 Cor 12:3? From each of the parallel sentences it can be deduced what the respective addressees thought.

The first clause presupposes that the speaking is indeed done in the Spirit: "No one speaking in the Spirit . . ." Paul does not discuss the issue of whether the words are spoken in the Spirit or not. Of course there are statements that are not spoken in the Spirit, but these is not the apostle's concern. What he wants to clarify is the *possible content* of what is spoken in the Spirit. Paul expresses it as a negation: it would *not be a curse*.[150]

---

149. First Corinthians 13:1–3 is also an argument of negation, since the absolute status ascribed to glossolalia and prophecy is corrected by the reference to love.

150. Vos, "Rätsel," 257: "In 3b Paul does not formulate a prerequisite for the

The emphasis is placed on the curse and underlined by its position as the conclusion of the statement. The logic of the argument is that the power and efficacy of the Spirit allow us to draw conclusions about the content of what would or would not be spoken in the Spirit (*argumentatio e causa ad effectum*).[151]

If Paul is rejecting the way of thinking of a certain group in Corinth, then this way of thinking must be based on the same premise (i.e. speaking in the Spirit) but draw an opposite conclusion. It could be formulated like this: "Certain people, who are speaking in the Spirit, are cursing Jesus." Whether Jesus is really being cursed or not is not so unequivocal that opinions could not differ on the subject. If some of the Corinthians had uttered a curse understandable for all present in the church service, as Schmithals and van Unnik suspect, then Paul would not have been able to dispute it.[152]

How can one imagine the situation in which there was disagreement about whether some of the church members in Corinth had uttered a curse when speaking in the Spirit or not? The context is also helpful here. A basic assumption contained in chapters 12 and 14 is the fact that glossolalia, which was so highly esteemed in Corinth, was not understandable in the church unless an interpreter was actively involved, which was probably seldom the case; otherwise Paul would not have required that speaking in tongues must be translated. So it would have been those speaking in tongues whose utterances were under dispute. After a solemn introduction, Paul, with his statement concerning the contents of what is spoken in the Spirit, addresses those church members who are skeptical about glossolalia. The accusations or at least misgivings that those

---

cursing of Jesus but rather a thesis concerning the content of speaking in the Spirit" (my translation).

151. In contrast, many interpretations, especially those that see a criterion in the text for differentiating between the spirits, reason from effect to cause and presuppose the following wording: οὐδεὶς λέγων Ἀνάθεμα Ἰησοῦς ἐν πνεύματι θεοῦ λαλεῖ ("No one who says 'Jesus is cursed' is speaking in the Holy Spirit").

152. Schmithals, *Gnosis*, 117; van Unnik, "Jesus," 119–21. Cullmann, *Christologie*, 225 also argues that the curse as well as the confession must have been understandable. Holtz, "Kennzeichen des Geistes," 370 follows him. Thereby it is overlooked that the two sentences containing the quoted statements are not parallel in one important point: In the first sentence the curse is not the presupposed fact; the presupposed fact is rather that the speaking is done in the Spirit. The content of what is being said is only the result of an inference. By contrast, the presupposition in the second sentence is the confession: that is, the content of what is being said is taken as a given fact from which it is implied that the speaker must possess the Spirit.

speaking in tongues could be cursing Jesus with their incomprehensible words would have arisen among these members. Paul rejects this, thereby requiring acceptance of this working of the Spirit.

The second clause presumes a different situation. Here the presupposition is not that the speaking is done in the Spirit, presupposed is the confession to the Lord Jesus: "No one can say, Jesus is Lord . . ." It is not a question of whether someone confesses Jesus to be Lord or not, neither is it a question of the full validity of the confession—although these questions could be asked. Rather Paul is declaring that confessing Jesus as *Kyrios* is only possible through the working of the Spirit. The emphasis is on the conclusion of the clause, and the sole condition that enables somebody to utter the confession. The logic of the argument begins with the fact of the spoken confession and concludes that the Spirit must be working (*argumentatio ex effectu ad causam*).[153] This leads to the following structure:

διὸ γνωρίζω ὑμῖν ὅτι

| οὐδεὶς | ἐν πνεύματι θεοῦ λαλῶν | λέγει· Ἀνάθεμα Ἰησοῦς, |
| καὶ οὐδεὶς | δύναται εἰπεῖν· Κύριος Ἰησοῦς, | εἰ μὴ ἐν πνεύματι ἁγίῳ. |

Sentence 1:
"No one"   Cause (Holy Spirit)   →   Effect (spoken formula)

Sentence 2:
"No one"   Effect (spoken formula)   →   Cause (Holy Spirit)

Paul's move from the Spirit's activity to the content of the utterance in the first clause, and in the second clause his move in exactly the opposite direction (i.e., from what had been said to the workings of the Spirit) contradict the interpretation that Paul had composed the negated curse formula as a contrast to the following confession.[154] The Corinthi-

---

153. Vos, "Rätsel," 255: Paul makes "possessing the Holy Spirit to a prerequisite for confessing the Lord" (my translation). That is factually correct. However, it would distort the emphasis in Paul's statement if the focus is placed on the question of whether the confession of the Lord was spoken genuinely or not. That is not Paul's concern, but rather whether the Spirit was effective in this believer—and continues to be so—or not.

154. If Paul wanted to compose a contrast to the confession, the first sentence (cause → statement) "No one who speaks in the Spirit says, 'Jesus is cursed,'" should have been followed by ". . . but who speaks in the Spirit says: 'Jesus is Lord.'" Or as a contrast to the second sentence (statement → cause), "No one can say 'Jesus is Lord,'

ans, whom Paul repudiated here, assume, as he does, that certain church members have uttered the confession "Jesus is Lord." Now this has, of course, been confessed by *every* believer upon baptism. What was in dispute was whether or not a particular group of Corinthian Christians had the Holy Spirit. And here Paul solemnly makes clear that no one can confess Jesus without the Holy Spirit. In this sentence Paul is addressing church members who are revealing glossolalia or other impressive workings of the Spirit. Because of them, church members without such gifts were being held in low esteem; even their church membership was being called into question (12:15–16: "I do not belong to the body"). Paul counters this by appealing to the confession that all Christians had made. Paul in fact declares that church members without impressive spiritual gifts also have the Holy Spirit, since they could not otherwise have spoken the baptismal confession.

Thus it becomes clear why Paul refers to the Corinthians' background in verse 2 and to baptism in verse 13. That they, through baptism, had put their past behind them, was in fact true for all members. Paul appealed to the Corinthians' common non-Christian past in order to encourage mutual acceptance, which verse 3 and the rest of the passage seek to foster among them.

What was the effect Paul wanted to achieve with the performance of 1 Cor 12:3? His arguments are logical. He brings clarity of thought into a dispute troubling the church. But he also achieves an emotional effect. Each group is raised in esteem in the eyes of the other. On the one hand, those speaking in tongues are freed from the accusation that they are cursing Jesus. Even when one does not understand what they are saying, Paul argues, one can be sure they are not cursing Jesus. On the other hand, glossolalia is relativized: it is not the only, and indeed not the decisive, working of the Spirit. Those who do not have this gift nevertheless have the Holy Spirit. Paul here acts as mediator. Just as his representative—the one presenting the letter—stands apart facing both parties, so does Paul. He shows understanding for both sides. He offers himself as example, since he confesses practicing glossolalia himself yet still lays value on understandable speech in which God's own presence is felt (which is the effect of prophetic speech, according to 14:25). The aim

---

unless through the Spirit," Paul should have written, "Whoever curses Jesus does not have the Holy Spirit," or (Vos, "Rätsel," 257) "None can say 'Jesus is cursed' except through an *evil* spirit" (my translation, italics added).

of this strategy is positive interaction between the groups, and this right at the beginning of the passage.

This interpretation of 1 Cor 12:3 is certainly not new. Carl Friedrich Georg Heinrici (1880) has already interpreted the sentence with the curse formula as a concession to those speaking in tongues: it may not be intelligible, but what they are saying can only be a confession of Jesus.[155] Philipp Bachmann's (1905) interpretation was, Paul was arguing against a mistrust of glossolalia.[156] When we consider the performance of Paul's letter in the church assembly in Corinth, this old suggestion gains new weight and appears to be the most plausible explanation of this difficult text.

The Relationship of the Leaders to Those Being Led

Using examples from 1 Thess 5:12–15 and Gal 6:1–10, the following sections will show how Paul, by means of the one presenting his letter, achieves interaction among the listeners that serves to promote a friendly relationship between members of different social groups in the church, between those who are leading out and those who are being led. It will again be seen that as Paul was writing the letter he had mentally anticipated its performance in the church meeting. Paul wrote the performance—as if writing a theater script—into the text. Thereby he knew how to encourage a certain kind of interaction among the audience members, and how to use it to serve his own ends.

1 Thessalonians 5:12–15

1 Thess 5:12–15 is interesting from the viewpoint of the performance of the letter, since Paul does not address the whole church in verse 12, but rather a specific group. This may not be recognizable in how they are addressed, because Paul uses the otherwise common ἀδελφοί, which is used in other parts of the letter to designate the whole church (2:1, 17; 4:1, 13; 5:1). But, quite clearly, the admonition that follows cannot be applied to all:

---

155. Heinrici, *Erste Sendschreiben an die Korinther*, 360.
156. Bachmann, *Erster Korintherbrief*, 386.

Ἐρωτῶμεν δὲ ὑμᾶς, ἀδελφοί, εἰδέναι τοὺς κοπιῶντας ἐν ὑμῖν καὶ προϊσταμένους ὑμῶν ἐν κυρίῳ καὶ νουθετοῦντας ὑμᾶς.

But we request of you, brethren, that you appreciate those who diligently labor among you, and have charge over you in the Lord and give you instruction.

Those who are being admonished and led by some church members should accept and respect them as leaders. Listeners are divided into two groups by this sentence. One group is described by οἱ κοπιῶντες καὶ προϊστάμενοι καὶ νουθετοῦντες. These are verbs that denote leadership functions. Using only one article for three participles shows that there are not three different leadership groups, but that Paul is separating one group of church members from the audience, who performs the three different tasks.[157] The other group consists of those to whom the sentence is directed. They are the ones who profit from the efforts of the first group.

What effect would this sentence have when it was read out by the one presenting the letter? Since nobody is specifically named, its message cannot be clearly assigned to any specific person. It is also improbable that the tasks mentioned are a description of a formal administrative structure.[158] This means that there is no clear delineation between the groups being described here. Each listener must decide for himself or herself whom he or she perceives to be performing the leadership duties described and whether or not he or she sees himself or herself as belonging to that group. However, experience would make a correlation possible for the church, since certain personalities would have assumed leadership duties because of their abilities or social position. Paul assumes that it would be possible to correlate the statement to a leadership group as described. However, it could be that individual listeners find themselves in both groups, since they sometimes work for the church and at other times receive care and admonishment.

It should be noted that Paul phrases both his exhortations in verse 12 and in verse 14 in the *we*-form. This adds a third group separate from the two groups into which he has divided the audience, namely, the apostle and his coworkers. In the salutation at the beginning of the letter,

---

157. Cf. Ellis, "Paul and His Co-Workers," 441.

158. On the situation of administrative offices in Thessalonica, cf. Malherbe, *Thessalonians*, 66: "They would have had functional, if not institutionalized authority." Also pp. 312-13. Cf. Laub, *Eschatologische Verkündigung*, 70-71. On the natural leadership authority of the first converts in churches, cf. Schmitt, *Paroikie*, 104-5.

Silvanus and Timothy are identified by name as cosenders who probably stand as representatives of Paul's entire team.[159] This third group is represented by an *individual* person in the performance situation. Every time the presenter as an individual speaks the verb in the form of the first-person plural, indicating Paul and his coworkers (here ἐρωτῶμεν and παρακαλοῦμεν) the listeners would experience a break in the illusion that it was actually Paul's voice they were hearing. They would become aware that they were the audience in a performance of Paul's letter. They thus had to imagine Paul's coworkers as being gathered around Paul, although in reality they saw only a single person standing before them. The result would be that they—in the typical role of an audience—would evaluate the performance, that is, decide whether the presenter has presented himself and spoken in way that in their opinion corresponded to how the apostle would. That of course put the reader under pressure to give his best performance.

In verse 14 comes a second injunction.

Παρακαλοῦμεν δὲ ὑμᾶς, ἀδελφοί, νουθετεῖτε τοὺς ἀτάκτους, παραμυθεῖσθε τοὺς ὀλιγοψύχους, ἀντέχεσθε τῶν ἀσθενῶν, μακροθυμεῖτε πρὸς πάντας.

We urge you, brethren, admonish the unruly, encourage the fainthearted, help the weak, be patient with everyone.

Again we find ἀδελφοί used as address. This time it is for those who encourage and admonish other church members.[160] In principle, these tasks could be exercised by any church member. So, for example, notice the inference in 5:11: "encourage one another" (παρακαλεῖτε ἀλλήλους). Nevertheless, Ernest Best and others are not convincing when they argue that the admonition in verse 14 is addressed to all church members.[161]

Ernest Best presents five arguments:

1) The position of leader was not a clearly defined role. It is probably true that leadership positions were not established as permanent offices. Nevertheless, there would have been persons who had accepted special

---

159. Stirewalt, *Paul*, 37–44. See also Ollrog, *Paulus und seine Mitarbeiter*, 184; Loubser, "Media Criticism." Malherbe, *Thessalonians*, 88 thinks of a "majestic plural." Ellis, "Paul and His Co-Workers" understands the "brothers" spoken of in Paul's Epistles as referring to the apostle's local coworkers.

160. Masson, *Thessalonicians*, 73; Holmstrand, *Markers and Meaning*, 66–67.

161. Best, *Thessalonians*, 229; cf. Holtz, *Erster Thessalonicher*, 250; Malherbe, *Thessalonians*, 311, 316.

responsibility for the church, and these could be meant here. Although listeners could not always exactly define the boundaries of the leadership group, they would have had in minds a core group of those responsible.

2) In verse 16 and perhaps also verse 15 the whole church is addressed. Best finds no indication of Paul changing addressees from verse 14 to verse 15 or from verse 15 to verse 16. This argument of silence overlooks the fact that in the situation of the oral presentation, there was no need to explicitly formulate a change of addressee. The performer could make clear who was being spoken to by his gaze and posture.

3) Best judges the verb parallels in verses 12 and 14, ἐρωτῶμεν and παρακαλοῦμεν, as a sign that there is no change of addressee. But the content of the two admonitions clearly shows that the respective situations of those being addressed are different. It will become clear that the parallelism has another function.

4) Best takes the vocative ἀδελφοί in verses 12 and 14 as a sign that the whole church is being addressed. Not only verse 12 but also such texts as Rom 10:1 and 11:25 show that this is not justified. There Paul directs the message to Gentile believers and not to all of the recipients. In 1 Cor 10:14 (cf. also 2 Cor 7:1), Paul speaks to only part of the Corinthian church using ἀγαπητοί, namely, to those who are prepared to participate in public meals in heathen temples and not those who avoid meat because it could have been dedicated to heathen gods. In other texts Paul uses the same manner of address for the whole church (e.g., 1 Cor 15:58; 2 Cor 12:19).

5) Finally, Best cites other texts where Paul speaks about mutual exhortation and care (e.g., Rom 15:14; Phil 2:4; Col 3:16). Of course, Paul can urge mutual exhortation among church members. Even he as an apostle can receive encouragement from ordinary church members (1 Thess 3:7). However, that does not exclude the possibility that in 1 Thess 5:14 he is admonishing a few leading personalities in particular to do this task.

The fact that in verse 14 Paul turns to those who have taken on leadership duties becomes clear when the section's two-part structure is considered.[162] Both parts form a perfect parallelism.[163] Each begins by

---

162. In the words of Malherbe, *Thessalonians*, 309, "This section is divided in two parts, the first giving directions on how to treat those individuals who provide 'pastoral care' (vv. 12–13), the second directing the individuals who provide the care (vv. 14–15)."

163. Cf. Holmstrand, *Markers and Meaning*, 66–67; Malherbe, *Thessalonians*, 309–10.

expressing the apostle's desire (ἐρωτῶμεν/παρακαλοῦμεν), has the address ἀδελφοί, and then describes the appropriate behavior and correct attitude for members of the one group toward the other. In this way Paul addresses two social groups in a reciprocal relationship. The reciprocal relationship is also shown by the repetition of the verb νουθετεῖν in verses 12 and 14. At the end of each part is a generalization that is applicable not only to the group being addressed, but that can be valid for all: "Live in peace with one another" (v. 13b). And: "See that no one repays another with evil for evil, but always seek after that which is good for one another and for all people" (v. 15). The parallels ἐν ἑαυτοῖς (v. 13) and εἰς ἀλλήλους (v. 15) must also be taken into consideration. Verse 15 is expanded with an additional statement: καὶ εἰς πάντας. This changes the focus from the reciprocal relationship of the two groups and extends the perspective to others in general, ultimately encompassing all people.

A	Address to first group	v. 12	Ἐρωτῶμεν δὲ ὑμᾶς, ἀδελφοί,
B	Threefold admonition: Appreciate!		εἰδέναι τοὺς κοπιῶντας ἐν ὑμῖν καὶ προϊσταμένους ὑμῶν ἐν κυρίῳ καὶ νουθετοῦντας ὑμᾶς
C	Additional admonition: Love!	v. 13	καὶ ἡγεῖσθαι αὐτοὺς ὑπερεκπερισσοῦ ἐν ἀγάπῃ διὰ τὸ ἔργον αὐτῶν.
D	General admonition as transition		εἰρηνεύετε ἐν ἑαυτοῖς.
A'	Address to second group	v. 14	Παρακαλοῦμεν δὲ ὑμᾶς, ἀδελφοί,
B'	Threefold admonition, concrete problems		νουθετεῖτε τοὺς ἀτάκτους, παραμυθεῖσθε τοὺς ὀλιγοψύχους, ἀντέχεσθε τῶν ἀσθενῶν
C'	Additional admonition, general problem		μακροθυμεῖτε πρὸς πάντας.
D'1	General admonition	v. 15	ὁρᾶτε μή τις κακὸν ἀντὶ κακοῦ τινι ἀποδῷ,
D'2	General admonition as transition, outsiders in view		ἀλλὰ πάντοτε τὸ ἀγαθὸν διώκετε καὶ εἰς ἀλλήλους καὶ εἰς πάντας.

Each part has a structure including three elements and an addition. In the first part there are three participles, which represent the three objects for the imperative (v. 12). An additional sentence (v. 13a) underlines and emphasizes the admonition. The second part has three imperatives, each with its own object describing a weakness or deficiency. There again follows an additional element, a fourth imperative, which has a more general object. This generalization also creates a further intensification.

The fact that Paul does not specifically say who is being addressed in the parallel admonitions can be explained by the performance situation.[164] If during the performance specific groups sat together, then the presenter could turn to them or look in their direction. This would be enough to demonstrate who was being addressed. The leaders probably had prominent places in the church meeting. (In Jas 2:2–3, we find polemics against social discrimination expressed in a seating arrangement[165] conforming to social conventions. Such polemics would not have been necessary had this not been a widespread practice.[166]) In the first of the parallel sections (1 Thess 5:12–13), the presenter speaks to those on the back benches or at the feet of the reclining distinguished guests. These would have been the majority. And while he is exhorting them to honor and love those leading and caring for them, he throws a glance towards the small group of dignitaries in the middle or gestures with his hand toward them. Of course everyone present would know who was meant anyway. The audience follows his glance and looks at the leaders whose work is then described.

With three participles—probably with acknowledgement in his voice—the presenter outlines the leaders' work. The triad is a symbol for completeness. A further imperative follows, that not only in word choice (ὑπερεκπερισσοῦ ἐν ἀγάπῃ) but also in sentence length and probably through the tone of voice as well, distinctly indicates an increase in importance. The linguistic form, the bodily gestures, and the content of what is being said form a coherent unit and turn the presentation into an event in which the listeners immediately experience what they are being admonished to do themselves: to show esteem for their leaders.

Paul indicates that respect is required of them by using the word εἰδέναι, which here has the meaning of "acknowledge" and includes obeying what leaders say. Paul points out the great effort these people invest

---

164. For example, it is different in 1 Cor 7:10, 12: "To the married I give this command . . . To the rest I say . . ." It is quite possible that married people and singles did not sit together in the performance and therefore could not be localized as groups in the room. Therefore they could not be indicated by the direction of the gaze or the body position, but had to be explicitly named.

165. Cf. Klinghardt, *Gemeinschaftsmahl*, 75–83 on seating order.

166. Cf. Luke 14:7–11; 1 Cor 11:21 also assumes that those who had enough to eat were sitting together. Cf. Theissen, "Soziale Integration" on the problems with the Lord's Supper.

(κοπιῶντες), acknowledges that their work is done at the Lord's commission (ἐν κυρίῳ), and points out that everything the leaders do is done for those being addressed (ἐν ὑμῖν/ὑμῶν/ὑμᾶς).[167] Verse 13 heightens the acknowledgement: "Esteem them very highly in love." This positive attitude toward the leaders would not only improve the relationship of church members to their leaders, but would also be good for the listening leaders to hear, and would encourage them in their work.

Verse 13b speaks directly to the mutual relationship of the groups that the performance has created: Live in peace with one another! Unlike the previous sentences, the content of this one is not aimed at a particular group but is meant for all. With this short sentence, the presenter would in a sense disengage from the group being addressed in the back seats: he would look around the room and then turn to the leaders. Here again the speech and actions of the presenter would complement each other. The transition would not happen abruptly but at the speed that corresponded to the performer's bodily orientation toward the second group.[168]

Now the presenter addresses the group of dignitaries on the places of honor. The congregation assembled on the rear seats is listening and watching the leaders.[169] There are four imperatives. Each has three words, which would result in a rhythmic presentation. The first two form an end rhyme. The presenter's voice resonates with appreciation and understanding.

The very first admonition has a positive undertone: the unruly (ἄτακτοι) must be admonished. There is still hope for them, so one should not withdraw from them (cf. 2 Thess 3:6). Second, Paul asks that the fainthearted be comforted (παραμυθεῖσθαι).[170] They are not being accused of disbelief or inconsistency. They reveal human weakness as could happen to anyone. The third admonition continues the positive basic at-

---

167. Malherbe, *Thessalonians*, 311 interprets οἱ κοπιῶντες ἐν ὑμῖν as missionary work, not service for the church members, which should, in his opinion, have been expressed with εἰς ὑμᾶς. But the section's parallel structure shows clearly that the groups are reciprocally connected.

168. Cf. above on p. 178 on Rom 14:13.

169. Malherbe, *Thessalonians*, 316.

170. Paul himself had provided comfort to church members in Thessalonica, cf. 1 Thess 2:12. The word παραμυθία is used by Paul in 1 Cor 14:3 for the work of the prophets. It could be that the leaders being addressed in the Thessalonian church saw themselves as charismatic leaders, or that Paul understood their work in the light of prophetic service. Whatever the case, Paul reminds them that their work serves to edify the church.

titude toward some problematic church members who are described as weak and therefore in need of help (οἱ ἀσθενεῖς). The stronger ones should attend to them.[171] The final admonition (μακροθυμεῖτε) also requires seeing the others in a positive way, namely, to hope for them and to trust the good in them. The generalization at the end (πρὸς πάντας) signals that this sequence also, as in verses 12–13, concludes with a fourth, more comprehensive element. Here also we find a progression, in that the first admonition speaks of a serious failure of some members (ἄτακτος); in the second and third only certain human weaknesses are mentioned (ὀλιγόψυχος, ἀσθενής), while finally the fourth mentions nothing that would have to be criticized or corrected. The positive basic attitude toward the believers with whom the leaders should do their work gradually becomes more and more clear.

How would the normal church members have reacted when they heard Paul's admonitions to the leaders? Even if most of them would not have considered themselves idle, fainthearted or weak, it would have been helpful for them to hear Paul encouraging a more positive attitude to the weak. Having heard these words, the followers might have found it much easier to accept the ministry of the leaders. By using this strategy, Paul helps foster mutual understanding between the leadership and the other church members.

Toward the end (v. 15), after speaking to the church leaders, the reader widens the perspective to encompass the whole church and admonishes them not to repay evil with evil but rather to do good to one another and—in a further widening of the perspective—also to those outside the church.[172] This, as in verse 13b, is also a very appropriate concluding signal and transition to what follows.

---

171. According to Malherbe, *Thessalonians*, 318–19 (there also pertinent literature), this is part of the psychagogic tradition of the philosophers. The description "weak" is used again by Paul in 1 Cor 8–9 and Rom 14–15, not in a pejorative manner, but rather to encourage help and care as exemplified by Christ. Cf. what has been said above on pp. 158–60 about the weak in Rom 14–15.

172. Barclay, "Conflict," 520–25 presumes that Paul is urging the Christians to have a positive attitude toward those outside of the church because there was a real danger of their taking revenge for the wrongs experienced in their heathen surroundings. The tension on the side of the Christians could have been expressed through harsh criticism and provocative missionizing. Barclay thus makes a connection between the reference to the outsiders (καὶ εἰς πάντας) and 1 Thess 5:15a, which is not justified linguistically.

The two parallel admonitions that Paul gives the Thessalonian church have the goal of fostering a healthy relationship between the church members and their leaders, who are working on their behalf. Paul's words engage two fronts simultaneously and so have a double effect. The performance first divides the church into two groups. The dividing border may not have been very clearly demarcated but could have easily turned into a battlefront. The letter acknowledges this possibility, very likely only a latent one, and deals with it.[173] The audience would have experienced the division immediately while listening. They would have been made acutely aware of the social differences in the church. But these were acknowledged in a way that enabled all to develop and practice the mutual acceptance and positive attitude demanded of them toward the other group. At the end of the performance the division would have been overcome and unity created despite social role differences. Therefore the members have not only heard about a positive attitude toward those in another group within the church, but it has also experienced and practiced this attitude while listening. After this the entire church is immediately admonished to exercise the positive attitude thus gained by doing good *to all*. With this admonition, the church as a whole is placed in juxtaposition to those outside.[174] Through the performance, listeners experience that it is possible to live in a healthy way with social differences and overcome the danger of disunity. This experience would help the church in future situations where the unity is threatened. The performance is practice for real life.

The presenter of the First Letter of Thessalonians plays an important role in this process. He embodies Paul, gives him his voice, and takes his position in the performative space.[175] The performer stands apart from all the other groups as the representative of the apostolic authority and of the church's founder. Because he wants to achieve a good relation-

---

173. The urgent instruction in 1 Thess 5:27 shows also that Paul's objective is to strengthen unity in the church. On this see also Oestreich, "Leseanweisungen."

174. Cf. von Lips, "Haustafeln," 273.

175. In this connection, Ward, "Pauline Voices," 95–96 writes: "Oral performance is a means of transforming silent texts into sounds and movement through the mediums of speech and gesture. It is a way in which the author-in-the-work becomes an audible person by means of the speech and movement of the presenter." Also p. 101: "Through the skillful use of voice and gesture, the representation of felt emotional values, and the thorough knowledge of the style and content of a given text, the oral performer in Greco-Roman culture embodied potent voices present in both oral and written material."

ship between both groups being spoken to, the performer takes care to address them in the same manner. That is the reason that he uses the same manner of address (ἀδελφοί) and arranges his admonitions in two parallel-structured sections. An imbalance would create the impression that Paul favored one of the sides. So the parallelism had the function of approaching both groups in the same manner. At the same time this strategy has the effect of setting Paul apart from *all* listeners, facing them all as an admonishing authority. During the performance of his letter, his authority would be recognized and confirmed by all attending.[176]

Galatians 6:1–10

We now turn to Gal 6:1–10, a part of the exhortation section of the Letter to the Galatians, and will compare it with 1 Thess 5:12–15.[177] This section at the end of the letter[178] has often been described as difficult and enigmatic. Paul presents a whole series of apparently unconnected admonitions, whose links to the rest of the letter have been questioned.[179] John Barclay, however, sees it differently. He explains the connection between the ethical admonitions and the main theme of the Letter to the Galatians—the controversy concerning some agitators' demands for circumcision—as follows: Paul's teaching that the law has lost its

---

176. In 2 Cor 13:11, at the end of the letter, we find an admonition that reminds us of 1 Thess 5:12–15. Paul again begins with the address ἀδελφοί and ends with the call to unity (τὸ αὐτὸ φρονεῖτε) and peace (εἰρηνεύετε). The church members are urged to let themselves be corrected (καταρτίζεσθε) and admonished (παρακαλεῖσθε). This call is comparable to 1 Thess 5:12, where the normal church members are being addressed. The passive imperatives presuppose that there is someone correcting them. But a corresponding admonition given to the authorities of the church, like in 1 Thess 5:14, is missing. The context of 2 Cor 13 makes it clear that Paul is thinking about his own authoritative role here. The Corinthians are being called to follow Paul's instructions. That shows that Paul's admonition to unity and peace in the church is closely bound up with his apostolic authority (cf. Wolff, *Zweiter Korinther*, 267).

177. Becker, *Galater*, 94 sees an exhortation in 1 Thess 5:12 that is "factually related" (my translation) to Gal 6:6.

178. In contrast to many other expositors, I see a new section beginning in Gal 6:1 marked by the use of the vocative ἀδελφοί.

179. It has often been said that the admonishing section at the end of the Letter to the Galatians conveys paraenetic tradition and has nothing to do with the actual intention of the letter, so e.g., Dibelius, *Formgeschichte*, 239; Eckert, *Urchristliche Verkündigung*, 149–52. By contrast, see Matera, "Culmination." Cf. Barclay, *Obeying*, 9–26; Schrage, "Probleme," 160–66; Schewe, *Galater*, 12–26 for a presentation and discussion of such interpretations.

relevance caused ethical uncertainty among the Galatians, resulting in immoral behavior. Because of this, the demand for obedience to the law became more attractive in Galatia, since the law promised the orientation in practical, everyday questions, which the Galatians had missed in the freedom of the gospel.[180] Paul, therefore, in order to bring the Galatians back away from the path of legalism, had to show how the power of the gospel brings order into the believers' lives. For Barclay, the admonishing part of the letter is not an appendix but actually the climax.[181] Barclay is certainly right when he sees the relationships between the believers in Galatia as being the topic in Gal 6:1–10. But it would seem that the paraenetic section of the Letter to the Galatians—despite the list of sins and virtues in 5:19–23—is not comprehensive enough to provide answers for a church seeking moral orientation. The emphasis lies too clearly on the relationships between the church members.

For Susanne Schewe, the admonishing sections are also an integral element of the Galatian Epistle. For her, the start of a return to the Jewish law is not the result of ethical insecurity and moral misconduct, as it is for Barclay. Rather, the moral deficit in Galatia, which is to be seen above all in the breakdown of fellowship, is a result of returning to the law. Paul shows in his admonitions in Gal 5 and 6 that the internal church difficulties are the consequence of relying on the law and thus on human σάρξ.[182]

On the other hand, Dieter Mitternacht has presented an interpretation of the Letter to the Galatians that emphasizes the relationship of the Galatian Christians to their apostle.[183] Mitternacht understands the Letter to the Galatians as an indirect call from Paul to the Galatians to bring proper order back into their relationship with him—after all, Paul had converted them—and to show this by obeying his gospel. We must concur with Mitternacht when he says that the relationship of the Galatians to the apostle is an important theme of the Letter to the Galatians. However, the relationship between the Galatians themselves is too prominent to be set aside. Performance criticism appears to be capable of connecting the two aspects.

180. Barclay, *Obeying*, 70–72, 106–7. Similarly Betz, *Galatians*, 8–9, 273–74; Longenecker, *Galatians*, xcviii; Schrage, "Probleme," 159 is skeptical.

181. Barclay, *Obeying*, 108–45; similarly Matera, "Culmination."

182. Schewe, *Galater*, 185–86, cf. also what is said on pp. 82–101 concerning σάρξ in Gal 5:13. For Schewe, the quarrel is not a second independent theme in Galatians (cf. pp. 110, 113 on 5:15).

183. Mitternacht, *Forum*.

Just as in 1 Thess 5:12–15, the structure of Gal 6:1–10 also implies that Paul is addressing two different groups of listeners.[184] We find a total of eight admonitions.[185] If we consider the degree of generality of the admonitions, then two of them are very specific: In verse 1 there is an admonition to gently help a person who has fallen into error (or whose sin has been uncovered).[186] Verse 6 calls listeners to support those who teach with (financial) goods.[187] These two imperatives appear to be a crucial instrument for structuring this section.[188]

Each of the admonitions is followed by a warning: "Each one looking to yourself, so that you too will not be tempted" (v. 1b), and "do not be deceived, God is not mocked" (v. 7a). Each of these warnings is connected to the previous imperative,[189] serving to emphasize it. Then, the tone changes. It follows a very general rule (vv. 2 and 7b), which is presented in the style of a proverb and is substantiated by a statement with "for if anyone . . ." (v. 3) and "for the one who . . ." (v. 8), respectively. The

---

184. There is no consensus concerning the structure of Gal 6:1–10. It has often been said that this section is lacking any logical order (Eckert, *Urchristliche Verkündigung*, 149; Mussner, *Galaterbrief*, 396, 408; Rohde, *Galater*, 257). See Barclay, *Obeying*, 147–49 for a discussion of the various suggested structures. Especially v. 6 seems to resist every attempt at meaningful integration into the section. Dunn, *Galatians*, 326 speaks of a "sudden thought"; Schrage, "Probleme," 167 of an "erratic block"; Lambrecht, "Paul's Coherent Admonition," 51 of an "afterthought"; Becker, *Galater*, 93 finds no logical connection. An interesting suggestion comes from Barclay (*Obeying*, 149–50; supported by Witherington, *Grace*, 418), who assumes a constant alternation between two general themes: mutual nurturing in the church ("corporate responsibility") and "individual accountability" to God. Gal 5:25–26 would therefore be a heading followed by seven sections (1a, 1b, 2, 3–5, 6, 7–8, 9–10). But this structure has the disadvantage that the fairly obvious division of the section into two halves, either before or after v. 6 (the commentators are unsure in that point), no longer plays a role.

185. Three imperatives in 2nd pers. pl., two in 3rd pers. sing., two adhortatives, and a participle with imperative sense.

186. Cf. Schewe, *Galater*, 144–45, n. 403 on the translation of προλημφθῇ.

187. A financial sense is assumed by Mussner, *Galaterbrief*, 402–3; Strelan, "Burden-Bearing"; Bruce, *Galatians*, 263; Rohde, *Galater*, 264–65; Matera, *Galatians*, 222; Dunn, *Galatians*, 326–28; Richardson, "Temples," 90, 92; Becker, *Galater*, 94; and Witherington, *Grace*, 429–30 (the last two also interpret φορτίον in v. 5 as financial); behavior fitting for fellowship, i.e., a more general sense, is assumed by Schlier, *Galater*, 275–76; Schewe, *Galater*, 169, n. 510. Eckert, *Urchristliche Verkündigung*, 146 considers the financial interpretation to be "fully isolated from the context, without a recognizable connection or occasion" (my translation).

188. Harnisch, "Einübung," 292; Dunn, *Galatians*, 316; and Schewe, *Galater*, 144, 168 argue differently.

189. Cf. Lambrecht, "Paul's Coherent Admonition," 44.

presence of maxims or proverbs, which draw on knowledge stored in the collective memory, is a typical feature of discourses in orally oriented societies.[190] In each case there is a further admonition at the close, which has been derived from the general principle.[191] These admonitions point to the eschatological judgment (vv. 4 and 9).[192] The final admonition is doubled in the second part (v. 10). We therefore have a parallel construction of both parts of the passage, whereby we find a supplement at the end providing a closing signal.

The structure of Gal 6:1-10, which has a notable similarity to 1 Thess 5:12-15, can be depicted as follows:

A	First specific admonition	v. 1	Ἀδελφοί, ἐὰν καὶ προλημφθῇ ἄνθρωπος ἔν τινι παραπτώματι, ὑμεῖς οἱ πνευματικοὶ καταρτίζετε τὸν τοιοῦτον ἐν πνεύματι πραΰτητος,
B	Warning		σκοπῶν σεαυτὸν μὴ καὶ σὺ πειρασθῇς.
C	General principle	v. 2	Ἀλλήλων τὰ βάρη βαστάζετε καὶ οὕτως ἀναπληρώσετε τὸν νόμον τοῦ Χριστοῦ.
D	Application of the rule: "If anyone..."	v. 3	εἰ γὰρ δοκεῖ τις εἶναί τι μηδὲν ὤν, φρεναπατᾷ ἑαυτόν.
E	Derived gen. admonition as transition with eschatological perspective	v. 4	τὸ δὲ ἔργον ἑαυτοῦ δοκιμαζέτω ἕκαστος, καὶ τότε εἰς ἑαυτὸν μόνον τὸ καύχημα ἕξει καὶ οὐκ εἰς τὸν ἕτερον· ἕκαστος γὰρ τὸ ἴδιον φορτίον βαστάσει.
A'	Second specific admonition	v. 6	Κοινωνείτω δὲ ὁ κατηχούμενος τὸν λόγον τῷ κατηχοῦντι ἐν πᾶσιν ἀγαθοῖς.
B'	Warning	v. 7	Μὴ πλανᾶσθε, θεὸς οὐ μυκτηρίζεται.

---

190. Betz, *Galatians*, 291-311 finds no less than eleven maxims or proverbs in Gal 5:25—6:10. Cf. North, "Sowing and Reaping" on the proverb concerning seed and harvest.

191. Rohde, *Galater*, 266 does not recognize any connection between the content of v. 7 and the previous verse, that is, the injunction to financially support those who teach, since it is not worded "*how* a man sows" (i.e., abundantly or sparsely), but rather "*whatever* a man sows." This subtle shift in the imagery of seed and harvest (cf. Schrage, "Probleme," 178) could be an indication that the lack of financial support for those teaching was only a symptom of a more fundamental tension in the church.

192. Mussner, *Galaterbrief*, 401-6; Kuck, "Each Will Bear His Own Burden," 296, n.47; Schrage, "Probleme," 176-79; Martyn, *Galatians*, 544-45; Rohde, *Galater*, 263. Schewe, *Galater*, 167, n.503, in contrast to the majority of expositors, rejects the position that not only vv. 7-8 but also v. 5 have an eschatological meaning and interprets the future in a gnomic sense. Lambrecht, "Paul's Coherent Admonition," 50 takes a similar view.

C'	General rule (proverb)		ὃ γὰρ ἐὰν σπείρῃ ἄνθρωπος, τοῦτο καὶ θερίσει·
D'	Application of the rule: "The one who . . ."	v. 8	ὅτι ὁ σπείρων εἰς τὴν σάρκα ἑαυτοῦ ἐκ τῆς σαρκὸς θερίσει φθοράν, ὁ δὲ σπείρων εἰς τὸ πνεῦμα ἐκ τοῦ πνεύματος θερίσει ζωὴν αἰώνιον.
E'1	Derived general admonition as transition with eschatological perspective	v. 9	τὸ δὲ καλὸν ποιοῦντες μὴ ἐγκακῶμεν, καιρῷ γὰρ ἰδίῳ θερίσομεν μὴ ἐκλυόμενοι.
E'2	Derived general admonition repeated with a view toward outsiders	v. 10	Ἄρα οὖν ὡς καιρὸν ἔχομεν, ἐργαζώμεθα τὸ ἀγαθὸν πρὸς πάντας, μάλιστα δὲ πρὸς τοὺς οἰκείους τῆς πίστεως.

Who is being addressed? The general principles and admonitions are meant for all. If, however, we ask who is being targeted by the two specific imperatives, then we have a clear answer for the second one (v. 6). It addresses those church members who are receiving instruction and should be supporting their teachers, including financially.[193] We again have a situation where Paul is addressing only part of the audience, without using a special form of address to indicate it.

What can we say about the *first* specific admonition (v. 1)? It is said to the ἀδελφοί. That could mean the complete church or just a group in it.[194] As we have seen in 1 Thess 5:12–15, that the addressees are not explicitly named does not prove that Paul is not thinking of a specific group. But another expression in Gal 6:1 deserves consideration: ὑμεῖς οἱ πνευματικοί.

---

193. Cf. Borse, *Standort*, 145; Matera, *Galatians*, 222; Becker, *Galater*, 93–94; Witherington, *Grace*, 430. Mussner, *Galaterbrief*, 402–3 and Rohde, *Galater*, 11 consider it to be the collection for the church in Jerusalem. That is rather improbable since the imperative in Gal 6:6 and also the two participles are in the present tense and therefore express a continuous arrangement and do not indicate a special one-time act. And neither in Gal 2:1 nor elsewhere in the letter do we find any mention of the Galatians being involved in the collection that is reported in 1 Cor 16:1 (on this, cf. also Schrage, "Probleme," 163). Schewe, *Galater*, 169–70 rejects the interpretation as an internal differentiation in the church between the teachers and those being instructed and places the injunction solely in the context of the relationship between Paul (who is teaching the church through the letter) and the recipients. The unspecific wording would at first suggest that local church teachers are meant, and then only in a second step the specific role of Paul.

194. Since Gal 6:2 is a "call to the believers' sense of solidarity" (my translation) and therefore applies to all, Eckert, *Urchristliche Verkündigung*, 144 concludes that all the admonitions are meant for all. Dunn, *Galatians*, 319 assumes that it is not the whole church that is being addressed: "Presumably, Paul did not expect the whole congregation do descend on the guilty fellow member." Dunn presents an overview of possible interpretations (pp. 319–20).

It has been repeatedly said that this salutation can only mean all Christians since Paul is convinced that all Christians have received the Holy Spirit.[195] But it would appear that Paul had a special reason for reminding those being addressed that they are "spiritual." Perhaps Paul speaks with an ironic undertone.[196] They are people full of self-confidence in their possession of the Holy Spirit. The warning "look to yourself" (v. 1b), which follows, and the derived admonition to test one's own work (v. 4) clearly show that they have a high opinion of themselves (v. 3: εἰ γὰρ δοκεῖ τις εἶναί τι).[197] Here we are dealing with church members, who have the authority and doubtless the zeal to take the matter of the fallen Christian into their own hands.[198] Paul is not prompting them to take up the matter of a sinning brother in the first place, but he is rather concerned with the way it is being done. The πραΰτης is the emphasized part of the sentence, not the helpful correction. The position of those being addressed would make it possible for them to pass judgement on the mistakes of others with a harsh tone and a hard hand. That is the reason Paul instructs them to be gentle. This must be a group in the Christian church that is higher in rank than the others. The warnings in verses 3–5 show that status thinking was very important to them.[199] It does not make sense to think of all believers here. Those receiving instruction (v. 6) are certainly in a different position. They belong to the lower social ranks. So we can say that two different social classes among the audience are being addressed in the two sections of Gal 6:1–10.

Hitherto we have found two very conspicuous parallels between Gal 6:1–10 and 1 Thess 5:12–15, which point to a comparable performance situation: the sections' parallel structures and the fact that Paul addresses

---

195. Barclay, *Obeying*, 157; Witherington, *Grace*, 422; Schewe, *Galater*, 151. Differently, Rohde, *Galater*, 259.

196. Cf. Schlier, *Galater*, 270; Martyn, *Galatians*, 546; Nanos, *Irony*, 36–38 and passim. Mussner, *Galaterbrief*, 398 finds no irony. Of course, it could be addressing those in need of encouragement to live up to their spiritual potential. Schewe, *Galater*, 251 interprets it thus, assuming that Paul, in this part of the letter, defines the rhetorical position of the recipients as if he has won the Galatians back for the "pneuma-sphere." However, the way the section continues points more towards irony. Cf. Nikolakopoulos, "Aspekte," 198 on the presentation of irony in the performance of the Letter to the Galatians. However, he only analyzes Gal 1:6; 2:6; and 5:12.

197. Martyn, *Galatians*, 544 sees those being addressed in v. 3 as the ones who have accepted the law and so think that they are better than the others.

198. Also in 1 Thess 5:12–14 it is the task of those with authority to correct straying church members.

199. Cf. Schewe, *Galater*, 160–65.

two different groups in each respective audience. A third characteristic must be mentioned that is also found in both passages. After giving appropriate admonitions specific to each of the groups, Paul returns to general statements or considerations at the end of each section. The general directive in 1 Thess 5:13b serves as a transition from one group to the other. Paul ends the first part of Gal 6:5 in a similar manner, using a very general statement, which is not only appropriate for those being addressed, but for everybody. The word ἕκαστος, in verses 4 and 5, should be noted here. The second section also ends with a general admonition (vv. 9–10). As in 1 Thess 5:15, where the whole passage ends by extending the viewpoint beyond the church, Gal 6:10 also includes those outside the church (v. 10: πρὸς πάντας).[200]

In both texts we have studied here, Paul is speaking *to* one group *about* another. A clear relationship between the groups is drawn in 1 Thess 5:12–15. The mutual relationship is not so obvious in Gal 6:1–10, although the groups being addressed have different social standings. The first group consists of self-confident spiritual authorities and perhaps also teachers. The second group consists of members receiving instruction or in some other way subordinate to those with authority.

If we ask about the manner in which each respective group (or an individual from each) is being spoken about, we again find a clear parallel between Gal 6:1–10 and 1 Thess 5:12–15: In each case, Paul shows a very positive attitude toward the one he is *talking about* and not the one he is *talking to*. The fallen member is not judged or shut out of the church.[201] Paul is not thinking of intransigence or an unrepentant spirit. If the word προλαμβάνω is used here with the meaning of "surprised" or "unexpectedly assailed" by a sin, then that would play down the mistake even more. If one considers the whole section, it quickly becomes clear that Paul only makes a short reference to the brother's mistake, while discussing in detail the sin of spiritual pride among those of higher social status. In other words, the sin of the *other* should be able to be overcome through

---

200. Cf. Becker, *Galater*, 96.

201. It is not said just what the transgression was. Schewe, *Galater*, 147 argues the case that the member has fallen away from grace and accepted circumcision and adherence to the Jewish law. Thus also Nanos, *Irony*, 195, but more cautiously. However, the openness of the language appears to have been consciously chosen, because Paul is concerned with behavior that promotes fellowship, and illustrates it using the case of transgression in the church.

the help of spiritual persons, while one's own sin is the real problem.[202] However, in the second part, where Paul turns to the group with a lower status, he speaks in support of teachers and gives distinct admonitions to the normal church members.

What effect would this strategy have had when the letter was presented in the various home churches?[203] The audience would be divided into two groups that differed in social ranking within the church. The groups might not necessarily have been formally distinguished, such as by church offices. When the presenter spoke to those acting with authority in the church, then the others, who were subject to this authority, would join in solidarity with one another and listen to what Paul had to say to the other group. It would also work that way when the members of the group were not sitting together. Church members in good standing would feel accepted and appreciated thanks to Paul's positive attitude toward the fallen church member, and thanks to Paul's indirect reproach of those with authority on the topic of their spiritual pride. But then those members with less status in the church were themselves given admonitions and warnings having to do with financial and other forms of support for teachers. This time the teachers and the authorities in the church would listen to what Paul had to say to the majority of church members, and they would feel accepted in their efforts. Each group would learn to think positively about the other. Each group was given the injunction to accept the other one, to support them, and to help them carry their burden. Each group was urged to take their own mistakes and temptations more seriously than those of others.

Here performance criticism recognizes how the admonition in Gal 6:6, which is often felt to be unconnected, fits into the context.[204] Two reciprocal groups in the audience—those correcting the others (that is, the ones who have and act with authority [v. 1]) and those who receive

---

202. Cf. Harnisch, "Einübung," 293.

203. Loubser, *Oral and Manuscript Culture*, 45 speaks of the "cybernetics," which accompany the presentation of the text, and which are written into the text: "In the case of the Epistle to the Galatians, the anticipated reaction of the Galatian congregations is already reflected in the text."

204. Schewe, *Galater*, 168–70 does not understand Gal 6:6 as a reference to the support of the teachers in the Galatian churches but rather as a directive instructing the Galatians to cultivate a positive relationship to Paul, who is indeed using this letter to teach them. It remains unclear in this interpretation just why the apostle begins to speak about his own relationship to the churches in v. 6 although he has thematized the relationship of the church members to one another in vv. 1–5.

instruction (v. 6)—are successively admonished, and positive bonds are established between the groups.[205]

By treating both groups alike, a treatment displayed in the carefully structured parallelism, Paul helps both groups to mutual acceptance. At the same time, he claims a special role for himself. In the same way that the presenter stands across from the audience during the performance of Paul's letter, so Paul also takes up a position that differs from that of both groups in the audience. Paul claims the same kind of authority over both the leaders and the other church members. He assumes responsibility for the unity and inner harmony of the church. Paul thereby also defines his role as an apostle.

The Letter to the Galatians reveals Paul's struggle to reassert his authority as an apostle in the Galatian churches. Improving relationships between the different groups, and among individuals within these churches, also appears to be an urgent concern. The tone of the passage being studied, with its warnings and corrections, is more earnest than the tone of 1 Thess 5:12–15. The context of the sixth chapter of Galatians points to difficult conflicts in the churches.[206] This becomes most obvious through sarcasm in Gal 5:15, which is comparable in sharpness to Gal 5:12.[207] In addition, commentators observe, chapter 5 emphasizes the ethics of relationships.[208] This situation is likely connected with the problem of returning to the Jewish law. Probably the emergence of those demanding circumcision had caused social order in the church to disintegrate.[209] The church was deeply divided over the question of circumcision. The fact that Paul never addresses an opposition group cannot be interpreted to mean that such a group did not exist or that the churches were all in agreement in the matter. It is much rather a strategy of Paul that should be studied from the performance perspective.[210]

---

205. If Gal 6:6 like 6:1 is concerned with the mutual relationships of the believers in Galatia, then it is hardly probable that Paul is thinking about support for the church in Jerusalem, as Hurtado, "Jerusalem Collection" has suggested.

206. Cf. Schlier, *Galater*, 246; Bruce, *Galatians*, 242; Barclay, *Obeying*, 71–72.

207. Gal 5:12 and 5:15 have a similar structure and function. It is generally accepted that Gal 5:12 was read and spoken because of the situation in Galatia. So despite the rhetorical character of Gal 5:15, we can assume that a current problem lies behind Gal 5:15; cf. Dunn, *Galatians*, 293.

208. Ibid., 304–6.

209. Ibid., 293. According to Kuck, "Each Will Bear His Own Burden," 296–97, there were status conflicts in the church; similarly Nanos, *Irony*, 54, 229 and *passim*.

210. On this, see the discussion in the next chapter pp. 233–34 concerning the opponents in the Letter to the Galatians.

4

Strategies in Letter Writing to Achieve Separation

The performance of a letter elicited not only conciliatory reactions. It also exacerbated differences or caused divisions in the audience. Using the example of the Letter to the Galatians, this study will now show that Paul also wrote such effects into the text of his letters as a performative strategy. For comparison, an analysis of Clement's first letter will follow, which, as with the Letter to Galatians, was designed to cause a group present in the audience to be ostracized. The performance criticism applied in this study will not only reveal the performative text strategy but also deepen the understanding of the content of certain statements such as the unspecific description of the opponents in the Letter to the Galatians and the emphasis on hospitality in the First Letter of Clement.

Winning Back the Listeners (Galatians)

Reason for the Letter

Paul dictated the Letter to the Galatians because the churches he had founded in Galatia, which were largely composed of former Gentiles (4:8), were at the point of acknowledging the Jewish law—or at least parts of it (5:3)—as binding and were about to let themselves be circumcised (5:2-4; 6:12). Paul understands such a change as a departure from the gospel he had proclaimed (1:6). At the same time, he sees his own missionary endeavors fundamentally in question (2:2; 3:4; 4:11). For him, this change nullifies the Galatians' reconciliation with God that was achieved through Jesus's self-sacrifice (2:21; 5:2). God's grace is thus being despised and forsaken (5:4).

With his letter, Paul enters a debate already in full swing in Galatia. Since the emergence of this issue, harmony in the churches had been disturbed. Each opinion had its spokesmen. The churches were deeply divided, the arguments fierce (5:15).[1] Every available method was used in the dispute: factual arguments,[2] the influence of socially important personalities,[3] flattery (4:17: ζηλοῦσιν ὑμᾶς), and social pressure (4:17: ἐκκλεῖσαι).[4]

The question that arose in Galatia was not about how the *individual* believers understood and lived their relationship with God (that is, whether they relied on God's gracious promises or if they sought to strengthen their claim to belong to God by obedience to God's law [3:18]). The discussion was not about *individual* choices.[5] While Paul does cite the example of a decision Peter made in a similar situation, his focus is not on Peter and his personal position on law and grace, but rather

---

1. This is also indicated by the emphasis on vices that damage the community in Gal 5:19-21 and by the list of virtues that all promote fellowship in Gal 5:22. Cf. on this aspect, Schewe, *Galater*, 125-34. She provides both a theological and a pragmatic textual analysis of Gal 5 and 6. Her main goal is to show how these final chapters fit into the letter as a whole and how they relate to Paul's main concern, namely, to counteract his opponents' demand for circumcision. For Schewe, the intrachurch dispute (5:15) is not a second and independent subject of the Letter to the Galatians (pp. 110 and 113). This makes it unnecessary to assume that Paul is fighting on two fronts (Lütgert, *Gesetz und Geist*; Ropes, *Singular Problem*). It is also unnecessary to consider that Paul, after rejecting the demand for Torah observance, is at the same time being forced to counteract existing libertine tendencies (Jewett, "Agitators," 209; Longenecker, *Galatians*, xcix-c; Dunn, *Galatians*, 11), or that Paul needs to compensate for a lack of social identity and ethical orientation among the Galatians that would have made subjection to the Torah appear attractive to them (Betz, *Galatians*, 8-9, 273-74; Barclay, *Obeying*, 58-60; Wolter, "Ethos," 439).

2. It seems that the supporters of circumcision have based their argument on Abraham, cf. "the opponents' sermon" as presented by Martyn, *Galatians*, 302-6.

3. The opponents of circumcision have probably cited Paul as the founder of the church whereas the proponents may have referred to James.

4. On Gal 4:17, cf. Betz, *Galatians*, 229-31. Martyn, *Galatians*, 124, 423 believes that one faction (the circumcision faction) puts pressure on those not in their faction by claiming that those without circumcision will be excluded from salvation.

5. Cf. Schrage, "Probleme," 189-94 on the question of a social or individual ethic in Gal 5-6.

on the consequences for the church in Antioch (2:11–14). One does not do justice to the Letter to the Galatians if reading it individualistically, as if it were a message for private study to help one to trust grace and understand the role of the law. Such an approach is anachronistic since it does not bear in mind that the letter is a witness to a performance event in a community. The letter would have been read out in front of all in the church assemblies, that is, where the dispute was taking place. It is concerned with the pivotal decisions being made by the *churches of a whole region*. At the end of the decision-making process, these churches would either take the path of "freedom," as Paul desired (5:1), or they would find their identity in the law as the synagogues did. Whatever the decision would be, in the end there would be some who had not been able to assert their opinion. They would have to concede if they did not want to be ostracized. Their reputation would be damaged to the extent that they had supported the defeated conviction. If the law was introduced as binding, then the Gentile believers would be the losers—and Paul as the apostle to the Gentiles with them.[6] If the Pauline position asserted itself, then the losers would be those who have followed the Jewish law as their way of life and custom from birth or since they had become proselytes by their own decision.

Paul's Opponents Belong to the Churches in Galatia

The letter does not say how a change of course came about in Galatia. Only the review of the happenings in Antioch in Syria could give some indications (2:12). There guests[7] from the church in Jerusalem, whom Paul characterized as τινὲς ἀπὸ Ἰακώβου, had induced a change in church practice. That was only possible because—truly or allegedly—the great authority of the church in Jerusalem, with James at its head, stood behind them. Peter, Barnabas, and other Jewish Christians broke off their

---

6. Paul describes this case in Gal 5:1 from the perspective of the churches being addressed by calling it "bondage." Gal 2:5 is worded likewise, i.e., that a victory for the representatives of those supporting the validity of the law appears to be a defeat for the addressed church members.

7. Are they inspectors? For a cautious discussion of this see Schäfer, *Paulus*, 231. Are they agitators? Schäfer, *Paulus*, 232: "They would hardly have tried to win the Gentile Christians in Antioch over for a gospel of circumcision" (my translation).

previous table fellowship with Gentile Christians.[8] According to Paul, they were behaving as though the Jewish law was still valid (2:18: they rebuild that which had been destroyed). On the one hand, they thus classified their previous behavior as wrong (2:18: they make themselves to be transgressors); on the other hand, they ostracized Gentile Christians (2:14: they force the Gentiles to live like Jews if they want to belong).

It is possible and very probable that influence from outside also encouraged the Galatians to rethink their position on the Jewish law. That would explain why the question of circumcision arose after Paul's departure.[9] Such an influence could have been the visit of a Galatian to another church, a guest in Galatia, or a letter. We do not know what happened. It appears that this is not important to Paul. It is striking that Paul attaches little importance to the guests from Jerusalem in his report on the events in Antioch. He only mentions them once in a subordinate clause (2:12).[10] He does *not* take issue with them. In contrast, his description of Peter's inconsistent behavior and his public criticism of Peter are quite detailed. And he makes clear that Peter is a prominent *representative of a complete group* in the Antioch church (2:13), and even that he is the *seducer* of this group.[11] Peter had come to Antioch some time before and had *repeatedly* (2:12: συνήσθιεν, imperfect) had table fellowship with the Gentile Christians. So he, like Barnabas, had been part of the church of Antioch for a considerable time.[12] All this leads to the assumption that in his Letter to the Galatians, Paul is also not concerned with those infiltrating the

---

8. Schewe, *Galater*, 114 rightly draws parallels between this behavior and the destruction of fellowship through the reinstatement of the law in Galatia. That fellowship is ruined is made drastically clear in Gal 5:15.

9. I can certainly concur with the arguments of Jewett, "Agitators," 204 and Dunn, *Galatians*, 11 thus far.

10. Schäfer, *Paulus*, 232–33: "In the presentation, the people of James are not parallel with the 'infiltrated false brothers' of the apostolic council (cf. Gal 2:4) and also cannot simply be equated with Paul's Galatian opponents" (my translation). Likewise Schlier, *Galater*, 71; Nanos, *Irony*, 5. According to Nanos, "Intruding Spies," the false brothers in Gal 2:4, are representatives of non-Christian Jewish lobby groups.

11. Betz, *Galatians*, 110: "Cephas managed to get 'the other Jews' to join him in the withdrawal [from the table fellowship with Gentile Christians] . . . Barnabas was 'carried away with them' (συναπήχθη)." Paul sees *Peter*, not the people of James, as the prototype of the opponents in Galatia. Barnabas is the prototype of the seduced addressees in Galatia.

12. Cf. Mussner, *Galaterbrief*, 137; Schäfer, *Paulus*, 229: "His stay in Antioch probably lasted for longer period of time" (my translation). However, Schäfer speaks of Peter's "visitor status."

church but with certain *members of the local churches* who believe that circumcising the Gentile believers is right and are campaigning for it.[13]

Admittedly, Paul does report a dispute with ψευδάδελφοι in Jerusalem in Gal 2:4-5. But they belonged to the local church there, to its Jewish legalistic wing.[14] They did not come from the outside and infiltrate the *church*, but they infiltrated the *negotiations* concerning the mission to the Gentiles that were conducted κατ' ἰδίαν (2:2).[15] The fact that Paul resisted them certainly parallels the situation in Galatia, since it had also been brothers *from within* the church there who had been resisting Paul's gospel.[16]

A frequently advanced argument for the opinion that Paul's opponents in Galatia did not belong to the Galatian churches but must have infiltrated from outside the churches is the fact that Paul never directly speaks to them and that Paul clearly distinguishes them from the letter's addressees. James Dunn states it as follows:

> But the fact that Paul always refers to the troublemakers in the third person, while addressing his converts in the second person, strongly suggests that the two groups were distinct.[17]

Robert Jewett argues likewise:

---

13. The fact that Paul is speaking of some who came from outside into the Christian church in Antioch in Syria (2:12) and caused the table fellowship to be discontinued leads many interpreters to conclude that Paul's opponents did not belong to the Galatian churches. This explanation presupposes that Paul refers specifically to the incident in Antioch because the Jewish troublemakers from *outside* (τινὲς ἀπὸ Ἰακώβου) make the Antioch event parallel to the situation in Galatia. However, a parallel is improbable since Paul only mentions the troublemakers in passing. Van Os, "Jewish Recipients," 62 is right when he writes, "If the opponents are like Peter, then we do not need to introduce new players on the scene, like Jewish outsiders or Gentile Judaizers."

14. Rohde, *Galater*, 82; Thurén, "Was Paul Angry," 313-14.

15. Thus correctly Witherington, *Grace*, 135-36; Das, *Paul and the Jews*, 30; cf. Suhl, *Paulus und seine Briefe*, 50.

16. That they are identical to those who, according to Acts 15:1, 24 and Gal 2:13, came to Antioch is just an assumption and contradicts the statement in Gal 2:4. There it concerns an event that happened *in Jerusalem*; cf. Mussner, *Galaterbrief*, 109; Rohde, *Galater*, 83; Martyn, *Galatians*, 196, 218.

17. Dunn, *Theology*, 8; cf. also Walter, "Paulus und die Gegner," 355; Barclay, *Obeying*, 43; Longenecker, *Galatians*, xciv; Martyn, *Galatians*, 120-21; Martyn, "Law-Observant Mission," 352; Rohde, *Galater*, 8-9 speaks about "intruders" without further substantiation; likewise Schlier, *Galater*, 18-19.

That they came from outside the congregation seems to be indicated by the fact that a sudden and unexpected shift of mind came over the Galatians (i.6) and that there was a struggle for the congregation's allegiance (iv.17). Paul always refers to the agitators (i.8–10; v.12; vi.12–13) as if they were separate from the Galatians themselves (iii.1–5; iv.8–16; v.7–8).[18]

Also the fact that Paul initially calls their message a "different gospel" (1:6) does not necessarily lead to the conclusion that his opponents were travelling missionaries.[19]

To assume that since the opponents remain indefinite, they are not present, is only plausible[20] when modern reading customs determine the interpretation of Paul's letters. If, however, the Letter to the Galatians is understood to be part of an oral letter event, then it becomes clear that Paul can *construct* the audience to his own liking. He can separate the very diverse listeners in groups using criteria of his own choosing by having the reader address one specific group while ignoring another. It is exactly in this way that he can *manipulate* them.[21] By not mentioning any names and not addressing the opponents directly he degrades his opponents.[22] He alienates the Galatians he is addressing from those

---

18. Jewett, "Agitators," 204. In addition, Jewett argues that the opponents must have come from outside because they had information concerning Paul's relationship to Jerusalem, which could not have been known in Galatia if Paul hadn't mentioned it. However, this is circular reasoning. Jewett can only assume that Paul's opponents had this knowledge because he understands Gal 1:16–20 as Paul's defense against attacks from his opponents, who had come from Jerusalem and had themselves argued that Paul was dependent on Jerusalem. However, Gal 1:16–20 can be interpreted otherwise—e.g., as a contrast to *Peter's* dependence on the opinions of those in Jerusalem. Vouga, "Galaterbrief" comes to a completely different conclusion: Since the opponents remain indeterminate and the addressees are presented as unified, Vouga presumes that Paul is not addressing a concrete situation in the Letter to the Galatians but is summarizing his theological thoughts in a fictional letter as an appendix to the collection of his main letters (Romans, 1 and 2 Corinthians).

19. As, e.g., Martyn, *Galatians*, 121–22 argues. Cf. Nanos's argumentation in *Irony*, 295.

20. Cf. Nanos's similar criticism in *Irony*, 169–83. However, he does not consider the presentation of a performance, but assumes that the opponents were a *Galatian* out-group, namely, non-Christian Jews in Galatia. Similarly Walter, "Paulus und die Gegner." Cf. the criticism of this interpretation in Das, *Paul and the Jews*, 24–29.

21. Cf. Botha, "Letter Writing," 28–30: In Galatia, it was Paul's goal to confront the opponents through an "effective counter-performance."

22. "Presumably the choice of the indefinite τινες to describe the opponents expresses on the one hand their relatively small number and on the other hand the

demanding circumcision and binds them to himself.²³ In his rhetorical analysis of the Pauline epistles, Thurén describes what he calls a "dynamic view of the text," which asks not only what the text communicates, but also what it *brings about*.²⁴ What is important is the interaction, through it "the performative nature of the text becomes evident."²⁵ However, if the performance event is not taken into consideration, the misunderstanding arises that the *constructed* audience is taken as a description of the *real* audience. Such a misunderstanding was impossible during the original reading of the letter to the church communities, since all could see who was present no matter if they were specifically addressed in the performance or not.

The purpose of Paul's letter was to instigate performance events in the various Galatian churches and to ensure that the debates would be channeled in the direction Paul desired. That would only be possible if nothing had been decided yet. That is why the Galatians are presented in the letter as if all of them are still looking for the right solution. Paul consciously constructs his implicit listeners in this way because he wants the decision to remain open. He wants to create a situation in the performance of the letter that provides (nearly) all listeners the possibility to side with the Pauline "freedom," independent of their previous standpoint. How open the question really was cannot be gathered from Paul's depiction here. The fact that the Galatians already observed certain feasts

---

contempt the apostle had for them: it wasn't worth the effort to name them!" (my translation), thus Mussner, *Galaterbrief*, 11, cf. also p. 57. Cf. Schlier, *Galater*, 38; Martyn, *Galatians*, 111, 121; Betz, *Galatians*, 49, n. 65 (with the reference to Ign. *Smyrn.* 5.3 and others): Paul avoids "the use of names and the providing of free publicity," also pp. 107 and 268. Du Toit, "Vilification," 406–7 also interprets the indefinite reference to the opponents as a disparagement.

23. Du Toit, "Alienation," 279: "rhetorical strategies to estrange his audience from his adversaries and to regain their association with him." Cf. also ibid., 286 and *passim*. Barclay, *Obeying*, 43, n. 15 had already suggested such a possibility: "But it is possible that Paul deliberately distinguishes them in this way to drive a wedge between 'the agitators' and Galatian Christians who had not yet accepted circumcision." With a similar argument, Thurén, "Was Paul Angry," 313 explains the fact that Paul only speaks of the opponents in the third person: "If the antagonists were a group within the congregation, such a distinction is precisely what Paul should have made in order to protect the addressees from their influence." See also ibid., 317 and Thurén, *Derhetorizing*, 67.

24. Thurén, *Derhetorizing*, 23–27.

25. Ibid., 24. Cf. Hardin, *Galatians and the Imperial Cult*, 93–94. Mitternacht, *Forum*, 64–66 and Schewe, *Galater*, 60–65 also consider the text's pragmatic dimension but without considering the performance, which includes the orality, the physical presence, and the interaction of the listeners.

(4:10)[26] points to a leaning toward the law (cf. also the aorist form in 3:1: ἐβάσκανεν). That is also supported by the urgent tone of the whole letter. In any case, one must expect—as with Peter and Barnabas in Antioch—that many Galatians had already long decided *for themselves* on which side of the debate they stood. There must have been energetic advocates of the law *in the Galatian churches*. Only this would explain why the observance of the Jewish law found such strong resonance. And this is the only possible explanation for the fierce conflicts in Galatia (5:15).[27] Apparently there was a clash of opinions. It was a conflict *within* the Galatian churches (note the double ἀλλήλους/ἀλλήλων in 5:15), not between the Galatians and a few visitors from outside.[28] That means that Paul's opponents are not to be found outside the Galatian churches, but were *within* the churches Paul himself had founded.[29]

---

26. Usually it is considered to be the Jewish ceremonial law since the letter is about the Jewish law. Hardin, *Galatians and the Imperial Cult*, 122-27 points to the feast calendar regarding the imperial cult.

27. According to Schlier, *Galater*, 246; Bruce, *Galatians*, 242; Stanley, "Under a Curse," 490; Martyn, *Galatians*, 491; Esler, *Galatians*, 225-26, there were real conflicts. Becker, *Galater*, 84, 87, however, considers it to be a more preventive exhortation. Schewe, *Galater*, 108-16 discusses the various possible interpretations and comes to the conclusion that Paul uses the latent or incipient destruction of the fellowship as an argument for his position: whoever relies on the flesh (that is, on the law) will have strife and destroy the church, but whoever relies on the Spirit (on grace) has peace.

28. Paul always refers to them in the present tense, so he reckons with their presence or ongoing activities: Gal 1:7; 3:10; 4:17; 5:4, 10, 12; 6:12, 13; the only exception is 3:1. Cf. Martyn, *Galatians*, 118: "Specifically, Paul knows that the Galatians will listen to his letter with the Teachers' sermon still ringing in their ears, and almost certainly with the Teachers themselves at their elbows." Unfortunately he doesn't draw any consequences for the identity of the teachers and the performance of the letter. Cf. Stirewalt, *Paul*, 106: "Some opponents may have been present at the meeting [in Galatia] or even in the delegation." By "the delegation," he means the brothers who, according to Gal 1:2, are with Paul. Similarly Stanley, "Under a Curse," 489-90.

29. Hardin, *Galatians and the Imperial Cult*, 92-94, following Winter, "Civic Obligations"; and Winter, "Imperial Cult" also advocates that Paul's opponents are Jewish Jesus-believers from Galatia. He interprets the fact that Paul only refers to them in the third person as evidence that they do not belong to the letter's recipients (p. 93): "Perhaps originally coming from within Galatian churches, the agitators later broke ties with Paul's readers or excluded themselves (or the Galatians) from fellowship (4.17)." So he understands the *constructed* audience of the letter to be the real one. According to Nanos, *Irony*, 6-9, 85, 135 and *passim*, the opponents are Galatians. However, according to him they are not Christians but members of the local Jewish community who are pressuring the Gentile Christians to become members of the Jewish community.

Paul's Opponents Are Prominent Jewish Christians

What do the references in the Letter to the Galatians reveal about Paul's opponents?[30] To begin with, it can be assumed that those promoting the validity of the law for Gentile Christians are Jews or proselytes. This situation not only is found in the book of Acts, but also appears in the Pauline epistles where Paul speaks of conflicts over questions about the law (Rom 14:1—15:13; Phil 3:2; 1 Thess 2:16; cf. Col 2:16-23). In his dispute with Peter, Barnabas, and other brethren in Antioch, which Paul uses as a comparison in the Letter to the Galatians, it was also Jews who were propagating the observance of the law. This assumption is supported by further evidence found in the Letter to Galatians. It has often been observed[31] that Paul reacts more to the Jews in his arguments: he refutes their arguments,[32] adopts their way of thinking,[33] does not question the validity of the law (3:21), emphasizes repeatedly that someone who is Spirit-led would not act against the real purpose of the law (5:14, 23; also 6:2), and generally presupposes detailed scriptural knowledge. Since the opponents invoke the Jewish law, Paul speaks of his own past in which he was, more than any other, a zealous supporter of his ancestral traditions (1:14: περισσοτέρως ζηλωτὴς ὑπάρχων τῶν πατρικῶν μου παραδόσεων). In this way he makes clear that he can understand the Galatian zealots only too well, but that his life had been turned around through God's intervention. No one is in a better position to correct a wrong opinion as someone who himself has experienced such a correction and who had been corrected by no one less than God himself.[34] It is also conspicuous that Paul never evaluates circumcision negatively but describes it in the same indifferent manner as noncircumcision (5:6; 6:15; cf. 3:28). Apparently,

---

30. Overviews of the hypotheses about the identity of Paul's opponents in the Letter to the Galatians are found e.g., in Mussner, *Galaterbrief*, 14–24; Rohde, *Galater*, 14–21; Longenecker, *Galatians*, lxxxix–xcvi; Mitternacht, *Forum*, 26–36; Nanos, *Irony*, 110–92; Howard, *Crisis in Galatia*, 1–7; Sumney, "Studying," 17–24.

31. Cf. Dunn, *Galatians*, 9; Dunn, *Theology*, 8; van Os, "Jewish Recipients," 61–62.

32. For example, the argument with Peter, which imperceptibly becomes an argument with Paul's opponents in Galatia, in Gal 2:15-21, the argument about Abraham in Gal 3:15-20, and about Jerusalem in Gal 4:21-27.

33. For example, the argument of the later arrival of the law Gal 3:17 and generally the question in Gal 3:19.

34. Cf. Sampley, "Paul's Frank Speech," 298–305 to παρρησία and ἦθος in the Epistle to the Galatians.

despite all his polemic against the plans for circumcision, he does not want the Galatians who have already been circumcised to feel ostracized. So Paul's opponents were indeed Jewish Christians in Galatia.[35]

One might object that the thesis that it was Jews in the Galatian churches (and possibly also proselytes) who pressured their Gentile brothers to be circumcised is contradicted by the fact that Paul addresses the recipients as former Gentiles in Gal 4:8. It appears as if *all* the believers in Galatia had formerly been serving "those which by nature are not gods." Furthermore, by addressing the Galatians as the ones having to decide whether to be circumcised, it appears that Paul is speaking to all the recipients as former Gentiles (5:2–3; 6:12). However, before conclusions can be drawn from this manner of speech, one must consider that the verbal address in a document designed for performance does not have to be unambiguous.[36] Like anyone who communicates orally, the presenter of a Pauline letter had many ways of making clear whom he was momentarily addressing: for instance glances, the direction the body is facing, finger pointing or other genstures, or proximity or distance in the room. The presenter could also deliberately avoid addressing specific persons present. He could ignore them thereby making them practically invisible. Despite passages where recipients of the letter are addressed as Gentile believers, it is still quite possible that there were Jewish Christians in Galatia, although they were probably only a minority.[37] That Paul's mention of Gentile believers might be ambiguous can be seen in the Letter to the Romans. There we also find Paul addressing the recipients as Gentile believers without differentiation (Rom 1:6, 13), although there were Jewish Jesus-believers in Rome (e.g., Rom. 16:7, 11).

---

35. Cf. Dix, *Jew and Greek*, 41; Tyson, "Paul's Opponents," 252–54; Winter, "Civic Obligations," 133–43; Esler, *Galatians*, 73: "It seems most likely that its [circumcision's] advocates are Israelite members of the Galatian communities, but that they are themselves being threatened—either by Israelite Christ-followers from elsewhere . . . , or by local Galatian Israelites, or by a coalition of both of these groups." Breytenbach, *Paulus und Barnabas*, 143 also reckons with a local problem in Galatia between Jewish Christians with connections to the synagogue and Gentile Christians, and concludes: "The attempt of the Jewish Christian troublemakers to integrate the Gentile Christians into the synagogue and make them keep the law . . . is incomprehensible if it does not take place within the context of the Jewish community. The hypothesis of newcomers, independent wandering Jewish Christian missionaries, does not fit well into the picture" (my translation).

36. Cf. above pp. 104–105 and the examples on pp. 212–14 and 223–24.

37. Cf. Schnelle, *Einleitung*, 117: "mainly Gentile Christians."

There are further clues in Paul's letter concerning his Jewish opponents in the Galatian churches. They probably held positions of respect in the churches. That would explain their significant influence, which enabled them to convince so many in the church of the validity of the law. Gal 3:28 shows that there were social differences in the churches. Those of higher social standing (the hosts of the house churches, the wealthier, the better educated) would have had the most say. The prominence of Jewish Christians favoring circumcision also makes it possible to comprehend why Paul plays down the importance of those of significant rank in the Jerusalem church: ὁποῖοί ποτε ἦσαν οὐδέν μοι διαφέρει· πρόσωπον ὁ θεὸς ἀνθρώπου οὐ λαμβάνει (2:6).[38] This parenthetical phrase is conspicuous because it appears to contradict Paul's purpose in this passage, in which he is emphasizing that his mission to the Gentiles is legitimized by the authority of those in Jerusalem (v. 6: δοκοῦντες twice, v. 9: οἱ δοκοῦντες στῦλοι εἶναι).[39] In view of the situation in Galatia, however, it was important to the apostle that listeners not shrink from criticizing distinguished personages. That is why Paul emphasizes two times that he was not afraid to openly challenge such a venerated figure as Peter when Peter, together with others, reestablished the Jewish law (2:12, 14). Paul's wording in in Gal 5:10 when he speaks of the opponents in the Galatian churches throws a light on the situation in Galatia: ὁ δὲ ταράσσων ὑμᾶς βαστάσει τὸ κρίμα, ὅστις ἐὰν ᾖ.[40] Here again the thought appears from Gal 2:6: a person will be judged without regard for the person's reputation.[41] Paul relativizes the reputations of church leaders also in Gal 6:3.[42] Everything points to Paul's opponents being respected people in Galatia. This would result in such Galatians having a similar standing to Peter, who belonged to the στῦλοι in Jerusalem and was later an important personality in Antioch. Paul tells of his courageous speech against him (2:11–14) in order to encourage the (Gentile) Galatians to risk contradicting the prominent Jewish brothers who were trying to enforce observance of the law.

---

38. "What they were makes no difference to me; God shows no partiality."

39. Cf. Walter, "Paulus und die Gegner," 353.

40. "But the one who is disturbing you will bear his judgment, whoever he is."

41. Cf. Mussner, *Galaterbrief*, 358.

42. Harnisch, "Einübung," 294 understands Gal 6:2-3 as being worded with a view to the opponents who "boast of their own efforts and continually revolve around themselves . . . who mirror themselves and celebrate the achievements of their own ego" (my translation).

It has repeatedly been said that Paul was being discredited by his opponents and that he had to defend his apostolic office.[43] Others suppose that those requiring circumcision did not see themselves as opposing Paul but thought they were completing the work he had begun in his spirit and as he would have done it (3:3).[44] However, this does not appear to explain adequately the reason why Paul emphasizes the independence of his apostolic office (1:15-24). This emphasis is more an attack than a defense. Probably the opponents in Galatia had invoked the apostles in Jerusalem as part of their argument for circumcision. However, since the Galatians had received from Paul a gospel authorized by *God*, they could oppose the opponents' demands, which—rightly or wrongly—were based on the apostles in Jerusalem. In this way Paul again encouraged the Galatians to resist those who were campaigning for circumcision for Gentile Christians based on the Jerusalem traditions.

A further indication about Paul's Galatian opponents is found in Gal 6:12-13 where he reveals their real motivation for their law offensive.[45] His opponents must have been personalities who on the one hand had something to lose, and on the other hand also had something to gain if the churches subjected themselves to the Jewish law. The possible loss is named in Gal 6:12: μόνον ἵνα τῷ σταυρῷ τοῦ Χριστοῦ μὴ διώκωνται.[46] It is not the persecution of the *whole* church addressed here;[47] neither is it that the Galatian Christians *as a whole* wanted to improve their status in society by accepting the law because they would then be accepted as Jews, thereby achieving a recognized social position.[48] The opponents are not concerned with the welfare of their brothers and sisters. For then Paul

---

43. For example, Betz, *Galatians*, 24-25, 28-30.

44. For example, Longenecker, *Galatians*, xciii; Howard, *Crisis in Galatia*, 9-11.

45. On the question of whether the Epistle to the Galatians provides reliable information about the opponents, cf. the discussion in Sumney, *Servants of Satan*; and in Hardin, *Galatians and the Imperial Cult*, 94-97.

46. "That they will not be persecuted for the cross of Christ."

47. This is the assumption of Mitternacht, *Forum*, 31.

48. So e.g., Barclay, *Obeying*, 58; Rohde, *Galater*, 274. Hardin, *Galatians and the Imperial Cult*, 111-12, 142-44 does speak of the opponents who want to avoid persecution for themselves but does so in the context of social disadvantages that result from an "ambiguous status in society" (p. 112) and from not participating in the emperor cult. This, however, was a problem that *all* believers had to face. In Hardin's opinion, the issue was *not* the status of *religio licitia* and therefore the *exemption* from the emperor cult, since also the Jews—just like the Gentiles—in many ways have been involved in it; cf. Hardin, *Galatians and Imperial Cult*, 102-10.

would have had to use ἵνα μὴ διώκησθε. What Paul writes about his Jewish opponents serves to reveal their egoism. The feared "persecution" must therefore have threatened specifically them. In that they acted out of fear, they are like Peter, who out of fear of losing his reputation in Jerusalem terminated his table fellowship with the Gentile Christians, thereby indirectly forcing them to convert to Judaism (2:12, 14).[49]

That becomes understandable if the opponents were distinguished Jews who lost their reputation—and their business relationships—in Jewish society due to the acceptance of the gospel of the Crucified One.[50] Having a good reputation was important to them (6:12 θέλουσιν εὐπροσωπῆσαι ἐν σαρκί). They possibly even had to fear being punished by the synagogue for socializing with Gentiles in the Christian church.[51] This is the situation that Paul suffers through as one who was once a distinguished Jew. By using ἐγὼ δέ at the beginning of Gal 5:11, Paul emphasizes his person in contrast to his opponents. It is hard to imagine a clearer antithesis to them: *Paul* no longer preaches circumcision and is persecuted because of this by his own folk.[52] By contrast his opponents in Galatia urged Gentile Christians to be circumcised to avoid just these difficulties.[53] Notice must be taken of the sarcasm Paul uses towards the opponents (5:12): they should castrate themselves (ἀποκόψονται) right away.

---

49. Cf. Betz, *Galatians*, 109: Peter feared "the 'political' consequences of losing his position of power." Cf. Schäfer, *Paulus*, 230–31.

50. The fact that there were Jewish communities in "Galatia" does not compel us to advocate the South-Galatia thesis as do, e.g., Longenecker, *Galatians*, lxx–lxxii; van Os, "Jewish Recipients"; and, more cautiously, Dunn, *Theology*, 16. Betz, *Galatians*, 5 points out that the presence of Jews in central Anatolia has been proven. The issue of localizing the Galatians is not essential for the analysis of the letter's performance.

51. Cf. Muddiman, "Anatomy," 261; Esler, *Galatians*, 74. Munck, *Paulus und die Heilsgeschichte*, 79–126; Harvey, "Opposition to Paul," 319–32; Richardson, *Israel*, 96 suggest persecution by local Jews. However, they assume that Paul's opponents were proselytes who had become Christians.

52. On the formulation using the conditional clause, cf. Rohde, *Galater*, 222–23.

53. It is not necessary to assume that this is about fearing Zealots' activities in Palestine; so Jewett, "Agitators," 204–6; Suhl, *Paulus und seine Briefe*, 17–20; Bruce, *Galatians*, 269; Becker, *Galater*, 13, 99. The opponents are not guests from Jerusalem as has been widely assumed (e.g., Longenecker, *Galatians*, xcv) but are to be found in the Galatian churches. Persecution by Jews was possible not only in Palestine, as, e.g., Becker, *Galater*, 99 assumes when he says, "the atmosphere of Jewish zeal is at home in Judea" (my translation). Acts 13:45; 14:2–5, 19; 17:5, 13; 19:12–13 report credibly about Jewish opposition against Christians in Hellenistic cities.

Up to now, the possibility of more sarcasm in Gal 6:13 has been overlooked: ἵνα ἐν τῇ ὑμετέρᾳ σαρκὶ καυχήσωνται.[54] The opponents would improve their reputation in the Jewish community of Galatia if through their influence Gentile Christians would become proselytes.[55] This is commented upon by Paul with the help of an Old Testament custom in warfare: just as David presented the foreskins of the defeated Philistines as trophies (1 Sam 18:25-27), so Paul's opponents also boast about the "flesh" of the brothers they have compelled to be circumcised.[56]

Another statement from Paul about his opponents sheds light on their situation: they themselves are not keeping the law (6:13: οὐδὲ γὰρ οἱ περιτεμνόμενοι αὐτοὶ νόμον φυλάσσουσιν). What does Paul mean by this?[57] Apparently Paul wants to vilify his opponents here as he already has done in the previous sentence, accusing them of egotism and shrinking from suffering. Here he accuses them of being inconsistent.[58] But it is difficult to comprehend why zealots of the Jewish law should themselves fail to keep it.[59]

The widespread explanation that Paul refers to the idea that absolutely no one can truly observe the law (2:16; 3:11) is not helpful[60] because the accusation regarding the lack of consistency is only meaningful if consistent acts were possible.[61] Mark D. Nanos argues that Paul's opponents are breaking the spirit of the law, because they are following

---

54. ". . . so that they may boast in your flesh."

55. Literature on this in Schewe, *Galater*, 196, n. 38.

56. On "circumcision flesh," cf. Mussner, *Galaterbrief*, 413; Martyn, *Galatians*, 561; Schewe, *Galater*, 84-85, 197; all these do not see the connection to 1 Sam 18.

57. Hirsch, "Zwei Fragen," 192-97 used this statement in particular as his basis and assumed that Paul's opponents are Judaizing Gentile Christians from Antioch. Michaelis, "Judaistische Heidenchristen," 87-89 and Munck, *Paulus und die Heilsgeschichte*, 79-126 followed him in this.

58. This is reminiscent of Paul's accusation against Peter: Gal 2:14; cf. 5:3. Cf. Howard, *Crisis in Galatia*, 15-16.

59. It has frequently been established that this does not fit Jewish Christian missionaries coming from Jerusalem, e.g., Howard, *Crisis in Galatia*, 11-12; cf. Das, *Paul and the Jews*, 20-21. This is why Hirsch, "Zwei Fragen" and Michaelis, "Judaistische Heidenchristen" presume they were proselytes.

60. This explanation is found e.g., in Rohde, *Galater*, 274; cf. the literature in Schewe, *Galater*, 198, n. 43.

61. The realization that no one can keep the law would not cohere with the accusation of inconsistency, but rather with that of an exaggerated opinion of themselves: they would have been proud of trying something that could not even be achieved. This accusation is implied by Paul in Rom 3:27; cf. also 1 Cor 1:29-31; Eph 2:9.

their own self-interest.⁶² Susanne Schewe interprets this verse to say that Paul's opponents were not observing the law as *newly* defined by the law of love (5:14) and the law of Christ (6:2).⁶³ But this interpretation also does not fit the context, because if this were the meaning, Paul would not be accusing the opponents of anything but rather would be explaining facts to the listeners, facts that had long become clear. This statement is only then an accusation when there is an inconsistency according to the *opponents* intentions.⁶⁴

We can make progress if we consider the contexts in which those acknowledging and observing the law are being accused of not keeping it. Such accusations arose in the disputes between various Jewish persons or groups who remained true to the law—for example, between the Qumran community and the priests in Jerusalem, between Jesus and the official Jewish teachers (Matt 23:23; John 7:19), between the official Jewish teachers and Jesus (Matt 5:17; John 7:23), between leaders and Pharisees on the one hand and the common people on the other (John 7:49), between the Jews of Jerusalem and the diaspora. Here the *Jew* Paul speaks about other Jews and considers their obedience to the law to be deficient.⁶⁵ This throws light on the provenance of the opponents: They belong to a kind of Judaism that a Pharisee educated in Jerusalem had reason to object to.⁶⁶ Obviously then, the conclusion is that they were

62. Nanos, *Irony*, 226–29.

63. Schewe, *Galater*, 197. She reasons as follows: Law and circumcision are marked as opposites by ἀλλά, which does not fit well. But the ἀλλά introduces the *complete* statement in v. 13b and refers to the opponents' intentions.

64. Kwon, *Eschatology*, 207: "He accuses them on their own ground." Hardin's explanation (*Galatians and Imperial Cult*, 89) also weakens Paul's arguments. His interpretation is that Paul accuses them of not really being interested in the law but only in their own reputations. Thus the accusation of factual inconsistency (οὐδὲ . . . αὐτοὶ νόμον φυλάσσουσιν) becomes an accusation of false motivation. Kwon, *Eschatology*, 207–12 explains that the law as moral authority was not the agitators' concern at all, and that they observed the law very selectively. Becker, *Galater*, 100 interprets the accusation as follows: If the law were properly understood, it would support Paul's position, since in Paul's argument "the law unmasks itself as obsolete and inapt for salvation" (my translation). Then, however, the opponents would have been accused of not *understanding* the law and not of *nonobservance*.

65. Paul judges the agitators from the perspective of a former Pharisee: Barclay, *Obeying*, 65; Longenecker, *Galatians*, 293; Witherington, *Grace*, 449; Howard, *Crisis in Galatia*, 15–16; Martyn, *Galatians*, 563 with reference to the fact that it would have hardly been possible for proselytes to observe the law completely.

66. Hirsch, "Zwei Fragen," 194 interprets this passage similarly as an intra-Jewish accusation: The Judaizing Gentile Christians—so is his thesis concerning the

diaspora Jews whose manifold adaption to Hellenistic culture had frequently aroused the criticism of the scribes in Jerusalem.[67]

Performance Situation in Galatia

We can now summarize the performance situation in Galatia when Paul's letter was being presented: After Paul's messengers—probably Galatian church members who had come to see Paul because of the controversial questions in Galatia and whom he had sent back—had arrived in a Galatian city,[68] a church meeting would have been called. This would have included the Gentile majority, the Jewish Christian minority (whose wealthy and esteemed representatives in particular were supporting the demand for circumcision), as well as the letter carriers and messengers from Paul. Which faction those presiding over the meeting would have belonged to remains undetermined and would have differed from church to church. Paul would have had to expect that under certain circumstances the presentation of his letter would be met with heavy resistance, or that some reader would be chosen who would not represent Paul's concerns in an optimal way when performing the letter.[69] All those present would have been aware that the issue was the dispute about how the Galatian churches should position themselves concerning the observance of the Jewish law. They would also have known who among those present had, up to that point, spoken in favor of the one or the other position concerning this question. During the performance of Paul's letter, those attending not only would have observed the one reading it but also would have perceived the effect of what was being said on the representatives of the opposing parties, especially on the leading personalities. This would have been easy to observe because of the seating arrangements.

---

opponents in the Letter to the Galatians—would as proselytes only insufficiently fulfil the law.

67. Cf. Hengel, *Judentum und Hellenismus*, 561–64.

68. According to Schnelle, *Einleitung*, 112–13, the education required to understand the Letter to the Galatians and the initial effect of the message of freedom point to urban circles interested in cultural and religious emancipation. Additionally, one could say that a Jewish population, and probably a synagogue, would also point to an urban setting.

69. Cf. above on pp. 147–51 on the description of Paul's strategy of challenging the listeners to assess the presenter's performance for themselves.

The Course of the Performance

How would the performance in the Galatian churches have proceeded? Performance is an event that not only unfolds by drawing on a script—in Galatia, on the script that is Paul's letter—but also brings about changes through the interaction among those present. We will now proceed through the presentation of the letter and pay special attention to the passages that specifically address the audience and to the passages in which Paul refers to himself. The interaction as it is written into the letter can be recognized most clearly in these passages.

Galatians 1:1–2

In the salutation of the letter, Paul claims a high authority for himself as an apostle appointed by Jesus and by God (1:1). In this way he energetically demands the listeners' attention. At the same time, he names the brothers who are with him as cosenders. Stirewalt has suggested that these brothers are members of the official Galatian delegation who have informed him about the situation in Galatia and who have helped prepare the letter. Paul acknowledges them as an official Galatian delegation and sends them back as messengers to deliver the letter.[70] That means that they are present in the Galatian assembly during the reading of the letter, are available for questions and can eventually report how the assembly reacted to Paul's letter (cf. 1 Clem 63:3). So the letter is designed in such a way that lends its performance in Galatia an official character. So Paul ensures that the event will have great significance. Apparently he wants decisions to be made—after the reading of the letter and the following discussion. Whatever the situation may have been in Galatia before the presentation, whatever majorities had been formed, whichever faction was setting the tone, whatever facts had already been created concerning the observance of the law (cf. 4:10), Paul ensures with the letter's introduction that the decision is open—that there is a chance for the assembly to return to the Pauline gospel.[71]

---

70. Cf. Stirewalt, *Paul*, 94–101, 105 with reference to official letters of which Josephus reports; this presumption concerning the co-senders can be found already in Eckert, *Urchristliche Verkündigung*, 235; cf. also Betz, *Galatians*, 1.

71. According to van Voorst, "Why Is There No Thanksgiving," 171, the "amen" at the end of v. 5 is the usual formula with which the listeners customarily answered to prayers, praise, blessings etc.: "Hellenistic letters familiar to the Galatians typically did not call for a verbal response as the letter was read, and Paul has been implicitly but

Galatians 1:6–7

Immediately after the introduction Paul divides the audience into two groups.[72] The presenter addresses the church meeting in the second-person plural, thereby forming the first group (1:6): μετατίθεσθε ἀπὸ τοῦ καλέσαντος ὑμᾶς.[73] He confronts this group with a second group, which he does not address but defines by describing their actions and intentions (1:7): τινές εἰσιν οἱ ταράσσοντες ὑμᾶς καὶ θέλοντες μεταστρέψαι τὸ εὐαγγέλιον τοῦ Χριστοῦ.[74] This second group remains unspecified.[75] They influence the first group; they "confuse" the church being addressed (1:7). This puts the first group into the role of victims. The μετατίθεσθαι of the first group stands in contrast to the μεταστρέψαι of the second one. The similar sounds of the prefixed prepositions create a parallel between the groups, while the verbs make the difference between them clear. The church being addressed turns—in confusion—to "another gospel," the τινές, by contrast, are *distorting* the gospel. That makes it clear to those present as to who is being more strongly indicted.

The presenter, if he remains true to the directions for the performance inherent in the text, turns to the majority of Gentile Christians, that is, to the majority of the believers in general. By looking at them and by speaking to them, he provokes a typical audience reaction: comments, glances and gestures that signal approval or at least inner involvement and understanding. All those present in the room perceive these reactions, since the normal seating arrangement makes it possible for all to observe

---

clearly critical of the Galatians in this prescript; now he wants them to agree with him, out loud in fact... The letter reader may have paused here before continuing, listening as he/she drew a breath for what kind of 'amen' might come."

72. Cf. Das, *Paul and the Jews*, 18.

73. "That you are so quickly deserting him who called you."

74. "There are some who are disturbing you and want to distort the gospel of Christ."

75. The fact that the opponents are not addressed and remain indeterminate (τινές in Gal 1:7 et al.) does not mean that Paul did not know who the opponents were, e.g., Longenecker, *Galatians*, xciv; Stanley, "Under a Curse," 489; Witherington, *Grace*, 23; Mitternacht, *Forum*, 62. Stirewalt, *Paul*, 94–99 argues plausibly that the brothers who were with Paul as the letter was written, and whom he mentions among the senders (1:2) constitute a delegation from Galatia. These brothers had been involved in the entire process of preparing the letter. Thus any uncertainties on Paul's side concerning the situation in Galatia were eliminated. Cf. Schlier, *Galater*, 212 to Gal 4:17: "He knows who the guilty ones are, and the Galatians know that too" (my translation).

one another. Whoever responds to the performance with approval shows openly that he or she wants to belong to this majority group.

By contrast, the presenter does not turn to the prominent Jewish Christians, the representatives of the demand for circumcision. He speaks to them "over his shoulder," so to speak. He does not give them opportunity to make their presence felt. Their reactions are ignored and thus annulled.[76] In this way this group not only remains verbally indeterminate (τινές); it also cannot be said who of those in the room belong to it and how many they are—of course, apart from the fact that the group's spokesmen are known. This means that the group will find it difficult to affect the performance by influencing the audience. This also means that no one has to reveal that he or she belongs to this group. It is possible to leave the group unobserved, so to speak. Paul uses this performance strategy to allow the less prominent members of the circumcision party to change sides without losing face.

Of course, the opponents could react loudly and vigorously to the performance, bringing themselves to the forefront and drawing many in the audience to their side. That is, they could immediately begin the discussion and dispute that according to the normal protocol was to come only after the reading of the letter.[77] This would cause a scandal since it would leave the framework of the letter event and break up the meeting. Thus Paul's performance strategy uses the advantage which the letter protocol offers and makes it difficult for the opponents to exert their influence.

Galatians 1:8–9

After Paul has addressed the audience and divided it into two groups, there follows a twofold cursing of all who are perverting the gospel (1:8–9). Here Paul makes his position in the dispute recognizable for all. He takes the side of those who are against circumcision.[78] Probably the

---

76. Of course the presenter could observe the prominent Jewish Christians during the reading. This would result in a strong discrepancy between the words (the address to the Gentile majority) and the nonverbal gesture (looking towards the prominent Jewish Christians). That would heighten the tension of the dramatic situation. The Jewish Christians would be encouraged to intervene, but the Gentile Christians would feel—despite being addressed—that they were not being taken seriously and would themselves be more strongly prone to assert themselves.

77. Cf. however the explanation on Gal 6:17 below on p. 257.

78. In contrast to the letters analyzed in the previous chapter where Paul was

apostle was an important identification figure for this group, although they are weakened by his absence. The letter now creates Paul's quasi-presence, thereby strengthening those opposing circumcision.

Through the curse, he makes enemies of the group supporting circumcision, right from the beginning. He begins the controversy by drastic means.[79] With the first curse Paul still considers the theoretical possibility that he himself or an angel could proclaim another gospel (conditional sentence with ἐάν). The second concerns the false proclamation of a τις (now singular!), with which Paul refers back to the previously used τινές. In this case he words the conditional sentence using εἴ τις, thus emphasizing the inescapability of the curse.

Whilst the first group of listeners, the addressed group, is confronted with a reproach that reveals Paul's disappointment,[80] the second is cursed for actively perverting the gospel. The performance of the letter uses enticement and threats to compel the listeners to take sides with those being addressed and not with the τινές, i.e., the enticement of remaining a partner in dialogue with Paul and bearing a lesser guilt for being the victims of confusion; the threat of becoming nameless and irrelevant and finally falling under God's curse.[81]

Galatians 1:11—2:10

In the following autobiographic section, Paul demonstrates his competence and, in addition, strengthens his authority. He presents himself as one who has personally lived through both possible positions concerning the law's validity. He also presents himself as a model for the principle that in this question, one should not judge those who are advocating the wrong opinion by considering their social status. Even if the στῦλοι from Jerusalem were to betray the gospel (or if heavenly angels were to pervert the gospel), one must resist them. With this, Paul sets the signal for confrontation. Everyone in the room knows which camp is now being

---

concerned with achieving reconciliation, here Paul is not a neutral mediator facing two hostile groups.

79. Thurén, "Was Paul Angry," 317–19. Page 317: "It was the apostle who sought trouble and controversy."

80. Concerning θαυμάζω ὅτι οὕτως ταχέως μετατίθεσθε cf. Nanos, *Irony*, 39–49.

81. Cf. Becker, *Galater*, 98: "The churches are immediately separated from the opponents, who were to receive the curse" (my translation).

attacked and knows who its most important representatives are. Verbally, however, the opponents remain undefined.

Galatians 2:11–21

In the section Gal 2:11–21, Paul initially reports about his dispute with Peter, that is, with the representative of the Jewish Christians, whom he had rebuked in Antioch at that time. Peter serves as a model of Paul's opponents in Galatia.[82] From verse 14 we find Paul's discourse with Peter and the theological reasons why the validity of the law is out of the question. Of course, this discourse is particularly suited for showing the Galatians why those wanting to enforce circumcision are wrong. So in this section Paul makes an imperceptible transition from a historical report to the current argumentation.[83]

Galatians 3:1

In Gal 3:1, Paul again addresses the listeners directly. The parallels to Gal 1:6–7 should be noted. Again the listeners are divided into two groups: The group of Galatians being addressed whose ignorance Paul deplores, and the indeterminate group of those who have bewitched the Galatians. The indeterminateness is expressed here using the τίς-question. Again the group being addressed is presented as the victims and the undefined group as perpetrators. The reproach of the foolish Galatians cannot be overheard. However, through earnest instruction—actually by means of a few very basic questions (3:2–6)—their failure can be overcome. But the guilt of those who had bewitched them (τίς ὑμᾶς ἐβάσκανεν) is quite another matter, since φαρμακεία is among those vices which, according to Gal 5:20, exclude one from God's kingdom.[84] But a further aspect of this confrontation should be noted: Only a few people can work magic. Although the opponents are indeed powerful, they are only a minority.

What was said about the opponents would move each listener to distance themselves from that group. Everyone likes to side with the majority. Everyone prefers to side with the victims, and not with the perpetrators when there are problems in the church community. No one

---

82. Cf. Schewe, *Galater*, 74–75.
83. Schäfer, *Paulus*, 224.
84. φαρμακεία and βασκαίνειν belong to the same word field, cf. Longenecker, "Until Christ," 93–99; Schewe, *Galater*, 126.

wants to belong to those who are practicing a vice such as witchcraft. No one wants to be under the curse (3:10; cf. 1:9). And, since Paul has not addressed the opponents (that is, has not challenged them to reveal themselves), many of them have the opportunity to change sides without losing face. That Paul is also expressly inviting Jewish Christians to side with him becomes plain by the fact that for him the boundary does not coincide with ethnic, social, or gender differences (3:27–28). Only the few who had been the spokespersons in behalf of the demand for circumcision remain. So when Paul indirectly indicates that the undefined opposition party are a minority, it is not just a description of the reality. (The Jewish Christians, despite their great influence, actually were in the minority.) It is also a manipulation of the listeners. Paul *makes* them a minority in the course of the performance.

Galatians 4:8–20

This situation repeats itself after a long section of theological arguments. In Gal 4:8 Paul addresses the listeners again—this time as Gentile Christians.[85] He calls to mind his earlier Galatian visit and the hearty relationship between them and him, the sick apostle (4:13–15). Memories come alive and strengthen the emotional bonding with Paul that has developed during the performance.[86] Paul had labored for them; they have helped him. Paul urges them to continue to support him and be on his side, not only when he is present.[87]

The opponents are again referred to in this context. Once again they are only mentioned in the third person, and are again depicted in a bad light.[88] They are zealous about the addressed church members, but out

---

85. Because Gal 4:8–9 speaks of the Galatians' falling off as a return to their Gentile past and Paul otherwise describes the falling off as a move towards the Jewish law, Witulski, *Adressaten*, 71–81 considers Gal 4:8–20 to be a part of another letter inserted by an editor.

86. Cf. Sampley, "Paul's Frank Speech," 302–4.

87. Cf. Schlier, *Galater*, 213; Mussner, *Galaterbrief*, 311. Rohde, *Galater*, 189 recognizes that Paul could be the subject of the passive infinitive ζηλοῦσθαι (v. 18) but finds in this connection that "an eagerness, whose object is Paul" (my translation) is missing. Thereby he overlooks that the verb ζηλοῦν picks up and summarizes what has been said in vv. 14–15 about the Galatians' behavior toward the apostle.

88. On the negative depiction of the opponents, cf. Johnson, "New Testament Anti-Jewish Slander"; Du Toit, "Alienation," 285, 287, 290 and *passim*; Du Toit, "Vilification"; Thurén, "Was Paul Angry," 312–14; Thurén, *Derhetorizing*, 66.

of self-interest (4:17–18).[89] Thus there is good zeal (i.e., that of Paul and that of the Galatians in the past) and bad zeal (i.e., that of the opponents).

Here, in comparison with earlier references of the opponents (1:6–7 and 3:1), there is a change in the way the opponents are mentioned in the performance. They are juxtaposed not only with those being addressed but also with the apostle. When listeners had previously been divided into two groups—one with a positive assessment, and the other, remaining undefined, with a negative assessment—then in a certain sense Paul stood in juxtaposition to *both* groups. This constellation was also reflected in the room during the performance: the presenter performed in front of the congregation and turned to one part while ignoring the other part and only addressing the second group "over his shoulder." Now, the perspective is turned upside-down, as it were. Now the Galatians who are being addressed have to become active. Now *they* are facing two parties who are both expecting to be courted: on the one hand, there is Paul and his gospel embodied in the person of the presenter, and on the other hand, there are the leading Jewish Christians who are present and who are trying to enforce the validity of the law. Paul, for the first time, risks an open competition with the opponents for the favor of the Galatians. This might suggest, on the one hand, that the group of opponents is only small in number and therefore fits as a counterpart to Paul (i.e., the presenter) as an individual; on the other hand, this might suggest that the members of the audience *being addressed* constitute the majority in the room. Paul apparently thinks he has won many of the listeners to his side by this time, not least through the emotional memories (4:13–15; cf. also the mother as illustration in 4:19). By this change in perspective, which becomes increasingly prevalent throughout the remainder of the performance (cf. 5:10–12; 6:12–13), the Galatians are being conditioned to be more active in their dealings with the crisis in Galatia.[90]

---

89. On the difficult expression ἀλλ' ἐκκλεῖσαι ὑμᾶς θέλουσιν, cf. Schlier, *Galater*, 212; Mussner, *Galaterbrief*, 310–11.

90. Paul could not be sure that each of the readers in the churches in Galatia would present the letter as he expected it to be presented. By the references to his bodily condition (4:13–15) and his tone of voice (4:20), he challenges the listeners to evaluate the performance and to find their own standpoint. On this, see above pp. 136–51. On the physical body in the performance, see above pp. 52–57 and 84–86.

Galatians 4:29-30

Paul's Jewish Christian opponents have become so decimated, isolated and vilified in the course of the performance—at least in Paul's opinion at the time he dictated the letter—that he can risk a cautious attack. After contrasting Hagar and Ishmael with Sarah and Isaac (4:22-28), Paul explicitly applies part of their story to the contemporary situation in Galatia (4:29): "As at that time he who was born according to the flesh persecuted him who was born according to the Spirit, so it is now also."[91] This detail appears like an appendix. Already in the previous sentence, Paul had conclusively established that the Galatian believers were children of the promise. Paul's appendix here is added in view of the Galatian situation.

What persecution is he thinking of? It could be a persecution by the Jewish synagogue. That would presuppose that the local Jews were making it difficult for the Galatians, which according to Gal 6:12 is quite probable at least for the Jewish Christians.[92] However, the scriptural reference, introduced with emphasis (4:30), must then be understood to mean that Paul is maintaining that *God* has excluded the Jews from salvation. This would mean that Paul is advocating a different position in the Letter to the Galatians than in Rom 11:25-32.[93] Although it is not impossible for Paul to change his opinion during the course of time, there is another possibility which fits the context of the Letter to the Galatians better. In this case, the persecution Paul is thinking of is the pressure prominent Jewish Christians were putting on Gentile Christians who were resisting the demand for circumcision (6:12: ἀναγκάζουσιν). Jewish Christians were using their social position to threaten (4:17: ἐκκλεῖσαι ὑμᾶς θέλουσιν) and disadvantage those who did not agree with them (5:7: ἐγκόπτειν).[94] The severe conflicts in the churches (5:15) could be connected to that. Then the scriptural reference would be an indirect appeal to the *churches* to disfellowship the few incorrigible Jewish Christians who continued to

---

91. Cf. Strack and Billerbeck, *Kommentar*, 3:575-76 as cited in Rohde, *Galater*, 203-4 and Mussner, *Galaterbrief*, 329-30 on the rabbinical background of this tradition.

92. See above pp. 239-40.

93. Cf. Rohde, *Galater*, 205 who explains this difference by pointing to the different situations in Galatia and Rome. Mussner, *Galaterbrief*, 332 argues against such a contradiction.

94. Cf. Mussner, *Galaterbrief*, 331; Hansen, *Abraham*, 141-54; Martyn, *Galatians*, 444-45.

demand circumcision after the performance of the letter.[95] This correlates to the use of the leaven illustration in Gal 5:9[96] and the remark that the opponents have to pay the penalty (5:10: βαστάσει τὸ κρίμα).

Paul has explicitly established a connection between the *persecution* that Ishmael caused and the contemporary situation (4:29: οὕτως καὶ νῦν). He is not explicit concerning the *expulsion* of Hagar and her son. That is not because Paul normally hesitates to order that someone be disfellowshipped (cf. 1 Cor 5:5). More probably, he is not entirely sure that the listeners will move to his side during the performance. A direct command to disfellowship someone could go too far for the situation in Galatia and turn the listeners against Paul, thus causing the performance to escalate in a direction he does not desire. Paul therefore prefers to leave it to the Galatians to deal with those among them who are continuing to demand circumcision.

Galatians 5:7–12

The next passage dealing with Paul's opponents is found in Gal 5:7–12. Again, they are not directly addressed but remain indeterminate in the question "Who hindered you?" (τίς ὑμᾶς ἐνέκοψεν). Again, this indeterminacy is a rhetorical strategy, because Paul is indeed aware that they are putting obstacles in the path[97] of the church and are themselves using rhetorical methods (5:8: πεισμονή). Again the addressed church members are first criticized (τῇ ἀληθείᾳ μὴ πείθεσθαι) and then immediately exonerated and depicted as victims. Thus a strategy is repeated that divides the listeners into a positively evaluated group (although they had been disobedient, they were victims of the reprehensible acts of others) and a negatively evaluated group which remains indefinite. This strategy enables one to leave the negatively evaluated group without being noticed.[98]

Again we find the strategy of threats and enticements serves to win many of the listeners to Paul's side. As a threat, Paul repeats the illustration of the leaven in verse 9, a veiled recommendation to disfellowship the members of the negatively evaluated group that remain in opposition

---

95. Mussner, *Galaterbrief*, 332; Schlier, *Galater*, 227 interprets this differently.

96. Cf. 1 Cor. 5:6, where Paul also uses the leaven illustration in connection with disfellowshipping. Cf. Hardin, *Galatians and the Imperial Cult*, 94.

97. Paul used a military or sports image but would have had concrete acts of the opponents in mind.

98. Schewe, *Galater*, 74 emphasizes the parallels to Gal 1:6–9.

and reveal themselves at the end of the performance.[99] On the other hand, in verse 10, Paul woos the church being addressed by expressing his trust in them. In this way Paul not only states his trust but also gives a strong impulse for the listeners not to betray his trust.[100] Paul returns to the opponents with the remark that those causing the confusion will pay the inevitable penalty. The ὅστις ἐὰν ᾖ is again indefinite. Thus it is also implied that the judgment will fall independent of the person's position.[101]

It is conspicuous that Paul again uses the singular here.[102] Paul has already spoken of the opponents so that they appear to be a minority. He conveys the picture here that it is only a few individual Jewish Christians who are campaigning for circumcision. The opposing party has now been reduced to a few prominent individuals. From this perspective, the opponents lose even more importance in the eyes of the larger audience. The fact that they are to be judged is, on the one hand, an indirect invitation to the Gentile Christian majority to pass such a judgment and, on the other hand, an indirect appeal to the tacit followers and sympathizers of the Jewish Christians to change sides.[103]

In Gal 5:11–12, as previously in Gal 4:17–18, Paul emphasizes his position in contrast to his opponents' (ἐγὼ δέ),[104] and thus confronts the audience he is addressing (ἀδελφοί) with the decision between himself and his opponents. Since Paul is being persecuted by the Jewish side, it is indisputably clear that he no longer preaches circumcision.[105] This makes

99. Cf. Gal 4:30; cf. ibid., 76: "appelative undertone" (my translation); cf. Becker, *Galater*, 79.

100. What Schewe, *Galater*, 72 says on Gal 5:5 is equally applicable to 5:10: "In 5:5, the author places his audience in the position where he wants them to be . . . By using 'we', the author constructs *the* commonality between himself . . . and his addressees that is not yet reality but is his intention to reestablish with his letter" (my translation).

101. Mussner, *Galaterbrief*, 358.

102. Longenecker, *Galatians*, xciv interprets it as a "generic singular"; also Mussner, *Galaterbrief*, 358; Martyn, *Galatians*, 475 thinks of the leader of the opposing group.

103. Martyn, *Galatians*, 476: "differentiating all of the Galatians from the Teachers and openly inviting them to stand at his side rather than at the side of the Teachers."

104. Barclay, "Mirror-Reading," 79; Hardin, *Galatians and the Imperial Cult*, 98–99.

105. The background behind the conditional sentence using εἰ is not the idea or accusation that Paul is perhaps still preaching circumcision. In that case, the conjunction ἐάν would have had to be used, which expresses that one must weigh the truth of the condition. On the other hand, in a conditional sentence using εἰ, the stress lies on the consequence, thus emphasizing how compelling the reasoning is. The irreal nature of the condition does not always need to be indicated by ἄν, as seen in 1 Cor 15:13, 14. Cf. Blass and Debrunner, *Grammatik*, §371, 1, with n. 1.

it obvious that Paul is on the side of the "free" who are being persecuted (4:29), that is, on the side of the listeners being addressed: Paul portrays them as hindered in their race by their opponents (5:7), as incited by agitators (5:12), and generally as victims. In sharp contrast to this, Paul disparages the opponents, using in fact a form of sarcasm for the first time here that could hardly be outdone: he says he wishes his opponents would castrate themselves (5:12).[106] Both this sarcasm and the term οἱ ἀναστατοῦντες show that Paul is increasingly relying on confrontation. Of course, such grim irony is a strong stimulus, provoking a reaction among the listeners. Such a reaction is well suited to end the ambiguity concerning which group each person in the audience belongs to. Whoever makes himself or herself noticed positions himself or herself in front of all those present. Paul's sarcasm might have provoked a derisive sneer or a vocal utterance from those who had been on his side the whole time, or who in the meantime have joined his side again. The opponents could have been recognized by their expressions of indignation. However, that did not have to happen. Here, as throughout the letter, the opponents are not spoken to directly. The strategy of speaking indirectly to them still makes it possible for them to change sides.

Galatians 5:13-26

The unity in the church was damaged by the circumcision dispute (5:15). The church was dominated by strivings for privilege and influence (5:21). Susanne Schewe has, in my opinion, convincingly argued that in his admonitions in Gal 5 and 6 Paul shows that internal difficulties of the church were a consequence of uplifting reliance on the law and with that turning to reliance on human σάρξ.[107] Paul calls listeners to return to a life in the Spirit, which does not destroy fellowship (cf. the majority of the vices in 5:19–21), but in which love, peace and all the other virtues that foster fellowship thrive (5:22).

---

106. It must be left open as to whether Paul is alluding to the ecstatic castration of the Attis and Cybele cults. Cf. Elliott, *Cutting Too Close*.

107. Schewe, *Galater*, 185–86. Cf. also what she says about Gal 5:13 and σάρξ on ibid., 82–101.

Galatians 6:1–10

If the most important personalities among Paul's opponents were prominent Jewish Christians, as evidence suggests, then Paul's strategy of defamation and decimation, and the call to resist their opinions, would have contributed to destabilizing the leadership structures in the Galatian churches. The question can remain open whether there were specific institutional structures or offices or if there were certain personalities to whom leadership tasks had fallen: perhaps to the church's hosts, to people with better education and higher social standing, or to people with a longer church membership,[108] or to members with the charisma of leadership ability. In Gal 6:1–10 Paul consecutively addresses leading personalities and ordinary church members. In Gal 6:1–5 he addresses those who could sharply reprimand others and were therefore in danger of thinking too highly of themselves.[109] He calls them οἱ πνευματικοί and expressly reminds them of the life in the Spirit that was just treated in chapter 5.[110] In Gal 6:6–10 he addresses those who were receiving instruction and so were obligated to support their leaders.[111] The aim of this section is to provide for renewal of church leadership structures and to strengthen fellowship in the churches *after* the removal of those who had been abusing their leadership roles to enforce the demand for circumcision.

Galatians 6:11–17

The last section is once again a strong attack on the opponents, laying bare their inconsistency and self-interest. Paul makes two accusations (6:12–13). First, his opponents want to avoid disadvantages (μὴ διώκωνται); and, second, they are seeking to make a good outward impression (εὐπροσωπῆσαι) and gain something to boast about (καυχήσωνται).[112] The

---

108. Cf. Schmitt, *Paroikie*, 104–5.

109. Witherington, *Grace*, 426–29 surmises that Paul is alluding to the agitators in Gal 6:3–5.

110. Depending on the situation, the address ἀδελφοί can mean only some of the listeners (contrary to Witherington, *Grace*, 422), which the presenter would make clear through his direction of view and body language. The seating was normally organized according to social rank, with leading people sitting in prominent places.

111. See the discussion of the strategy of Gal 6:1–10 above on pp. 219–27.

112. Cf. Harnisch, "Einübung," 280–81.

accusations are massive and not without sarcasm (6:12).[113] Here, as in the rest of the letter, the opponents are not addressed directly.

The church members being addressed are again depicted as victims: "that they may boast in *your* flesh." In other words, "you are being used." In contrast to earlier passages in the letter, here there is no more criticism of those Paul is addressing.

At the end of the letter Paul again places himself in opposition to his opponents,[114] and once more invites the listeners to choose between himself and those demanding circumcision. Paul makes a twofold contrast between himself and them. In order to do this he unfolds his two accusations (6:12–13), taking them up in the opposite order.

First Paul deals with an accusation that he is seeking glory. In contrast Paul emphasizes strongly (6:14a: ἐμοὶ δὲ μὴ γένοιτο) that he himself is in no way interested in his own prestige. The emphasis on ἐμοὶ and the repetition of καυχᾶσθαι make the contrast to the opponents clear. Then Paul speaks in very fundamental terms with a clear allusion to the previous chapter: The fact that the world is crucified to him, and he to the world (cf. 5:24) stands in contrast to the worldly interests of his opponents, which can be seen both in their striving for glory and their avoidance of persecution. In chapter 5, Paul had called this living according to the flesh. Being "crucified to the world" is a negatively worded description of the believing Christian's existence. The positive wording is, "walking in the Spirit," or "being led by the Spirit" (5:16, 18). The Galatians must choose: they have before them Paul, embodied by the presenter, and they also see the prominent Jews in their midst who are so forcefully propounding circumcision.

For Paul, it was important that calling for a decision was not a way to drive a wedge between the Gentile and the Jewish Christians. The Jewish Christians present should not feel shut out and should not identify themselves with Paul's prominent opponents. Rather Paul aimed to invite them to join his own side. This is why he repeats, Circumcision is actually irrelevant (6:15; cf. 5:6; 3:28). Being re-created by God is the only thing that matters. Then he pronounces a blessing on those who will concur (στοιχήσουσιν) with the conviction Paul has been expressing. The use of the future tense is a clear invitation to accept this conviction.[115] The bless-

---

113. On sarcasm, see above on pp. 240–41.
114. Cf. Tolmie, *Persuading*, 223.
115. Cf. Rohde, *Galater*, 277: "because Paul includes those in his wish, who, in the future, will act according to his rule, rejecting the preachers of circumcision and living

ing is for "the Israel of God." Paul makes clear that he understands his way not as a contradiction of Israel's tradition but rather as a re-turning to what was inherent in this tradition from the very beginning. In the believing Abraham, all are blessed who believe the gospel (cf. 3:9): Jews and also Gentiles (3:14). The fact that Paul reiterates this once again is a sign of his appreciation for Israel's tradition and a renewed invitation to the Jewish Christians to join his side.

Finally Paul takes up once more his first accusation against his opponents, namely, their strivings to avoid persecution. He points out that, in contrast to his opponents, he bears the marks of Jesus on his own body. These are the marks of persecution for Jesus' sake, the scars of mistreatment and suffering.[116] It can be seen from his body that he has not shrunk back from persecution.[117]

His appeal that no one trouble him any longer is the apostle's dramatic concluding signal. He has spoken. His labor for the churches (4:19), his emphatic writing (6:11: πηλίκα γράμματα), and his scars that witness to his suffering for Christ (6:17) give him great authority. Now he puts an authoritative end to the debate over the observance of the law in Galatia.[118] With this sentence, Paul once again strategically intervenes in the performance of the letter in the Galatian churches: Normally, a discussion followed the reading of the letter, whereby the carriers of the letter had the task of orally explaining the letter's content. But in Galatia, this discussion—according to Paul's instructions—should be reduced to a minimum, that is, the opponents should be given little room for a dispute over the issue.

Summary

When we review the performance written into the Letter to the Galatians, a fourfold strategy is revealed:

---

without observing the provisions of the Jewish law" (my translation).

116. Ibid., 279–80; Hardin, *Galatians and the Imperial Cult*, 98. Cf. the overview of interpretations in Tolmie, *Persuading*, 227–32.

117. Paul's pointing to his scars brings the presenter to the limits of what he can embody in his own person in the performance, since he himself probably had no such scars. Even in the most skillful presentation, the audience would be reminded that they are experiencing a performance and not Paul himself. See above pp. 150–51 on the distancing effect of this strategy and the challenge to the audience to make its own decisions.

118. Cf. Becker, *Galater*, 102–3.

1) Throughout the entire letter, the question concerning circumcision is presented as an open question independent of any decisions that had previously been made. The Galatians must decide, or decide anew.

2) Throughout the letter, the audience is divided into two parts. On the one side are those who have left the right path, foolish church members who are victims of manipulation and confusion. For them, there is hope (5:10). On the other side there are Paul's opponents, who are always described negatively. They are the perpetrators and responsible for the problems in the churches.

3) Paul addresses the church members belonging to the first group directly and seeks to win them over. The criticism against them subsides in the second half of the letter. Instead, Paul more forcefully urges them to make their own decision by repeatedly contrasting himself with his opponents (4:18; 5:11; 6:14, 17).

4) The members of the second group, the opponents, are never spoken to directly by Paul, although he knows very well that they are listening. To be sure, the words and arguments he chooses are certainly meant for their ears too, but he only addresses them "over his shoulder," as it were. It is consciously left unclear who belongs to this group. They receive no impulse to reveal themselves. Over the course of the performance, the depictions of the size of this group become smaller and smaller, even the singular is used (5:10). The accusations against this group become ever more pointed and are directed against their personal motivations (4:17; 6:12–13); even an element of sarcasm is used (5:12; 6:13). In the second half of the letter there is also the threat of consequences for leading church members astray (4:30; 5:10, 21). This all serves to pull as many as possible out of the second group—especially the sympathizers, tacit followers, and lower-ranking people. Since they do not have to reveal themselves, they can leave this group without losing face.

Of course we do not know whether the performance in the individual churches was carried out as Paul would have wished, or whether the debate really ceased after the performance. We do not know how the (perhaps few remaining) opponents behaved after this letter event. If the brothers named at the beginning as coauthors (1:1) were the ones delivering the letter, then they must have—as was usual—explained and enlarged upon some of the contents after the performance. The fact that the letter has been preserved could be an indication of the fact that, at least in some of the churches, the performance did indeed have the results that Paul desired.

Expelling the Opponents
(First Letter of Clement)

A comparable performance to that of the Epistle to the Galatians can be found in the First Letter of Clement. This letter was written by the Roman Christians[119] to the church in Corinth at the end of the first or the beginning of the second century CE.[120] As with the Letter to the Galatians, it was written to Christians in order to solve an acute problem that had broken out among them. For this purpose, the letter was to be read out in a church assembly.[121]

Performance Situation in Corinth

In Corinth there were some leading personalities, called ἐπίσκοποι or πρεσβύτεροι,[122] who had been disempowered (44:3, 6).[123] This was only possible because there was a superior power that pushed this change through. Leading personalities were dependent on having a strong following in order to enforce their demands.[124] In a performance situation,

---

119. Concerning the authorship, cf. the detailed discussion in Lona, *Erste Clemensbrief*, 66–75 and Schmitt, *Paroikie*, 7–21. In the tradition of the church, authorship by Clement of Rome is well testified. There are, however, no references to a single author within the letter itself so that the designation, in the following, will be "the authors."

120. This letter is usually dated to the time of Domitian, because of the sudden series of occurrences, referred to in 1 Clem 1:1, which befell the Roman Christians. This has, however, been disputed by Welborn, "Date" and others since the scarcely specific terms (συμφοραὶ καὶ περιπτώσεις) point more to the traditional wording of an excuse, justifying why the Roman Christians did not become active sooner. Besides, the positive attitude to ruler and state (37:2-3; 60:2; 61:1-2; cf. von Harnack, "Schreiben der römischen Kirche," 71–72; but differently Schmitt, *Paroikie*, 21–31) does not fit well with a persecution situation. Cf. also Bakke, *Concord and Peace*, 8–11. On the possibility of an earlier date, cf. Erlemann, "Datierung." Lona, *Erste Clemensbrief*, 77 and Schmitt, *Paroikie*, 117–25 argue for the traditional dating.

121. Lona, *Erste Clemensbrief*, 23.

122. Used synonymously according to ibid., 474; cf. von Harnack, "Schreiben der römischen Kirche," 73; Mikat, *Bedeutung*, 15; Schmitt, *Paroikie*, 75.

123. 1 Clemens 44:3: ἀποβάλλεσθαι τῆς λειτουργίας; v. 6: ἐνίους ὑμεῖς μετηγάγετε καλῶς πολιτευομένους ἐκ τῆς ἀμέμπτως αὐτοῖς τετιμημένης λειτουργίας.

124. Cf. von Harnack, "Schreiben der römischen Kirche," 41–42: the church had agreed to the degradation. Lindemann, *Clemensbriefe*, 26: "Probably the Corinthian events were based on a majority decision of the local ἐκκλησία" (my translation). Similarly Mikat, *Bedeutung*, 18: "*Clement* takes his stand against these revolutionaries and

perhaps a public speech, the fight for a position of power was often decided through the acclamation of the congregation.[125] The fact that the audience has a considerable influence on what happens in a performance has not only been confirmed by performance research,[126] but it has also been substantiated for the ancient world.[127] The new wielders of power in Corinth had apparently understood how to obtain a numerical majority[128] or social dominance for their own objectives through persons with rank and influence in the church.[129] However, it must be assumed that the deposed presbyters also had a group of sympathizers behind them who had lost the power struggle.

The reason for the uprising cannot be found in the letter.[130] It has been deduced from 1 Clem 48:5-6 that there were opposing points of view concerning the leadership of the church. One was characterized more by a formal office, and the other was more charismatic.[131] But if the uprising was carried out by those resistant to formal offices, then it is difficult to explain why some bishops were able to retain their offices after the uprising (44:6).[132] There does not appear to have been a doctrinal dispute behind the conflict, since the rebels were not accused of

---

therewith against the attitude of many of the church members" (my translation). First Clem 44:3 also presupposes that the ἐπίσκοποι were elected by agreement of the whole church.

125. Cf. Schmitt, *Paroikie*, 80, there also the appropriate literature.

126. See above pp. 59–61 and 89–94 on the role of the audience.

127. Cf. Korenjak, *Publikum und Redner*, 100–14 (he calls the section of his book "Die emotionale Macht des Publikums"); and Aldrete, *Gestures*, 159–64 concerning the unpredictability of the public encounter between the emperor and the plebs. Cf. also Bartsch, *Actors*, 63–97.

128. Thus von Harnack, "Schreiben der römischen Kirche," 75; Mikat, *Bedeutung*, 13.

129. Schmitt, *Paroikie*, 101 reads in 1 Clem 54:2 that the insurrection's leaders were able to assert themselves, but were unable to gather a majority behind them. Therefore he does not perceive that the letter presupposes that the majorities had been changed through the performance by this time. On this, see below pp. 266–67.

130. Cf. Lona, *Erste Clemensbrief*, 79–80 for a list of explanations researchers have posited.

131. Knopf, *Erster Clemensbrief*, 42; similarly Schneider, "Einleitung," in Clemens von Rom, *Epistola ad Corinthios*, 8, who assumes that the rebels were not claiming an office but rather wanted to abolish it. Rhode, "Häresie," 219 also thinks of charismatics and on p. 222 bases his view on the fact that towards the end of the letter the rebels are also credited with a positive attitude. On this, see below pp. 271 and 273–74.

132. Cf. von Harnack, "Schreiben der römischen Kirche," 73; Schmitt, *Paroikie*, 101–2.

false teaching and were accepted by Christians in other places after their "emigration" (54:2–3).[133] It cannot be deduced that the dispute in Corinth was about church office based on the fact that the Roman letter tries to *solve* the problem in Corinth by invoking the power of the bishop's office as it was understood by the authors.

Odd Magne Bakke conjectures that members of the lower classes, who were striving for honor, were behind the revolt in Corinth.[134] He deduces this from 1 Clem 3:3 and evaluates these statements as indirect descriptions of the events, albeit in traditional language (also drawing on Isa 3:5). This thesis needs some correcting for two reasons: First, if 1 Clem 3:3 is a description of events, then most of the common people would have understood it as a description of their success. However, the context has the function of describing the church's current situation as negatively as possible for the majority of listeners and to make clear to them what a terrible business they have let themselves be drawn into. Second, the letter presumes that there were leaders in the revolt (57:1–2). They would have only been able to bring the majority behind them if they were qualified for leadership roles by their higher social standing.[135] If those now wielding power were perhaps younger and until that point less prominent, they nevertheless belonged to the church's higher social class.[136] Adolf von Harnack's assessment that it is "a fully-fledged quarrel among cliques" remains entirely plausible.[137]

When the First Letter of Clement arrives in Corinth, the dispute has already been decided, but the parties are still not reconciled. The various groups are attending the church meeting.[138] The church is split (46:9:

133. Rohde, "Häresie," 224, 226; Lindemann, *Clemensbriefe*, 16; Schneider, "Einleitung," in Clemens von Rom: *Epistola ad Corinthios*, 8.

134. Bakke, *Concord and Peace*, 289–317.

135. Cf. Schmitt, *Paroikie*, 21: "in relation to their (former?) position in the Roman colony" (my translation).

136. Schneider, "Einleitung," in Clemens von Rom, *Epistola ad Corinthios*, 7; and Schmitt, *Paroikie*, 100 interpret this same passage as a rebellion of the young against the old. Differently Lona, *Erste Clemensbrief*, 141–42.

137. Von Harnack, "Schreiben der römischen Kirche," 76 (my translation). Cf. Mikat, *Bedeutung*, 18, n. 43. He presumes that the senders are afraid that the disturbances in Corinth could lead to state persecution (ibid., 24, 28, 36–39). Schmitt, *Paroikie*, 103 also assumes that the specific dispute over persons in Corinth is connected to the dispute over church office, especially concerning its lifetime validity.

138. It is improbable that there were two centers of worship, as von Harnack concluded from chs. 40–41, "Schreiben der römischen Kirche," 76, because the

σχίσμα and στάσις). Many are supporting the new leaders; others have resigned themselves to accepting the new situation. Some are opponents of the new leaders and likely fear personal disadvantages for siding with the losers in the fight for dominance in Corinth. Because of this situation, the theme of the letter is peace and unity (63:2: ἔντευξις περὶ εἰρήνης καὶ ὁμονοίας).[139]

In accordance with the customs of the ancient world for delivering official letters to a group of people (e.g., to the inhabitants of a city), the letter is brought by emissaries who are named in the letter (65:1) and recommended to the recipients.[140] It is a three-man delegation. They are of a mature age (ἕως γήρους ἀμέμπτως) and are described (63:3) as faithful (πιστοί) and as having a proven judgment (σώφρονες). The emissaries are familiar with the contents of the letter, when requested give supplementary information (cf. Acts 15:23–32), and do their best so that the letter achieves the effect desired.[141]

The manner in which the messengers are received is decisive. If the letter was not read out because the new holders of power suppressed it, the sender's purpose would be lost. That is the reason why the virtue of hospitality is so strongly stressed in Clement's first letter (e.g., 1:2-3; 10:7—12:8; 35:5).(Commentators have often noted this fact without being able to give a plausible explanation for it.[142]) However, from the viewpoint of the performance, it becomes clear that the author wanted

---

performance of the letter presupposes that the opposing groups are listening conjointly. Similarly van Unnik, "Studies," 138, who also rejects the idea of spatial separation, referring to 1 Clem 34:7.

139. Cf. van Unnik, "Studies," 129–30 and *passim*; also Mikat, *Bedeutung*; Bakke, *Concord and Peace, passim*.

140. Stirewalt, *Paul*, 6–8, 16.

141. Van Unnik, "Studies," 172–75 compares the task of the Roman delegation with that of mediators in political disputes, as attested to in inscriptions. Cf. Welborn, "Date," 213.

142. Do we have here a traditional theme of admonition not connected to the purpose of the letter? E.g., von Harnack, "Schreiben der römischen Kirche," 91: "Christian hospitality must have involved such high costs, dangers and sacrifice in those times that it was considered to be a cardinal virtue and a specific test of the Christian life (πίστις)" (my translation). Was hospitality used for partisan politics? Did the guests therefore seek accommodation by the deposed bishops? Or was the hospitality neglected because of the divisions? Thus argues e.g., Lona, *Erste Clemensbrief*, 27–28, 122, 210, who builds upon Chadwick, "Justification," 284–85. Schmitt, *Paroikie*, 92–95 points to hospitality—practiced beyond the limits of the Christian community—as an important factor in mission.

to ensure that the messengers would be well received, since the public presentation, and thereby the letter's success, depended upon it.

A new performance situation suited to reorder the power structures again is created by the appearance of the Roman delegation and the reading of the letter. The letter repeatedly suggests that there is currently strife in Corinth (46:5). These statements could be a rhetorical strategy to keep the situation open for a new decision. Horacio Lona interprets the future tense in 1 Clem 44:4 (ἔσται) as follows: "If the author nevertheless [although the dismissal of the bishops has already been accomplished] alludes to it [the decision] in the future tense, then [it is] with the intention of motivating the Corinthians to revise this step, which can only mean the reinstatement of the officeholders."[143] Thus, the letter is about the future course of the Corinthian church.[144]

Hence we must assume that for the delivery of the First Letter of Clement the Christians in Corinth have come together according to the protocol for the reception of an official letter in order to hear what was in the letter and subsequently to listen to what the messengers from Rome had to say. Those assembled are seated so that they can see one another. The commoners are gathered in the places allotted to them. There are some seats of honor for the leaders. These are occupied by those who have newly come to power.[145] Those who are assembled know who voted for the new order and who were against it. The messengers from Rome are also sitting in prominent seats and are visible to all. After the formal greeting of the messengers and the official presentation of the letter, the letter is read out by the one chosen to read it.

The Course of the Performance

In the following, the course of the performance of the First Letter of Clement is presented, although not section by section but rather in a comprehensive summary. It will become apparent that the performance progressed in three stages.

---

143. Lona, *Erste Clemensbrief*, 465 (my translation).

144. In this sense the presentation of the letter is defined by van Unnik, "Studies," 159–63 and Bakke, *Concord and Peace*, 203 and *passim* as deliberative speech.

145. Mikat, *Bedeutung*, 23 speaks wrongly of a church "which is, for all practical purposes, without leadership" (my translation).

Distance between the New Leaders and the Church Members

In the first section, distance is created between the common church members and the initiators of the leadership changes. The new leaders are isolated. The authors use the following means to achieve this:

1) Right from the start, two groups are created in the audience.

> Owing to the sudden and repeated misfortunes and calamities which have befallen us, we consider that our attention has been somewhat delayed in turning to the questions disputed among you, beloved, and especially the abominable and unholy sedition, alien and foreign to the elect of God, which a few rash and self-willed persons have made blaze up to such a frenzy that your name, venerable and famous, and worthy as it is of all men's love, has been much slandered (1:1).[146]

One group is the majority of the church members, who are referred to as the "elect of God." The other group is made up of the leaders of the insurrection, the "few rash and self-willed persons." In the given situation one could assume that there are six groups among the listeners: three groups in the upper class (namely, the deposed bishops, those who had retained their offices, and the new leaders), three groups among the lower class (namely, the new leaders' supporters, probably in the majority; then the opponents of the change, a minority; and also the group of undecided members). But the authors speak of only two groups. They never address the deposed bishops, although these are referred to as blameless (44:3–6). The authority of these bishops is too badly impaired for them to be able to influence the crowd. It is this crowd, however, that the authors are trying to win over with their letter. The authors also never address those bishops who were able to stay in office.[147]

The common church members are taken together as *one* group, although they were certainly divided over the deposing of some of their bishops (cf. 56:2). Why didn't the authors call attention to the opponents of the leadership change even though the authors were on their side as far as the dispute was concerned? Why did the authors not address them? When a group is directly addressed in a performance situation, its members must react in front of the rest of the listeners (for example, through

---

146. Here and in the following: text according to Schneider: Clemens von Rom. *Epistola ad Corinthios*, translation by Lake, *Apostolic Fathers*.

147. Lona, *Erste Clemensbrief*, 471: not all bishops had been deposed.

signals—if only slight—of approval, which could be expected when the writers spoke to the opponents of the insurgency). That means that because of their reaction, the opponents of the change would be recognized by all attending the performance. That is, the authors would have visibly defined a minority among the listeners, namely, the defeated group of opponents to the change. At the same time, they would have defined the majority of the members, those who had brought about the change, as their opponents. The Romans wanted to avoid such a positioning of the church members and leave it open as to who stood on which side. In this way, they made it possible for those who had supported the leadership changes to rethink their position and possibly change sides.

In the same way as with the opponents of the leadership change, the writers do not at first address the instigators of the change and their supporters. Instead, they only speak *about* them.[148] With this strategy they prevent them from making themselves recognizable by their reactions (e.g., by a protest). As not present, as it were, they do not need to react. Of course, all the listeners know who is meant because they know the ones who caused the change of leadership. But those being alluded to by the letter writers could signal through their inconspicuous behavior that they did not feel that they were being targeted. So they too still have the possibility to change sides.

2) The authors address the commoners throughout most of the letter (cf. the workers in 34:1). They are being stirred up against the new leaders. In the end, the goal is to bring about a decision against the instigators of the change with the help of this majority. The authors use the power of the crowd whose protest, especially in a performance situation, could be dangerous to those in power.

For the normal church members, the revolt of the lower classes against the upper classes, the underprivileged against the privileged, the young against the old (3:3) upsets the established and necessary social order. The common people do not like the idea of a revolt from below. They love order, which gives them a feeling of security.[149] That is why the authors can reckon with approval when they call to mind the divine order in nature (19:3—20:12; 33) and in Israel's sacrificial system (40:1—41:4).

---

148. Chadwick, "Justification," 285 interprets it thus: The author refuses to recognize the new leadership.

149. Lona, *Erste Clemensbrief*, 220 on 1 Clem 14:2: "They [the instigators] want to estrange the commoners from the 'proper order'" (my translation).

The commoners are used to leading their lives in a way that acknowledges those with authority and is of no offense to those in high positions. Since it is not easy to get the simple church members to distance themselves from the new church leaders, the authors must argue using *God's* authority: "Let us offend foolish and thoughtless . . . men rather than God" (21:5; similarly 14:1-2).

The authors address the recipients as such who are used to obeying. They are expressly praised for their role as those who are faithfully obedient. This can be seen in the comparison with military service, where not all are leaders, and where, above all, the higher ranks are unable to achieve anything without the lower ones (37:1-4). The praise of the common people can also be seen in the traditional illustration of the body (37:5). Now they should obey God and the Roman emissaries, not the leaders in "abominable jealousy" (14:1-2). One authority is being replaced by another authority. Throughout the letter there is a wealth of references to God's authority and his judgment (28:1: God sees everything, cf. 21:3, 9; 27:6-7).[150] God hates not only those who do wrong but also those who consent to it (35:6: συνευδοκοῦντες). This argument is aimed at the followers of the new holders of power.

On the one hand the masses are given a new orientation (i.e., God's authority), which at the same time is being brought to them by the Roman church. The listeners are to recognize the authorities over them. On the other hand, they are also addressed as authorities, who themselves give directions to the youth, women, and children (1:3; 21:6-8).[151] Throughout this letter, they are viewed as men with the right to vote in an assembly (ἐκκλησία). By using this term for them, the authors of 1 Clement are preparing them to make a decision against the leaders of the uprising.

3) By means of the letter, the authors pit the majority of church members against a minority, who promoted deposing bishops. Right from the beginning, they say that the instigators of the revolt are only a few: "a few persons" (1:1). Later the authors reduce the number even more: "that on account of one or two persons the steadfast and ancient church of the Corinthians is being disloyal to the presbyters" (47:6).[152]

---

150. Ibid., 320 to 1 Clem 28:1: "If this assumption [that 28:1 is alluding to the situation in Corinth] is true, then the author is pleading for the Corinthians to distance themselves clearly from the leaders of the disturbance (cf. 14:1-2)" (my translation).

151. Ibid., 123 speaks of an "orientation by this fictional 'middle' of the church" (my translation).

152. Von Harnack, "Schreiben der römischen Kirche," 99 understands the passage as realistic depiction: "Therefore the number of ringleaders was very small"

The leaders of the revolt must clearly have been more numerous, since otherwise they would not have been able to carry it through. However, with this wording, the authors of 1 Clement *make* a small group out of them. In this way they induce the listeners to side with the larger crowd. The group of those responsible for the change of power still has not been addressed, so they are not visibly distinguishable.

4) A positive characterization is set against a negative one. Throughout the letter, there is a wealth of negative evaluations of the instigators of the power change. They have become rash, self-willed, frenzied (ἀπόνοια) (1:1).[153] They are driven by envy and jealousy, by the lusts of their evil hearts (3:1–4; 4:7; 14:1); they are foolish (ἄφρονες), irrational (ἀνόητοι),[154] arrogant (ἐπαιρόμενοι), and boasters (ἐν ἀλαζονείᾳ τοῦ λόγου αὐτῶν).[155] They have instigated a revolt (3:2, στάσις); they rush into strife and sedition (14:2). The fact that they are breaking from the traditional order sounds very negative to the ears of the ordinary people, for whom it is difficult to break free from their place in the system of order.

The negative phrase in 1 Clem 15:1 τοῖς μεθ' ὑποκρίσεως βουλομένοις εἰρήνην[156] is also a characterization of those causing the disturbance.[157] The authors are therefore aware that the new leaders are also speaking of wanting to overcome division and strife, but the senders of the letter

---

(my translation). In contrast, Lindemann, *Clemensbriefe*, 26 more correctly refers to a "deliberate understatement." Similarly Lona, *Erste Clemensbrief*, 511 (cf. also p. 118): "The small number should rather testify to the unimportance of the movement, even though the results are clearly not so unimportant." However, it reads differently on p. 78: "The conflict's originators are only very few people (1:1; 54:2; 57:1)" (my translations).

153. Cf. Lona, *Erste Clemensbrief*, 118 on the background.

154. Following Malina, Witherington, *Grace*, 201 points out that the ἀνόητος has a moral deficit, and that he is "one who lacks respect for or understanding of social boundaries, and so is capable of being guilty of crossing these boundaries from time to time and so bringing shame upon himself."

155. First Clement 21:5; 39:1. Lona, *Erste Clemensbrief*, 424 sees in the ἡμᾶς in 1 Clem 39:1 a reference to the public reading of the letter. "The text, from the very beginning, was written for the situation and with the expectation that it would be read out before the church" (my translation). Thus the authors join forces with the Corinthians, more exactly—and Lona misses this—with the group of Corinthian listeners, who have distanced themselves from those creating the disturbance.

156. ". . . whose wish for peace is hypocrisy."

157. Lona, *Erste Clemensbrief*, 223–24 reckons with two groups *in Corinth* seeking peace, one μετ' εὐσεβείας and another μεθ' ὑποκρίσεως. However, according to Lona, the ones seeking peace μετ' εὐσεβείας could be the Romans.

deny their sincerity.[158] That the instigators are accused of using boastful words shows that they have won over the people by rhetorical methods (15:4–5; 17:5).[159] Thus, the negative characterization does not serve to demonstrate differences but to defame in a conflict by rhetorical means.

The church members being addressed are characterized in a completely different way. Admittedly, they have deposed some legitimately appointed bishops. This "sin is not small" (44:4). But at the same time they are exonerated. They have been led astray; someone called the adversary is to blame: "our transgressions and . . . what we have done through any attacks of the adversary" (51:1).[160] Through repentance everything can be made right. They are called "brothers" (ἀδελφοί) and "beloved" (ἀγαπητοί), who once had a good reputation (1:2—2:8), who are prudent and can be reasoned with, who are knowledgeable of the Scriptures (45:2; 53:1), and who are even "faithful and distinguished" (62:3). The negative evaluation of the opponents and the positive evaluation of the church members being addressed also serve to inspire as many as possible to take sides with the "good" and distance themselves from the leaders of the revolt.

In the first and longest section of the letter, the authors divide the listeners into two groups. The crowd of commoners in the back rows is described positively, despite the fact that the deposing of bishops had been carried out with their backing. The presenter speaks directly to them, in a certain sense, gathering as many as possible with his eyes and gestures. The other group is described as a minority and characterized by many negative attributes.[161] Since they are not being addressed and only spoken *about*, it is not established who belongs to this group. Nobody needs to reveal themselves as belonging to it.

Sanctions for the Instigators

The second step in the performance identifies the culprits in Corinth and demands that they be punished.

---

158. Schmitt, *Paroikie*, 100–101 sees evidence in 1 Clem 15:1 "that there had been negotiations over the settlement of the dispute, and that also those whom the Roman church branded as 'instigators' were interested in resolving the conflict" (my translation).

159. Lona, *Erste Clemensbrief*, 226: "The issue is easy to understand, if, from the Romans' point of view, the 'new circumstances' had been facilitated by the *eloquence* of one group, i.e., if for just that reason the instigators were able to assert themselves" (my translation, emphasis added). Similarly p. 278.

160. On the uncertain textual tradition, cf. ibid., 540–41.

161. Rohde, "Häresie," 221–22.

The identification of the guilty comes first. In the second part of the letter (from ch. 40 onwards) the authors deal with the specific problems in Corinth. After having presented the divine order of church leadership and denouncing the deposing of the bishops in Corinth (ch. 44), they identify, for the first time, the guilty parties. This is initially done with a question: "Who then were they who did these things [the deposing and persecution of the righteous as with e.g., Daniel]?" (45:7).[162]

During the reading, the crowd would certainly cast a few glances at some of the persons who had been leading out in the power change. Now, the question, who are they? encourages them to identify the instigators of the revolt by glances or hand signs. They were probably sitting in the front row and in the seats of honor. A few moments later, after a reference to Paul's First Letter to the Corinthians, the presenter calls out, "But now consider [literally: observe] who they are who have perverted you!" (47:5: νυνὶ δὲ κατανοήσατε τίνες ὑμᾶς διέστρεψαν . . .).[163] All eyes are turned to the instigators of the revolt. If the meeting hall had rows of benches on three or four walls, as was usual in ancient times, then they found themselves surrounded by hostile faces. It is even possible that some hostile gestures were made that some abusive shouts could be heard. The separating distance the presenter had created now becomes visible. Many of those who had endorsed the power change are now on the other side, so that there really are only a few of the main culprits remaining, just "one or two persons" (47:6: δι' ἓν ἢ δύο πρόσωπα). The performance of the letter has achieved what it postulated. It has identified and isolated the main culprits behind the power change.

Sanctions for the guilty ones follow. Now the presenter can finally deal with the question of how to solve the problem in Corinth (ch. 51). Here, in this section, an interesting structure underlines the already implemented division of the listeners into two groups. Two parallel sentences are formulated; one for each group, expressing what each must do (51:1).

---

162. Lona, *Erste Clemensbrief*, 486: "The answer is important because the expression presents the culprits of the past in a way that makes an analogy with the instigators in Corinth unavoidable" (my translation). Cf. also 1 Clem 1:1.

163. Of course, κατανοεῖν also has the meaning of "a mental observation." But the reference to the leaders of the revolt is too obvious as not to have drawn the looks of the listeners to them.

A	Let us then pray that for our transgressions, and for what we have done through any attacks of the adversary, forgiveness may be granted to us.
B	And those also who were the leaders of sedition and disagreement are bound to consider the common hope.

Each sentence would have been spoken in the direction of the respective group being referred to, with the speaker probably turning to face them physically. Nevertheless, the sentence for the leaders of the revolt is again indefinite since they are not being addressed directly. The church members should ask for forgiveness. They are those who have been misled, and not the main culprits. Repentance and a change of ways will heal the damage. In contrast, the leaders of the revolt must face what can be done for the common hope of betterment. What they can do is introduced and explained by the example of the self-sacrificing Moses. This allusion to Moses implies that they should be prepared to leave the church and go into exile (54:2): "If sedition and strife and divisions have arisen on my account, I will depart, I will go away whithersoever you will, and I will obey the commands of the people."

Although the exodus is presented as an honorable decision (54:1: "Who then among you is noble, who is compassionate, who is filled with love?"), it is in fact a banishment.[164] This is primarily recognizable by the fact that the *church* decides where the guilty ones should go (54:2: "I will go away whithersoever you will, and I will obey the commands of the people").[165] Once again, the crowd is juxtaposed against the few insurgents. The Roman authors' goal becomes obvious: It is the majority of church members—whom the authors have now won over for their own position—who should take action, namely, who should impose banishment.[166] That the exile was imposed by a church decision is also made clear in chapter 56, which speaks of chastisement.

---

164. Cf. the parallels in Mikat, *Bedeutung*, 31–34; and Lona, *Erste Clemensbrief*, 555–56.

165. By contrast Schmitt, *Paroikie*, 85, n. 59: He argues that the place is not stipulated by the Corinthian church but has already been decided by the Romans in consultation with other churches. First Clement 54:2 should therefore be interpreted: "I will go into exile, *if* that is what you want" (my translation; italics added).

166. Differently Mikat, *Bedeutung*, 31–33, who does not see a majority shift during the performance, and therefore must postulate that the Romans include themselves in the majority referred to in 1 Clem 54:2.

Why are the sanctions against those responsible for the revolt described so positively? Words are put into the mouths of the insurgents (54:2) through which they save face, and through which their guilt is veiled by a conditional sentence: "If sedition and strife and divisions have arisen on my account . . ."[167] Why is their expatriation presented as an honorable decision, as a sacrifice for the people (54:1–3)?[168] Moses is cited as a biblical example, and other nonbiblical examples from history are also cited (ch. 55). Why this strategy?[169] The authors apparently expect that the sanctions against the leaders of the revolt will be difficult to implement. The Romans know that there are many among the church members in Corinth who had once sided with the insurgents. For that reason, they make it as easy as possible for them to pronounce the banishment. It should appear that the church is doing what is best for itself *and* for the troublemakers with the verdict they pass concerning the leaders of the revolt. They are conceded an honorable departure. Since the exodus is depicted as a heroic act, the exiles do not completely lose face. Additionally, they are given the prospect that they will be well received anywhere they may go (54:3). This probably meant they would be provided with letters of recommendation.[170]

The subsequent prayer for the "guilty" and the scriptural citations on the value of chastisement (ch. 56) legitimize the verdict of banishment as a God-guided act. This section also is not for convincing the troublemakers but is addressed very explicitly to the majority of the church (56:2 and 16: ἀγαπητοί). This has not been sufficiently taken into consideration by interpreters.[171] The *church members* being addressed must be the first

---

167. On the mild language, cf. Lona, *Erste Clemensbrief*, 554–55.

168. Lindemann, *Clemensbriefe*, 153 says: "It is striking that the authors do not demand that the church distance itself from the 'troublemakers,' but instead hope for their 'noble-mindedness' (v. 1)" (my translation). Schmitt, *Paroikie*, 73: "Focus on winning back the brother who has sinned" (my translation); cf. Lindemann, *Clemensbriefe*, 153. These authors do not reckon with the dynamics of a performance, even if Lona, *Erste Clemensbrief*, 557, n. 1 refers to the power of language.

169. Lona, *Erste Clemensbrief*, 558 finds it "peculiar" that after the threats and judgements such a positive tone is struck. Lindemann, *Clemensbriefe*, 154: It is "striking that the ringleaders of the στάσις are not really threatened with something, but that they—on condition that they do the right thing—are almost acknowledged as having exemplary character" (my translation).

170. Schmitt, *Paroikie*, 85 thinks of preparatory communication of the Roman church with churches that could potentially accept the exiled ones.

171. For example, Lindemann, *Clemensbriefe*, 157: "The leaders of the insurrection . . . should recognize the chastisement—pronounced and executed in 1 Clem—as a

to accept the role of disciplining (παιδεία) of the insurgents. They are promised that then their "house shall have peace" (56:13). With these remarks, the authors help those who still sympathize with the new leaders to agree to the banishment. With their positive description of the banishment and their decision to offer a prayer of intercession, the authors are not showing magnanimity toward the insurgents[172] but are rather making a concession to their sympathizers in order to avoid displeasure among the listeners in Corinth (56:2: ἀναλάβωμεν παιδείαν ἐφ' ᾗ οὐδεὶς ὀφείλει ἀγανακτεῖν).[173]

Calling upon the New Leaders to Submit

In the third step of the performance, the presenter turns directly to the new power holders in Corinth. Now, for the first and only time, he speaks directly to the leaders of the revolt (57:1–2):

> You therefore, who laid the foundation of the sedition, submit to the presbyters, and receive correction of repentance, bending the knees of your hearts. Learn to be submissive, putting aside the boastful and the haughty self-confidence of your tongue, for it is better for you to be found small but honourable in the flock of Christ, than to be preeminent in repute but to be cast out from his hope.

Only now in 1 Clem 57:1–2 do the authors believe they have the audience definitively on their side. Up to this point, the performance had been designed to distance the church from the leaders of the revolt and to bring as many of their followers as possible to secretly change sides. Now it is time to reap the fruits of this strategy. Both the length of the letter and the verbosity of the first part, which has remained incomprehensible to many commentators,[174] must been seen from the viewpoint of the performance. Time is needed to win the Corinthians over to the

---

work of divine love" (my translation).

172. Although it sounds thus, cf. Schmitt, *Paroikie*, 66–67.

173. Lona, *Erste Clemensbrief*, 570 correctly recognizes that 1 Clem 56:2 shows that the authors are expecting resistance in the Corinthian church. However, he does not differentiate clearly enough between the resistance of the insurgents and that of the rest of the church members. The rest of the church members are meant here.

174. For example, Chadwick, "Justification," 285: "Clement is assumed to have been an industrious and well-meaning, but rather stupid fellow, who stuffed his long letter with a mass of rambling and irrelevant matter."

authors' position. It is not only a matter of arguments, whose plausibility can quickly be evaluated. It is first and foremost a striving for trust and emotional agreement, which, in ancient rhetoric, fell in the domain of ἦθος and πάθος.

After the church members' glances have been directed several times to those mainly responsible for the troubles (e.g., 45:7; 47:5), these men are finally confronted with a decision, with all those present looking on. They must submit to the church officials, or they must expect to be separated from the "flock," i.e., expelled from the church (57:2). A comprehensive quote from Prov 1:23–33 underlines the seriousness of the divine judgment (57:3–7).

According to 1 Clem 54:2, submission means to go into exile, where supremacy of any kind is at an end (57:2: μικροὺς καὶ ἐλλογίμους εὑρεθῆναι). No soft reprimand is being made here, no watering down of the misdemeanor. Here where the guilty parties are being addressed directly, there is no longer talk of their own self-sacrificing decision. Instead, we again find the clear language of condemnation, which has been used time and again to brand the leaders of the disturbances in Corinth (1:1; 3:1–4; 4:7; 14:1; 21:5; 39:1). The "boastful and proud arrogance of the tongue" (ἀποθέμενοι τὴν ἀλαζόνα καὶ ὑπερήφανον τῆς γλώσσης ὑμῶν αὐθάδειαν) is especially emphasized, with pleonasm underlining the drastic condemnation. This silences the leaders of the revolt. Any attempt to defend themselves or to contradict the sentence is condemned beforehand as arrogance.

An admonition to obedience follows, which is connected with a promise of belonging to the saved (ch. 58). This section again turns away from the leaders of the revolt to the whole congregation, a move shown by the use of the first-person plural. Hence, those who are guilty of the revolt are being *spoken of* again (59:1: τινές). The long prayer, which closes the main part of the performance,

> urges through form and content to acceptance. The 'thou' addressed to God, the 'we' of the pleaders, the 'amen' expected at the end of the doxology, are intended to draw the listeners into the act of prayer ... More importantly, it is up to the Corinthians, who have already so often been included in the Roman letter by the use of the mutual 'we', ... to accept the letter's content and to make the concern their own. The prayer at the end of

the text, which has now become a common prayer, implies this acceptance and at the same time, expresses it.[175]

The alternatives of banishment—softened by the letters of recommendation and the image of heroic sacrifice for the good of the church—or being cast out of the church not only are presented to the troublemakers but also outline the actions possible for the Corinthians. Hence, they have the choice between a softened or a radical solution. The possibility that the Corinthians would acquiesce to the permanent deposing of the presbyters and that they would take no actions against the instigators is not given any consideration. In this way, the Romans press for a solution to the problem according to their wishes. They probably would have known that excluding the instigators of the insurrection in Corinth could not be achieved. For that reason, the authors not only offer a practical way to restore peace but at the same time provide an interpretation of the banishment for those who are to enforce it that would help them to legitimize their action, even if it is directed against those they had previously supported.

The reception of Clement's first letter allows the conclusion that it was successful according to the intentions of the senders. Tassilo Schmitt reflects on the success of Clement's letter and discusses two possible reasons for it: the reputation of the sender and the convincing power of the arguments unfolded.[176] Performance criticism adds a third reason, which has been neglected so far: the power of the performance that is written into the letter. Performance criticism is a tool well suited for bringing to life this aspect of early Christian letter literature. It promotes a better understanding of texts that belong to a culture where pieces of writing did not primarily present information to the eyes of a single reader, but were rather designed to guide a reader through a powerful and effective oral performance before a small or large group of listeners.

---

175. Lona, *Erste Clemensbrief*, 623 (my translation).
176. Schmitt, *Paroikie*, 2–5.

Summary and Perspectives

The study of the performance of early Christian letters presented her continues what the founders of the performance-criticism method have begun.[1] Based on the foundation they have laid, certain general questions on performance were discussed, and then various examples from New Testament letters and other ancient and early Christian letters were presented. The goal of this study will have been achieved if the potential found in the method of performance criticism has become clear. In summary, five aspects are to be highlighted.

1) Performance criticism is a historical analysis. The established historical interpretation of the New Testament sought to explain the content of texts with regard to the time of origin. It has exploited the findings of historical research concerning the respective material, financial, cultural, social, political, and religious environments of the New Testament documents. Performance criticism goes one step further and also examines the texts as *communication mediums* in their historical contexts. That is nothing but consistent, and complements the historical understanding by adding a hitherto neglected aspect. After all, historical research into the ancient society from which the texts came has established that the culture of those times was particularly shaped by oral communication. Written language was recorded orality. Written texts did not replace but rather served oral communication. More precisely, written texts were designed for the experience of a performance situation.

Of course this study's description of the performance of early Christian letters cannot bring back the unique and unrepeatable event of the letter presentation. Instead, the reconstructions offered here

1. Cf., e.g., Rhoads, "Performance Criticism"; Foley, *How to Read*; Loubser, *Oral and Manuscript Culture*.

serve as models to help us understand what happened when the letters reached their recipients and were read out. Such models are necessary in order to prevent the anachronism of making our present written culture the basis for understanding the impact the historical texts had. Textual studies have shown that knowledge of the typical letter events in the culture of those times can enrich our understanding of the texts we are dealing with.

2) Performance criticism frees the texts from the disembodied abstraction of language, which is the result of the modern culture of writing. The written word, which actually only had an intermediate position in New Testament times and served to facilitate the *direct* interaction between people, drew all attention to itself and finally became the determining form of language in the nineteenth century.[2] Since the written word exists independently from the author and the recipients (that is, it is no longer bound to the time and place of the oral exchange), the bodily side of the language has been lost from view. This is especially true because a large part of oral communication can hardly be encoded in writing: this large part includes the voice, the pauses, and the taking of breaths; the facial expression, the gestures, and the movements of the body; the age, experiences, and everything that life has written into the appearance of the speaker. In addition, there are the bodies and experiences of the listeners and the social roles of all those present. Moreover, the setup of the performance location, the time of the performance, the sensory impressions (such as certain smells, the temperature and light), and many more factors belong to the bodily experience of language. These aspects did not appear important for the interpretation of the text. The meaning of the text was sought only in what could be derived from the semantics of the written text.

Performance criticism opens up a fundamentally different perspective on the New Testament texts. They are no longer only signs of something extralinguistic identified and understood by interpreting the written words. Corresponding to a culture shaped by orality, and corresponding to where the texts originated, these texts are witnesses to communicative *events* in which speakers and listeners were involved. The narrow focus on the reference function of language is broken open. Thus a very important dimension of oral language is recovered, namely, the dimension of experience. In particular, this includes the long-neglected

---

2. Knoop, "Zum Verhältnis von geschriebener und gesprochener Sprache."

material side of language, with the interaction of those involved and the mimesis of bodily expression. The voice and the sound of the language, the presenter's use of the body, measures to steer the viewing direction of the audience, and the many other elements that constitute a performance event are part of the phenomenon. The information contained in the text is only *one* building block in the overall event, and the information can therefore be incomplete—to the regret of today's reader. What really matters is the *effect* the performance achieves: for example, strengthening fellowship, isolating false teachers, reassuring believers of faith and hope, reorienting believers toward Christian living. Performance criticism makes visible how these effects are achieved with language.

The change of perspective on the texts has considerable consequences for understanding them. During the experience of the performance, the text, e.g., a letter of Paul, takes effect as a whole entity, more precisely, in the chronological consecutiveness of all its parts. Questions about the meaning of individual statements must always take account of the connection of an individual statement to the whole letter in performance, and of the impact of the performance as an event in time. The experience of the speech event may narrow the scope of interpretation of individual statements. Performance criticism will eliminate some suggested and semantically possible meanings, as has been shown for 1 Cor 12:3 and Gal 6:1–10. On the other hand, performance criticism will suggest textual interpretations that have up to now escaped the notice of modern commentators because what is said in a performance situation takes on a meaning that the words do not have in other situations. We have seen this, for example, in the references to hospitality in the First Letter of Clement.

During the performance the audience also had no chance to look up comparison texts or to apply later statements in the interpretation of earlier ones—apart from sentences that react to statements just read.[3] If links within the text to other texts, or to nontextual knowledge, were necessary for comprehension, then these links had to have been created during the listening process, perhaps through explicit references, through text structures such as repetition and framing, and through allusions to well-known traditions (Immanent Art). It is therefore important to be familiar with the tradition that grounds the culture and society in which the text was formed. The texts work through the ears and the memory of

---

3. See, e.g., what was said above on pp. 164–65 on Rom 14:2.

the recipient. They do not achieve their effect through the comparative study of books.

3) Performance criticism draws attention to the medial side of communication. For a long time, research into the New Testament texts proceeded without reflection from the assumption that it was dealing with written communication as we know it in modern times. Writing, as a medium of communication, was taken completely for granted so that little thought was given to it. Only the emergence of new media—first film and television, then the Internet and all forms of electronic communication—raised a new awareness of the role of media (McLuhan), which then also proved to be fertile for the interpretation of biblical texts (Kelber). Performance criticism picks up this thread and includes the media aspect of communication in text analysis. The medium comes into view with its own effect, namely, with its contribution to the event experience and the generation of meaning.

The medial side of communication does not only comprise the written text, not even primarily. In antiquity, a document (for example a letter or a Gospel) was only one part of a complex communicative event that was particularly characterized by orality. However, it would also be inadequate to speak of oral language as the medium of the New Testament texts, as is often done. The medium is much rather the *performance*—that is, the event that encompasses the presenter in his corporeality, the text being presented with its aesthetic quality, the multifaceted audience, the performance space, the social setting, the actualized tradition, and much, much more.

The performance-critical method, by paying attention to the medial side of communication, moves a person into focus who had previously scarcely played a role in textual interpretation: the person presenting the text to the audience. It becomes clear that this person, by means of the way he speaks, through his body language, and through the story life has written upon his body, has a decisive influence not only on the performance event but also on how what is being said is understood and on the effect it achieves. For example, only through performance criticism does it become apparent how the letter writer can bring about an alienation effect by referring to his own body, because the audience thus becomes aware of the difference between the body of the writer and the body of the presenter. In this way the audience is challenged to form its own judgment of what has been said and to make its own decisions.[4] It has become apparent in this regard that the epistolary topos of the physical presence or absence of the sender takes on a new significance.

In a performance, the audience evaluates the medial side of the event, that is, the skill of the actors and the aesthetic quality of what is being offered. Whether it finds favor or not influences the overall effect and thereby also the success of the performance. Previously, if any attention was paid to the aesthetic side of the New Testament texts at all—which was seldom enough—then it was more of peripheral interest, with little relevance to the understanding of the text. By contrast, performance criticism gives consideration to the aesthetic quality of the text because important performative strategies for the text are revealed therein, which also influence the interpretation of what was being said. How important it is, for example, to recognize the hymnic parts of a text has been demonstrated in the interpretation of Rom 14:7–10.

The language structures in the text not only reveal the poetry of the text,[5] they also make the rhythm of the performance accessible to the interpreter. For example, it has been shown that parallelism is able to structure not only thought contents but above all the addressing of specific groups and persons. Parallelism is therefore a means of steering the course of action in a performance. In such text structures, performance criticism detects the performative strategies written into the text and evaluates them for interpretation.[6]

4) Performance criticism sees texts as evidence bearing witness to social events. Performance is a *collective* experience. For that reason, in the analysis of the New Testament texts, performance criticism will always consider what effect the texts would have had on the community. This also applies when individuals are named or being addressed directly. The focus is not on an individual reader. The analysis of the Letter to the Galatians has shown that Paul was not concerned with the individual's understanding of law and salvation in Christ but with the path taken by the churches in a whole region.[7]

---

4. See above on pp. 136–51 the section on the reader as medium of the communication.

5. Foley, *How to Read*, 95–108.

6. Cf. above pp. 153–57 and the remarks on parallelism as found in Rom 14:1–15:13, similarly in the section on 1 Cor 12 on pp. 199–205.

7. See above on pp. 229–30.

The cultural preconditions for the performance of the New Testament texts are an important foundation for performance criticism. Of course, the language heard in the performance is the cultural achievement of a society. It is, however, the societal framework that primarily constitutes the performance. This includes not only the external conditions under which those present see and understand themselves as performers and listeners, but also the expectations linked to the performance and the interpretative framework created by it. Performance criticism takes a fresh look at what form criticism was looking for with the question about the *Sitz im Leben*, but from a new perspective. In this study it was in particular the reception protocol for an official letter that cast light on the performance events of the Pauline letters.[8]

5) Performance criticism gives careful consideration to the interaction of all persons involved in the performance. The leading question for exegetes is no longer what is being transmitted to the reader, but rather what is happening. This study of the performance of early Christian letters presented to listeners of differing backgrounds or to listeners who were quarreling has shown that these texts are not just about transmitting information or teachings to the addressees. The presentation of the texts had an effect on all those involved, an effect that occurred immediately during the performance. This experience would affect thoughts and deeds in everyday life outside of the performance, at least that was the intention.

The presentation of the New Testament letters shaped the relationships between the sender and the addressees, between the reader and the listeners, and also the reletionships within the audience. Performance is a mutually influencing upon the presenter and the audience which can change majorities and balances of power. Thus the performance can help to overcome tensions in the audience, as has been demonstrated with 1 Cor 12:3, Rom 14–15, and 1 Thess 5:12–14. Performance criticism not only sees an *admonition* to unity in the text but also uncovers the strategy for organizing a unifying *event*. On the other hand, the performance can also increase tension and ostracize particular persons or groups, as can be seen in the Letter to the Galatians or in the First Letter of Clement.

Since performance criticism not only gives consideration to the author, but also to the presenter and the audience as well, strategies also receive attention through which individuals or certain groups in the

---

8. See above on pp. 73–79 on the procedure for reception of an official letter.

audience are put into the public focus and, therefore, come under pressure.[9] However, it is not the author alone, or the presenter representing him, who acts in such a strategy—although the author certainly could benefit in the sense of *divide et impera*.[10] Such an act much rather always involves *all* those who are involved in the performance. The audience plays an active role. Previously the fact that directly addressing or indirectly referring to specific persons in the audience could have such an effect has been largely disregarded.

The audience's active participation in the performance also manifests itself in the fact that the author of the text must be mindful not to demand too much from the audience, because he doesn't want to risk the performance taking an undesired turn. The fact that Paul does not demand or command but rather pleads and relies on voluntary reactions in the Letter to Philemon, or the fact that in the Letter to the Galatians he only insinuates the expulsion of the opponents but does not demand it explicitly, have, for example, been shown to be out of regard for the audience.[11] These examples also demonstrate that the performance-critical method can change and enrich the understanding of the texts.

Performance criticism is still in the early stages. What has been offered here on the theory of this method is only a small contribution to a very rewarding and necessary discussion and an invitation to further dialog. The examples given here of how performance criticism can be applied in the interpretation of the Pauline letters introduce possibilities, but they are only a part of what should be the object of research.

In this study, the Letter to the Galatians and Clement's first letter were analyzed as complete entities in harmony with the ancient custom of regarding texts in their entirety and experiencing and understanding them in performance. It must be conceded that thereby certain aspects were given prominence (forming the relationship between opposing groups, constructing majorities or minorities), while other aspects were only touched on insufficiently (e.g., euphony, or the recourse to the common tradition that Foley has called Immanent Art). From other letters, only certain parts were examined or specific hypotheses tested

---

9. See above the section on singling out individual listeners, especially on pp. 113–32.

10. See above pp. 121–23 on 2 Cor 2:5–11 and pp. 132–35 on Ign. *Pol.*

11. See above pp. 131–32 on Phlm 8–9 and p. 252 on Gal 4:30. Cf. also the demands for banishment clothed as honorable emigration in 1 Clem 54:1–3, found above on pp. 270–72.

(exerting pressure on individuals, dividing the audience for one's own benefit, alienation effects, reconciliation strategies). A wealth of passages is available for further study. Ideally, a comprehensive examination of the performative effect should be conducted for each of the New Testament letters.

The *performative strategies* presented here are also only first steps into uncharted terrain. For example, John M. Foley points out that the structure of the text is the key to the elements that are not encoded in writing, such as rhythm, pace, pauses, gestures, and so on (ethnopoetics). This has been shown concerning parallelism in the text analyses in this work. Many other language structures (framing, chiastic or ring patterns, series or sequences, anacoluthon, acrostics, anadiplosis, stanzas and refrain) would lend themselves to further study. The effects of the sounds of language have also not been comprehensively evaluated for performance (assonance, alliteration, hiatus, rhyme, and paronomasia).[12] In the examination of the Letter to the Galatians, the impact of sarcasm during the reading to an audience was mentioned. Other rhetorical figures of speech (e.g., puns, irony, and hyperbole) should also be examined.

This study in no way claims to have even named all possible strategies in the performance of a letter. Many are probably yet to be discovered. The better our understanding of the nature of a performance becomes (performance theory), the more will come to light.

The social framework, which is so important for the performance, provides scope for further studies. While this study has focused on the moment when the letter was received, it is also repeatedly interested in the *author* and those involved in authoring the letter. The New Testament letters were not designed solely according to the will of the authors. They were also designed to correspond to the cultural and particular expectations of the audience. A more exact knowledge of these expectations—not just the letter conventions reflected in the manuscript,[13] but particularly the expectations regarding the letter performance—could help clarify our understanding of the letters from the perspective of the *recipients*.

In contrast to this study with its focus on the events surrounding the reception of a letter, the cooperation between the author and his co-authors, scribes, and advisors during the *composition of the letter* would

---

12. Cf. Lee and Scott, *Sound Mapping*.

13. Cf. Koskenniemi, *Studien*; Thraede, *Grundzüge*; White, *Form and Function*; White, "New Testament Epistolary Literature."

be a rewarding area for research.[14] This aspect would include things that originate from the secretary (e.g., Rom 16:22), the role of the "brothers" accompanying Paul in Gal 1:2, and the alternation between the *we*-form and *I*-statements, for instance as in the First Letter to the Thessalonians. It would be helpful to develop a model that describes the drafting process for an apostolic letter "composed in performance"—to borrow a phrase from the title of Antionette C. Wire's book about the origin of the Gospel of Mark.[15]

In a performance, the meaning of what is said is generated by several sources: by what the listeners experience physically through mimesis; by the social framework of the performance through which it becomes clear that what is said is not to be understood as "normal" communication, but rather according to the context of performance; by the pleasure of enjoying aesthetically successful communication—or just the opposite; by tradition, which is brought to the mind of those familiar with it through formulas and allusions; by the things that the language points to semantically; by the emotional impulses the performance conveys; and of course by the interaction between the presenter and the listeners, and the interaction of the listeners among themselves. Understanding a text in a performance is a collective process in which the whole wealth of human communication is involved. Depending on the situation and the audience, different presentations of the texts would generate different meanings but remain within certain boundaries. Performance criticism helps today's readers gain access, at least in part, to this wealth of meaning and impact inherent in the oral events to which the texts of the New Testament bear witness.

---

14. Cf. Ellis, "Paul and His Co-Workers"; Byrskog, "Co-Senders"; especially Loubser, "Media Criticism."

15. Wire, *Case for Mark*.

Bibliography

Achtemeier, Paul J. "*Omne Verbum Sonat*: The New Testament and the Oral Environment of Late Western Antiquity." *JBL* 109 (1990) 3–27.
Albright, William F., and C. S. Mann. "Two Texts in 1 Corinthians." *NTS* 16 (1969/1970) 271–76.
Aldrete, Gregory S. *Gestures and Acclamations in Ancient Rome*. Ancient History and Society. Baltimore: Johns Hopkins University Press, 1999.
Alexander, Loveday. "Ancient Book Production and the Circulation of the Gospels." In *The Gospels for All Christians: Rethinking the Gospel Audiences*, edited by Richard Bauckham, 71–111. Grand Rapids: Eerdmans, 1998.
———. "Hellenistic Letter-Forms and the Structure of Philippians." *JSNT* 37 (1989) 87–101.
———. "The Living Voice: Scepticism towards the Written Word in Early Christian and in Graeco-Roman Texts." In *The Bible in Three Dimensions: Essays in Celebration of Forty Years of Biblical Studies in the University of Sheffield*, edited by D. J. A. Clines et al., 221–47. JSOTSup 87. Sheffield: JSOT Press, 1990.
Amador, J. David Hester. *Academic Constraints in Rhetorical Criticism of the New Testament: An Introduction to a Rhetoric of Power*. JSNTSup 174. Sheffield: Academic, 1999.
Andersen, Øivind. "How Good Should an Orator Be?" In *The Orator in Action and Theory in Greece and Rome*, edited by Cecil W. Wooten, 3–16. Mnemosyne Sup 225. Leiden: Brill, 2001.
Anderson, Roger Dean, Jr. *Ancient Rhetorical Theory and Paul*. CBET 18. Leuven: Peeters, 1998.
Andresen, Carl. "Zum Formular frühchristlicher Gemeindebriefe." *ZNW* 56 (1965) 233–59.
———. "Zum Formular frühchristlicher Gemeindebriefe." *ZNW* 56 (1965) 233–59.
Aristotle. *Aristotelis ars rhetorica*. Edited by Rudolf Kassel. Berlin: de Gruyter, 1976.
Arzt, Peter. "The 'Epistolary Introductory Thanksgiving' in the Papyri and in Paul." *NovT* 36 (1994) 29–46.

Arzt-Grabner, Peter. *Philemon*. Papyrologische Kommentare zum Neuen Testament 1. Göttingen: Vandenhoeck & Ruprecht, 2003.

Assmann, Aleida et al., eds. *Schrift und Gedächtnis: Archäologie der literarischen Kommunikation*. Beiträge zur Achäologie der literarischen Kommunikation 1. Munich: Fink, 1998.

Assmann, Aleida, and Jan Assmann. "Einleitung." In *Schriftlichkeit: Das griechische Alphabet als kulturelle Revolution*, by Eric A. Havelock, 1–35. Weinheim: VCH, Acta Humaniora, 1990.

Assmann, Jan. *Das kulturelle Gedächtnis: Schrift, Erinnerung und politische Identität in frühen Hochkulturen*. C. H. Beck Kulturwissenschaft. Munich: Beck, 1992.

Aune, David E. *The New Testament in Its Literary Environment*. LEC 8. Philadelphia: Westminster, 1987.

———. "Romans as a Logos Protreptikos." In *The Romans Debate*, edited by Karl P. Donfried, 278–96. Rev. and exp. ed. Edinburgh: T. & T. Clark, 1991.

Austin, John L. *How to Do Things with Words*. Oxford: Clarendon, 1962.

Bachmann, Philipp. *Der erste Brief des Paulus an die Korinther*. Kommentar zum Neuen Testament 7. Leipzig: Deichert, 1905.

Bahn, Eugene. "Interpretative Reading in Ancient Greek." *Q J Speech* 18 (1932) 432–40.

Bahr, Gordon J. "Paul and Letter Writing in the Fifth Century." *CBQ* 28 (1966) 465–77.

———. "The Subscription in the Pauline Letters." *JBL* 87 (1968) 27–41.

Bailey, Kenneth D. *Sociology and the New Systems Theory: Toward a Theoretical Synthesis*. Albany: State University of New York Press, 1994.

Bakke, Odd Magne. *"Concord and Peace": A Rhetorical Analysis of the First Letter of Clement with an Emphasis on the Language of Unity and Sedition*. WUNT 2/143. Tübingen: Mohr/Siebeck, 2001.

Bakker, Egbert J. "How Oral is Oral Composition?" In *Signs of Orality: The Oral Tradition and Its Influence in the Greek and Roman World*, edited by E. Anne Mackay, 29–47. Mnemosyne Sup 188. Leiden: Brill, 1998.

Bakker, Egbert J., and Ahuvia Kahane, eds. *Written Voices, Spoken Signs: Tradition, Performance, and the Epic Text*. Center for Hellenic Studies Colloquia. Cambridge: Harvard University Press, 1997.

Balogh, Josef. "Voces Paginarum: Beiträge zur Geschichte des lauten Lesens und Schreibens." *Philologus* 82 (1927) 83–109, 202–40.

Barclay, John M. G. "Conflict in Thessalonica." *CBQ* 55 (1993) 512–30.

———. "Mirror-Reading a Polemical Letter: Galatians as a Test Case." *JSNT* 31 (1987) 73–93.

———. *Obeying the Truth: A Study of Paul's Ethic in Galatians*. Studies of the New Testament and Its World. Edinburgh: T. & T. Clark, 1988.

Bar-Ilan, Meir. "Illiteracy in the Land of Israel in the First Centuries C.E." In *Essays in the Social Scientific Study of Judaism and Jewish Society*, edited by S. Fishbane et al., 46–61. Hoboken, NJ: Ktav, 1992.

Barrett, C. K. *A Commentary on the First Epistle to the Corinthians*. BNTC. London: Black, 1968.

Bartsch, Hans-Werner. "Die Empfänger des Römerbriefes." *ST* 25 (1971) 81–89.

Bartsch, Shadi. *Actors in the Audience: Theatricality and Doublespeak from Nero to Hadrian*. Revealing Antiquity 6. Cambridge: Harvard University Press, 1994.

Bassler, Jouette M. "1 Cor. 12:3: Curse and Confession in Context." *JBL* 101 (1982) 415–18.

Bateson, Gregory. "A Theory of Play and Fantasy." In *The Performance Studies Reader*, edited by Henry Bial, 141–51. New York: Routledge, 2007 [article first published 1955].
Bauman, Richard. *Folklore, Cultural Performances, and Popular Entertainments: A Communications-Centered Handbook.* New York: Oxford University Press, 1992.
———. *Story, Performance, and Event: Contextual Studies in Oral Narrative.* Cambridge Studies in Oral and Literate Culture 10. Cambridge: Cambridge University Press, 1986.
Bauman, Richard, ed. *Verbal Art as Performance.* Prospect Heights, IL: Waveland, 1977.
Baumann, Jürgen, et al., eds. *Homo scribens: Perspektiven der Schriftlichkeitsforschung.* Germanistische Linguistik 134. Tübingen: Niemeyer, 1993.
Beacham, Richard C. *The Roman Theatre and Its Audience.* London: Routledge, 1995.
Becker, Eve-Marie. *Schreiben und Verstehen: Paulinische Briefhermeneutik im Zweiten Korintherbrief.* Neutestamentliche Entwürfe zur Theologie 4. Tübingen: Francke, 2002.
Becker, Jürgen, and Ulrich Luz. *Die Briefe an die Galater, Epheser und Kolosser.* NTD 8. Göttingen: Vandenhoeck & Ruprecht, 1998.
Berger, Klaus. "Apostelbrief und apostolische Rede: Zum Formular frühchristlicher Briefe." *ZNW* 65 (1974) 190–231.
———. "Hellenistische Gattungen im Neuen Testament." In *ANRW* II 25.2, 1031–432. Berlin: de Gruyter, 1984.
Best, Ernest. *A Commentary on the First and Second Epistles to the Thessalonians.* New York: Harper & Row, 1972.
Betz, Hans-Dieter. *2 Corinthians 8 and 9: A Commentary on Two Administrative Letters of the Apostle Paul.* Hermeneia. Philadelphia: Fortress, 1985.
———. *Galatians: A Commentary on Paul's Letter to the Churches in Galatia.* Hermeneia. Philadelphia: Fortress, 1979.
———. "The Literary Composition and Function of Paul's Letter to the Galatians." *NTS* 21 (1975) 353–79.
Bieberstein, Sabine. "Disrupting the Normal Reality of Slavery: A Feminist Reading of the Letter to Philemon." *JSNT* 79 (2000) 105–16.
Binder, Herrmann. *Der Brief des Paulus an Philemon.* ThHKNT 11/2. Berlin: Evangelische Verlagsanstalt, 1990.
Birge, M. K. *The Language of Belonging: A Rhetorical Analysis of Kinship Language in First Corinthians.* CBET 31. Leuven: Peeters, 2002.
Bitzer, Lloyd F. "The Rhetorical Situation." *Philosophy and Rhetoric* 1 (1968) 1–14.
Black, C. Clifton. "Keeping up with Recent Studies XVI: Rhetorical Criticism and Biblical Interpretation." *Expository Times* 100 (1989) 252–58.
Blass, Friedrich, and Albert Debrunner. *Grammatik des neutestamentlichen Griechisch.* 15th ed. Revised by Friedrich Rehkopf. Göttingen: Vandenhoeck & Ruprecht, 1979.
Boedeker, Deborah. "Amerikanische Oral-Tradition-Forschung: Eine Einführung." In *Vergangenheit in mündlicher Überlieferung*, edited by Jürgen von Ungern-Sternberg and Hansjörg Reinau, 34–53. Colloquium Rauricum 1. Stuttgart: Teubner, 1988.
Bohle, Ulrike, and Ekkehard König. "Zum Begriff des Performativen in der Sprachwissenschaft." In *Theorien des Performativen*, edited by Erika Fischer-Lichte and Christoph Wulf, 13–34. Paragrana 10. Berlin: Akademie, 2001.

Bonner, Stanley F. *Education in Ancient Rome: From the Elder Cato to the Younger Pliny.* London: Methuen, 1977.

Boomershine, Thomas E. "Biblical Storytelling and Biblical Scholarship." *Journal of Biblical Storytelling* 12 (2002-2003) 5-13.

———. "Jesus of Nazareth and the Watershed of Ancient Orality and Literacy." In *Orality and Textuality in Early Christian Literature,* edited by Joanna Dewey, 7-36. Semeia 65. Atlanta: Scholars, 1995.

———. "Peter's Denial as Polemic or Confession: The Implications of Media Criticism for Biblical Hermeneutics." In *Orality, Aurality and Biblical Narrative,* edited by Lou H. Silberman, 47-68. Semeia 39. Decatur, GA: Scholars, 1987.

———. *Story Journey: An Invitation to the Gospel as Storytelling.* Nashville: Abingdon, 1988.

Borse, Udo. *Der Standort des Galaterbriefes.* BBB 41. Cologne: Hanstein, 1972.

Bosenius, Bärbel. *Die Abwesenheit des Apostels als theologisches Programm: Der zweite Korintherbrief als Beispiel für die Brieflichkeit der paulinischen Theologie.* TANZ 11. Tübingen: Francke, 1994.

Botha, J. Eugene. "Exploring Gesture and Nonverbal Communication in the Bible and the Ancient World: Some Initial Observations." *Neot* 30 (1996) 1-20.

Botha, Pieter J. J. "Greco-Roman Literacy as Setting for New Testament Writings." *Neot* 26/1 (1992) 195-215.

———. "Letter Writing and Oral Communication in Antiquity." *Scriptura* 42 (1992) 17-34.

———. "Living Voice and Lifeless Letters: Reserve towards Writing in the Graeco-Roman World." *HTS* 49 (1993) 742-59.

———. "Mark's Story as Oral Traditional Literature: Rethinking the Transmission of Some Traditions about Jesus." *HTS* 47 (1991) 304-31.

———. "New Testament Texts in the Context of Reading Practices of the Roman Period: The Role of Memory and Performance." *Scriptura* 90 (2005) 621-40.

———. *Orality and Literacy in Early Christianity.* BPCS 5. Eugene, OR: Cascade Books, 2012 [collected essays].

———. "The Verbal Art of the Pauline Letters: Rhetoric, Performance and Presence." In *Rhetoric and the New Testament: Essays from the 1992 Heidelberg Conference,* edited by Stanley E. Porter and Thomas H. Olbricht, 409-28. JSNTSup 90. Sheffield: Sheffield Academic, 1993.

Bowman, Alan K., and Greg Woolf, eds. *Literacy and Power in the Ancient World.* Cambridge: Cambridge University Press, 1994.

Brecht, Bertolt. "Aus einem Brief an einen Schauspieler." In *Schriften zum Theater: Über eine nicht-aristotelische Dramatik,* by Bertolt Brecht, 281-85. Edited by Sigfried Unseld. Bibliothek Suhrkamp 41. Frankfurt: Suhrkamp, 1983.

———. "Kleines Organon für das Theater." In *Schriften zum Theater: Über eine nicht-aristotelische Dramatik,* by Bertolt Brecht, 128-73. Edited by Sigfried Unseld. Bibliothek Suhrkamp 41. Frankfurt: Suhrkamp, 1983.

———. "Neue Technik der Schauspielkunst." In *Schriften zum Theater: Über eine nicht-aristotelische Dramatik,* by Bertolt Brecht, 106-14. Edited by Sigfried Unseld. Bibliothek Suhrkamp 41. Frankfurt: Suhrkamp, 1983.

———. *Schriften zum Theater: Über eine nicht-aristotelische Dramatik.* Edited by Sigfried Unseld. Bibliothek Suhrkamp 41. Frankfurt: Suhrkamp, 1983.

———. "Die Strassenszene." In *Schriften zum Theater: Über eine nicht-aristotelische Dramatik*, by Bertolt Brecht, 90–105. Edited by Sigfried Unseld. Bibliothek Suhrkamp 41. Frankfurt am Main: Suhrkamp, 1983.

———. "Über experimentelles Theater." In *Schriften: Ausgewählte Werke in sechs Bänden*, 6:403–21. Frankfurt: Suhrkamp, 1997.

———. "Verfremdungseffekte in der chinesischen Schauspielkunst." In *Schriften zum Theater: Über eine nicht-aristotelische Dramatik*, by Bertolt Brecht, 74–89. Edited by Sigfried Unseld. Bibliothek Suhrkamp 41. Frankfurt: Suhrkamp, 1983.

———. "Vergnügungstheater oder Lehrtheater." In *Schriften zum Theater: Über eine nicht-aristotelische Dramatik*, by Bertolt Brecht, 60–73 . Edited by Sigfried Unseld. Bibliothek Suhrkamp 41. Frankfurt: Suhrkamp, 1983.

Breytenbach, Cilliers. *Paulus und Barnabas in der Provinz Galatien: Studien zu Apostelgeschichte 13 f.; 16,6; 18,23 und den Adressaten des Galaterbriefes*. AGJU 38. Leiden: Brill, 1996.

———. "Das Problem des Übergangs von mündlicher zu schriftlicher Überlieferung." *Neot* 20 (1986) 47–58.

Brown, Raymond E. "Not Jewish Christianity and Gentile Christianity but Types of Jewish/Gentile Christianity." *CBQ* 45 (1983) 74–79.

Brox, Norbert. "ΑΝΑΘΕΜΑ ΙΗΣΟΥΣ (1 Kor 12,3)." *BZ* 12 (1968) 103–11.

Bruce, Frederick F. *The Epistle to the Galatians: A Commentary on the Greek Text*. NIGTC 6. Grand Rapids: Eerdmans, 1982.

Bultmann, Rudolf. *Der Stil der paulinischen Predigt und die kynisch-stoische Diatribe*. FRLANT 13. Göttingen: Vandenhoeck & Ruprecht, 1984 [first published 1910].

Bünker, Michael. *Briefformular und rhetorische Disposition im 1. Korintherbrief*. GTA 28. Göttingen: Vandenhoeck & Ruprecht, 1983.

Burfeind, Carsten. "Wen hörte Philippus? Leises Lesen und lautes Vorlesen in der Antike." *ZNW* 93 (2002) 138–45.

Byrne, Brendan, SJ. *Romans*. SP 6. Collegeville, MN: Liturgical, 1996.

Byrskog, Samuel. "Co-Senders, Co-Authors and Paul's Use of the First Person Plural." *ZNW* 87 (1996) 230–50.

———. "Epistolography, Rhetoric and Letter Prescript: Romans 1:1–7 as a Test Case." *JSNT* 65 (1997) 27–46.

———. *Story as History—History as Story: The Gospel Tradition in the Context of Ancient Oral History*. WUNT 123. Tübingen: Mohr/Siebeck, 2000.

Campbell, Douglas A. "Determining the Gospel through Rhetorical Analysis in Paul's Letter to the Roman Christians." In *Gospel in Paul: Studies on Corinthians, Galatians and Romans for Richard N. Longenecker*, edited by G. P. Richardson and L. Ann Jervis, 315–336. JSNTSup 108. Sheffield: Sheffield Academic, 1994.

Carlson, Marvin. *Performance: A Critical Introduction*. 2nd ed. New York: Routledge, 2004.

Carr, David M. *Writing on the Tablet of the Heart: Origins of Scripture and Literature*. Oxford: Oxford University Press, 2005.

Chadwick, Henry. "Justification by Faith and Hospitality." In *Studia Patristica: Papers Presented to the Third International Conference on Patristic Studies, Held at Christ Church, Oxford, 1959*, part 2: *Biblica, Patres Apostolici, Historica*, edited by Frank L. Cross, 281–85. TU 79. Berlin: Akademie, 1961.

Chow, John K. *Patronage and Power: A Study of Social Networks in Corinth*. JSNTSup 75. Sheffield: JSOT Press, 1992.

Cicero, Marcus Tullius. *An seine Freunde: lateinisch-deutsch*. Edited and translated by Helmut Kasten. Sammlung Tusculum. Munich: Artemis, 1989.

———. *Atticus-Briefe: lateinisch-deutsch*. Edited and translated by Helmut Kasten. Sammlung Tusculum. Düsseldorf: Artemis & Winkler, 1998.

———. *Cicero's Brutus or History of Famous Orators: also, his orator, or accomplished speaker*. Translated by E. Jones. London: White, 1776.

———. *De Oratore: Über den Redner: lateinisch - deutsch*. Edited and translated by Theodor Nüsslein. Sammlung Tusculum. Düsseldorf: Artemis & Winkler, 2007.

———. *The Orations of Marcus Tullius Cicero*. Translated by C. D. Yonge. London: Bohn, 1856.

———. *Orator: lateinisch-deutsch*. Edited by Bernhard Kytzler. Sammlung Tusculum. Munich: Artemis, 1988.

———. *Die politischen Reden: lateinisch-deutsch*. Edited, translated, and explained by Manfred Fuhrmann. 3 vols. Munich: Artemis & Winkler, 1993.

———. *Die Prozessreden: lateinisch-deutsch*. Edited, translated, and explained by Manfred Fuhrmann. 2 vols. Munich: Artemis & Winkler, 1997.

———. *Sämtliche Reden*. Edited by Manfred Fuhrmann, 2 vols. Düsseldorf: Artemis & Winkler, 2000.

Clark, W. P. "Ancient Reading." *CJ* 26 (1930/31) 698–700.

Clarke, Andrew D. *Secular and Christian Leadership in Corinth: A Social-Historical and Exegetical Study of 1 Corinthians 1–6*. AGJU 18. Leiden: Brill, 1993.

Classen, Carl Joachim. "Paulus und die antike Rhetorik." *ZNW* 82 (1991) 1–33.

———. "St Paul's Epistles and Ancient Greek and Roman Rhetoric." In *Rhetoric and the New Testament: Essays from the 1992 Heidelberg Conference*, edited by Stanley E. Porter and Thomas H. Olbricht, 265–91. JSNTSup 90. Sheffield: Sheffield Academic, 1993.

Claudius. "Claudius to the Alexandrians." In *Light from Ancient Letters*, by John L. White, 133–37. FF. Philadelphia: Fortress, 1986.

Claussen, Carsten. *Versammlung, Gemeinde, Synagoge: Das hellenistisch-jüdische Umfeld der frühchristlichen Gemeinden*. SUNT 27. Göttingen: Vandenhoeck & Ruprecht, 2002.

Clemens von Rom. *Epistola ad Corinthios*. Translated and introduced by Gerhard Schneider. Fontes Christiani 15. Freiburg: Herder, 1994.

Conring, Barbara. *Hieronymus als Briefschreiber: Ein Beitrag zur spätantiken Epistolographie*. Studien und Texte zu Antike und Christentum 8. Tübingen: Mohr/Siebeck, 2001.

Cox, Claude E. "The Reading of the Personal Letter as the Background for the Reading of the Scriptures in the Early Church." In *The Early Church in Its Context: Essays in Honour of Everett Ferguson*, edited by Abraham J. Malherbe et al., 74–91. NovTSup 90. Leiden: Brill, 1998.

Crafton, Jeffrey A. *The Agency of the Apostle: A Dramatistic Analysis of Paul's Responses to Conflict in 2 Corinthians*. JSNTSup 51. Sheffield: JSOT, 1991.

———. "Paul's Rhetorical Vision and the Purpose of Romans: Toward a New Understanding." *NovT* 32 (1990) 317–39.

Culley, Robert C. "Oral Tradition and Biblical Studies." *Oral Tradition* 1 (1986) 30–65.

Cullmann, Oscar. *Die Christologie des Neuen Testaments*. Tübingen: Mohr/Siebeck, 1975.

Dabourne, Wendy. *Purpose and Cause in Pauline Exegesis: Romans 1.16—4.25 and a New Approach to the Letters*. SNTSMS 104. Cambridge: Cambridge University Press, 1999.

Das, A. Andrew. *Paul and the Jews*. Library of Pauline Studies. Peabody, MA: Hendrickson, 2003.

Davis, Casey Wayne. *Oral Biblical Criticism: The Influence of the Principles of Orality on the Literary Structure of Paul's Epistle to the Philippians*. JSNTSup 172. Sheffield: Sheffield Academic, 1999.

Dean, Margaret E. "The Grammar of Sound in Greek Texts: Toward a Method for Mapping the Echoes of Speech in Writing." *Australian Biblical Review* 44 (1996) 53–70.

———. "Textured Criticism." *JSNT* 70 (1998) 79–91.

Dederen, Raoul. "On Esteeming One Day Better Than Another." *AUSS* 9 (1971) 16–35.

Deissmann, Adolf. *Licht vom Osten: Das Neue Testament und die neuentdeckten Texte der hellenistisch-römischen Welt*. Tübingen: Mohr, 1923 [first published 1908].

Demetrius. "De Elocutione 223–35." In *Ancient Epistolary Theorists*, compiled and translated by Abraham J. Malherbe, 16–19. SBLSBS 19. Atlanta: Scholars, 1988.

———. *On Style*. Translated by Doreen C. Innes and W. Rhys Roberts. In *Aristotle*, Vol. 13: Aristotle: *Poetics*. Longinus: *On the Sublime*. Demetrius: *On Style*. LCL 199. Cambridge: Harvard University Press, 1995.

Demosthenes. *Orations*, Vol. 7: *Orations 60-61: Funeral Speech, Erotic Essay, Exordia, Letters*. Translated by Norman W. De Witt and Norman J. De Witt. LCL 374. Cambridge: Harvard University Press, 1949.

Derrett, J. Duncan M. "Cursing Jesus (I Cor. XII.3): The Jews as Religious 'Persecutors.'" *NTS* 21 (1975) 544–54.

———. "The Function of the Epistle to Philemon." *ZNW* 79 (1988) 63–91.

Dewey, Arthur J. "A Re-Hearing of Romans 10:1–15." In *Orality and Textuality in Early Christian Literature*, edited by Joanna Dewey, 109–27. Semeia 65. Atlanta: Scholars, 1995.

Dewey, Joanna. "Mark as Aural Narrative: Structures as Clues to Understanding." *STRev* 36 (1992) 45–56.

———, ed. *Orality and Textuality in Early Christian Literature*. Semeia 65. Atlanta: Scholars, 1995.

———. "Oral Methods of Structuring Narrative in Mark." *Int* 43 (1989) 32–44.

———. "Textuality in an Oral Culture: A Survey of the Pauline Traditions." In *Orality and Textuality in Early Christian Literature*, edited by Joanna Dewey, 37–65. Semeia 65. Atlanta: Scholars, 1995.

Dibelius, Martin. *Die Formgeschichte des Evangeliums*. Berlin: Evangelische Verlagsanstalt, 1969.

Dix, Gregory. *Jew and Greek: A Study in the Primitive Church*. London: Dacre, 1953.

Doan, William J., and Terry Giles. *Prophets, Performance, and Power: Performance Criticism of the Hebrew Bible*. New York: T. & T. Clark, 2005.

Donfried, Karl Paul, ed. *The Romans Debate*. Revised and expanded edition. Edinburgh: T. & T. Clark, 1991.

Dormeyer, Detlev. *Das Neue Testament im Rahmen der antiken Literaturgeschichte: Eine Einführung*. Darmstadt: Wissenschaftliche Buchgesellschaft, 1993.

Doty, William G. "The Classification of Epistolary Literature." *CBQ* 31 (1969) 183–99.

———. *Letters in Primitive Christianity*. 1973. Reprinted, Eugene, OR: Wipf & Stock, 2014.

Downing, F. Gerald. *Doing Things with Words in the First Christian Century*. JSNTSup 200. Sheffield: Sheffield Academic, 2000.

Du Toit, A. B. "Alienation and the Re-Identification as Pragmatic Strategies in Galatians." *Neot* 26 (1992) 279–95.

———. "Vilification as a Pragmatic Device in Early Christian Epistolography." *Bib* 75 (1994) 403–12.

Dunn, James D. G. "Altering the Default Setting: Re-invisaging the Early Transmission of the Jesus Tradition." *NTS* 49 (2003) 139–75.

———. *The Epistle to the Galatians*. BNTC 9. Peabody, MA: Hendrickson, 1993.

———. *The Epistles to the Colossians and to Philemon: A Commentary on the Greek Text*. NIGTC. Grand Rapids: Eerdmans, 1996.

———. *Jesus and the Spirit: A Study of the Religious and Charismatic Experience of Jesus and the First Christians as Reflected in the New Testament*. NTL. Philadelphia: Westminster, 1975.

———. *Jesus Remembered*. Christianity in the Making 1. Grand Rapids: Eerdmans, 2003.

———. *The Theology of Paul's Letter to the Galatians*. New Testament Theology. Cambridge: Cambridge University Press, 1993.

Eckert, Jost. *Die urchristliche Verkündigung im Streit zwischen Paulus und seinen Gegnern nach dem Galaterbrief*. Münchener Universitäts-Schriften; Katholische Fakultät, Biblische Untersuchungen 6. Regensburg: Pustet, 1971.

Elliott, Neil. *The Rhetoric of Romans: Argumentative Restraint and Strategy and Paul's Dialogue with Judaism*. JSNTSup 45. Sheffield: JSOT Press, 1990.

Elliott, Susan. *Cutting Too Close for Comfort: Paul's Letter to the Galatians in Uts Anatolian Cultic Context*. JSNTSup 248. London: T. & T. Clark, 2003.

Ellis, E. Earle. "Paul and His Co-Workers." *NTS* 17 (1970/71) 437–52.

Elmer, Ian J. *Paul, Jerusalem, and the Judaisers: The Galatian Crisis in its Broadest Historical Context*. WUNT 2/258. Tübingen: Mohr/Siebeck, 2009.

Epp, E. J. "New Testament Papyrus Manuscripts and Letter Carrying in Greco-Roman Times." In *The Future of Early Christianity: Essays in Honor of Helmut Koester*, edited by B. A. Pearson, 35–56. Minneapolis: Fortress, 1991.

Erlemann, Kurt. "Die Datierung des Ersten Klemensbriefes—Anfragen an eine communis opinio." *NTS* 44 (1998) 591–607.

Esler, Philip F. *Conflict and Identity in Romans: The Social Setting of Paul's Letter*. Minneapolis: Fortress, 2003.

———. *Galatians*. New Testament Readings. London: Routledge, 1998.

Fantham, Elaine. "Two Levels of Orality in the Genesis of Pliny's Panegyricus." In *Signs of Orality: The Oral Tradition and Its Influence in the Greek and Roman World*, edited by E. Anne Mackay, 221–37. Mnemosyne Sup 188. Leiden: Brill, 1998.

Farrell, Thomas J. "Kelber's Breakthrough." In *Orality, Aurality and Biblical Narrative*, edited by Lou H. Silberman, 27–45. Semeia 39. Decatur, GA: Scholars, 1987.

Finnegan, Ruth. "The How of Literature." *Oral Tradition* 20/2 (2005) 164–87.

———. *Literacy and Orality: Studies in the Technology of Communication*. Oxford: Blackwell, 1988.

———. "What Is Oral Literature Anyway? Comments in the Light of Some African and Other Comparative Material." In *Oral Literature and the Formula*, edited by Benjamin A. Stolz and Richard S. Shannon III, 127–76. Ann Arbor: Center for the Coordination of Ancient and Modern Studies, University of Michigan, 1976.

———. "What Is Orality—If Anything?" *Byzantine and Modern Greek Studies* 14 (1990) 130-49.
Fischer-Lichte, Erika. *Ästhetik des Performativen*. Edition Suhrkamp 2372. Frankfurt: Suhrkamp, 2004.
———. "Performance, Inszenierung, Ritual: Zur Klärung kulturwissenschaftlicher Schlüsselbegriffe." In *Geschichtswissenschaft und "Performative Turn": Ritual, Inszenierung und Performanz vom Mittelalter bis zur Neuzeit*, edited by Jürgen Martschukat and Steffen Patzold, 33-54. Norm und Struktur 19. Köln: Bohlau, 2003.
———. "Performativität und Ereignis." In *Performativität und Ereignis*, edited by Erika Fischer-Lichte et al., 11-37. Theatralität 4. Tübingen: Francke, 2003.
———. "Theater als Modell für eine Ästhetik des Performativen." In *Performativität und Praxis*, edited by Jens Kertscher and Dieter Mersch, 97-103. Munich: Fink, 2003.
Fischer-Lichte, Erika, and Jens Roselt. "Attraktion des Augenblicks - Aufführung, Performance, performativ und Performativität als theaterwissenschaftliche Begriffe." Special issue, *Theorien des Performativen*, edited by Erika Fischer-Lichte and Christoph Wulf, *Paragrana* 10 (2001) 237-53.
Fitzgerald, John T. "Paul, the Ancient Epistolary Theorists, and 2 Corinthians 10-13." In *Greeks, Romans, and Christians: Essays in Honor of Abraham J. Malherbe*, edited by David L. Balch et al., 190-200. Minneapolis: Fortress, 1990.
Fitzmeyer, Joseph A. *The Letter to Philemon*. AB 34C. New York: Doubleday, 2000.
Foley, John Miles. *Comparative Research on Oral Traditions: A Memorial for Milman Parry*. Columbus, OH: Slavica, 1987.
———. *How to Read an Oral Poem*. Urbana: University of Illinois Press, 2002 [e-companion at www.oraltradition.org/].
———. *Immanent Art: From Structure to Meaning in Traditional Oral Epic*. Bloomington: Indiana University Press, 1991.
———, ed. *Oral Traditional Literature: A Festschrift for Albert Bates Lord*. Columbus, OH: Slavica, 1981.
———. "Traditional Signs and the Homeric Art." In *Written Voices, Spoken Signs: Traditions, Performance, and the Epic Text*, edited by Egbert Bakker and Ahuvia Kahane, 56-82. Center for Hellenic Studies: Colloquia. Cambridge: Harvard University Press, 1997.
———. "Words in Tradition, Words in Text: A Response." In *Orality and Textuality in Early Christian Literature*, edited by Joanna Dewey, 169-80. Semeia 65. Atlanta: Scholars, 1995.
Forbes, Christopher. "Early Christian Inspired Speech and Hellenistic Popular Religion." *NovT* 28 (1986) 257-70.
Frede, Dorothea. "Mündlichkeit und Schriftlichkeit: Von Platon zu Plotin." In *Logos und Buchstabe: Mündlichkeit und Schriftlichkeit im Judentum und Christentum der Antike*, edited by Gerhard Sellin and Francois Vouga, 33-54. TANZ 20. Tübingen: Francke, 1997.
Friedrich, Gerhard. "Der erste Brief an die Thessalonicher." In *Die Briefe an die Galater, Epheser, Philipper, Kolosser, Thessalonicher und Philemon*, by Jürgen Becker et al., 203-51. NTD 8. Göttingen: Vandenhoeck & Ruprecht, 1990.
Frilingos, Chris. "'For My Child, Onesimus': Paul and Domestic Power in Philemon." *JBL* 119 (2000) 91-104.

Fuhrmann, Manfred. "Mündlichkeit und fiktive Mündlichkeit in den von Cicero veröffentlichten Reden." In *Strukturen der Mündlichkeit in der römischen Literatur*, edited by Gregor Vogt-Spira, 53–62. ScriptOralia, Altertumswissenschaftliche Reihe 4. Tübingen: Narr, 1990.

Funk, Robert W. "The Apostolic Parousia: Form and Significance." In *Christian History and Interpretation: Studies Presented to John Knox*, edited by W. R. Farmer et al., 249–68. Cambridge: Cambridge University Press, 1967.

———. *Language, Hermeneutic, and Word of God*. New York: Harper & Row, 1966.

Gäckle, Volker. *Die Starken und die Schwachen in Korinth und Rom: Zur Herkunft und Funktion der Antithese in 1 Kor 8,1—11,1 und Röm 14,1—15,13*. WUNT 2/200. Tübingen: Mohr/Siebeck, 2005.

Gagarin, Michael. "The Orality of Greek Oratory." In *Signs of Orality: The Oral Tradition and Its Influence in the Greek and Roman World*, edited by E. Anne Mackay, 163–80. Mnemosyne Sup 188. Leiden: Brill, 1998.

Gaius. *Institutiones, lateinisch und deutsch*. Edited, translated, and explained by Ulrich Manthe. Texte zur Forschung 81. Darmstadt: Wissenschaftliche Buchgesellschaft, 2004.

Gamble, Harry Y. *Books and Readers in the Early Church: A History of Early Christian Texts*. New Haven: Yale University Press, 1995.

Gardner, Jane F. *Women in Roman Law & Society*. London: Croom Helm, 1986.

Gärtner, H. A. "Die Gesten in der Darstellung. Beispiele zur Bedeutung des mündlichen Vortrags für das Verständnis der römischen Historikertexte." In *Strukturen der Mündlichkeit in der römischen Literatur*, edited by Gregor Vogt-Spira, 97–116. ScriptOralia, Altertumswissenschaftliche Reihe 4. Tübingen: Narr, 1990.

Gaventa, Beverly R. "The Maternity of Paul: An Exegetical Study of Galatians 4:19." In *The Conversation Continues: Studies in Paul & John in Honor of J. Louis Martyn*, edited by Robert T. Fortna and Beverly R. Gaventa, 189–201. Nashville: Abingdon, 1990.

Georgi, Dieter. *The Opponents of Paul in Second Corinthians: A Study of Religious Propaganda in Late Antiquity*. Philadelphia: Fortress, 1986 [German original: *Die Gegner des Paulus im 2. Korintherbrief: Studien zur religiösen Propaganda in der Spätantike*. WMANT 11. Neukirchen-Vluyn: Neukirchener, 1964].

Gerhardsson, Birger. *Memory and Manuscript: Oral Tradition and Written Transmission in Rabbinic Judaism and Early Christianity*. Acta Seminarii Neotestamentici Upsaliensis 22. Uppsala: Almqvist & Wiksell, 1961.

———. "The Secret of the Transmission of the Unwritten Jesus Tradition." *NTS* 51 (2005) 1–18.

Gestrich, Christof. "Die Sprache der Versöhnung: Theologie und Sprachphilosophie in Begegnung. Erwägungen zu G. W. F. Hegel und W. von Humboldt über die Frage der Verhinderung destruktiver Gewalt." *ZTK* 94 (1997) 488–510.

Giles, Terry, and William J. Doan. *Twice Used Songs: Performance Criticism of the Songs of Ancient Israel*. Peabody, MA: Hendrickson, 2009.

Gilliard, Frank D. "More Silent Reading in Antiquity: Non Omne Verbum Sonabat." *JBL* 112 (1993) 689–94.

Giomini, Remo, and M. S. Celentano. "Praefatio." In *Ars Rhetorica*, by G. Iulii Victoris, v–xxxii. Leipzig: Teubner, 1980.

Given, Mark D. *Paul's True Rhetoric: Ambiguity, Cunning, and Deception in Greece and Rome*. Emory Studies in Early Christianity 7. Harrisburg: Trinity, 2001.

Gleason, Maud. *Making Men: Sophists and Self-Presentation in Ancient Rome*. Princeton: Princeton University Press, 1995.
Godet, Frédéric. *Commentar zu dem Brief an die Römer*. Part 2. Hannover: Meyer, 1882.
Goetsch, Paul. "Der Übergang von Mündlichkeit zu Schriftlichkeit: Die kulturkritischen und ideologischen Implikationen der Theorien von McLuhan, Goody und Ong." In *Symbolische Formen, Medien, Identität: Jahrbuch 1989/90 des Sonderforschungsbereichs "Übergänge und Spannungsfelder zwischen Mündlichkeit und Schriftlichkeit,"* edited by Wolfgang Raible, 113–29. ScriptOralia 37. Tübingen: Narr, 1991.
Goffman, Erving. *Frame Analysis: An Essay on the Organization of Experience*. Harper Colophon Books. New York: Harper & Row, 1974.
———. *The Presentation of Self in Everyday Life*. Anchor Books. Garden City, NY: Dubleday, 1959.
Goldhill, Simon. "The Anecdote: Exploring the Boundaries between Oral and Literate Performance in the Second Sophistic." In *Ancient Literacies: The Culture of Reading in Greece and Rome*, edited by William A. Johnson and Holt N. Parker, 96–113. Oxford: Oxford University Press, 2009.
Goldstein, Jonathan. A. *The Letters of Demosthenes*. New York: Columbia University Press, 1968.
Goody, Jack, ed. *Literacy in Traditional Societies*. Cambridge: Cambridge University Press, 1968.
Goody, Jack, and Ian Watt. "The Consequences of Literacy." In *Literacy in Traditional Societies*, edited by Jack Goody, 27–68. Cambridge: Cambridge University Press, 1968.
Graham, William A. *Beyond the Written Word: Oral Aspects of Scripture in the History of Religion*. Cambridge: Cambridge University Press, 1987.
Günther, Hartmut, ed. *Schrift und Schriftlichkeit: Ein interdisziplinäres Handbuch internationaler Forschung*. 2 vols. Handbücher zur Sprach- und Kommunikationswissenschaft 10,1 and 10,2. Berlin: de Gruyter, 1994–1996.
Güttgemanns, Erhardt. *Offene Fragen zur Formgeschichte des Evangeliums: Eine methodologische Skizze der Grundlagenproblematik der Form- und Redaktionsgeschichte*. Munich: Kaiser, 1971.
Haacker, Klaus. *Der Brief des Paulus an die Römer*. ThHKNT 6. Leipzig: Evangelische Verlagsanstalt, 1999.
———. "Der Römerbrief als Friedensmemorandum." *NTS* 36 (1990) 25–41.
Habinek, Thomas. "Situating Literacy at Rome." In *Ancient Literacies: The Culture of Reading in Greece and Rome*, edited by William A. Johnson and Holt N. Parker, 114–40. Oxford: Oxford University Press, 2009.
Hackforth, Reginald. *The Authorship of the Platonic Epistles*. 1913. Publications of the University of Manchester. Classical Series 2nd ser. 72. Hildesheim: Olms, 1985.
Hájek, Milan. "Comments on Philippians 4:3—Who was 'Gnésios Syzygos?'" *Communio Viatorum* 7 (1964) 261–62.
Hall, Robert G. "The Rhetorical Outline for Galatians: A Reconsideration." *JBL* 106 (1987) 277–87.
Halverson, John. "Oral and Written Gospel: A Critique of Werner Kelber." *NTS* 40 (1994) 180–95.
Hansen, G. Walter. *Abraham in Galatians: Epistolary and Rhetorical Contexts*. JSNTSup 29. Sheffield: JSOT Press, 1989.

Hardin, Justin K. *Galatians and the Imperial Cult: A Critical Analysis of the First-Century Social Context of Paul's Letter.* WUNT 2/237. Tübingen: Mohr/Siebeck, 2008.
Hardmeier, Christoph. *Erzähldiskurs und Redepragmatik im Alten Testament: Unterwegs zu einer performativen Theologie der Bibel.* FAT 46. Tübingen: Mohr/Siebeck, 2005.
Harnack, Adolf von. "Das Schreiben der römischen Kirche an die korinthische aus der Zeit Domitians (I. Clemensbrief)." In *Encounters with Hellenism: Studies on the First Letter of Clement*, edited by Cilliers Breytenbach and Laurence L. Welborn, 1–103. AGJU 53. Leiden: Brill 2004 [first published: *Einführung in die Alte Kirchengeschichte: Das Schreiben der römischen Gemeinde an die korinthische aus der Zeit Domitians (I. Clemensbrief).* Leipzig: Hinrich, 1929].
Harnisch, Wolfgang. "Einübung des neuen Seins: Paulinische Paränese am Beispiel des Galaterbriefs." *ZTK* 84 (1987) 279–96.
Harris, William V. *Ancient Literacy.* Cambridge: Harvard University Press, 1989.
Hartman, D. "Epistolary Conventions and Social Change in Paul's Letters." In *Early Christianity, Late Antiquity and Beyond*, edited by T. W. Hillard et al., 195–204. Ancient History in a Modern University 2. Grand Rapids: Eerdmans, 1998.
Hartman, Lars. "On Reading Others' Letters." In *Text-Centered New Testament Studies: Text-Theoretical Essays on Early Jewish and Early Christian Literature*, edited by David Hellholm, 167–77. WUNT 102. Tübingen: Mohr/Siebeck, 1997 [article first published 1986].
Harvey, A. E. "The Opposition to Paul." In *Studia Evangelica*, vol 4.1, edited by F. L. Cross, 319–32. TU 102. Berlin: Akademie, 1968.
Harvey, John D. *Listening to the Text: Oral Patterning in Paul's Letters.* Evangelical Theological Society Studies. Grand Rapids: Baker, 1998.
———. "Orality and Its Implications for Biblical Studies: Recapturing an Ancient Paradigm." *JETS* 45 (2002) 99–109.
Haufe, Günter. *Der erste Brief des Paulus an die Thessalonicher.* ThHKNT 12/1. Leipzig: Evangelische Verlagsanstalt, 1999.
Havelock, Eric A. *The Literate Revolution in Greece and Its Cultural Consequences.* Princeton Series of Collected Essays. Princeton: Princeton University Press, 1982.
———. *The Muse Learns to Write: Reflections on Orality and Literacy from Antiquity to the Present.* New Haven: Yale University Press, 1986.
———. *Preface to Plato.* History of the Greek Mind 1. Cambridge: Harvard University Press, 1963.
———. *Schriftlichkeit: Das griechische Alphabet als kulturelle Revolution.* Translated by Gabriele Herbst, with an introduction by Aleida and Jan Assmann. Weinheim: VCH, Acta Humaniora, 1990.
Head, Peter M. "Named Letter-Carriers among the Oxyrhynchus Papyri." *JSNT* 31 (2009) 279–99.
Hearon, Holly E. "The Implications of Orality for Studies of the Biblical Text." In *Performing the Gospel: Orality, Memory, and Mark: Essays Dedicated to Werner Kelber*, edited by Richard A. Horsley et al., 3–20. Minneapolis: Fortress, 2006 [earlier version in *Oral Tradition* 19 (2004) 96–107].
Hearon, Holly E., and Philip Ruge-Jones, eds. *The Bible in Ancient and Modern Media: Story and Performance.* BPCS 1. Eugene, OR: Cascade Books, 2009.
Heil, Christoph. *Die Ablehnung der Speisegebote durch Paulus: Zur Frage nach der Stellung des Apostels zum Gesetz.* BBB 96. Weinheim: Beltz Athenäum, 1994.

Heil, John Paul. "The Chiastic Structure and Meaning of Paul's Letter to Philemon." *Bib* 82 (2001) 178–206.
Heiligenthal, Roman. "Methodische Erwägungen zur Analyse neutestamentlicher Gemeindekonflikte." *ZRGG* 48 (1996) 97–113.
Heinrici, Carl Friedrich Georg. *Das erste Sendschreiben des Apostels Paulus an die Korinther.* Berlin: Hertz, 1880.
———. *Das zweite Sendschreiben des Apostels Paulus an die Korinther.* Berlin: Hertz, 1887.
Henaut, Barry W. *Oral Traditions and the Gospels: The Problem of Mark 4.* JSNTSup 82. Sheffield: Sheffield Academic, 1993.
Hendrickson, G. L. "Ancient Reading." *CJ* 25 (1929/30) 182–96.
Hengel, Martin. *Judentum und Hellenismus: Studien zu ihrer Begegnung unter besonderer Berücksichtigung Palästinas bis zur Mitte des 2. Jh.s v. Chr.* WUNT 10. Tübingen: Mohr, 1988.
Hester, James D. "Speaker, Audience and Situations: A Modified Interactional Model." *Neot* 32 (1998) 75–94.
Hezser, Catherine. *Jewish Literacy in Roman Palestine.* TSAJ 81. Tübingen: Mohr/Siebeck, 2001.
Hibbitts, Bernard J. "Coming to Our Senses: Communication and Legal Expression in Performance Cultures." *Emory Law Journal* 4 (1992) 873–960.
Hirsch, Emanuel. "Zwei Fragen zu Galater 6." *ZNW* 29 (1930) 192–97.
Holland, Glenn S. *Divine Irony.* Sellinsgrove, PA: Susquehanna University Press, 2000.
———. "'Frightening You with Letters': Traces of Performance in the Letters of Paul." *Proceedings Eastern Great Lakes and Midwest Bible Society* 26 (2006) 1–21.
———. "Playing to the Groundlings: Shakespeare Performance Criticism and Performance Criticism of the Biblical Texts." *Neot* 41 (2007) 317–40.
Holloway, Paul A. *Consolation in Philippians: Philosophical Sources and Rhetorical Strategy.* SNTSMS 112. Cambridge: Cambridge University Press, 2001.
———. "Paul's Pointed Prose: The Sententia in Roman Rhetoric and Paul." *NovT* 40 (1998) 32–53.
Holmstrand, Jonas. *Markers and Meaning in Paul: An Analysis of 1 Thessalonians, Philippians, and Galatians.* ConBNT 28. Stockholm: Almqvist & Wiksell, 1997.
Holtz, Traugott. *Der erste Brief an die Thessalonicher.* EKKNT 13. Zurich: Benziger, 1986.
———. "Das Kennzeichen des Geistes (1 Kor. XII. 1–3)." *NTS* 18 (1971–72) 365–76.
Horsley, Richard A., and Jonathan A. Draper. *Whoever Hears You Hears Me: Prophets, Performance, and Tradition in Q.* Harrisburg, PA: Trinity, 1999.
Horsley, Richard A., et al., eds. *Performing the Gospel: Orality, Memory, and Mark.* Minneapolis: Fortress, 2006.
Howard, George. *Paul: Crisis in Galatia; A Study in Early Christian Theology.* SNTSMS 35. 2nd ed. Cambridge: Cambridge University Press, 2004.
Hübner, Hans. *An Philemon, an die Kolosser, an die Epheser.* HNT 12. Tübingen: Mohr/Siebeck, 1997.
———. "Der Galaterbrief und das Verhältnis von antiker Rhetorik und Epistolographie." *TLZ* 109 (1984) 241–50.
———. "Die Rhetorik und die Theologie: Der Römerbrief und die rhetorische Kompetenz des Paulus." In *Die Macht des Wortes: Aspekte gegenwärtiger Rhetorik-*

forschung, edited by C. J. Classen and H. J. Müllenbrock, 165–79. Ars rhetorica 4. Marburg: Hitzeroth, 1992.
Hughes, Frank Witt. *Early Christian Rhetoric and 2 Thessalonians*. JSNTSup 30. Sheffield: Sheffield Academic, 1989.
Hunt, Allen Rhea. *The Inspired Body: Paul, the Corinthians, and Divine Inspiration*. Macon, GA: Mercer University Press, 1996.
Hurtado, Larry W. "The Jerusalem Collection and the Book of Galatians." *JSNT* 5 (1979) 46–62.
Hymes, Dell. "Breakthrough into Performance." In *Folklore: Performance and Communication*, edited by Dan Ben-Amos and Kenneth S. Goldstein, 11–74. Approaches to Semiotics 40. The Hague: Mouton, 1975.
Ignatius. "An Polykarp." In *Die Apostolischen Väter*, edited by Joseph A. Fischer, 216–25. Schriften des Urchristentums 1. Darmstadt: Wissenschaftliche Buchgesellschaft, 1959.
———. "An Polykarp." In *Die Apostolischen Väter*, edited by Karl Bihlmeyer, 110–13. Tübingen: Mohr, 1970.
———. "Ignatius to Polycarp." In *The Apostolic Fathers with an English Translation*, edited by Kirsopp Lake, 1:266–77. Cambridge: Harvard University Press, 1975.
Imber, Margaret. "Practised Speech: Oral and Written Conventions in Roman Declamation." In *Speaking Volumes: Orality and Literacy in the Greek and Roman World*, edited by Janet Watson, 199–216. Mnemosyne Sup 218. Leiden: Brill, 2001.
Irenäus von Lyon. *Adversus Haereses: Gegen die Häresien*. Vol. 3. Translated and introduced by Norbert Brox. Freiburg: Herder, 1995.
Iser, Wolfgang. *Der Akt des Lesens: Theorie ästhetischer Wirkung*. Munich: Fink, 1976.
Isokrates. *Sämtliche Werke*. Vol. 2: *Reden IX–XXI, Briefe, Fragmente*. Translated by Christine Ley-Hutton. Bibliothek der griechischen Literatur 44. Stuttgart: Hiersemann, 1997.
Iulii Victoris, G.: *Ars rhetorica*. Edited by Remo Giomini and Maria Silvana Celentano. Leipzig: Teubner, 1980 [text and English translation also in Malherbe, *Ancient Epistolary Theorists*, 62–65].
Jaffee, Martin S. *Torah in the Mouth: Writing and Oral Tradition in Palestinian Judaism 200 BCE–400 CE*. Oxford: Oxford University Press, 2001.
Jeal, Roy. "Melody, Imagery and Memory in the Moral Persuasion of Paul." Heidelberg Conference on Rhetoric, Ethics, and Moral Persuasion in Biblical Discourse, July 22–25, 2002, http://www.ars-rhetorica.net/Queen/VolumeSpecialIssue2/Articles/Jeal.pdf/.
Jervell, Jacob. "Der Brief nach Jerusalem: Über Veranlassung und Adresse des Römerbriefes." *ST* 25 (1971) 61–73.
Jewett, Robert. "The Agitators and the Galatian Congregation." *NTS* 17 (1970/71) 198–212.
———. "Ecumenical Theology for the Sake of Mission: Romans 1:1–17 + 15:14—16:24." In *Romans*, edited by David M. Hay and E. Elizabeth Johnson, 89–108. Pauline Theology 3. Minneapolis: Fortress, 1995.
———. *Romans: A Commentary*. Hermeneia. Minneapolis: Fortress, 2007.
———. *The Thessalonian Correspondence: Pauline Rhetoric and Millenarian Piety*. FF. Philadelphia: Fortress, 1986.
Johanson, Bruce C. *To All the Brethren: A Text-Linguistic and Rhetoric Approach to I Thessalonians*. ConBNT 16. Uppsala: Almqvist & Wiksell, 1987.

Johnson, Lee A. "Titus' Tearful Performance: How Artful Presentations of Paul's Letter Produced Success in Corinth." Paper delivered at the SBL Annual Meeting, Performance Criticism of Biblical and Other Ancient Texts Section, New Orleans, November 23, 2009.

Johnson, Luke T. "The New Testament's Anti-Jewish Slander and the Conventions of Ancient Polemic." *JBL* 108 (1987) 419–41.

Johnson, William A., Jr. *Readers and Reading Culture in the High Roman Empire: A Study of Elite Communities*. Classical Culture and Society. New York: Oxford University Press, 2010.

Josephus, Flavius. *Antiquitates Judaicae*, books IX–XI, with an English translation by Ralph Marcus. LCL 326. Cambridge: Harvard University Press, 2001.

———. *Antiquitates Judaicae*, books XII–XIV, with an English translation by Ralph Marcus. LCL 365. Cambridge: Harvard University Press, 1966.

———. *Des Flavius Josephus Jüdische Altertümer*. Translated with introduction and notes by Heinrich Clementz. Wiesbaden: Fourier, 1990.

Julius Victor, C. "Ars rhetorica." In *Rhetores latini minores: ex codicibus maximam partem primum adhibitis*, edited by Karl Halm, 371–448. Leipzig: Teubner, 1863.

Karris, Robert J. "Rom 14:1—15:13 and the Occasion of Romans." *CBQ* 35 (1973) 155–78. Reprinted in *The Romans Debate*, edited by Karl P. Donfried, 75–99. Minneapolis: Augsburg, 1977.

Käsemann, Ernst. *An die Römer: Kommentar zum Paulusbrief.* HNT 8a. Tübingen: Mohr, 1974 [English translation: *Commentary on Romans*. Translated by Geoffrey W. Bromiley. Grand Rapids: Eerdmans, 1980].

Keck, Leander E. "Christology, Soteriology, and the Praise of God (Romans 15:7–13)." In *The Conversation Continues: Studies in Paul & John in Honor of J. Louis Martyn*, edited by Robert T. Fortna and Beverly R. Gaventa, 85–97. Nashville: Abingdon, 1990.

———. *Romans*. ANTC. Nashville: Abingdon, 2005.

Kelber, Werner H. "Biblical Hermeneutics and the Ancient Art of Communication: A Response." In *Orality, Aurality and Biblical Narrative*, edited by Lou H. Silberman, 97–105. Semeia 39. Decatur, GA: Scholars, 1987.

———. "Jesus and Tradition: Words in Time, Words in Space." In *Orality and Textuality in Early Christian Literature*, edited by Joanna Dewey, 139–67. Semeia 65. Atlanta: Scholars, 1995.

———. "Modalities of Communication, Cognition, and Physiology of Perception: Orality, Rhetoric, Scribality." In *Orality and Textuality in Early Christian Literature*, edited by Joanna Dewey, 193–216. Semeia 65. Atlanta: Scholars, 1995.

———. "Narrative as Interpretation and Interpretation of Narrative: Hermeneutical Reflections on the Gospels." In *Orality, Aurality and Biblical Narrative*, edited by Lou H. Silberman, 107–33. Semeia 39. Decatur, GA: Scholars, 1987.

———. *The Oral and the Written Gospel: The Hermeneutics of Speaking and Writing in the Synoptic Tradition, Mark, Paul, and Q*. Voices in Performance and Text. Philadelphia: Fortress, 1983.

Kennedy, George A. *Classical Rhetoric and Its Christian and Secular Tradition from Ancient to Modern Times*. 2nd ed., rev. and enl. Chapel Hill: University of North Carolina Press, 1999.

———. *New Testament Interpretation through Rhetorical Criticism*. Studies in Religion. Chapel Hill: University of North Carolina Press, 1984.

Kern, Philip H. *Rhetoric and Galatians: Assessing an Approach to Paul's Epistle.* SNTSMS 101. Cambridge: Cambridge University Press, 1998.

Kertscher, Jens. "Wittgenstein—Austin—Derrida: 'Performativität' in der sprachphilosophischen Diskussion." In *Performativität und Praxis,* edited by Jens Kertscher and Dieter Mersch, 35–58. Munich: Fink, 2003.

Keyes, Clinton W. "The Greek Letter of Introduction." *American Journal of Philology* 56 (1935) 28–44.

Kim, Chan-Hie. *Form and Structure of the Familiar Greek Letter of Recommendation.* SBLDS 4. Missoula: SBL, 1972.

Kindermann, Heinz. *Das Theaterpublikum der Antike.* Salzburg: Müller, 1979.

Kirshenblatt-Gimblett, Barbara. "Performance of Precepts/Precepts of Performance: Hasidic Celebrations of Purim in Brooklyn." In *By Means of Performance: Intercultural Studies of Theatre and Ritual,* edited by Richard Schechner and Willa Appel, 109–17. Cambridge: Cambridge University Press, 1990.

Klauck, Hans-Josef, with the collaboration of Daniel P. Bailey. *Ancient Letters and the New Testament: A Guide to Context and Exegesis.* Waco: Baylor University Press, 2006 [German original: *Die antike Briefliteratur und das Neue Testament.* UTB 2022. Paderborn: Schöningh, 1998].

———. *1. Korintherbrief, 2. Korintherbrief.* Leipzig: St. Benno, 1990.

Klijn, A. F. J. "Die Syrische Baruch Apokalypse." In *Himmelfahrt Moses / Die griechische Esra-Apokalypse / Die syrische Baruch-Apokalypse,* edited by E. Brandenburger et al., 101–91. JSHRZ 5/2. Gütersloh: Mohn, 1976.

Klinghardt, Matthias. *Gemeinschaftsmahl und Mahlgemeinschaft: Soziologie und Liturgie frühchristlicher Mahlfeiern.* TANZ 13. Tübingen: Francke, 1996.

Knoop, Ulrich. "Zum Verhältnis von geschriebener und gesprochener Sprache: Anmerkungen aus historischer Sicht." In *Homo scribens: Perspektiven der Schriftlichkeitsforschung,* edited by Jürgen Baumann et al., 217–29. Reihe Germanistische Linguistik 134. Tübingen: Niemeyer 1993.

Knopf, Rudolf. *Der erste Clemensbrief.* HNT Ergänzungsband. Tübingen: Mohr, 1923.

Knox, Bernard M. W. "Silent Reading in Antiquitiy." *GRBS* 9 (1968) 421–35.

Koch, Peter, and Wulf Oesterreicher. "Funktionale Aspekte der Schriftkultur." In *Schrift und Schriftlichkeit: Ein interdisziplinäres Handbuch internationaler Forschung,* edited by Hartmut Günther, 587–604. Handbücher zur Sprach- und Kommunikationswissenschaft 10.1. Berlin: de Gruyter, 1994.

———. "Sprache der Nähe—Sprache der Distanz: Mündlichkeit und Schriftlichkeit im Spannungsfeld von Sprachtheorie und Sprachgeschichte." *Romanistisches Jahrbuch* 36 (1985) 15–43.

Korenjak, Martin. *Publikum und Redner: Ihre Interaktion in der sophistischen Rhetorik der Kaiserzeit.* Zetemata 104. Munich: Beck, 2000.

Körtner, Ulrich H. *Der inspirierte Leser: Zentrale Aspekte biblischer Hermeneutik.* Göttingen: Vandenhoeck & Ruprecht, 1994.

Koskenniemi, Heikki. *Studien zur Idee und Phraseologie des griechischen Briefes bis 400 n. Chr.* Annales Academiae Scientiarum Fennicae, Ser. B. 102,2. Helsinki: Suomalainen Tiedeakatemian, 1956.

Krämer, Sybille. "Sprache—Stimme—Schrift: Sieben Gedanken über Performativität als Medialität." In *Performanz: Zwischen Sprachphilosophie und Kulturwissenschaften,* edited by Uwe Wirth, 323–46. STW 1575. Frankfurt: Suhrkamp, 2002.

———. "Was tut Austin, indem er über das Performative spricht? Ein anderer Blick auf die Anfänge der Sprechakttheorie." In *Performativität und Praxis*, edited by Jens Kertscher and Dieter Mersch, 19–33. Munich: Fink, 2003.
Krämer, Sybille, and Marco Stahlhut. "Das 'Performative' als Thema der Sprach- und Kulturphilosophie." In *Theorien des Performativen*, edited by Erika Fischer-Lichte and Christoph Wulf, 35–64. *Paragrana* 10, 2001.
Kremendahl, Dieter. *Die Botschaft der Form: Zum Verhältnis von antiker Epistolographie und Rhetorik im Galaterbrief*. NTOA 46. Göttingen: Vandenhoeck & Ruprecht, 2000.
Kuck, David W. "'Each Will Bear His Own Burden': Paul's Creative Use of an Apocalyptic Motif." *NTS* 40 (1994) 289–97.
Kwon, Yon-Gyong. *Eschatology in Galatians: Rethinking Paul's Response to the Crisis in Galatia*. WUNT 2/183. Tübingen: Mohr/Siebeck, 2004.
Lake, Kirsopp. *The Apostolic Fathers with an English Translation*, vol. 1. Cambridge: Harvard University Press, 1912. Reprinted, 1975.
Lambrecht, Jan. "Paul's Coherent Admonition in Galatians 6,1–6: Mutual Help and Individual Attentiveness." *Bib* 78 (1997) 33–56.
———. "Syntactical and Logical Remarks on Romans 15:8–9a." *NovT* 42 (2000) 257–61.
Lampe, Peter. "Der Brief an Philemon." In *Die Briefe an die Philipper, Thessalonicher und Philemon*, edited by Nikolaus Walter et al., 203–32. NTD 8/2. Göttingen: Vandenhoeck & Ruprecht, 1998.
———. "Keine 'Sklavenflucht' des Onesimus." *ZNW* 76 (1985) 135–37.
———. "Rhetorical Analysis of Pauline Texts—Quo Vadit?" In *Paul and Rhetoric*, edited by J. Paul Sampley and Peter Lampe, 3–21. New York: T. & T. Clark, 2010.
———. *Die stadtrömischen Christen in den ersten beiden Jahrhunderten: Untersuchungen zur Sozialgeschichte*. WUNT 2/18. Tübingen: Mohr, 1989.
Larson, Jennifer. "Paul's Masculinity." *JBL* 123 (2004) 85–97.
Laub, Franz. *Eschatologische Verkündigung und Lebensgestaltung nach Paulus: Eine Untersuchung zum Wirken des Apostels beim Aufbau der Gemeinde in Thessalonike*. Regensburg: Pustet, 1973.
Lee, Margaret Ellen, and Bernard Brandon Scott. *Sound Mapping the New Testament*. Salem, OR: Polebridge, 2009.
Lefèvre, Eckard. "Die römische Literatur zwischen Mündlichkeit und Schriftlichkeit." In *Strukturen der Mündlichkeit in der römischen Literatur*, edited by Gregor Vogt-Spira, 9–15. ScriptOralia, Altertumswissenschaftliche Reihe 4. Tübingen: Narr, 1990.
Lehmann, Reinhard G. "Brief oder Botschafter? Eine kontextuelle Annäherung an Lachisch Ostrakon 2 und 5." In *Bote und Brief: Sprachliche Systeme der Informationsübermittlung im Spannungsfeld von Mündlichkeit und Schriftlichkeit*, edited by Andreas Wagner, 75–101. Nordostafrikanisch/Westasiatische Studien 4. Frankfurt: Lang, 2003.
Lentz, Tony M. *Orality and Literacy in Hellenic Greece*. Carbondale: Southern Illinois University Press, 1989.
Lévi-Strauss, Claude. *Tristes Tropiques*. Terre humaine. Civilisations et sociétés. Paris: Plon, 1976.
Libanios. *Libanii Opera: Zwölf Bände*, vol. 10: *Epistulae 1–839*, edited by Richard Foerster. 1921. Reprinted, Hildesheim: Olms, 1963.

Liebert, Donald Hans. "The 'Apostolic Form of Writing': Group Letters Before and After 1 Corinthians." In *The Corinthian Correspondence*, edited by Reimund Bieringer, 433-40. BETL 125. Leuven: Leuven University Press, 1996.

Lindemann, Andreas. *Die Clemensbriefe*. HNT 17. Tübingen: Mohr, 1992.

Lips, Hermann von. "Die Haustafeln als 'Topos' im Rahmen der urchristlichen Paränese: Beobachtungen anhand des 1. Petrusbriefes und des Timotheusbriefes." *NTS* 40 (1994) 261-80.

Litfin, Duane. *St. Paul's Theology of Proclamation: 1 Corinthians 1-4 and Greco-Roman Rhetoric*. SNTSMS 79. Cambridge: Cambridge University Press, 1994.

Llewelyn, Stephen Robert. "Directions for the Delivery of Letters and the Epistles of St Paul." In *Early Christianity, Late Antiquity and Beyond*, edited by Thomas W. Hillard et al., 184-94. Ancient History in a Modern University 2. Grand Rapids: Eerdmans, 1998.

———. "Sending Letters in the Ancient World: Paul and the Philippians." *Tyndale Bulletin* 46 (1995) 337-56.

Lohmeyer, Ernst. *Die Briefe an die Philipper, an die Kolosser und an Philemon*. KEK 9. Göttingen: Vandenhoeck & Ruprecht, 1956.

Lohse, Eduard. *Der Brief an die Römer*. KEK 4. Göttingen: Vandenhoeck & Ruprecht, 2003.

———. *Die Briefe an die Kolosser und an Philemon*. KEK 9/2. Göttingen: Vandenhoeck & Ruprecht, 1977.

Lona, Horacio E. *Der erste Clemensbrief*. Kommentar zu den Apostolischen Vätern 2. Göttingen: Vandenhoeck & Ruprecht, 1998.

Long, Fredrick J. *Ancient Rhetoric and Paul's Apology: The Compositional Unity of 2 Corinthians*. SNTSMS 131. Cambridge: Cambridge University Press, 2008.

Longenecker, Bruce W. "'Until Christ Is Formed in You': Suprahuman Forces and Moral Character in Galatians." *CBQ* 61 (1999) 92-108.

Longenecker, Richard N. *Galatians*. WBC 41. Dallas: Word, 1990.

Lord, Albert Bates. "The Gospels as Oral Tradition Literature." In *The Relationships among the Gospels: An Interdisciplinary Dialogue*, edited by W. O. Walker, 33-91. Trinity University Monograph Series in Religion. San Antonio: Trinity University Press, 1978.

———. *The Singer of Tales*. Harvard Studies in Comparative Literature 24. Cambridge: Harvard University Press, 1960.

Loubser, J. A. "Media Criticism and the Myth of Paul, the Creative Genius, and His Forgotten Co-workers." *Neot* 34 (2000) 329-47.

———. *Oral and Manuscript Culture in the Bible: Studies on the Media Texture of the New Testament—Explorative Hermeneutics*. Stellenbosch: Sun, 2007 [2nd ed.: BPCS 7. Eugene, OR: Cascade Books, 2013].

———. "Orality and Literacy in the Pauline Epistles: Some New Hermeneutical Implications." *Neot* 29 (1995) 61-74.

———. "Orality and Pauline 'Christology': Some Hermeneutical Implications." *Scriptura* 47 (1993) 25-51.

———. "Reconciling Rhetorical Criticism with Its Oral Roots." *Neot* 35 (2001) 95-110.

Luhmann, Niklas. *Religious Dogmatics and the Evolution of Societies*. Translated with an introduction by Peter Beyer. Studies in Religion and Society 9. Lewiston, NY: Mellen, 1984.

———. *Social Systems*. Translated by John Bednarz Jr., with Dirk Baecker. Stanford: Stanford University Press, 1995.

Lütgert, Wilhelm. *Gesetz und Geist: Eine Untersuchung zur Vorgeschichte des Galaterbriefes*. BFCT 22/6. Gütersloh: Bertelsmann, 1919.

Luther, Martin. *Vorlesung über den Römerbrief 1515/1516*. Edited by Eduard Ellwein. Munich: Kaiser, 1928.

Lyons, Kirk D. "Paul's Confrontation with Class: The Letter to Philemon as Counter-Hegemonic Discourse." *Cross Currents* 55 (2006) 116–32.

Maassen, Irmgard. "Text und/als/in der Performanz in der frühen Neuzeit: Thesen und Überlegungen." In *Theorien des Performativen*, edited by Erika Fischer-Lichte and Christoph Wulf, 285–302. *Paragrana* 10, 2001.

Mack, Burton L. *Rhetoric and the New Testament*. GBSNTS. Minneapolis: Fortress, 1990.

Mackay, E. Anne, ed. *Signs of Orality: The Oral Tradition and its Influence in the Greek and Roman World*. Mnemosyne Sup 188. Leiden: Brill, 1998.

Malherbe, Abraham J., comp. and trans. *Ancient Epistolary Theorists*. SBLSBS 19. Atlanta: Scholars, 1988.

———. *The Letters to the Thessalonians: A New Translation with Introduction and Commentary*. AB 32B. New York: Doubleday, 2000.

Maly, Karl. "1 Kor 12,1–3, eine Regel zur Unterscheidung der Geister?" *BZ* 10 (1966) 82–95.

Martin, Dale B. *The Corinthian Body*. New Haven: Yale University Press, 1995.

Martyn, J. Louis. *Galatians: A New Translation with Introduction and Commentary*. AB 33A. New York: Doubleday, 1997.

———. "A Law-Observant Mission to Gentiles: The Background of Galatians." In *The Galatians Debate: Contemporary Issues in Rhetorical and Historical Interpretation*, edited by Mark D. Nanos, 348–61. Peabody, MA: Hendrickson, 2002 [first published in *Scottish Journal of Theology* 38 (1985) 307–24].

Marxsen, Willi. *Einleitung in das Neue Testament: Eine Einführung in ihre Probleme*. Gütersloh: Mohn, 1964.

Masson, Charles. *Les deux Épîtres de Saint Paul aux Thessaloniciens*. Commentaire du Nouveau Testament XIa. Neuchatel: Delachaux & Niestlé, 1957.

Matera, Frank J. "The Culmination of Paul's Argument to the Galatians: Gal. 5:11—6:17." *JSNT* 32 (1988) 79–91.

———. *Galatians*. SP 9. Collegeville, MN: Liturgical, 1992.

Maxey, James A. *From Orality to Orality: A New Paradigm for Contextual Translation of the Bible*. BPCS 2. Eugene, OR: Cascade Books, 2009.

McLuhan, Marshall. *The Gutenberg Galaxy: The Making of Typographic Man*. Toronto: University of Toronto Press, 1962.

———. *Understanding Media: The Extensions of Man*. New York: McGraw-Hill, 1964.

Meeks, Wayne A. *The First Urban Christians: The Social World of the Apostle Paul*. 2nd ed. New Haven: Yale University Press, 2003.

———. "Judgment and the Brother: Romans 14:1—15:13." In *Tradition and Interpretation in the New Testament: Essays in Honor of E. Earle Ellis*, edited by Gerald F. Hawthorne, 290–300. Grand Rapids: Eerdmans, 1987.

———. *The Origin of Christian Morality: The First Two Centuries*. New Haven: Yale University Press, 1993.

Mehat, A. A. "L'enseignement sur 'les choses de l'ésprit' (1 Cor 12:1–3)." *Revue d'histoire et de philosophie religieuses* 63 (1983) 395–415.
Meier, Samuel A. *The Messenger in the Ancient Semitic World.* HSM 45. Atlanta: Scholars, 1989.
Michaelis, Wilhelm. "Judaistische Heidenchristen." *ZNW* 30 (1931) 83–89.
Michel, Otto. *Der Brief an die Römer.* KEK. Göttingen: Vandenhoeck & Ruprecht, 1955.
Middleton, Peter. "How to Read a Reading of a Written Poem." *Oral Tradition* 20/1 (2005) 7–34.
———. "Poetry's Oral Stage." In *Performance and Authenticity in the Arts,* edited by Salim Kemal and Ivan Gaskell, 215–53. Cambridge Studies in Philosophy and the Arts. Cambridge: Cambridge University Press, 1999.
Mikat, Paul. *Die Bedeutung der Begriffe Stasis und Aponoia für das Verständnis des 1. Clemensbriefes.* Veröffentlichungen der Arbeitsgemeinschaft für Forschung des Landes Nordrhein-Westfalen: Geisteswissenschaften 155. Köln: Westdeutscher Verlag, 1969.
Millard, Alan. *Reading and Writing in the Time of Jesus.* New York: New York University Press, 2000.
Miller, Robert D. II. *Oral Tradition in Ancient Israel.* BPCS 4. Eugene, OR: Cascade Books, 2011.
Minear, Paul S. *The Obedience of Faith: The Purposes of Paul in the Epistle to the Romans.* Studies in Biblical Theology 19. London: SCM, 1971.
Mitchell, Margaret M. "New Testament Envoys in the Context of Greco-Roman Diplomatic and Epistolary Conventions: The Example of Timothy and Titus." *JBL* 111 (1992) 641–62.
———. *Paul and the Rhetoric of Reconciliation: An Exegetical Investigation of the Language and Composition of 1 Corinthians.* HUT 28. Tübingen: Mohr, 1991.
Mitternacht, Dieter. *Forum für Sprachlose: Eine kommunikationspsychologische und epistolär-rhetorische Untersuchung des Galaterbriefs.* ConBNT 30. Stockholm: Almqvist & Wiksell, 1999.
Moiser, Jeremy. "Rethinking Romans 12–15." *NTS* 36 (1990) 571–82.
Moo, Douglas J. *The Epistle to the Romans.* NICNT. Grand Rapids: Eerdmans, 1996.
Morgan, Teresa. *Literate Education in the Hellenistic and Roman World.* Cambridge Classical Studies. Cambridge: Cambridge University Press, 2000.
Morstein-Marx, Robert. *Mass Oratory and Political Power in the Late Roman Republic.* Cambridge: Cambridge University Press, 2004.
Muddiman, John. "An Anatomy of Galatians." In *Crossing the Boundaries: Essays in Biblical Interpretation in Honour of Michael D. Goulder,* edited by Stanley E. Porter et al., 257–70. Biblical Interpretation Series 8. Leiden: Brill 1994.
Müller, Markus. *Vom Schluss zum Ganzen: Zur Bedeutung des Briefkorpusabschlusses in Paulusbriefen.* FRLANT 172. Göttingen: Vandenhoeck & Ruprecht, 1997.
Müller, Roman. *Sprachbewusstsein und Sprachvariation im lateinischen Schrifttum der Antike.* Zetemata 111. Munich: Beck, 2001.
Mullins, Terence Y. "Benediction as a NT Form." *AUSS* 15 (1977) 59–64.
———. "Disclosure: A Literary Form in the New Testament." *NovT* 7 (1964) 44–50.
———. "Formulas in New Testament Epistles." *JBL* 91 (1972) 380–90.
———. "Greeting as a New Testament Form." *JBL* 87 (1968) 418–26.
———. "Visit Talk in New Testament Letters." *CBQ* 35 (1973) 350–58.

Munck, Johannes. *Paulus und die Heilsgeschichte*. Acta Jutlandica, Teologisk Serie 6. Aarhus: Universitetsforlag, 1954.

Murphy-O'Connor, Jerome. *Paul the Letter-Writer: His World, His Options, His Skills*. Good News Studies 41. Collegeville, MN: Liturgical, 1995.

Mussner, Franz. *Der Galaterbrief*. HThKNT. Leipzig: Benno, 1974.

Nanos, Mark D. "Intruding 'Spies' and 'Pseudo-Brethren': The Jewish Intra-Group Politics of Paul's Jerusalem Meeting (Gal 2:1–10)." In *Paul and His Opponents*, edited by Stanley E. Porter, 59–97. Pauline Studies 2. Leiden: Brill 2005.

———. *The Irony of Galatians: Paul's Letter in First-century Context*. Minneapolis: Fortress, 2002.

———. *The Mystery of Romans: The Jewish Context of Paul's Letter*. Minneapolis: Fortress, 1996.

Neyrey, Jerome H. "Acts 17, Epicureans, and Theodicy: A Study in Stereotypes." In *Greeks, Romans, and Christians: Essays in Honor of Abraham J. Malherbe*, edited by David L. Balch et al., 118–34. Minneapolis: Fortress, 1990.

Niditch, Susan. "Oral Tradition and Biblical Scholarship." *Oral Tradition* 18 (2003) 43–44.

———. *Oral World and Written World: Ancient Israelite Literature*. Library of Ancient Israel. Louisville: Westminster John Knox, 1996.

Nikolakopoulos, Konstantin. "Aspekte der 'paulinischen Ironie' am Beispiel des Galaterbriefes." *BZ* 45 (2001) 193–208.

Nimis, Stephan A. "Ring-Composition and Linearity in Homer." In *Signs of Orality: The Oral Tradition and its Influence in the Greek and Roman World*, edited by E. Anne Mackay, 65–78. Mnemosyne Sup 188. Leiden: Brill, 1998.

Nordling, John G. "The Gospel in Philemon." *CTQ* 71 (2007) 71–83.

———. "Onesimus fugitivus: A Defense of the Runaway Slave Hypothesis in Philemon." *JSNT* 41 (1991) 97–119.

———. *Philemon*. Concordia Commentary. Saint Louis: Concordia, 2004.

———. "Philemon in the Context of Paul's Travels." *CTQ* 74 (2010) 289–305.

———. "Some Matters Favouring the Runaway Slave Hypothesis in Philemon." *Neot* 44/1 (2010) 85–121.

North, J. L. "Sowing and Reaping (Galatians 6:7b): More Examples of a Classical Maxim." *JTS* 43 (1992) 523–27.

Nygren, Anders. *Der Römerbrief*. Göttingen: Vandenhoeck & Ruprecht, 1951.

O'Brien, Peter T. *Colossians, Philemon*. WBC 44. Waco: Word, 1982.

Oesterreicher, Wulf. "Types of Orality in Text." In *Written Voices, Spoken Signs: Tradition, Performance, and the Epic Text*, edited by Egbert J. Bakker and Ahuvia Kahane, 190–214. Center for Hellenic Studies Colloquia. Cambridge: Harvard University Press, 1997.

Oestreich, Bernhard. "Argumentation für den Frieden in Römer 14,1—15,13." In *Glaube und Zukunftsgestaltung: Festschrift zum hundertjährigen Bestehen der Theologischen Hochschule Friedensau: Aufsätze zu Theologie, Sozialwissenschaften und Musik*, edited by Bernhard Oestreich et al., 95–127. Frankfurt: Lang, 1999.

———. "Ethnische und religöse Spannungen in der Gemeinde Rom." In *Ethnische und religiöse Identität*, edited by Horst Friedrich Rolly and Matthias Dauenhauer, 194–207. Spes Christiana, Beiheft 3. Friedensau: Theologische Hochschule Friedensau, 2000.

———. "Leseanweisungen in Briefen als Mittel der Gestaltung von Beziehungen (1 Thess 5.27)." *NTS* 50 (2004) 224-45.

Olbricht, Thomas H. "An Aristotelian Rhetorical Analysis of 1 Thessalonians." In *Greeks, Romans, and Christians: Essays in Honor of Abraham J. Malherbe*, edited by David L. Balch et al., 216-36. Minneapolis: Fortress, 1990.

———. "Classical Rhetorical Criticism and Historical Reconstructions: A Critique." In *The Rhetorical Interpretation of Scripture: Essays from the 1996 Malibu Conference*, edited by Stanley E. Porter and Dennis L. Stamps, 108-24. JSNTSup 180. Sheffield: Sheffield Academic Press, 1999.

———. "Delivery and Memory." In *Handbook of Classical Rhetoric in the Hellenistic Period 330 B.C.-A.D. 400*, edited by Stanley E. Porter, 159-69. Leiden: Brill, 1997.

Ollrog, Wolf-Henning. *Paulus und seine Mitarbeiter: Untersuchungen zu Theorie und Praxis der paulinischen Mission*. WMANT 50. Neukirchen-Vluyn: Neukirchener, 1979.

Olson, David R. *The World on Paper: The Conceptual and Cognitive Implications of Writing and Reading*. Cambridge: Cambridge University Press, 1994.

Olson, David R., and Nancy Torrance, eds. *Literacy and Orality*. Cambridge: Cambridge University Press, 1991.

Ong, Walter J. *Orality and Literacy: The Technologizing of the Word*. London: Methuen, 1982.

———. *The Presence of the Word: Some Prolegomena for Cultural and Religious History*. The Terry Lectures. New Haven: Yale University Press, 1967.

Os, Bas van. "The Jewish Recipients of Galatians." In *Paul: Jew, Greek, and Roman*, edited by Stanley E. Porter, 51-64. Pauline Studies 5. Leiden: Brill, 2008.

Paige, Terence. "1 Cor 12:2: A Pagan Pompe?" *JSNT* 44 (1991) 57-65.

Parry, Milman. *L' épithète traditionelle dans Homère: Essai sur un problème de style homérique*. Paris: Les Belles Lettres, 1928.

———. "Studies in the Epic Technique of Oral Verse-Making: I. Homer and the Homeric Style." *HSCP* 41 (1930) 73-147.

———. "Studies in the Epic Technique of Oral Verse-Making. II. The Homeric Language as the Language of Oral Poetry." *HSCP* 43 (1932) 1-50.

Parunak, H. Van Dyke. "Oral Typesetting: Some Uses of Biblical Structure." *Bib* 62 (1981) 153-68.

Paulsen, Hennig. *Die Briefe des Ingatius von Antiochia und der Brief des Polykarp von Smyrna*. HNT 18. Tübingen: Mohr, 1985.

Pearson, Birger A. "Did the Gnostics Curse Jesus?" *JBL* 84 (1967) 301-5.

Perelman, Chaim, and Lucie Olbrechts-Tyteca. *The New Rhetoric: A Treatise on Argumentation*. Notre Dame: University of Notre Dame Press, 1969 [French original: *La Nouvelle Rhéthorique: Traité de l'Argumentation*. Paris: Presses Universitaires de France, 1958].

Person, Raymond F., Jr. "The Ancient Israelite Scribe as Performer." *JBL* 117 (1998) 601-9.

Peterlin, Davorin. *Paul's Letter to the Philippians in the Light of Disunity in the Church*. NovTSup 79. Leiden: Brill, 1995.

Petersen, Norman R. *Rediscovering Paul: Philemon and the Sociology of Paul's Narrative World*. 1985 [reprinted, Eugene, OR: Wipf & Stock, 2008].

Philodemus. *Volumina Rhetorica*. Vol. 1. Edited by Siegfried Sudhaus. Leipzig: Teubner, 1892.

Philostratus of Lemnos. "De Epistolis." In *Ancient Epistolary Theorists*, compiled and translated by Abraham J. Malherbe, 42–43. SBLSBS 19. Atlanta: Scholars, 1988.

Flavii Philostrati. *Opera*. Edited by Carl Ludwig Kayser. 1870–71. Reprinted, Hildesheim: Olms, 1985.

Piras, Antonio. "γνήσιε σύζυγε in Phil 4,3 und seine gotische Übersetzung: Ein Beitrag zur Text- und Interpretationsgeschichte." *ZNW* 101 (2010) 78–92.

Plato. *Plato in Twelve Volumes*. Vol. 7, *Theaetetus. Sophist*. Translated by R. G. Bury. Cambridge: Harvard University Press, 1966.

———. *Werke in 8 Bänden: griechisch und deutsch*. Vol. 5, edited by Gunther Eigler. Darmstadt: Wissenschaftliche Buchgesellschaft, 1990.

Plinius Caecilius Secundus, Gaius. *Briefe [Epistularum libri decem]: Lateinisch - deutsch*, edited by Helmut Kasten. Sammlung Tusculum. Munich: Artemis, 1984.

Plutarch. *Moralia*. Vol. 1, *The Education of Children. How the Young Man Should Study Poetry. On Listening to Lectures. How to Tell a Flatterer from a Friend. How a Man May Become Aware of His Progress in Virtue*. Translated by Frank Cole Babbitt. LCL 197. Cambridge: Harvard University Press, 1927.

———. *Moralia*. Vol. 14, *That Epicurus Actually Makes a Pleasant Life Impossible. Reply to Colotes in Defense of the Other Philosophers. Is 'Live Unknown' a Wise Concept. On Music*. Translated by Benedict Einarson. LCL 428. Cambridge: Harvard University Press, 1967.

Pogoloff, Stephen Mark. *Logos and Sophia: The Rhetorical Situation of 1 Corinthians*. SBLDS 134. Atlanta: Scholars, 1992.

Pokorný, Petr. *Der Brief des Paulus an die Kolosser*. ThHKNT 10/1. Berlin: Evangelische Verlagsanstalt, 1987.

Porter, Stanley E. "Paul as Epistolographer *and* Rhetorican?" In *The Rhetorical Interpretation of Scripture: Essays from the 1996 Malibu Conference*, edited by Stanley E. Porter and Dennis L. Stamps, 222–248. JSNTSup 180. Sheffield: Sheffield Academic, 1999.

———. "The Theoretical Justification for Application of Rhetorical Categories to Pauline Epistolary Literature." In *Rhetoric and the New Testament: Essays from the 1992 Heidelberg Conference*, edited by Stanley E. Porter and Thomas H. Olbricht, 100–122. JSNTSup 90. Sheffield: Sheffield Academic, 1993.

Poster, Carol. "A Conversation Halved: Epistolary Theory in Graeco-Roman Antiquity." In *Letter-Writing Manuals and Instruction from Antiquity to the Present: Historical and Bibliographic Studies*, edited by Carol Poster and Linda C. Mitchell, 21–51. Studies in Rhetoric/Communication. Columbia: University of South Carolina Press, 2007.

Probst, Hermann. *Paulus und der Brief: Die Rhetorik des antiken Briefes als Form der paulinischen Korintherkorrespondenz (1 Kor 8–10)*. WUNT 2/45. Tübingen: Mohr, 1991.

Pseudo-Demetrius. "Formae Epistolicae." In *Demetrii et Libanii qui τύποι ἐπιστολικοί et ἐπιστολιμαῖοι χαρακτῆρες*, edited by Valentin Weichert. Leipzig: Teubner, 1910 [text and English translation also in Malherbe, comp. and trans., *Ancient Epistolary Theorists*, 30–41].

Pseudo-Libanius. "Characteres Epistolici." In *Demetrii et Libanii qui τύποι ἐπιστολικοί et ἐπιστολιμαῖοι χαρακτῆρες*, edited by Valentin Weichert. Leipzig: Teubner, 1910 [text and English translation also in Malherbe, comp. and trans., *Ancient Epistolary Theorists*, 66–81].

Quintilianus, Marcus Fabius. *Institutio Oratoria. Ausbildung des Redners: Zwölf Bücher.* Edited and translated by Helmut Rahn. 2 vols. Texte zur Forschung 2 und 3. Darmstadt: Wissenschaftliche Buchgesellschaft, 1995.

———. *Institutio Oratoria*, with an English translation by Harold Edgeworth Butler. LCL. Cambridge: Harvard University Press, 1922.

Raible, Wolfgang. *Kulturelle Perspektiven auf Schrift und Schreibprozesse: Elf Aufsätze zum Thema Mündlichkeit und Schriftlichkeit.* ScriptOralia 72. Tübingen: Narr, 1995.

———. *Medienwechsel: Erträge aus zwölf Jahren Forschung zum Thema 'Mündlichkeit und Schriftlichkeit.'* ScriptOralia 113. Tübingen: Narr, 1998.

———, ed. *Symbolische Formen, Medien, Identität: Jahrbuch 1989/90 des Sonderforschungsbereichs "Übergänge und Spannungsfelder zwischen Mündlichkeit und Schriftlichkeit."* ScriptOralia 37. Tübingen: Narr, 1991.

Ramsaran, Rollin A. "From Mind to Message: Oral Performance in 1 Corinthians 15." Paper read at SBL Annual Meeting, Atlanta 2003, https://www.sbl-site.org/assets/pdfs/ramsaran.pdf/ [accessed November 24, 2003].

Rauer, Max. *Die "Schwachen" in Korinth und Rom nach den Paulusbriefen.* Biblische Studien 21. Freiburg: Herder, 1923.

Reasoner, Mark. *The Strong and the Weak: Romans 14,1—15,13 in Context.* SNTSMS 103. Cambridge: Cambridge University Press, 1999.

Reck, Reinhold. *Kommunikation und Gemeindeaufbau: Eine Studie zu Entstehung, Leben und Wachstum paulinischer Gemeinden in den Kommunikationsstrukturen der Antike.* SBB 22. Stuttgart: Katholisches Bibelwerk, 1991.

Reed, Jeffrey T. "Are Paul's Thanksgivings 'Epistolary'?" *JSNT* 61 (1996) 87–99.

———. "Using Ancient Rhetorical Categories to Interpret Paul's Letters: A Question of Genre." In *Rhetoric and the New Testament: Essays from the 1992 Heidelberg Conference*, edited by Stanley E. Porter and Thomas H. Olbricht, 292–324. JSNTSup 90. Sheffield: Sheffield Academic, 1993.

Reid, Marty L. "Paul's Rhetoric of Mutuality: A Rhetorical Reading of Romans." *SBLSP* 34 (1995) 117–39.

Rhetores latini minores: ex codicibus maximam partem primum adhibitis. Edited by Karl Halm. Leipzig: Teubner, 1863.

Rhetorica ad Herennium: Lateinisch–deutsch. Edited and translated by Theodor Nüsslein. Sammlung Tusculum. Munich: Artemis & Winkler, 1994.

Rhoads, David. "Performance Criticism: An Emerging Methodology on Biblical Studies." Two parts. *BTB* 36 (2006) 118–33, 164–84.

———. *Reading Mark: Engaging the Gospel.* Minneapolis: Fortress, 2004.

———. "What Is Performance Criticism?" In *The Bible in Ancient and Modern Media: Story and Performance*, edited by Holly E. Hearon and Philip Ruge-Jones, 83–100. BPCS 1. Eugene, OR: Cascade Books, 2009.

Richards, E. Randolph. *Paul and First-Century Letter Writing: Secretaries, Composition and Collection.* Downers Grove, IL: Inter-Varsity, 2004.

———. *The Secretary in the Letters of Paul.* WUNT 2/42. Tübingen: Mohr, 1991.

Richardson, Peter. *Israel in the Apostolic Church.* SNTSMS 10. Cambridge: Cambridge University Press, 1969.

———. "Temples, Altars and Living from the Gospel (1 Cor. 9.12b–18)." In *Gospel in Paul: Studies in Corinthians, Galatians and Romans for Richard N. Longenecker,* edited by L. Ann Jervis and Peter Richardson, 89–110. JSNTSup 108. Sheffield: Sheffield Academic, 1994.

Riepl, Wolfgang. *Das Nachrichtenwesen des Altertums: Mit besonderer Berücksichtigung auf die Römer.* Leipzig: Teubner, 1913.

Robb, Kevin. *Literacy and Paideia in Ancient Greece.* New York: Oxford University Press, 1994.

Robbins, Vernon K. *Exploring the Texture of Texts: A Guide to Socio-Rhetorical Interpretation.* Harrisburg: Trinity, 1996.

———. "Rhetoric and Culture. Exploring Types of Cultural Rhetoric in a Text." In *Rhetoric and the New Testament: Essays from the 1992 Heidelberg Conference,* edited by Stanley E. Porter and Thomas H. Olbricht, 443–63. JSNTSup 90. Sheffield: Sheffield Academic, 1993.

———. "Rhetorical Analysis of Biblical Documents in the Past Decade with Special Focus upon the Seven 'Pepperdine' Conferences." Heidelberg Conference on Rhetorics, Ethics and Moral Persuasion in Biblical Discourse, 22–25 Juli 2002, http://www.ars-rhetorica.net/Queen/VolumeSpecialIssue2/Articles/Robbins.pdf/ [accessed November 24, 2003].

Robertson, Charles Kevin. *Conflict in Corinth: Redefining the System.* Studies in Biblical Literature 42. New York: Lang, 2001.

Rohde, Joachim. *Der Brief des Paulus an die Galater.* ThHKNT 9. Berlin: Evangelische Verlagsanstalt, 1989.

———. "Häresie und Schisma im ersten Clemensbrief und in den Ignatius-Briefen." *NovT* 10 (1968) 217–33.

Ropes, James Hardy. *The Singular Problem of the Epistle to the Galatians.* Harvard Theological Studies. Cambridge: Harvard University Press, 1929.

Saenger, Paul. "Silent Reading: Its Impact on Late Medieval Script and Society." *Viator* 13 (1982) 367–414.

———. *Space between Words: The Origins of Silent Reading.* Stanford: Stanford University Press, 1997.

Sampley, J. Paul. "Foreword: Ruminations Occasioned by the Publication of These Essays and the End of the Seminar." In *Paul and Rhetoric,* edited by J. Paul Sampley and Peter Lampe, ix–xvii. T. & T. Clark Biblical Studies. New York: T. & T. Clark, 2010.

———. "Paul's Frank Speech with the Galatians and the Corinthians." In *Philodemus and the New Testament World,* edited by John T. Fitzgerald et al., 295–321. NovTSup 111. Leiden: Brill, 2004.

———. "The Weak and the Strong: Paul's Careful and Crafty Rhetorical Strategy in Romans 14:1—15:13." In *The Social World of the First Christians: Essays in Honor of Wayne A. Meeks,* edited by Michael White and O. Larry Yarbrough, 40–52. Minneapolis: Fortress, 1995.

Sass, Gerhard. "Röm 15,7–13—als Summe des Römerbriefs gelesen." *EvT* 53 (1993) 510–27.

Sauter, Willmar. *The Theatrical Event: Dynamics of Performance and Perception.* Studies in Theatre History and Culture. Iowa City: University of Iowa Press, 2000.

Schäfer, Ruth. *Paulus bis zum Apostelkonzil: Ein Beitrag zur Einleitung in den Galaterbrief, zur Geschichte der Jesusbewegung und zur Pauluschronologie.* WUNT 2/179. Tübingen: Mohr/Siebeck, 2004.

Schechner, Richard. *Between Theater and Anthropology*. Philadelphia: University of Pennsylvania Press, 1985.

———. "Magnitudes of Performance." In *By Means of Performance: Intercultural Studies of Theatre and Ritual*, edited by Richard Schechner and Willa Appel, 19–49. Cambridge: Cambridge University Press, 1990.

Schewe, Susanne. *Die Galater zurückgewinnen: Paulinische Strategien in Galater 5 und 6*. FRLANT 208. Göttingen: Vandenhoeck & Ruprecht, 2005.

Schlatter, Adolf. *Paulus: Der Bote Jesu; Eine Deutung seiner Briefe an die Korinther*. Stuttgart: Calwer, 1969.

Schlier, Heinrich. *Der Brief an die Galater*. KEK 7. Göttingen: Vandenhoeck & Ruprecht, 1965.

———. *Der Römerbrief*. HThKNT 6. Freiburg: Herder, 1977.

Schmeller, Thomas. *Paulus und die "Diatribe": Eine vergleichende Stilinterpretation*. NTAbh 19. Münster: Aschendorff, 1987.

Schmidt, Hans Wilhelm. *Der Brief des Paulus an die Römer*. ThHKNT 6. Berlin: Evangelische Verlagsanstalt, 1962.

Schmithals, Walter. *Die Gnosis in Korinth: Eine Untersuchung zu den Korintherbriefen*. FRLANT NF 48. Göttingen: Vandenhoeck & Ruprecht, 1965.

———. *Der Römerbrief: Ein Kommentar*. Gütersloh: Gerd Mohn, 1988.

———. "Zur Abfassung und ältesten Sammlung der paulinischen Hauptbriefe." In *Paulus und die Gnostiker: Untersuchungen zu den kleinen Paulusbriefen*, 175–200. Theologische Forschung 35. Hamburg: Reich, 1965.

Schmitt, Tassilo. *Paroikie und Oikoumene: Sozial- und mentalgeschichtliche Untersuchungen zum 1. Clemensbrief*. BZNW 110. Berlin: de Gruyter, 2002.

Schneider, Nélio. *Die "Schwachen" in der christlichen Gemeinde Roms*. Theologie 5. Münster: Lit, 1996.

Schnelle, Udo. *Einleitung in das Neue Testament*. UTB 1830. Göttingen: Vandenhoeck & Ruprecht, 2002.

Schnider, Franz, and Werner Stenger. *Studien zum neutestamentlichen Briefformular*. NTTS 11. Leiden: Brill, 1987.

Schoedel, William R. *Die Briefe des Ignatius von Antiochien: Ein Kommentar*. Munich: Kaiser, 1990 [English original: *Ignatius of Antioch: A Commentary on the Letters of Ignatius of Antioch*. Hermeneia. Philadelphia: Fortress, 1985].

Schoon-Janssen, Johannes. "On the Use of Elements of Ancient Epistolography in 1 Thessalonians." In *The Thessalonians Debate: Methodological Discord or Methodological Synthesis?*, edited by Karl P. Donfried and Johannes Beutler, 179–93. Grand Rapids: Eerdmans, 2000.

———. *Umstrittene "Apologien" in den Paulusbriefen: Studien zur rhetorischen Situation des 1. Thessalonicherbriefes, des Galaterbriefes und des Philipperbriefes*. GTA 45. Göttingen: Vandenhoeck & Ruprecht, 1991.

Schrage, Wolfgang. *Der erste Brief an die Korinther: 1 Kor 11,17—14,40*. EKKNT 8/3. Zurich: Benzinger, 1999.

———. "Probleme paulinischer Ethik anhand von Gal 5,25—6,10." In *La foi agissant par l'amour (Galates 4,12—6,16)*, edited by Albert Vanhoye et al., 155–200. Série Monographique de "Benedictina", Section Biblio-Oecuménique 13. Rom: "Benedictina" Abbaye de S. Paul, 1996.

Schreiber, Alfred. *Die Gemeinde in Korinth: Versuch einer gruppendynamischen Betrachtung der Gemeinde von Korinth auf der Basis des ersten Korintherbriefes.* NTAbh 12. Münster: Aschendorff, 1977.

Schröter, Jens. *Erinnerung an Jesu Worte: Studien zur Rezeption der Logienüberlieferung in Markus, Q und Thomas.* WMANT 76. Neukirchen-Vluyn: Neukirchener, 1997.

Schumacher, Eckhard. "Performativität und Performance." In *Performanz: Zwischen Sprachphilosophie und Kulturwissenschaften,* edited by Uwe Wirth, 383–402. STW 1575. Frankfurt: Suhrkamp, 2002.

Searle, John R. *Speech Acts: An Essay in the Philosophy of Language.* Cambridge: Cambridge University Press, 1969.

Sellin, Gerhard. "Ästhetische Aspekte der Sprache in den Briefen des Paulus." In *Paulus und Johannes: Exegetische Studien zur paulinischen und johanneischen Theologie und Literatur,* edited by Dieter Sänger and Ulrich Mell, 411–26. WUNT 198. Tübingen: Mohr/Siebeck 2006.

Sellin, Gerhard, and Francois Vouga, eds. *Logos und Buchstabe: Mündlichkeit und Schriftlichkeit im Judentum und Christentum der Antike.* TANZ 20. Tübingen: Francke, 1997.

Seneca, L. Annaeus. *Philosophische Schriften,* vol. 3: *Ad Lucilium Epistulae Morales I–LXIX, An Lucilius Briefe über Ethik 1–69.* Translated, introduced and annotated by Manfred Rosenbach. Darmstadt: Wissenschaftliche Buchgesellschaft, 1999.

———. *Philosophische Schriften,* vol. 4: *Ad Lucilium Epistulae Morales LXX–CXXIV, [CXXV], An Lucilius Briefe 70–124, [125].* Translated, introduced and annotated by Manfred Rosenbach. Darmstadt: Wissenschaftliche Buchgesellschaft, 1999.

Shiell, William David. *Reading Acts: The Lector and the Early Christian Audience.* Biblical Interpretation Series 70. Leiden: Brill, 2004.

Shiner, Whitney. *Proclaiming the Gospel: First-Century Performance of Mark.* Harrisburg, PA: Trinity, 2003.

Shogren, Gary Steven. "'Is the Kingdom of God about Eating and Drinking or Isn't It' (Romans 14:17)." *NovT* 42 (2000) 238–56.

Siegert, Folker. *Argumentation bei Paulus—gezeigt an Röm 9–11.* WUNT 34. Tübingen: Mohr, 1985.

Silberman, Lou H., ed. *Orality, Aurality and Biblical Narrative. Semeia* 39. Decatur, GA: Scholars, 1987.

Simmel, Georg. *Soziologie: Untersuchungen über die Formen der Vergesellschaftung,* complete edition, vol. 2. STW 811. Frankfurt: Suhrkamp, 1992 [first published 1908].

Slusser, Michael. "Reading Silently in Antiquity." *JBL* 111 (1992) 499.

Small, Jocelyn Penny. *Wax Tablets of the Mind: Cognitive Studies in Memory and Literacy in Classical Antiquity.* London: Routledge, 1997.

Smit, Joop. "Argument and Genre of 1 Corinthians 12–14." In *Rhetoric and the New Testament: Essays from the 1992 Heidelberg Conference,* edited by Stanley E. Porter and Thomas H. Olbricht, 211–30. JSNTSup 90. Sheffield: Sheffield Academic, 1993.

———. "The Letter of Paul to the Galatians: A Deliberative Speech." *NTS* 35 (1989) 1–26.

Smit, Peter-Ben. "A Symposium in Rom. 14:17? A Note on Paul's Terminology." *NovT* 49 (2007) 40–53.

Snyder, H. G. *Teachers and Texts in the Ancient World: Philosophers, Jews and Christians.* Religion in the First Christian Centuries. London: Routledge, 2000.

Sofsky, Wolfgang, and Rainer Paris. *Figurationen sozialer Macht: Autorität, Stellvertretung, Koalition.* STW 1135. Frankfurt: Suhrkamp, 1994.

Sonkowsky, Robert P. "An Aspect of Delivery in Ancient Rhetorical Theory." *Transactions and Proceedings of the American Philological Association* 90 (1959) 256–74.

———. "Oral Interpretation of Classical Latin Literature." In *Performance of Literature in Historical Perspectives,* edited by David William Thompson et al., 31–65. Lanham, MD: University Press of America, 1983.

———. "Oral Performance and Ancient Greek Literature." In *Performance of Literature in Historical Perspectives,* edited by David William Thompson et al., 1–30. Lanham, MD: University Press of America, 1983.

Stamps, Dennis L. "Rhetorical Criticism of the New Testament: Ancient and Modern Evaluations of Argumentation." In *Approaches to New Testament Study,* edited by Stanley E. Porter and David Tombs, 129–69. JSNTSup 120. Sheffield: Sheffield Academic, 1995.

———. "The Theological Rhetoric of Pauline Epistles: Prolegomenon." In *The Rhetorical Interpretation of Scripture: Essays from the 1996 Malibu Conference,* edited by Stanley E. Porter and Dennis L. Stamps, 249–59. JSNTSup 180. Sheffield: Sheffield Academic, 1999.

Standaert, Benoît. "Analyse rhétorique des chapitres 12 à 14 de 1 Co." In *Charisma und Agape (1 Co 12–14),* edited by Lorenzo De Lorenzi, 23–50. Monographic Series of "Benedictina," Biblical-ecumenical section 7. Rome: Abtei von St Paul vor den Mauern, 1983.

Standhartinger, Angela. *Studien zur Entstehungsgeschichte und Intention des Kolosserbriefs.* NovTSup 94. Leiden: Brill, 1999.

Stanley, Christopher D. "'Under a Curse': A Fresh Reading of Galatians 3.10–14." *NTS* 36 (1990) 481–511.

Starr, Raymond J. "Reading Aloud: Lectores and Roman Reading." *CJ* 86 (1991) 337–43.

Stegemann, Ekkehard W., and Wolfgang Stegemann. *Urchristliche Sozialgeschichte: Die Anfänge im Judentum und die Christusgemeinden in der mediterranen Welt.* Stuttgart: Kohlhammer, 1995 [English translation: *The Jesus Movement: A Social History of its First Century.* Translated by O. C. Dean Jr. Minneapolis: Fortress, 1999].

Stirewalt, M. Luther. *Paul, the Letter Writer.* Grand Rapids: Eerdmans, 2003.

———. *Studies in Ancient Greek Epistolography.* SBLRBS 27. Atlanta: Scholars, 1993.

Stolz, Benjamin A., and Richard S. Shannon III, eds. *Oral Literature and the Formula.* Ann Arbor: Center for the Coordination of Ancient and Modern Studies, University of Michigan, 1976.

Stowers, Stanley Kent. *The Diatribe and Paul's Letter to the Romans.* SBLDS 57. Chico, CA: Scholars, 1981.

———. *Letter Writing in Greco-Roman Antiquity.* LEC 5. Philadelphia: Westminster, 1986.

Strack, Hermann L., and Paul Billerbeck. *Kommentar zum Neuen Testament aus Talmud und Midrasch.* Vol 3. Munich: Beck, 1979.

Strange, James F. "Ancient Texts, Archaeology as Text, and the Problem of the First-Century Synagogue." In *Evolution of the Synagogue: Problems and Progress,* edited by Howard Clark Kee and Lynn H. Cohick, 27–45. Harrisburg: Trinity, 1999.

Strelan, J. G. "Burden-Bearing and the Law of Christ: A Re-Examination of Galatians 6.2." *JBL* 94 (1975) 266-76.
Stuhlmacher, Peter. "Der Abfassungszweck des Römerbriefs." *ZNW* 77 (1986) 180-93.
———. *Der Brief an Philemon*. EKKNT 18. Zurich: Benziger, 1981.
———. *Der Brief an die Römer*. NTD 6. Göttingen: Vandenhoeck & Ruprecht, 1989.
Suetonius Tranquillus, Gaius. *Werke in einem Band: Kaiserbiographien über berühmte Männer*, introduced and annotated by Werner Krenkel, from the Latin translated by Adolf Stahr and Werner Krenkel. Bibliothek der Antike: Römische Reihe. Berlin: Aufbau, 1965.
Suhl, Alfred. *Paulus und seine Briefe: Ein Beitrag zur paulinischen Chronologie*. SNT 11. Gütersloh: Mohn, 1975.
Sumney, Jerry L. *Identifying Paul's Opponents: The Question of Method in 2 Corinthians*. JSNTSup 40. Sheffield: JSOT Press, 1990.
———. *'Servants of Satan', 'False Brothers' and Other Opponents of Paul*. JSNTSup 188. Sheffield: Sheffield Academic, 1999.
———. "Studying Paul's Opponents: Advances and Challenges." In *Paul and His Opponents*, edited by Stanley E. Porter, 7-58. Pauline Studies 2. Leiden: Brill, 2005.
Surburg, Mark P. "Ancient Rhetorical Criticism, Galatians, and Paul at Twenty-five Years." *Concordia Journal* 30 (2004) 13-39.
Svenbro, Jesper. "Phrasikleia—An Archaic Theory of Writing." In *Literacy and Society*, edited by Karen Schousboe and Mogens Trolle Larsen, 229-46. Copenhagen: Akademisk, 1989.
Sykutris, Johannes. "Epistolographie." In *Pauly's Real-Encyclopädie der Classischen Altertumswissenschaft, Suppl.* Vol. 5, 185-220. Stuttgart: Metzler, 1931.
Tannen, Deborah. "The Oral/Literate Continuum in Discourse." In *Spoken and Written Language: Exploring Orality and Literacy*, edited by Deborah Tannen, 1-16. Advances in Discourse Processes 9. Norwood, NJ: Ablex, 1982.
Taussig, Hal. *In the Beginning Was the Meal: Social Experimentation and Early Christian Identity*. Minneapolis: Fortress, 2009.
Theissen, Gerd. "Soziale Integration und sakramentales Handeln: Eine Analyse von 1 Cor. XI 17-34." In *Studien zur Soziologie des Urchristentums*, 290-317. WUNT 19. Tübingen: Mohr, 1989.
———. *Social Reality and the Early Christians: Theology, Ethics, and the World of the New Testament*. Translated by Margaret Kohl. Minneapolis: Fortress, 1992.
———. "Soziale Schichtung in der korinthischen Gemeinde." In *Studien zur Soziologie des Urchristentums*, 231-71. WUNT 19. Tübingen: Mohr, 1989.
———. "Die Starken und die Schwachen in Korinth. Soziologische Analyse eines theologischen Streites." In *Studien zur Soziologie des Urchristentums*, 272-89. WUNT 19. Tübingen: Mohr, 1989.
Theon, Aelius. *Progymnasmata: Greek Textbooks of Prose Composition and Rhetoric*. Translated with introduction and notes by George A. Kennedy. Writings from the Graeco-Roman World 10. Leiden: Brill, 2003.
Thiselton, Anthony C. *The First Epistle to the Corinthians*. NIGTC. Grand Rapids: Eerdmans, 2000.
Thomas, Rosalind. *Literacy and Orality in Ancient Greece*. Key Themes in Ancient History. Cambridge: Cambridge University Press, 1992.
Thompson, David William et al., eds. *Performance of Literature in Historical Perspectives*. Lanham, MD: University Press of America, 1983.

Thompson, Paul. *The Voice of the Past: Oral History*. Oxford: Oxford University Press, 1988.

Thorsteinsson, Runar M. *Paul's Interlocutor in Romans 2: Function and Identity in the Context of Ancient Epistolography*. ConBNT 40. Stockholm: Almqvist & Wiksell, 2003.

Thraede, Klaus. *Grundzüge griechisch-römischer Brieftopik*. Zetemata 48. Munich: Beck, 1970.

Thucydides. *Geschichte des Peloponnesischen Krieges: Griechisch–deutsch*. Translated and introduced by Georg Peter Landmann. Darmstadt: Wissenschaftliche Buchgesellschaft, 1993.

Thurén, Lauri. *Argument and Theology in 1 Peter: The Origins of Christian Paraenesis*. JSNTSup 114. Sheffield: Sheffield Academic, 1995.

———. *Derhetorizing Paul: A Dynamic Perspective on Pauline Theology and the Law*. WUNT 124. Tübingen: Mohr/Siebeck, 2000 [reprinted, Harrisburg, PA: Trinity, 2002].

———. *The Rhetorical Strategy of 1 Peter: With Special Regard to Ambiguous Expressions*. Åbo: Åbo Akademis, 1990.

———. "Was Paul Angry? Derhetorizing Galatians." In *The Rhetorical Interpretation of Scripture: Essays from the 1996 Malibu Conference*, edited by Stanley E. Porter and Dennis L. Stamps, 302–20. JSNTSup 180. Sheffield: Sheffield Academic, 1999.

Tolmie, D. Francois. *Persuading the Galatians: A Text-Centered Rhetorical Analysis of a Pauline Letter*. WUNT 2, 190. Tübingen: Mohr/Siebeck, 2005.

Trobisch, David. *Die Entstehung der Paulusbriefsammlung: Studien zu den Anfängen christlicher Publizistik*. NTOA 10. Freiburg, Switzerland: Universitäts-Verlag, 1989.

Tsang, Sam. "Are We 'Misreading' Paul? Oral Phenomena and Their Implication for the Exegesis of Paul's Letters." *Oral Tradition* 24 (2009) 205–25.

Tyson, Joseph B. "Paul's Opponents in Galatia." *NovT* 10 (1968) 241–54.

Ueding, Gert. *Klassische Rhetorik*. Munich: Beck, 1995.

Unnik, Willem C. van. "Jesus: Anathema or Kyrios (1 Cor. 12: 3)." In *Christ and the Spirit in the New Testament*, edited by Barnabas Lindars and Stephen S. Smalley, 113–26. Cambridge: Cambridge University Press, 1973.

———. "Studies on the So-Called First Epistle of Clement. The Literary Genre." In *Encounters with Hellenism: Studies on the First Letter of Clement*, edited by Cilliers Breytenbach and Laurence L. Welborn, 115–81. AGJU 53. Leiden: Brill, 2004 [Dutch original: *Studies over de zogenaamde Eerste Brief van Clemens*, Chapter I: Het Litteraire Genre. Amsterdam: Noord-Hollandsche Uitg. Mij., 1970].

Vansina, Jan. *Oral Tradition as History*. London: Currey, 1985.

Vatz, Richard. "The Myth of the Rhetorical Situation." *Philosophy and Rhetoric* 6 (1973) 154–61.

Vegge, Tor. *Paulus und das antike Schulwesen: Schule und Bildung des Paulus*. BZNW 134. Berlin: de Gruyter, 2006.

Venetz, Hermann-Josef. "Stephanas, Fortunatus, Achaikus, Epaphroditus, Epaphras, Onesimus & Co: Die Frage nach den Gemeindevertretern und Gemeindegesandten in den paulinischen Gemeinden." In *Peregrini Curiositas: Eine Reise durch den orbis antiquus: Zu Ehren von Dirk van Dramme*, edited by Andreas Kessler et al., 13–28. NTOA 27. Freiburg, Switzerland: Universitätsverlag, 1994.

Vogt-Spira, Gregor, ed. *Strukturen der Mündlichkeit in der römischen Literatur*. ScriptOralia, Altertumswissenschaftliche Reihe 4. Tübingen: Narr, 1990.

Voorst, Robert E. van. "Why Is There No Thanksgiving Period in Galatians? An Assessment of an Exegetical Commonplace." *JBL* 129 (2010) 153–72.
Vos, Johan S. "Das Rätsel von 1 Kor 12:1–3." *NovT* 35 (1993) 251–69.
Vouga, François. *An die Galater*. HNT 10. Tübingen: Mohr/Siebeck, 1998.
———. "Der Galaterbrief: kein Brief an die Galater? Essay über den literarischen Charakter des letzten grossen Paulusbriefes." In *Schrift und Tradition: Festschrift für Josef Ernst zum 70. Geburtstag*, edited by Knut Backhaus and Franz Georg Untergassmair, 243–58. Paderborn: Schöningh, 1996.
———. "Zur rhetorischen Gattung des Galaterbriefes." *ZNW* 79 (1988) 291–92.
Wagner, Andreas. "Bote, Botenformel und Brief – einige sachliche und terminologische Klärungen." In *Bote und Brief: Sprachliche Systeme der Informationsübermittlung im Spannungsfeld von Mündlichkeit und Schriftlichkeit*, edited by Andreas Wagner, 1–10. Nordostafrikanisch/Westasiatische Studien 4. Frankfurt: Lang, 2003.
Wagner, J. Ross. "The Christ, Servant of Jew and Gentile: A Fresh Approach to Romans 15:8–9." *JBL* 116 (1997) 473–85.
Walter, Nikolaus. "Paulus und die Gegner des Christusevangeliums in Galatien." In *L'Apôtre Paul: Personnalité, Style et Conception du Ministère*, edited by A. Vanhoye, 351–56. BETL 73. Leuven: Leuven University Press, 1986.
Walters, James. *Ethnic Issues in Paul's Letter to the Romans: Changing Self-Definition in Early Roman Christianity*. Valley Forge, PA: Trinity, 1993.
Wanamaker, C. A. *The Epistles to the Thessalonians: A Commentary on the Greek Text*. NIGTC. Grand Rapids: Eerdmans, 1990.
Ward, Richard F. "Pauline Voices and Presence as Strategic Communication." In *Orality and Textuality in Early Christian Literature*, edited by Joanna Dewey, 95–107. Semeia 65. Atlanta: Scholars, 1995.
Warning, Rainer. *Rezeptionsästhetik: Theorie und Praxis*. Munich: Fink, 1975.
Watson, Duane F. "The Contributions and Limitations of Greco-Roman Rhetorical Theory for Constructing the Rhetorical and Historical Situations of a Pauline Epistle." In *The Rhetorical Interpretation of Scripture: Essays from the 1996 Malibu Conference*, edited by Stanley E. Porter and Dennis L. Stamps, 125–51. JSNTSup 180. Sheffield: Sheffield Academic, 1999.
———. *Invention, Arrangement, and Style: Rhetorical Criticism of Jude and 2 Peter*. SBLDS 104. Atlanta: Scholars, 1988.
———. "A Rhetorical Analysis of 2 John according to Greco-Roman Convention." *NTS* 35 (1989) 104–30.
———. "Rhetorical Criticism of the Pauline Epistles since 1975." *CurBS* 3 (1995) 219–48.
Watson, Duane F., and Alan J. Hauser. *Rhetorical Criticism of the Bible: A Comprehensive Bibliography with Notes on History and Method*. Biblical Interpretation Series 4. Leiden: Brill, 1994.
Watson, Janet, ed. *Speaking Volumes: Orality and Literacy in the Greek and Roman World*. Mnemosyne Sup 218. Leiden: Brill, 2001.
Weiss, Harold. "Paul and the Judging of Days." *ZNW* 86 (1995) 137–53.
Weiss, Johannes. "Beiträge zur paulinischen Rhetorik." In *Theologische Studien: Herrn Wirkl. Oberkonsistorialrath Professor D. Bernhard Weiss zu seinem 70. Geburtstage dargebracht*, edited by Caspar René Gregory et al., 165–247. Göttingen: Vandenhoeck & Ruprecht, 1897.

Weissenrieder, Annette, and Robert B. Coote. *The Interface of Orality and Writing: Speaking, Seeing, Writing in the Shaping of New Genres*. WUNT 260. Tübingen: Mohr/Siebeck, 2010.

Welborn, Laurence L. "The Date of First Clement." *Biblical Research* 19 (1985) 34–54. Reprinted as "The Preface to 1 Clement: The Rhetorical Situation and the Traditional Date." In *Encounters with Hellenism: Studies on the First Letter of Clement*, edited by Cilliers Breytenbach and Laurence L. Welborn, 197–216. AGJU 53. Leiden: Brill, 2004.

Wendland, Ernst R. *Finding and Translating the Oral-Aural Elements in Written Language: The Case of the New Testament Epistles*. Lewiston, NY: Mellen, 2008.

———. *LiFE-style Translating: A Workbook for Bible Translators*. SIL Publications in Translation and Textlinguistics 2. Dallas: SIL, 2006.

Wengst, Klaus. *Der Brief an Philemon*. Theologischer Kommentar zum Neuen Testament 16. Stuttgart: Kohlhammer, 2005.

White, John L. "Ancient Greek Letters." In *Greco-Roman Literature and the New Testament: Selected Forms and Genres*, edited by David E. Aune, 85–105. SBLSBS 21. Atlanta: Scholars, 1988.

———. *The Form and Function of the Body of the Greek Letter: A Study of the Letter-Body in the Non-Literary Papyri and in Paul the Apostle*. SBLDS 2. Missoula: Scholars, 1972.

———. *Light from Ancient Letters*. FF. Philadelphia: Fortress, 1986.

———. "New Testament Epistolary Literature in the Framework of Ancient Epistolography." *ANRW* II 25.2 (1984) 1730–56.

———. "Saint Paul and the Apostolic Letter Tradition." *CBQ* 45 (1983) 433–44.

Wick, Peter. *Die urchristlichen Gottesdienste: Entstehung und Entwicklung im Rahmen der frühjüdischen Tempel-, Synagogen- und Hausfrömmigkeit*. BWA(N)T 150. Stuttgart: Kohlhammer, 2002.

Wickert, Ulrich. "Der Philemonbrief – Privatbrief oder Apostolisches Schreiben?" *ZNW* 52 (1961) 230–38.

Wiefel, Wolfgang. "Die jüdische Gemeinschaft im antiken Rom und die Anfänge des römischen Christentums: Bemerkungen zu Anlass und Zweck des Römerbriefs." *Jud* 26 (1970) 65–88.

Wilckens, Ulrich. *Der Brief an die Römer*. 3 vols. EKKNT 6. Zurich: Benziger, 1978, 1980, 1982.

———. "Über Abfassungszweck und Aufbau des Römerbriefs." In *Rechtfertigung als Freiheit: Paulusstudien*, 110–70. Neukirchen-Vluyn: Neukirchener, 1974.

Wilder, Amos. *The Language of the Gospel: Early Christian Rhetoric*. New York: Harper & Row, 1964.

Wilhelmi, Gerhard. "ἀλλάξαι τὴν φωνήν μου (Gal 4,20)." *ZNW* 65 (1974) 151–54.

Wilke, Christian Gottlob. *Die neutestamentliche Rhetorik: Ein Seitenstück zur Grammatik des neutestamentlichen Sprachidioms*. Dresden und Leipzig: Arnoldische Buchhandlung, 1843.

Winter, Bruce W. "Civic Obligations: Galatians 6:11–18." In *Seek the Welfare of the City: Christians as Benefactors and Citizens*, 123–44. First-Century Christians in the Graeco-Roman World. Grand Rapids: Eerdmans, 1994.

———. "The Imperial Cult and Early Christians in Pisidian Antioch (Acts XIII 13–50)." In *Actes du 1er Congrès International sur Antioche de Pisidie*, edited by

Thomas Drew-Bear et al., 67–75. Collection Archéologie et Histoire de L'Antiquité, Université Lumière-Lyon 2.5. Lyon: Université Lumière-Lyon, 2002.

———. *Philo and Paul among the Sophists.* SNTSMS 96. Cambridge: Cambridge University Press, 1997.

———. "Philodemus and Paul on Rhetorical Delivery (hypocrisis)." In *Philodemus and the New Testament World,* edited by John T. Fitzgerald et al., 323–42. NovTSup 111. Leiden: Brill, 2004.

Winter, Sara B. C. "Methodological Observations on a New Interpretation of Paul's Letter to Philemon." *USQR* 39 (1984) 203–12.

———. "Paul's Letter to Philemon." *NTS* 33 (1987) 1–15.

Wire, Antoinette Clark. *The Case for Mark Composed in Performance.* BPCS 3. Eugene, OR: Cascade Books, 2011.

———. *The Corinthian Women Prophets: A Reconstruction through Paul's Rhetoric.* Minneapolis: Fortress, 1990.

———. "Performance, Politics, and Power: A Response." In *Orality and Textuality in Early Christian Literature,* edited by Joanna Dewey, 129–35. Semeia 65. Atlanta: Scholars, 1995.

Witherington, Ben III. *Conflict and Community in Corinth: A Socio-Rhetorical Commentary on 1 and 2 Corinthians.* Grand Rapids: Eerdmans, 1995.

———. *Grace in Galatia: A Commentary on St Paul's Letter to the Galatians.* Edinburgh: T. & T. Clark, 1998.

———. *The Letters to Philemon, the Colossians, and the Ephesians: A Socio-Rhetorical Commentary on the Captivity Epistles.* Grand Rapids: Eerdmans, 2007.

Witulski, Thomas. *Die Adressaten des Galaterbriefes: Untersuchungen zur Gemeinde von Antiochia ad Pisidiam.* FRLANT 193. Göttingen: Vandenhoeck & Ruprecht, 2000.

Wolff, Christian. *Der erste Brief des Paulus an die Korinther.* ThHKNT 7. Leipzig: Evangelische Verlagsanstalt, 2000.

———. *Der zweite Brief des Paulus an die Korinther.* ThHKNT 8. Berlin: Evangelische Verlagsanstalt, 1989.

Wolter, Michael. *Der Brief an die Kolosser. Der Brief an Philemon.* Ökumenischer Taschenbuchkommentar zum Neuen Testament 12. Gütersloh: Gerd Mohn, 1993.

———. "Ethos und Identität in paulinischen Gemeinden." *NTS* 43 (1997) 430–44.

Woolf, Greg. "Literacy or Literacies in Rome?" In *Ancient Literacies: The Culture of Reading in Greece and Rome,* edited by William A. Johnson and Holt N. Parker, 46–68. Oxford: Oxford University Press, 2009.

Wuellner, Wilhelm. "The Argumentative Structure of 1 Thessalonians as Paradoxical Encomium." In *The Thessalonian Correspondence,* edited by Raymond F. Collins, 117–36. BETL 87. Leuven: Leuven University Press, 1990.

———. "Greek Rhetoric and Pauline Argumentation." In *Early Christian Literature and the Classical Intellectual Tradition: In Honorem Robert M. Grant,* edited by W. R. Schoedel and R. L. Wilken, 177–88. Théologie Historique 54. Paris: Beauchesne, 1979.

———. "Hermeneutics and Rhetorics: From 'Truth and Method' to 'Truth and Power.'" Special issue 3, *Scriptura.* Stellenbosch: University of Stellenbosch, 1989.

———. "Paul as Pastor: The Function of Rhetorical Questions in First Corinthians." In *L'Apôtre Paul: Personnalité, Style et Conception du Ministère,* edited by A. Vanhoye, 49–77. BETL 73. Leuven: Leuven University Press, 1986.

———. "Paul's Rhetoric of Argumentation in Romans: An Alternative to the Donfried-Karris Debate over Romans." *CBQ* 38 (1976) 330–51.

———. "Rhetorical Criticism and its Theory in Culture-Critical Perspective." In *Text and Interpretation: New Approaches in the Criticism of the New Testament*, edited by Patrick J. Hartin and Jacobus H. Petzer, 171–85. NTTS 15. Leiden: Brill, 1991.

———. "Where Is Rhetorical Criticism Taking Us?" *CBQ* 49 (1987) 448–63.

Yaghjian, Lucretia B. "Ancient Reading." In *The Social Sciences and New Testament Interpretation*, edited by Richard L. Rohrbaugh, 206–30. Peabody, MA: Hendrickson, 1996.

Author Index

Achtemeier, Paul J., 37n153, 72n292, 75n310
Albright, William F., 196n126
Aldrete, Gregory S., 26n91, 77n327, 78n331, 85n360, 87n364, 91n376, 260n127
Alexander, Loveday, 4n10, 8n5, 37n154, 71n288, 72n294
Amador, J. David Hester, 28n103, 29n110, 47n201
Andersen, Øivind, 93n384
Anderson, Roger Dean, 18nn56–57, 19n59, 20n61, 20n64, 22n75, 23n81, 25nn86–87
Andresen, Carl, 14n35
Arzt, Peter, 8n5
Arzt-Grabner, Peter, 129n75, 138n100, 140n104
Assmann, Aleida, 32n121, 32n125, 34n129, 37n150
Assmann, Jan, 32n121, 32n125, 34n129, 37n150, 37n155
Aune, David E., 11n20, 13n31, 14n33, 14n35, 20n65, 21n66
Austin, John L., 52–54, 62, 186

Bachmann, Philipp, 210
Bahn, Eugene, 44n183, 75n310, 92n383
Bahr, Gordon J., 8n5, 11n17, 12n24

Bailey, Kenneth D., 45n192
Bakke, Odd Magne, 17n52, 259n120, 261, 262n139
Bakker, Egbert J., 35n138, 37n150
Balogh, Josef, 37n153
Barba, Eugenio, 56n232
Barclay, John M. G., 101nn16–17, 217n172, 219–20, 221n184, 224n195, 227n206, 229n1, 232n17, 234n23, 239n48, 242n65, 253n104
Bar-Ilan, Meir, 37n151, 74n303
Barrett, C. K., 197n131
Bartsch, Hans-Werner, 99n5, 158n20
Bartsch, Shadi, 260n127
Bassler, Jouette M., 198n135
Bateson, Gregory, 58
Bauman, Richard, 37n150, 51–53, 55, 57–59, 61–64, 136
Baumann, Jürgen, 37n150
Beacham, Richard C., 76n316, 78n331
Becker, Eve-Marie, 20n64, 25n88
Becker, Jürgen, 101n17, 146nn129–30, 148n139, 149n140, 149n143, 219n177, 221n184, 221n187, 223n193, 225n200, 235n27, 240n53, 242n64, 247n81, 253n99, 257n118
Berger, Klaus, 8n3, 20n66, 24, 24n84

Best, Ernest, 106n26, 212–13, 212n161
Betz, Hans-Dieter, 17, 19, 20n61, 24, 27, 28n106, 85n359, 101n17, 146n129, 148n137, 148n139, 149n142, 220n180, 222n190, 229n1, 229n4, 231n11, 234n22, 239n43, 240nn49–50, 244n70
Bieberstein, Sabine, 130n76, 131n82
Billerbeck, Paul, 251n91
Binder, Herrmann, 130n76, 131n82, 139n101, 139n103
Birge, Mary K., 88n367
Bitzer, Lloyd F., 29
Black, C. Clifton, 17n51
Blass, Friedrich, 253n105
Boedeker, Deborah, 32n121
Bohle, Ulrike, 53n221
Bollinger, T., 76n315
Bonner, Stanley F., 71n291, 78n331
Boomershine, Thomas E., 39n169, 40n171, 41, 51, 70
Borse, Udo, 223n193
Bosenius, Bärbel, 25n88
Botha, J. Eugene, 30, 85n360
Botha, Pieter J. J., 4n10, 12n24, 15n41, 28n105, 37n153, 40n171, 48, 71n284, 73n301, 74nn303–4, 111n34, 233n21
Bowman, Alan K., 74n305
Brecht, Bertolt, 142–44
Breytenbach, Cilliers, 39n170, 237n35
Brown, Raymond E., 163n41
Brox, Norbert, 197n132
Bruce, Frederick, 101n17, 148n139, 221n187, 227n206, 235n27, 240n53
Bultmann, Rudolf, 176n66, 189n108
Bünker, Michael, 2n5, 11n18, 21n67
Burfeind, Carsten, 37n153
Byrne, Brendan, 158n21, 163n38, 178n72, 185n99, 187n101
Byrskog, Samuel, 2n5, 20n64, 37n155, 112, 283n14

Campbell, Douglas A., 88n365
Carlson, Marvin, 52n220, 56n232, 58n239, 64nn264–65, 64nn267–68, 65n272, 66n273, 136n97

Carr, David M., 37n154
Celentano, M. S., 23n81
Chadwick, Henry, 262n142, 265n148, 272n174
Chow, John K., 146n128
Clark, W. P., 37n153
Clarke, Andrew D., 118
Classen, Carl Joachim, 16n43, 18n56, 19n59, 20n64, 178n75
Claussen, Carsten, 76, 77n321
Conring, Barbara, 8n3
Coote, Robert B., 34n130, 40n171, 41n177
Cox, Claude E., 13n30, 73n301, 74n308
Crafton, Jeffrey A., 19n58, 99n5, 161n32, 163nn40–41, 188n107
Culley, Robert C., 38n157
Cullmann, Oscar, 197n130, 207n152

Dabourne, Wendy, 20n65, 40n175
Das, A. Andrew, 232n15, 233n20, 241n59, 245n72
Davis, Casey Wayne, 40
Dean, Margaret E., 5n15, 30, 75n311, 83n352
Debrunner, Albert, 253n105
Dederen, Raoul, 169n53
Deissmann, Adolf, 7–8, 14
Derrett, J. Duncan M., 129n74, 197n129
Derrida, Jaques, 64n267
Dewey, Arthur J., 39n169, 47n199, 107n29
Dewey, Joanna, 34n131, 40n171, 41n177, 71n284, 71nn289–90, 74n305, 74n308, 75n313
Dibelius, Martin, 219n179
Dix, Gregory, 237n35
Doan, William J., 41n179, 51n214
Donfried, Karl Paul, 99n2
Dormeyer, Detlev, 3n9, 14n35, 24n82
Doty, William G., 8n2, 8n4, 10nn14–15, 11n17, 14n35, 78n336
Downing, F. Gerald, 71n286, 71n290
Draper, Jonathan A., 40n171, 48, 70n283, 81
Du Toit, A. B., 234nn22–23, 249n88
Dunn, James D. G., 39n170, 127n66, 128, 129n70, 129n75, 130n77,

Author Index

130n80, 132n85, 138n100, 139n101, 140n104, 147, 197n132, 221n184, 221nn187–88, 223n194, 227n207, 229n1, 231n9, 232, 236n31, 240n50

Eckert, Jost, 219n179, 221n184, 221n187, 223n194, 244n70
Eigler, Gunther, 191n115
Elliott, Neil, 19n58
Elliott, Susan, 254n106
Ellis, E. Earle, 105n26, 211n157, 212n159, 283n14
Elmer, Ian J., 101n16
Epp, Eldon J., 73n300
Erlemann, Kurt, 259n120
Esler, Philip F., 6n15, 103, 106, 176n68, 235n27, 237n35, 240n51

Fantham, Elaine, 3n9
Farrell, Thomas J., 38n157
Finnegan, Ruth, 32n122, 34, 35n139, 36n141, 71n285
Fischer-Lichte, Erika, 54, 55, 56n233, 59n243, 60, 61n256, 62, 65nn269–70, 66n275, 67n275, 69, 84n358, 86n362, 136nn97–98, 186
Fitzgerald, John T., 11n20
Fitzmeyer, Joseph A., 129n70, 129n75
Foley, John Miles, 5, 34n129, 35–37, 41, 48, 57–58, 59n245, 64, 68, 71n285, 80–81, 94, 178, 181n81, 275n1, 279n5, 281–82
Forbes, Christopher, 197n131
Frede, Dorothea, 4n10
Friedrich, Gerhard, 102n19
Frilingos, Chris, 129n70, 129n75, 130nn77–78, 132n85
Fuhrmann, Manfred, 3n9, 25n87, 26n90, 34n131, 78n334, 103n23, 123n62
Funk, Robert W., 8n6, 10n16, 13n31, 29n107, 38, 39n166, 48n203, 72n295

Gäckle, Volker, 99nn1–2, 99nn5–6, 154nn10–11, 158n22, 159nn24–25, 160n26, 163nn37–39, 164nn42–43, 169nn52–53, 173n58, 174n64, 182n87, 187n101
Gagarin, Michael, 22n71
Gamble, Harry Y., 37n154, 71n285, 74n303, 75
Gardner, Jane F., 118n47
Gärtner, Hans A., 83n355
Gaventa, Beverly R., 148n135
Georgi, Dieter, 40n176, 41n176, 101n14
Gerhardsson, Birger, 37n155, 39n170, 77n322
Gestrich, Christof, 168n50, 189n109
Giles, Terry, 41n179, 51n214
Gilliard, Frank D., 37n153
Giomini, Remo, 23n81
Given, Mark D., 86n361
Gleason, Maud, 84n357
Godet, Frédéric, 160n28, 178n72
Goetsch, Paul, 32n125
Goffman, Erving, 58
Goldhill, Simon, 71n285
Goldstein, Jonathan A., 25n85
Goody, Jack, 32, 33n128
Graham, William A., 38n157
Günther, Hartmut, 37n150
Güttgemanns, Erhardt, 14n35, 38n158, 39n170

Haacker, Klaus, 99n5, 153n4, 160n28, 187n10
Habinek, Thomas, 20n62, 71n285, 74n306
Hackforth, Reginald, 191n114
Hájek, Milan, 124n65
Hall, Robert G., 19n59
Halverson, John, 39n169
Hansen, G. Walter, 19n59, 251n94
Hardin, Justin K., 234n25, 235n26, 235n29, 239n45, 239n48, 242n64, 252n96, 253n104, 257n116
Hardmeier, Christoph, 41n179
Harnack, Adolf von, 259n120, 259n122, 259n124, 260n128, 260n132, 261, 262n142, 266n152

Harnisch, Wolfgang, 221n188, 226n202, 238n42, 255n112
Harris, William V., 37n151, 71n287, 71n291, 74nn303–4, 74n308
Hartman, D. 8n5
Hartman, Lars, 129n70
Harvey, A. E., 240n51
Harvey, John D., 5n15, 31n118, 40, 84n356
Haufe, Günter, 102n20
Hauser, Alan J., 17nn46–47, 17n49, 19n58, 20n63
Havelock, Eric A., 32–33, 34n129, 38
Head, Peter M., 16n42, 74, 78n336
Hearon, Holly E., 13n28, 41n177, 41n179
Heil, Christoph, 153, 185n99
Heil, John Paul, 84n356
Heiligenthal, Roman, 104n25
Heinrici, Carl Friedrich Georg, 16n44, 210
Henaut, Barry W., 39nn169–70, 44n182
Hendrickson, G. L., 37n153, 51n216
Hengel, Martin, 243n67
Herrmann, Max, 54, 60n252, 61n256
Hester, James D., 19n58, 47, 89
Hezser, Catherine, 37n151, 71n284, 71n287, 73n300, 74n303, 75n310, 75n313, 78n336, 79n340
Hibbitts, Bernard J., 72n293
Hirsch, Emanuel, 241n57, 241n59, 242n66
Holland, Glenn S., 28n105, 78nn332–33, 85n359, 86n361, 93n385, 94n386, 97, 144n119, 145n126
Holloway, Paul A., 91n379, 102n18
Holmstrand, Jonas, 212n160, 213n163
Holtz, Traugott, 106n26, 195n121, 196nn123–24, 197, 207n152, 212n161
Horsley, Richard A., 40n171, 41n177, 48, 70n283, 81
Howard, George, 236n30, 239n44, 241nn58–59, 242n65
Hübner, Hans, 20n61, 21n66, 24, 137n100

Hughes, Frank Witt, 19n58, 21n66, 25n86, 26
Hunt, Allen Rhea, 204
Hurtado, Larry W., 227n205
Hymes, Dell, 48, 63, 64n264

Imber, Margaret, 26n94
Iser, Wolfgang, 12n27, 67n276

Jaffee, Martin, 37n154, 39n170, 44n186
Jeal, Roy, 83n352
Jervell, Jacob, 189n108
Jewett, Robert, 19n58, 99nn5–6, 154n9, 157n16, 157n18, 158n21, 159n25, 162n34, 162n36, 173n61, 183n93, 185n97, 229n1, 231n9, 232, 233n18, 240n53
Johanson, Bruce C., 19n58, 21n67
Johnson, Lee A., 6n16, 49n206, 140n105
Johnson, Luke T., 249n88
Johnson, William A., 37n153

Kahane, Ahuvia, 37n150
Karris, Robert J., 99n2, 163n41, 169n53
Käsemann, Ernst, 153n5, 184n96, 187n101, 188n106
Keck, Leander E., 160n26, 163n39, 187n101
Kelber, Werner H., 28n105, 31n119, 38–39, 41, 278
Kennedy, George A., 16n43, 17, 18nn53–54, 19n59, 20n66, 25n87, 27n97, 29
Kern, Philip H., 16n43, 18n57, 20n64
Kertscher, Jens, 64n276
Keyes, Clinton W., 79n338, 115n43
Kim, Chan-Hie, 79n338, 115n43
Kindermann, Heinz, 59n246, 61nn254–55, 76n315, 90n373
Kirshenblatt-Gimblett, Barbara, 60
Klauck, Hans-Josef, 1nn1–2, 2n3, 11n20, 13n29, 20n63, 21n70, 22n75, 24n81, 25n85, 74n303, 121, 122n60, 144n119, 193n117, 195n119
Klijn, A. F. J., 96n390
Klinghardt, Matthias, 77n322, 162n35, 166n46, 215n165

Knoop, Ulrich, 71n286, 71n291, 276n2
Knopf, Rudolf, 260n131
Knox, Bernard M. W., 37n153
Koch, Peter, 35
König, Ekkehard, 53n221
Korenjak, Martin, 59n246, 61nn254–55, 76n317, 78n335, 86n363, 87, 91n378, 92n381, 103n24, 175n65, 181n82, 260n127
Körtner, Ulrich H., 67n276
Koskenniemi, Heikki, 2, 8, 12n22, 15n41, 23n81, 26, 27n95, 72n294, 144, 145n125, 282n13
Krämer, Sybille, 53n221, 54n224, 65n272
Kremendahl, Dieter, 11n17, 20n63, 21n67, 22n75, 25n86, 27n96
Kuck, David W., 222n192, 227n209
Kwon, Yon-Gyong, 242n64

Lambrecht, Jan, 186n100, 187n101, 221n184, 221n189, 222n192
Lampe, Peter, 16n43, 21n67, 99, 129n74, 138n100, 139n101, 140n104
Larson, Jennifer, 84n357
Laub, Franz, 211n158
Laughton, Charles, 143n113
Lee, Margaret Ellen, 30, 131n81, 139n101, 282n12
Lefèvre, Eckard, 72n292
Lehmann, Reinhard, 79n340
Lentz, Tony M., 37n151, 71n284, 71n291, 75n311
Lévi-Strauss, Claude, 74n305
Liebert, Donald Hans, 111
Lindemann, Andreas, 259n124, 261n133, 267n152, 271nn168–69, 271n171
Lips, Hermann von, 218n174
Litfin, Duane, 19n58
Llewelyn, Stephen Robert, 12n25, 16n42, 73n300
Lohmeyer, Ernst, 124n64
Lohse, Eduard, 130n76, 131n82, 139n101, 187n101
Lona, Horacio E., 259nn119–21, 260n130, 261n136, 262n142, 263, 264n147, 265n149, 267nn152–53, 267n155, 267n157, 268n159, 269n162, 270n164, 271nn167–69, 272n173, 274n175
Long, Fredrick J., 14n34, 17n52, 20n62, 25nn85–87, 26n94
Longenecker, Bruce W., 248n84
Longenecker, Richard N., 18n53, 19n59, 220n180, 229n1, 232n17, 236n30, 239n44, 240n50, 240n53, 242n65, 245n75, 253n102
Lord, Albert Bates, 31–34, 38n157
Loubser, J. A., 28n105, 41n177, 45, 46, 47, 50n213, 71n284, 212n159, 226n203, 275n1, 283n14
Luhmann, Niklas, 45n192
Lütgert, Wilhelm, 101n17, 229n1
Luther, Martin, 160n28, 173n60
Lyons, Kirk D., 130n80, 139n102

Maassen, Irmgard, 70n281, 80, 81n346, 82nn349–50, 156n14
MacAloon, John, 64n265
Mack, Burton L., 16n43, 18n53, 19n58
Mackay, E. Anne, 37n150
Malherbe, Abraham J., 1n1, 2n7, 3n8, 4n12, 8n3, 23n80, 24n81, 145n124, 149n141, 211n158, 212n159, 212n161, 213nn162–63, 216n167, 216n169, 217n171
Malina, Bruce J., 267n154
Maly, Karl, 195n121, 196n124, 197n133
Mann, C. S., 196n126
Martin, Dale B., 201mn142
Martyn, J. Louis, 222n192, 224nn196–97, 229n2, 229n4, 232nn16–17, 233n19, 234n22, 235nn27–28, 241n56, 242n65, 251n94, 253nn102–3
Marxsen, Willi, 99n5
Masson, Charles, 102n19, 212n160
Matera, Frank J., 219n179, 220n181, 221n187, 223n193
Maxey, James A., 49n208
McLuhan, Marshall, 32, 45, 51, 278

Meeks, Wayne A., 99n7, 153n5, 155n13, 159n24, 163n37, 167n48, 168n49, 176n69
Mehat, A. A., 197n131
Meier, Samuel, 15n40, 74n302, 77n323, 79n341
Michaelis, Wilhelm, 241n57, 241n59
Michel, Otto, 99n3, 153n5, 157n18, 160n27, 161n33, 167n48, 173n61, 174n64, 180n80, 181n85, 183n94, 185n98, 187n102
Middleton, Peter, 35n139, 56, 57n237, 62n260, 63, 70n281
Mikat, Paul, 259n122, 259n124, 260n128, 261n137, 262n139, 263n145, 270n164, 270n166
Millard, Alan R., 37n154
Miller, Robert D., 38n157
Minear, Paul S., 157n15, 157n18, 162n34, 179n77
Mitchell, Margaret M., 13n32, 15n39, 16n42, 17n47, 17n50, 17n52, 18n56, 49n206, 73n299, 79n337, 100, 153n2, 191n112, 199n139, 205n148
Mitternacht, Dieter, 220, 234n25, 236n30, 239n47, 245n75
Moiser, Jeremy, 99n5, 154n8, 188n104
Moo, Douglas J., 154n10, 163n37, 176n67, 178n72, 180n79, 182n89, 187n101
Morgan, Teresa, 37n152
Morstein-Marx, Robert, 3n9, 59n246, 61n255, 87n364, 91n376, 91n380, 92n382
Muddiman, John, 240n51
Müller, Markus, 8n5
Müller, Roman, 22n76, 23n78
Mullins, Terence Y., 8nn5-6, 72n295, 148n137
Munck, Johannes, 240n51, 241n57
Murphy-O'Connor, Jerome, 12nn24-26, 84n356, 130n76
Mussner, Franz, 101n17, 147n132, 148n139, 149n143, 150n144, 221n184, 221n187, 222n192, 223n193, 224n196, 231n12,
232n16, 234n22, 236n30, 238n41, 241n56, 249n87, 250n89, 251n91, 251nn93-94, 252n95, 253nn101-2

Nanos, Mark, 86n361, 173n63, 224n196, 225n201, 227n209, 231n10, 233nn19-20, 235n29, 236n30, 241, 247n80
Neyrey, Jerome H., 109n33
Niditch, Susan, 4n11, 38n157, 71n284, 74n303
Nikolakopoulos, Konstantin, 224n196
Nimis, Stephan, 84
Nordling, John G., 129n74, 131n82, 138n100, 139n101, 142n108
North, J. L., 222n190
Nygren, Anders, 153n5, 167n48, 183n91, 189n109

O'Brien, Peter, 129n73, 138n101, 141n106
Oesterreicher, Wulf, 35
Oestreich, Bernhard, 78n332, 96n389, 152n1, 163n39, 176n68, 193n116, 218n173
Olbrechts-Tyteca, Lucie, 5n13, 18, 28
Olbricht, Thomas H., 19n58, 27n100, 30, 77n328
Ollrog, Wolf-Henning, 212n159
Olson, David R., 37n150
Ong, Walter J., 33, 34n130, 38, 71n286, 181n81, 181n83
Os, Bas van, 232n13, 236n31, 240n50

Paige, Terence, 198n136
Paris, Rainer, 113n41
Parry, Milman, 31–33, 38
Parunak, H. Van Dyke, 31n118
Paulsen, Hennig, 133n92
Pearson, Birger A., 197n132
Perelman, Chaim, 5n13, 18, 28
Person, Raymond F., 38n157
Peterlin, Davorin, 102n18
Petersen, Norman R., 130nn79-80, 131, 132nn83-84, 138n101, 139n102, 141n106, 142n107, 142n109
Pfister, Manfred, 82n350

Author Index

Piras, Antonio, 124
Pogoloff, Stephen Mark, 19n58, 92n383
Pokorný, Petr, 127n66
Porter, Stanley E., 2nn5–6, 3n8, 18n53,
    18n57, 19n58, 20n64, 21n70,
    28n106
Poster, Carol, 1n1, 23n81
Probst, Hermann, 23n79, 25n85,
    191n113

Raible, Wolfgang, 32n121, 37n150
Ramsaran, Rollin A., 48, 73n301
Rauer, Max, 163n41
Reasoner, Mark, 99nn1–2, 159n25,
    164n42, 169n53, 183n93
Reck, Reinhold, 78n336, 115n43
Reed, Jeffrey T., 8n5, 20n64, 21n70,
    28n106
Reid, Marty L., 163n41
Reinhardt, Max 60n248
Rhoads, David, 5n14, 40n171, 41–43,
    50n213, 51, 70, 82n351, 87n364,
    89n370, 90n374, 110–11,
    137n99, 275n1
Richards, E. Randolph, 12nn23–26,
    16n42, 72n296, 73n301, 78n336
Richardson, Peter, 221n187, 240n51
Riepl, Wolfgang, 12n25, 73n300,
    77n326, 78n336
Robb, Kevin, 37n152
Robbins, Vernon K., 19, 28n103, 30
Robertson, Charles Kevin, 100
Rohde, Joachim, 101n16, 148n139,
    149n143, 221n184, 221n187,
    222nn191–92, 223n193,
    224n195, 232n14, 232nn16–17,
    236n30, 239n48, 240n52,
    241n60, 249n87, 251n91,
    251n93, 256n115, 261n133,
    268n161
Ropes, James, Hardy, 229n1
Roselt, Jens, 54n224, 65n269, 136n97
Ruge-Jones, Philip, 41n179

Saenger, Paul, 37n153, 51n216, 75n310
Sampley, J. Paul, 24n82, 26n88, 158n22,
    160n29, 168n51, 169n53, 170,
    182n88, 236n34, 249n86

Sass, Gerhard, 187n101
Sauter, Willmar, 54–55, 59n245,
    60nn249–50
Schäfer, Ruth, 230n7, 231n10, 231n12,
    240n49, 248n83
Schechner, Richard, 57n236, 60n248, 65
Schewe, Susanne, 101nn16–17,
    219n179, 220, 221nn186–88,
    222n192, 223n193, 224nn195–
    96, 224n199, 225n201, 226n204,
    229n1, 231n8, 234n25, 235n27,
    241nn55–56, 241n60, 242,
    248n82, 248n84, 252n98,
    253n100, 254
Schlatter, Adolf, 197n128
Schlier, Heinrich, 101n17, 148n139,
    149n143, 174n64, 221n187,
    224n196, 227n206, 231n10,
    232n17, 234n22, 235n27,
    245n75, 249n87, 250n89,
    252n95
Schmeller, Thomas, 88n365, 176n66
Schmidt, Hans Wilhelm, 153n5,
    157n18, 161n31, 167n48,
    173n62, 183nn90–91, 184n96,
    187n101
Schmithals, Walter, 97n391, 153n6,
    157n18, 158n21, 164n42,
    167n48, 173n57, 178n71,
    178n74, 180n79, 182n87, 197,
    206–7
Schmitt, Tassilo, 116n44, 211n158,
    255n108, 259nn119–20,
    259n122, 260n125, 260n129,
    260n132, 261nn135–37,
    262n142, 268n158, 270n165,
    271n168, 271n170, 272n172,
    274
Schneider, Gerhard, 260n131, 261n133,
    261n136, 264n146
Schneider, Nélio, 158n23, 159n24,
    163nn37–38, 164n42
Schnelle, Udo, 237n37, 243n68
Schnider, Franz, 9n9, 10n15, 11n17,
    14n35, 20n65, 72n295, 73n297,
    78n332, 145n120
Schoedel, William R., 132n88, 132n90,
    134n93

Schoon-Janssen, Johannes, 8n6, 21n67
Schrage, Wolfgang, 196n127, 197n134, 219n179, 220n180, 221n184, 222nn191–92, 223n193, 229n5
Schreiber, Alfred, 105n26
Schröter, Jens, 39n170
Schumacher, Eckhard, 64n265
Scott, Bernard Brandon, 30n115, 131n81, 139n101, 282n12
Searle, John R., 47, 52n220, 53n222, 64n267
Sellin, Gerhard, 6n15, 27n101, 31n118, 37n150, 40n174, 48, 49n205, 83n352, 83n354
Shannon, Richard S. III, 37n150
Shiell, William David, 44–45, 71n284, 71n291 73n301, 74n306, 75n309, 78n330
Shiner, Whitney, 44, 46n195, 50n213, 67n277, 70, 82n349, 91, 175n65, 202n143
Shogren, Gary Steven, 163n37
Siegert, Folker, 19n58, 28n102
Silberman, Lou H., 40n171
Simmel, Georg, 112–17, 122, 125, 130, 134, 136
Slusser, Michael, 37n153
Small, Jocelyn Penny, 37n154, 75n312
Smit, Joop, 17n52, 19n59, 198n135
Smit, Peter-Ben, 162n35, 181n84
Snyder, H. Gregory, 37n152
Sofsky, Wolfgang, 113n41
Sonkowsky, Robert P., 22n71, 26n94, 77n329, 81
Stahlhut, Marco, 53n221
Stamps, Dennis L., 2n5, 16n43, 18n57, 19n58, 20n61, 21n68, 21n70
Standaert, Benoît, 198n138
Standhartinger, Angela, 119n54
Stanley, Christopher D., 235nn27–28, 245n75
Starr, Raymond J., 37n153, 75n310
Stegemann, Ekkehard W., 99n7, 176n69
Stegemann, Wolfgang, 99n7, 176n69
Stenger, Werner, 9n9, 10n15, 11n17, 14n35, 20n65, 72n295, 73n297, 78n332, 145n120

Stirewalt, M. Luther, 4n10, 10n15, 12nn24–25, 13–16, 21n69, 24n82, 25n88, 27n99, 73, 75n313, 77nn323–24, 78n333, 85n359, 105n26, 107, 112n39, 129n75, 130n78, 212n159, 235n28, 244, 245n75, 262n140
Stolz, Benjamin A., 37n150
Stowers, Stanley Kent, 8n2, 11, 21n67, 88n365, 176n66
Strack, Hermann L., 251n91
Strange, James F., 76n320
Strelan, John G., 221n187
Stuhlmacher, Peter, 99n5, 127n67, 130n76, 131n82, 138n101, 142n109, 153n5, 163n41, 167n47, 169n53, 178n73, 181n86, 182n87, 183n91, 188n103
Suhl, Alfred, 232n15, 240n53
Sumney, Jerry L., 101n14, 236n30, 239n45
Surburg, Mark P., 19n59
Svenbro, Jesper, 75n312
Sykutris, Johannes, 8n3, 21n69, 78n336

Tannen, Deborah, 34n130, 37n150
Taussig, Hal, 162n35
Theissen, Gerd, 6n17, 76n315, 99–100, 102, 105–7, 159n25, 215n166
Thiselton, Anthony C., 196, 197n132, 198n136
Thomas, Rosalind, 37n151, 71n291, 74n303, 74n305, 75n311, 92n383
Thompson, David William, 37n150
Thompson, Paul, 37n155
Thorsteinsson, Runar M., 99n5, 185n99
Thraede, Klaus, 1n2, 8n5, 9, 13n29, 15n41, 27n98, 85n359, 144–45, 282n13
Thurén, Lauri, 19n58, 20, 21n67, 232n14, 234, 247n79, 249n88
Tolmie, D. Francois, 19n59, 256n114, 257n116
Torrance, Nancy, 37n150
Trobisch, David, 97n391

Tsang, Sam, 13n31, 15n40, 47n199, 73n298, 75n310
Tyson, Joseph B., 237n35

Ueding, Gert, 27n100
Unnik, Willem C. van, 196n125, 206–7, 262nn138–39, 262n141, 263n144

Vansina, Jan, 32n121, 37n155
Vatz, Richard, 29n110
Vegge, Tor, 8n7, 23n79, 71n291, 75n313
Venetz, Hermann-Josef, 79n339
Vogt-Spira, Gregor, 37n150
Voorst, Robert E. van, 244n71
Vos, Johan S., 196n122, 196n124, 197n135, 198nn137–38, 200n141, 205n148, 206n150, 208n153, 209n154
Vouga, Francois, 19n58, 37n150, 101n17, 233n18

Wagner, Andreas, 73n300
Wagner, J. Ross, 186n100, 187n101
Walter, Nikolaus, 232n17, 233n20, 238n39
Walters, James, 103n21, 176n68
Wanamaker, Charles A., 19n58
Ward, Richard F., 48n202, 78n330, 218n175
Warning, Rainer, 12n27, 67n276
Watson, Duane F., 17nn46–47, 17n49, 17nn51–52, 19n58, 20n63, 29n110
Watson, Janet, 37n150
Watt, Ian, 32, 33n128
Weiss, Harold, 169n53
Weiss, Johannes, 16n44, 83n353, 155n13, 173n59, 189n108
Weissenrieder, Annette, 34n130, 40n171, 41n177
Welborn, Laurence L., 259n120, 262n141
Wendland, Ernst R., 31n118, 47n197, 49–50, 73n301, 75n313, 82n350

Wengst, Klaus, 137n100, 139n101
White, John L., 8n3, 8n5, 8n7, 9–11, 14n36, 16n42, 21n70, 24n83, 144n119, 193n117, 194n118, 195n120, 282n13
Wick, Peter, 76n314
Wickert, Ulrich, 129n70
Wiefel, Wolfgang, 99
Wilckens, Ulrich, 99n5, 153nn5–7, 154n8, 154n10, 157n18, 158n19, 158n23, 163n37, 163n40, 180n80, 182n87, 187n101, 188nn104–5, 190n111
Wilder, Amos, 17n45
Wilhelmi, Gernhard, 148n136
Wilke, Christian Gottlob, 16n44
Winter, Bruce W., 20n62, 25n87, 28n104, 92n383, 235n29, 237n35
Winter, Sara B. C., 129n70, 129n74, 138n100
Wire, Antoinette Clark, 19n58, 44n186, 48n202, 49n206, 204n145, 283
Witherington, Ben III, 101n17, 107n29, 129n70, 130n76, 130n80, 132n83, 137n100, 139n101, 147n133, 148n139, 149n143, 196n125, 221n184, 221n187, 223n193, 224n195, 232n15, 242n65, 245n75, 255nn109–10, 267n154
Witulski, Thomas, 249n85
Wolff, Christian, 101nn14–15, 121n56, 122n58, 196n127, 197n134, 219n176
Wolter, Michael, 137n100, 139n101, 140n104, 229n1
Woolf, Greg, 71n284, 74n305
Wuellner, Wilhelm, 17n51, 18nn56–57, 19n58, 21n66, 27n101, 28n102, 30

Yaghjian, Lucretia B., 37n151

Subject Index

addressing listeners, 87, 89–90, 104–13, 119, 123–25, 132–34, 153–54, 164, 176–77, 180–81, 182, 184, 187–89, 191–92, 194, 203–16, 219n176, 221, 223–25, 233–34, 237, 245–50, 255, 258, 264–67, 273, 279
alienation effect, 93, 139–41, 143–44, 146–51, 212, 278
Antioch incident, 230–31, 232n13, 236, 238, 248
aphorism, maxim, 91, 174–75, 178, 180–81, 182n89, 222
applause, 44, 59, 91–92, 175
audience
    activated for action, 118, 142–43, 146, 250–51, 256, 266, 274
    actively generates meaning, 47, 55, 60n249, 283
    consideration given to the audience, concession, 118, 132, 252, 271–72, 274
    constructed, 47n201, 87, 157, 201, 233–34, 235n29, 249, 253n100, 264–66, 268, 281
    disunited, 47, 98–103, 107, 156–57, 201–2
    dividing, 110, 117–18, 122, 130, 134, 211, 218, 226, 233, 245, 250, 252, 258, 266–69
    evaluates the performance, 30, 52, 57, 59, 63–65, 91–94, 136–37, 141, 146–47, 150–51, 175, 186, 212
    inciting the audience, 117, 119, 238–39, 255, 265
    influences the performance, 4n13, 16, 36, 43, 50, 55, 59–62, 82, 89, 94, 98, 112, 136, 259–60
    in rhetorical interpretation, 30, 40
    interaction between parts, 30, 40, 47, 61–62, 76, 89–91, 98, 108–111, 114, 152, 167, 190, 210, 234, 244, 276
    majority/minority, 91, 117–18, 122, 125, 127, 166, 215, 226, 243–46, 248–50, 253, 259n124, 260–61, 264–66, 270–71, 280–81
    own interpretation, 141, 143, 147, 150
    protest, 105, 168, 265
    reaction, 13, 30–31, 44, 49, 55–57, 59–63, 65, 76n316, 77–78, 89–92, 98, 103–5, 107–9, 112, 115, 120, 137, 140–41, 152, 161, 175–76, 179, 217, 228, 245–46, 254, 265

autopoietic feedback-loop, 60–62, 67n276, 136

banishment, expatriation, 118, 270–72, 274
baptism, 174n64, 199, 209
Bible translation and performance, 49
boasting, 160, 183n92, 238n42, 241, 255–56, 267–68, 273

captatio benevolentiae, 179
charismata, spiritual gifts, 100, 195, 198–99, 202–4, 209
church offices, 211–12, 226, 255, 260–64
circumcision, 85, 90, 101n17, 150–51, 219, 227, 229nn1–4, 231, 234, 236–40, 246–49, 251–56, 258
competition, 92–93, 107n29, 250
confession, Christian, 164n64, 173, 177, 197, 200, 205, 207n152, 208–9
control function of the audience, 77, 126, 128
controversy
   1 Clement, 259–62
   1 Corinthians, 99–100, 199, 201–2
   Alexandria, 193–95
   Galatians, 101, 219, 227, 229, 235, 247, 251, 254
   opportunity to change sides, 246, 249, 253–54, 260n129, 265, 272
   Philippians, 90, 124–26
   Romans, 98–99, 161, 163n36, 170n56
corporeality of the letter's author, 84, 93, 138–42, 144–51, 257, 278
corporeality in performance, 52–57, 66, 70, 81–85, 136–37, 186, 278
coworkers of Paul, 102, 105n26, 112, 124–25, 127n66, 211–12
culture of written language, modern, 12, 30–31, 33, 42, 51, 57
curse, 196–97, 206–8, 246–47, 249

degrading, vilification, blackguarding, 233–34, 249, 255, 258, 267–68, 273
divide et impera, 113–14, 116–18, 120, 125, 130, 136, 281

embodiment, 27, 43, 47, 54–55, 66, 78, 84, 140, 142, 146, 150, 186, 218, 250, 256, 257n117
emergence, 61–62, 67–68
emotions, 44, 48, 90, 92, 148, 166, 183, 202, 209, 218n175, 249–50, 260n127, 273
ephemerality, 61–62, 67–68
epic theater (Brecht), 142–44
ethos, 93, 139n102, 147, 190, 273
expulsion from the church, 118, 146, 251–52, 273, 281

fellowship, strenghtening of the, 126, 128, 157, 210, 255
form criticism, 38–39, 280
freedom, 184, 220, 230, 234, 243n68, 254

gesture, 30, 36, 42, 44–46, 47n199, 55–56, 58, 63, 72, 77, 82n349, 85, 104–5, 117, 142, 146, 149n142, 150, 162, 164, 176, 201, 215, 218n175, 245, 246n76, 268–69, 276, 282
glossolalia, speaking in tongues, 100, 148n139, 202–7, 209–10

Holy Spirit, 180, 196, 199, 202–9, 224, 235n27, 254–56
hospitality, 153, 162, 262
house church, 10n15, 14, 45, 88–89, 99, 103–4, 105n26, 107–8, 115, 127–31, 132n84, 135, 137–39, 141–42, 162, 226, 238

irony, 49, 85–86, 224n196, 224, 254, 282

James, 229n3, 230. 231nn10–11
Jews and Gentiles, relationship between, 98–99, 106, 151, 153, 158, 163, 178, 184–88, 193–95, 198, 203n144, 230–31, 235n29, 236–38, 240, 243, 251, 256–57
judgment, eschatological, 167, 177, 222, 266

Subject Index

language
  language concept, 35
  performative use, 52–53, 58, 69, 186, 188
  poetic, hymnic, 174–75, 181, 185, 188, 216, 279
  voice and sound, 11, 30–31, 42, 44–45, 55–56, 63, 70n281, 72, 75, 78n331, 82n349, 83–85, 90, 92, 95, 103n23, 104, 137–39, 142, 146–52, 174, 186, 193, 205, 215–16, 218, 250n90, 276–77
law, Jewish, 99, 118, 151, 163, 167, 169–71, 179n76, 220, 225n201, 227–31, 235–39, 241–44, 247–50, 257, 279
leaders of the church, 87, 96, 102–3, 112, 115, 118, 126, 134, 210–27, 238, 250, 255, 259–63, 266, 269
letter
  ancient epistolary theory, 1–2, 2n7, 22, 23n81
  and oral communication, 1, 9–10, 13, 15, 22–23
  experience of a mental vision, a virtually seeing, 9, 145
  forms and conventions, 8–9, 144–45
  in ancient text on rhetorics, 21–22
  protocol of receiving, 15–16, 73–79, 166, 193, 243, 246, 257, 263, 280
  social event, 4, 9, 11–13, 15–16, 21, 26–27, 45, 47–48, 72, 75, 89–90, 106, 215, 230, 234, 276, 278–79
  style, 1–3, 22–23
letters of Paul
  and oral preaching, 24
  as an alternative to oral communication, 25
  comparable to official letters, 14–15, 73, 75, 244
literacy, 74

meal, table fellowship, 76, 161–62, 172, 213, 231
media and media aspects of communication, 32, 35, 42, 46, 51, 54–55, 57, 69, 82, 91, 95, 136–37, 140–42, 146–47, 278

mediation, 104, 113–16, 121–22, 125–26, 130, 136, 168, 192, 203, 209, 262n141
memory, 47, 50n211, 77, 83–84, 165, 172, 222, 277
messenger
  literacy not necessary, 74
  recommendation, 79, 85, 115–16, 117n45, 262
  role, 15, 16n42, 49, 73, 77–79, 117, 243–44, 257
messenger formula, 21
metaphor, 49, 56, 147–48, 167–69, 199
mimesis, mirroring, 56, 84, 137, 140, 277

observance of days, 96, 169–71
opponents of Paul, 26, 90, 101n16, 150–51, 176, 229nn1–3, 230–42, 245n75, 246, 248–59
orality
  culture dominated by orality, 4, 12–13, 15–16, 31–33, 35–39, 41–42, 44–45, 71, 275–76
  interaction between oral and written communication, 22, 31n117, 34, 71
  preference of oral communication, 3–4, 26, 41–42, 71
  traces in texts, 25n87, 36, 49, 80–82, 94, 124

parallelism, 40, 44n182, 48–49, 83–84, 87, 90, 92, 104, 124, 153–57, 162, 164–66, 169–80, 185–87, 189–90, 195, 199–201, 203–7, 213–15, 218–19, 222, 227, 269, 279, 282
pathos, 185, 273
Paul
  age, 84, 93, 95, 138–39, 151
  apostolic authority, 10–11, 14, 115, 122–23, 132n84, 138n101, 2049, 85, 103, 109, 185, 197, 204–5, 218–19, 227, 239, 244, 247
  example, 209, 247, 256
  illness, 146–47, 249
  marks of Jesus, 149, 257

Paul (continued)
  presence and absence, 9n9, 10, 48, 84–85, 93, 140, 144–49, 151, 247, 279
  rhetorical competence, 49, 92–93
  voice, 84–85, 93, 148
  zealot, former, 236
performance
  addressing one group while speaking up for another, 166–67, 177, 179, 182, 187–89, 192, 194, 202, 205, 209, 218, 225–26
  awareness of a doubleness, 65–66
  changes relationships, 6, 43, 90, 108–9, 111n35, 190, 210, 216, 218, 227, 281
  definition, 52, 54–55
  directs gazes, 85, 108–9, 115, 117, 126, 166, 176, 182, 202, 215, 269, 273
  enticement and threat, 195, 247, 252, 267–68
  framed through social conventions, 57–59, 64, 70
  generates meaning, 43, 57, 66, 70, 82, 137
  indirect address, "over one's shoulder", 246, 250, 254, 258, 265, 270
  medial aspect, 64–65, 69–70, 82, 85, 91–92, 95–96, 136–37, 140–42, 146–51, 175, 186, 193, 278
  public pressure on individuals, 125–27, 130, 134, 132, 272
performance culture, 41, 72n293
performance of texts, 21, 26, 77–78
performance of New Testament texts, 41n180, 43–44, 70
performative space, 43, 58, 63, 86–88, 129n75, 161–62, 164, 172, 218, 278
persecution, 43, 149–50, 197, 206, 239–40, 251–52, 256–57, 259n120, 261n137
Peter, 39, 41n178, 100, 229–31, 232n13, 233n18, 235–36, 238, 240, 248
position of the performer, 36, 72, 86–87, 104, 117, 164, 218, 227, 250

praise (of humans), 23, 75n310, 78n331, 93, 105, 123, 126, 133, 191, 266
praise of God, 155, 157, 177, 187–88
presence, spiritual, parusia in letters, 8–9, 15, 24, 48, 78, 81, 85, 144–45, 148–49, 247, 279
presenter, reader of the text, 11, 28n106, 40, 42–45, 47–50, 53n223, 63, 75, 78, 83–87, 92–95, 104–5, 112–17, 124–25, 134, 136–42, 146–51, 162, 164–66, 174–75, 178, 186, 188, 194–95, 212, 215–16, 218, 226–27, 237, 243, 245–46, 250, 257n117, 268–69, 272, 277–78, 280
prophecy, 198, 202–6, 209, 216n170
propositio, 197–99, 205–6
proverb, 2, 52, 84, 180, 181n81, 182n89, 221–22
pseudo-apostles, 232

reading instructions in letters, 96, 193, 218n173
reconciliation, 107n32, 111, 124, 126, 131, 152–227
rhetoric
  and actors, 2, 22, 78
  and interpretation of the New Testament, 16–21, 27–28
  oral communication improved by writing, 3, 22, 34
  rhetorical situation, 29
  speeches submitted in written form, 24–25
  transition, 154, 171, 178, 203, 216, 225

sarcasm, 163n36, 204–5, 227, 240–41, 254, 256, 258, 282
save face, 122, 130, 132, 246, 249, 258, 271
script, 36n144, 56–57, 64–65, 67n275, 68, 81–82, 94, 142, 150, 210, 244
scriptio continua, 75, 83, 138
seating order, 76–77, 109, 114, 166n46, 176, 215, 243, 245, 255n110, 263, 269
self-referentiality, 52, 54, 62, 94, 186

slaves, 74, 75n310, 100, 104, 107–8, 118, 129–31, 133, 137–42, 167–69
social order, 86, 227, 265, 267
sociocultural situation, 11n18, 13, 19, 29n110, 43, 51, 64, 67
status, higher social, 99, 102–4, 107, 118, 132, 139, 141, 146, 151, 180, 211, 225, 229, 238–39, 251, 255, 261

text
    abstraction of language event, 66–67, 69, 276
    performative text strategies, 81–82, 87, 114, 119, 135, 142, 151, 156, 190, 227–28
    reception by the ear, 11, 16, 29–30, 31n117, 39, 51, 79–80, 83, 277
theater, 2, 40n176, 51, 54, 58–60, 65, 76, 78n331, 86, 114, 142–44

tradition
    Immanent Art, 36, 64, 94, 160, 177–78, 180, 184, 277
    oral transmission, 32–33, 38–39, 42, 46
trust, 130n76, 253, 273

understanding with the body, 56–57, 84
understanding vs. experience, 56–57, 68–69

weak, 99n1, 102, 104, 110, 154n10, 157–62, 165–67, 183, 212, 217
witchcraft, magic, 248–49
writing
    encoding the spoken word, 71, 75, 138
    reification of language, 4

Ancient Document Index

Old Testament

Genesis

32:43	188

Leviticus

18:8	118
19:14	160

Numbers

23:19	189

1 Samuel

18:25–27	241

Psalms

51:4	189
69:9	184

Proverbs

1:23–33	273

Isaiah

3:5	261
45:20	177
45:22	177
45:23	177, 184
53:4	183

New Testament

Matthew

5:17	242
23:23	242
27:34	184n95

Mark

13:14	89n371

Luke

9:51–56	46
14:7–11	215n166
14:8	76n315

John

2:17	184n95
7:19	242
7:23	242
7:49	242
13:20	162
19:35	89n371

Acts

13:45	240n53
14:2–5	240n53
14:19	240n53
15:1	232n15
15:23–32	262
15:23–29	14n35
15:23	117n45
15:24	232n15
15:25–29	79
15:30–32	15
15:30	73
17:5	240n53
17:13	240n53
17:18	109
17:31	109
18:26	162
19:9	88
19:12–13	240n53
19:32	91
19:34	91, 181n82
23:6–10	110
28:2	162

Romans

1–11	153n6
1:5–6	106n28
1:6	237
1:9–12	72
1:9	95n387
1:11–12	164n44
1:13	106n28, 237
1:14	103
1:16—4:25	40n175
1:16–17	98
1:23	188
3:3–4	189
3:23	188
3:26	91n379
3:27	241n61
4	98
4:25	91n379
5:2	95n388, 188
5:21	94
6:11	94
6:23	94, 95
7:1	105n26
7:25	95
8:1–2	94
8:18	188
8:21	188
8:29	95
8:32–39	185
9–11	98
9:1	94
9:23	188
10:1	213
10:15–21	47n199
10:16–17	39
11:13–24	187
11:13	104, 105n26
11:25–32	251
11:25	213
11:29	189
11:33–36	88n366, 185
12:1—15:7	153n6
12:3—13:14	153
12:3	153
12:3	95n388
12:4–5	153
12:5	94
12:6	95n388
12:9–21	83n354
12:9–10	153
12:13	153
12:16	153
12:18	153

12:19–21	153	2:1–4	72
13:1–7	153	2:1	93
13:8–10	153	2:3	84
14–15	98, 109, 217n171, 280	3	105n26
14:1—15:13	153n5, 279n6, 99n2, 152–91, 236	3:2	88
		3:4—4:5	93
14	105n26	3:10	95
14:1–4	104	4:3	93
14:1	153	4:5	177
14:2	90, 153, 277n3	4:10–13	85
14:3	85, 87	4:14–15	88
14:5	153	4:14	94n386
14:6	153	4:15	95
14:7–10	279	4:17	73n299
14:23	153n7	5:1–5	118
15:1–7	153	5:1	90, 112
15:1	153	5:3–5	144, 145n126
15:7–12	103	5:3	5, 9n9, 84–85, 145, 147, 149
15:7	94, 153		
15:8–13	153n6	5:5	252
15:8	153	5:6	252n96
15:13	88n366, 153	6	106
15:14–15	164n44	7	100
15:14	213	7:1	87
15:15	94n386, 95n388	7:8	87
15:30	164n44	7:10	215n164
15:33	185	7:12	215n164
16:1–2	79n339, 115	7:24–27	84
16:1	73, 85	8–10	100, 106n27, 179n76
16:3	94, 163	8–9	217n171
16:7, 11	237	8	159
16:21–23	153n6	8:1	180n78
16:22	283	8:6	205n148
16:25–27	153n7	8:7	158–59
		8:7–12	104
		8:9	106n27

1 Corinthians

		8:10–11	106n27
1:2	96	9:3	106
1:4	95n388	9:15	94n386
1:10–12	99	9:22	91n379
1:10–11	99	10:14	213
1:10	6	10:15	106n27
1:11	100n11, 112	10:23	90
1:12	87	10:23a	104
1:18	100n11	10:30	180n80
1:29–31	241n61	10:31	106n27
2:1–5	93	11	6, 100
		11:16	88

1 Corinthians (continued)

11:17–22	106
11:18	99, 100n11
11:20–22	105n26
11:21	76n315, 100n8, 104, 215n166
11:23–25	88
12	6, 279n6
12:1–3	205
12:2	203n144
12:3	80n343, 195–200, 205–10, 277, 280
12:4–27	205
12:4–6	199
12:7	199
12:8–11	199
12:9	95n387
12:12–27	199–201
12:15–21	206
12:15–16	209
12:22	159
12:26	84
12:27–30	200
12:29–30	204n145
12–14	100, 195, 197–99
13	203
13:11	88
14	203
14:2–14	203
14:3	216n170
14:5	203
14:15	203
14:18–19	203
14:25	209
14:26–33	203–4
14:36–38	88
14:37–39	205
14:37–38	204
14:37	94n386
14:39–40	205
15	48
15:3–6	88
15:3–4	173
15:10	95n388
15:12	104, 197n132
15:13	253n105
15:14	253n105
15:42–44	84
15:58	213
16:1	223n193
16:10–11	79n339
16:21	10
16:22	88n366

2 Corinthians

1:5	94
1:12–2:11	25
1:12—2:4	93
1:12	95n388
1:13	94n386
2	134
2:4	26, 49, 84
2:5–11	101, 121–22, 281n10
2:5	101n15
2:6	122
2:6	121
2:7–8	121
2:9	121
2:10	122
2:12–13	73n299
2:12	95n387
2:17	46n194
3:1–6	39
3:4	94
3:6b	84
4:2	93
4:10	84
5:6–8	84
5:18	94
5:20	138n101
6:1	95n388
7:1	213
7:6–7	121
7:8	121
7:12	101, 121
7:13–15	121
8:1	95n388
8:2	102n20
8:16–24	73n299
9:6	84
9:13	95n387
9:14	95n388
10:1	140n104

10:7	88n368
10:10–11	46n194, 84
10:10	26
10:11	92
10:14	95n387
11:7	95n387
11:12–15	93
11:23–30	84
11:30	84
12:5–10	84
12:7	84
12:19	213
13:1	72
13:10	84, 94n386
13:11	219n176
16:10–11	115

Galatians

1	88
1:1–2	244
1:1	258
1:2	235n28, 245n75, 283
1:5	244n71
1:6–9	110, 252n98
1:6–7	245–46, 248, 250
1:6	224n196, 228, 233
1:7	95n387, 235n28, 245n75
1:8–10	233
1:8–9	246–48
1:9	249
1:10	93
1:11—2:10	247–48
1:14	236
1:15–24	239
1:16–20	233n18
1:20	94n386
1:27—2:11	102
2:1	223n193
2:2	229, 232
2:4–5	232
2:4	231n10, 232n16
2:5	230n6
2:6	224n196, 238
2:9	238
2:11–21	248
2:11–14	230, 238
2:12	230–31, 232n13, 238, 240
2:13	231, 232n15
2:14	231, 238, 240, 241n58
2:15–21	236n32
2:16	241
2:18	231
2:21	95n388, 229
3:1–5	233
3:1	48, 89, 235, 248–50
3:2–6	248
3:3	239
3:4	229
3:9	257
3:10	235n28, 249
3:11	241
3:13	196
3:14	257
3:15–20	236n32
3:17	236n33
3:18	229
3:19	236n33
3:21	236
3:27–28	249
3:28	103, 236, 238, 256
4:2–3	102
4:4–7	88
4:8–20	249–50
4:8–16	233
4:8–9	249n85
4:8	228, 237, 249
4:10	170n55, 235, 244
4:11	229
4:13–20	93n385, 146–49
4:13–15	84, 249, 250
4:14–15	249n87
4:15	85
4:17–18	250, 253
4:17	151, 229, 233, 235nn28–29, 245n75, 251, 258
4:18–20	149n142
4:18	258
4:19	250, 257
4:20	84–85, 93, 250n90
4:21–27	236n32
4:22–28	251
4:29–30	251–52
4:29	251–52, 254

Galatians (continued)

4:30	251, 253n99, 258, 281n11
5–6	229n5
5	254
5:1	230
5:2–4	228
5:2–3	237
5:2	140n104, 229
5:3	228, 241n58
5:4	229, 235n28
5:5	253n100
5:6	236, 256
5:7–12	252–54
5:7–8	233
5:7	251, 254
5:8	252
5:9	252
5:10–12	250
5:10	85, 238, 235n28, 252, 253n100, 258
5:11–12	253
5:11	149, 240, 258
5:12	224n196, 227, 233, 235n28, 240, 254, 258
5:13–26	254
5:13	220n182, 254n107
5:14	236, 242
5:15	101, 227, 229, 231n8, 235, 251, 254
5:16, 18	256
5:19–23	220
5:19–21	229n1, 254
5:20	248
5:21	254, 258
5:22	229n1, 254
5:23	236
5:24	256
5:25–26	221n184
6	254
6:1–10	210, 219–24, 255, 277
6:1–5	255
6:1	182, 183n92
6:2–3	238n42
6:2	159, 236, 242
6:3–5	255n109
6:3	238
6:6–10	255
6:6	89
6:11–17	255–57
6:11	10, 46n194, 94, 11n17, 257
6:12–14	93
6:12–13	151, 233, 235n28, 239, 250, 255–56, 258
6:12	149–50, 228, 237, 239–40, 251, 256
6:13	241, 258
6:14	256, 258
6:15	236, 256
6:17	84, 149–50, 246n77, 257, 258

Ephesians

2:9	241n61
3:1	139n102, 140n104
3:3	94n386
4:1	139n102
6:20	93, 139nn101–2
6:21–22	78n336, 115

Philippians

1:2	90
1:4	88n366
1:7	139n102
1:13	93, 139n102
1:15–18	102
1:15–17	93
1:17	146n127, 139n102
1:20–24	84
1:27	84
2:12	84, 146n127
2:25–30	73n299, 115
2:4	213
2:6–11	88n366, 177
3:2	236
3:18	84–85, 93
4:1–2	105n26
4:2–3	104, 105n26, 107, 124–26
4:2	87, 112
4:11–13	84
4:11	102n20
4:16	102n20

Colossians

1:6	95n388
1:23–24	140n104
1:24	84
2:16–23	236
2:16	170n55
2:5	84–85
3:16	213
4:3	93, 139n102
4:7–9	73n299, 79n339, 115
4:7–8	78n336
4:16	78n332, 79, 96
4:17	89, 105n26, 107, 127–28
4:18	10, 93, 139n102

1 Thessalonians 8n6

1:5	93n385
1:12	95n388
2:1–12	93
2:1–8	93
2:1–2	93n385
2:1	210
2:9–12	93n385
2:11–12	88, 95
2:13	39
2:16	236
2:17	210
2:18	140n104
2:2	95n387
2:3–7	93
2:5	93
2:7	88
2:8	95n387
2:9	95n387
3:2	95n387
3:7	213
3:11–13	88n366
3:12	102
4:1	106n26, 210
4:9–10	102
4:13	106n26, 210
4:18	97
5:1	106n26, 210
5:10	173
5:11	106n26, 212
5:12–15	210–19, 221–25, 227
5:12–14	87, 280
5:12	102
5:13	225
5:14	102, 106n26, 213
5:15	225
5:23	88n366
5:26–27	11
5:27	13, 218n173, 73, 78n332, 96

2 Thessalonians

2:5	93n385
3:6	216
3:7	93n385
3:17	11

1 Timothy

4:13	73, 76

2 Timothy

1:8	139n102
1:16	139n102

Philemon 105n26, 128–32

1–2	89
2	107, 111, 127
8–9	137–42, 281n11
9	72, 84, 93, 138n101
10	95
11	138n101
19	10, 94, 95
21	94n386
22	72
25	107

1 John

4:2	197

2 John

10	162

Hebrews

11:26	184n95

James

2:2–3	215
2:2	76n315

Revelation

1:3	76

Greco-Roman Writings

Aristotle, *Poetics*

6	142

Aristotle, *Rhetoric*

1.3.3	17n48
2.12–17	103n22
3.5.6	75n313
3.12	22n71

Cicero, *Epistulae ad Atticum*

8.14.1	2n8, 72n294
9.10.1	13n29, 72n294

Cicero, *Epistulae ad familiares*

2.4.1	13n29
9.21.1	22
15.16.1	145

Cicero, *De Lege agraria* 119–20

2.22, 31, 63–64, 66–67	119n53
2.63–64	120
2.66–67	120
2.74	119

Cicero, *De oratore*

1.31.142	27n100
1.33.150	20n62
1.33.152	34n132
3.56.213	20n62, 28n104

Cicero, *Orator ad Brutum*

14.45–46	170n56
56	28n104

Cicero, *Pro Cluentio*

14–15	118n47

Cicero, *Pro Flacco*

66	103n23

Cicero, *Pro Lege Manilia*

37	120–21
69	123–24, 134

Cicero, *Pro Milone* 103n23

Cicero, *Pro rege Deiotaro*

6	87n364

Ancient Document Index

Claudius,
To the Alexandrians 193–95

Demetrius, *De elocutione*

223–35	23n81
223–29	1–3
224	22, 73
227	145n125
232	2

Demosthenes, *Epistulae*

3.35	25

Gaius, *Institutiones*

1.63	118n47

Isocrates, *Epistulae*

1.2–3	4n10
2.13	23n81

Julius Victor, *Ars Rhetorica*

27	23

Libanius, *Epistulae*

528.4	24n81

Petronius, *Satyrikon*

75	75n310

Philodemus, *De Rhetorica*

4, col. 15, ll. 3–6	28n104

Philostratus of Lemnos,
De epistolis 3n8

2.257.29–258.28	24n81

Platon, *Epistulae*

6.322–23	190–93

Plinius minor, *Epistulae*

5.19.3	78n331
9.34	74n307

Plutarch, *De musica*

1131d	75n311

Plutarch,
De recta ratione audiendi

41c	91n380

Pseudo-Demetrius,
Formae epistolicae

1–21	11, 22
1	145n122

Pseudo-Libanius, *Characteres epistolici* 11, 22, 46–50

Quintilian, *Institutio oratoria*

1.1.28–29	3n9
1.8.2	78n331
1.11.6–12	78n331
1.11.14	77n328
2.10.13	78n331
9.4.19–22	3n8
9.4.19–20	22

Quintilian, *Institutio oratoria*
(continued)

10.1.1–3	3n9
10.1.2–3	34n132
10.1.2	3n9
10.1.16–131	3n9
10.3	20n62
10.3.1–18	3n9
10.3.1	34n132
10.3.21	3n8
10.6.3	3n9
10.7.26	3n8
10.7.28–29	3n9
10.7.30–31	3n9
10.7.31–32	77n329
11.2.33	78n331
11.3.4	78n331
11.3.6	20n62, 28n104
11.3.57	78n331

Rhetorica ad Herennium

1.3	27n100

Seneca, *Epistulae*

40.1	4n12, 145n124, 149n141
75.1–2	2n8

Suetonius, *Divus Augustus*

48	26n91
49.3	16n42

Theon, *Progymnasmata*

1.84–92	3n9
8	119n54

Thukydides, *Historiae*

7.10	15

Jewish Literature

2 Baruch

86:1–2	96

2 Maccabees

10:15	162

Josephus, *Antiquitates*

11.8.3	79n341
13.5.8	79n341
13.9.2	79n341

Early Christian Writings

1 Clement

1:1	117, 259n120, 264, 266–67, 269n162, 273
1:2—2:8	268
1:2–3	262
1:3	266
3:1–4	267, 273
3:2	267
3:3	261, 265
4:7	267, 273
10:7—12:8	262
14:1–2	266
14:1	117, 267, 273
14:2	265n149, 267
15:1	117, 267, 268n158
15:4–5	268
17:5	268
19:3—20:12	265
21:3, 9	266

21:5	266, 267n155, 273	59:1	273
21:6–8	266	60:2	259n120
27:6–7	266	61:1–2	259n120
28:1	266	62:3	268
33	265	63:2	262
34:1	265	63:3	77n325, 79, 116, 244, 262
34:7	262n138	65:1	77n325, 79, 116, 262
35:5	262		
35:6	266		
37:1–4	266		

Ignatius, *To the Ephesians*

37:2–3	259n120
37:5	266
39:1	267n155, 273
40–41	261n138
40:1—41:4	265
44	269
44:3–6	264

11:2	139n102

Ignatius, *To the Philadelphians*

10	135

44:3	259, 260n124
44:4	263, 268
44:6	259, 260
45:2	268
45:7	269, 273
46:5	263
46:9	261
47:1–4	96
47:5	117, 269, 273
47:6	117, 266, 269
48:5–6	260
51	269
51:1	268–69
53:1	268
54	118
54:1	270
54:1–3	271, 281n11
54:2–3	261
54:2	260n129, 267n152, 270–71, 273
54:3	271
55	271
56	270–71
56:2	264, 272
56:2	271
56:13	272
56:2, 16	271
57:1–2	261, 272
57:1	117, 267n152
57:2	273
57:3–7	273
58	273

Ignatius, *To the Philippians*

1:1	139n102
14	115

Ignatius, *To Polycarp* 95, 132–35

1:2	133, 135
2:1	135
4:1	133, 135
4:3	133, 135
6	134
6:1	133n92
7:2	133
7:3	133
8:1	133
8:3	133

Ignatius, *To the Smyrnaeans*

5.3	234n22
11	133, 135

Irenaeus, *Adversus haereses*

3.7.1	75n313

Polycarp, *To the Philippians*

1:1	139n102
14	115

www.ingramcontent.com/pod-product-compliance
Lightning Source LLC
Chambersburg PA
CBHW032013300426
44117CB00008B/1007